D0897558

Arc of Containment

A VOLUME IN THE SERIES

THE UNITED STATES IN THE WORLD

edited by Mark Philip Bradley, David C. Engerman,
Amy S. Greenberg, and Paul A. Kramer

A list of titles in this series is available at cornellpress.cornell.edu.

STUDIES OF THE WEATHERHEAD EAST ASIAN INSTITUTE, COLUMBIA UNIVERSITY

The Studies of the Weatherhead East Asian Institute of Columbia University
were inaugurated in 1962 to bring to a wider public the results of significant
new research on modern and contemporary East Asia.

Arc of Containment

Britain, the United States, and
Anticommunism in Southeast Asia

Wen-Qing Ngoei

Cornell University Press
Ithaca and London

First published 2019 by Cornell University Press

Library of Congress Cataloging-in-Publication Data

Names: Ngoei, Wen-Qing, 1976– author.
Title: Arc of containment : Britain, the United States, and anticommunism in Southeast Asia / Wen-Qing Ngoei.
Description: Ithaca : Cornell University Press, 2019. | Series: The United States in the world | Includes bibliographical references and index.
Identifiers: LCCN 2018040259 (print) | LCCN 2018040973 (ebook) | ISBN 9781501716416 (epub/mobi) | ISBN 9781501716423 (pdf) | ISBN 9781501716409 | ISBN 9781501716409 (cloth)
Subjects: LCSH: United States—Foreign relations—Southeast Asia. | Southeast Asia—Foreign relations—United States. | Great Britain—Foreign relations—Southeast Asia. | Southeast Asia—Foreign relations—Great Britain. | Communism—Southeast Asia—History—20th century. | Nationalism—Southeast Asia—History—20th century. | Postcolonialism—Southeast Asia—History—20th century. | Chinese—Southeast Asia—History—20th century.
Classification: LCC DS525.9.U6 (ebook) | LCC DS525.9.U6 N36 2019 (print) | DDC 327.73059—dc23
LC record available at https://lccn.loc.gov/2018040259

To my family

Contents

Abbreviations

AMDA	Anglo-Malayan Defense Agreement (Anglo-Malaysian Defense Agreement after 1963)
ANZUS	Australia, New Zealand, United States Security Treaty
ASA	Association of Southeast Asia
ASEAN	Association of Southeast Asian Nations
ASPAC	Asia Pacific Council
ATOM	*Conduct of Anti-Terrorist Operations in Malaya*
BRIAM	British Advisory Mission
CCP	Chinese Communist Party
CIA	Central Intelligence Agency
FPDA	Five Power Defense Arrangement
GMD/KMT	Guomindang/Kuomintang (Chinese Nationalist Party)
MAAG	Military Assistance Advisory Group
MCA	Malayan Chinese Association
MCP	Malayan Communist Party
NATO	North Atlantic Treaty Organization
NLF	National Liberation Front (known also as the Viet Cong)
NSC	National Security Council
PAP	People's Action Party (Singapore)
PKI	Partai Komunis Indonesia (Indonesian Communist Party)
PRRI	Revolutionary Government of the Republic of Indonesia
RAF	Royal Air Force

SEATO	Southeast Asia Treaty Organization
UMNO	United Malays National Organization
UN	United Nations
ZOPFAN	Zone of Peace, Freedom and Neutrality

Arc of Containment

Introduction

Recovering the Regional Dimensions of U.S. Policy toward Southeast Asia

The war in the Pacific was finally over. Now, the western powers—battered, licking their wounds—entered the colossal wreck of Japan's Co-Prosperity Sphere to reclaim their Southeast Asian territories. Some of these campaigns went badly. France's recolonization dream in Indochina, sustained almost entirely by U.S. aid, became a nightmare. The Viet Minh had the French reeling by early 1954. And just a week into that new year, U.S. president Dwight Eisenhower met with senior officials of the National Security Council (NSC) to discuss France's flagging military efforts. Director of Central Intelligence Allen Dulles was the first to speak. He informed Eisenhower that the French garrison was "locked up" at Dien Bien Phu, "surrounded by approximately three Viet Minh divisions" as "fresh Viet Minh battalions were en route." Admiral Arthur Radford, chairman of the Joint Chiefs of Staff, thought— wrongly, as it turned out—that the Viet Minh would "avoid an all-out assault on Dien Bien Phu." Dulles was less sure. He believed that the Viet Minh might attack this French "fortress" and accept severe military losses if only to inflict "psychological damage" on the French "will to continue" the war. As talk lurched toward how the United States might respond to the prospect of a French withdrawal, Eisenhower became agitated. Though none in the NSC dared say it, he could sense that they waited on his answer to one question above all: would he commit U.S. troops to Indochina? On record, he declared "with great force" that he "could not imagine the United States putting ground troops anywhere in Southeast Asia, except possibly in Malaya."[1]

At the time, Britain and its local allies in Malaya as well as Singapore were six years into counterinsurgency operations and political campaigns against the mostly Chinese Malayan Communist Party (MCP). Like the Viet Minh, the MCP had been the backbone of a popular anti-Japanese resistance army in occupied Malaya during World War II. In 1948, MCP guerrillas launched an armed revolt against British authorities, attempting to leverage support from the hundreds and thousands of ethnic Chinese who constituted nearly 40 percent of Malaya's population. In Singapore, affiliates of the MCP infiltrated workers' unions and middle schools, mounting frequent labor strikes and student protests that paralyzed the country. British leaders had named these troubles an "Emergency." But Eisenhower considered them critical Cold War contests with wider regional ramifications. Throughout his first year in office, he had agonized over communist aggression in Malaya and Indochina. In his inaugural speech of 1953 and others that year, he held that Malaya was "indefensible" if Indochina went to the Viet Minh, that should Malaya fall, then Indonesia would also quickly succumb to communism. In April 1954, he envisioned the states of Southeast Asia as a row of dominoes, their fates all interconnected in the Cold War struggle.[2]

Little wonder, then, that the Singapore domino also preoccupied Eisenhower's officials. Singapore Island was host to Britain's most important naval and air installations in Asia and vital to the U.S.-led Southeast Asia Treaty Organization (SEATO) military alliance. In March 1955, Kenneth Young of the State Department returned from Southeast Asia to report not only that Malaya would soon become a "Chinese state" but also that Singapore faced "real danger of communist subversion." He explained: "80% of Singapore was Chinese" and more than half of them under the age of twenty-one—the communists had already made such "headway" in the country's middle schools that in the coming years most of Singapore's labor force would be "oriented toward and under the control of Peking."[3] Months later, U.S. strategists still grappling with Young's assessment warned that in the interconnected region, losing Singapore ensured "the power of the West to influence events in Burma, Thailand, Indonesia, Laos, Cambodia and Vietnam would be greatly reduced."[4] Recently declassified documents show, furthermore, that until 1959 NSC officials so feared an "internal takeover by the Communists or the extreme leftists" in Singapore that they resolved to "take all feasible measures to thwart the attempt, including even military action."[5] It did not come to this. Britain and Singapore's anticommunist nationalists managed in the early 1960s to suppress the country's socialist movement. Yet it was never a remote prospect given

Eisenhower's track record of covert maneuvers against the left-leaning governments of Iran, Guatemala, and Indonesia.

These Cold War anxieties explain why Eisenhower was relieved when Malayan and British efforts ultimately sent a tattered MCP fleeing north to the Malayan-Thai border in the late 1950s.[6] He was cheered also that Britain had cultivated anticommunist Malayan nationalists who won popular legitimacy at the ballot box in the mid-1950s, led their country to independence in 1957, and continued thereafter to align their nation with the West. In 1960, Eisenhower would hail the end of the Malayan Emergency as a "victory" against communism "in all its forms."[7] U.S. officials entertaining the possibility of Southeast Asia's dominoes falling for the West sought to adapt Britain and Malaya's example for the United States' Cold War playbook.

The Kennedy and Johnson administrations, too, invested high stakes in the smooth decolonization, stability, and avowed anticommunism of Malaya and Singapore.[8] In 1962, Roger Hilsman, adviser to President John F. Kennedy, judged that the creation of Malaysia—the merger of Malaya, Singapore, and Britain's Borneo territories scheduled for 1963—would complete a "wide anticommunist arc" that linked Thailand, Malaya, Singapore, and the Philippines, encircling China and its Vietnamese allies.[9] Kennedy, with the entire region in view, soon acclaimed Malaysia as "the best hope for security in that very vital part of the world."[10] In September 1964, with President Lyndon Johnson poised to send U.S. troops to Vietnam, RAND Corporation delivered (per the State Department's commission) five detailed studies of British-Malayan counterinsurgency and jungle warfare tactics.[11] As U.S. involvement in Southeast Asia deepened, U.S. leaders clutched at those older hands, the British, from which world power was slipping, as if to seize some cache of imperial knowledge that might be brought to bear on the once heavily colonized region. Britain's empire would cast a long shadow on U.S. relations with Southeast Asia, dissolving only in the 1970s when the British finally vacated their military bases in Singapore.

So what? Of course British decolonization, the progress of Malaya and Singapore toward independence, and their victories over communism shaped U.S. Cold War policy. Every domino in Southeast Asia was critical to the United States—by the domino logic their destinies were all intertwined. For good or ill, Eisenhower's idiosyncratic depiction of Southeast Asian security had flattened the distinctions between the countries of the region. As dominoes of identical dimensions, all must have appeared equally important to U.S. strategy.

Yet most studies of the United States' involvement in Southeast Asia have focused on the U.S. war in Vietnam. Indeed, historian Robert McMahon's decades-old remonstrance about the literature concerned with U.S.-Vietnam relations could easily have been penned today—it is still "dauntingly voluminous" and liable to "overwhelm virtually all other regional issues."[12] There are far more histories of the Vietnam War than of U.S. relations with the rest of Southeast Asia combined. And as long as Vietnam's fraught decolonization dominates our perspective, the history of U.S. intervention in Southeast Asia traces familiar narratives of the United States' best and brightest feeding their hubris and meeting ultimate failure, or the irony of U.S. leaders' reluctant, pessimistic, and irrevocable slide into an unwinnable conflict in Vietnam. Fixation with Vietnam also burrows into the psychological wounds of U.S. defeat, the "Vietnam Syndrome" that for decades haunted U.S. citizens' perceptions of their armed forces as well as shook their confidence in their leaders and the nation. Consequently, the views and responses of Southeast Asian actors closest to the war itself, besides those of the Vietnamese, have curiously escaped detailed study.

A number of historians have responded to this imbalance by delving into the United States' other bilateral relations within the region. The work they do is invaluable. But these studies also tip the scales in the opposite direction, claiming the primacy of another Southeast Asian domino instead of Vietnam. One scholar has called Indonesia the "largest domino" in postwar U.S. foreign policy because of its "demographic weight . . . geographical expanse . . . [and] abundance of natural resources."[13] Another reminds us that Eisenhower voiced exceptional concern about Laos when he handed the reins of government to Kennedy in 1961; that U.S. officials thought Laotians more susceptible to communism than all other Southeast Asians, making Laos the domino that teetered at the head of the line, its position not "interchangeab[le]" with any other.[14] One other historian has suggested that U.S. leaders actually viewed Burma and Vietnam as Southeast Asia's "two most threatened" states, and that at certain junctures in the early Cold War, Burma seemed like it "might well be the first domino to fall."[15]

This creates a paradox. Designating any single domino as the most important to U.S. policy relies on as well as repudiates the domino theory. The regional dynamic that so captured the strategic imagination of U.S. leaders—the interconnectedness of the Southeast Asian states—is lost. Furthermore, using a bilateral relationship as one's basic unit of analysis risks descending into a kind of intellectual silo, obscuring the proper (and larger) dimensions of the U.S. Cold War project within and beyond Southeast Asia. Perhaps this explains why

studies of U.S.–Southeast Asian relations with a "broad, regional focus" remain, as McMahon once observed, "surprisingly rare."[16]

Would our understanding of the U.S. encounter with Southeast Asia change if we pivoted from Vietnam to U.S. relations with Britain, Malaya, and Singapore (one, a declining empire; the other two, dominoes that historians have left at the margins of U.S. foreign relations)? Does a new international history come to light when we examine how the fortunes of these four nations became entangled with each other and that of the wider region?

These general questions underpin the particulars of this study: How did the presence of Chinese communities in Malaya, in Singapore, and throughout Southeast Asia figure in U.S. and British Cold War policies? What impact did the persistence of British imperial power in Malaya and Singapore exert on U.S. involvement in the region? In what ways did the heartening trajectories of Malaya and Singapore (to the United States, at least) influence U.S. strategies and prospects in and outside Vietnam? Indeed, how did all the regional dominoes that never fell affect Vietnam, each other, and the broader patterns of decolonization and the Cold War in Southeast Asia? In answering these, my book recasts the history of U.S. empire in Southeast and East Asia from World War II through the end of U.S. intervention in Vietnam.

Arc of Containment argues that anticommunist nationalism in Southeast Asia intersected with preexisting local antipathy toward China and its diaspora to usher the region from European-dominated colonialism to U.S. hegemony. Between the late 1940s and the 1960s, Britain and its indigenous collaborators in Malaya and Singapore overcame the mostly Chinese communist parties of both countries by crafting a pro-West nationalism that was anticommunist by virtue of its anti-Chinese bent. London's neocolonial schemes in Malaya and Singapore would prolong its influence in the region. But as British power waned, Malaya and Singapore's anticommunist leaders cast their lot with the United States, mirroring developments in the Philippines, Thailand, and (in the late 1960s) Indonesia.

This pro-U.S. trajectory was more characteristic of Southeast Asian history after World War II than Indochina's temporary embrace of communism. By the early 1970s, these five anticommunist nations had quashed Chinese-influenced socialist movements at home and established, with U.S. support, a geostrategic arc of states that contained the Vietnamese revolution and encircled China. In the process, the Euro-American colonial order of Southeast Asia passed through Anglo-American predominance into a condition of U.S. hegemony.

In effect, the Cold War in Southeast Asia represented but one violent chapter in the continuous history of western imperialism in the twentieth century. Tracing this relatively seamless imperial transition, my book draws inspiration from Mark Bradley's attempt to "reconceptualize the international history of the twentieth century in ways that more fully transcend the traditional Cold War narrative."[17] It elaborates Anne Foster's insightful study of pre-1941 Southeast Asia, which has revealed how easily and often U.S. colonial officials cooperated with their Dutch, French, and British counterparts to preserve the colonial order, from capturing Southeast Asian communists to blunting the anticolonial edge of nationalist movements, to containing the burgeoning Japanese empire.[18] I show that these imperial tendencies recurred after 1945, challenging notions of World War II as a decisive watershed in world affairs. Indeed, Britain's neocolonial ambitions were mutually constitutive with U.S. empire; Southeast Asian collaborators upheld them both. To borrow from Charles Maier's analyses of the U.S. empire and its predecessors, Southeast Asia's anticommunist nationalists chose to "acquiesce" to Anglo-American predominance first and, later on, the U.S. empire alone. And it was an empire, one "built on a congeries of client states (or 'friendly kings') . . . [rather than] direct rule." In practical terms, the "friendly kings" of the anticommunist arc "enlist[ed] against common enemies" they shared with the U.S. hegemon, solicited U.S. support for their regimes (with conspicuous success), linked their economies to that of the United States, and, where possible, tried to influence U.S. policy.[19] The anticommunist arc offered the United States an "international empire" in Asia, one to succeed formal colonialism, a new "order produced through the coordination of multiple, 'legitimate' nation-states."[20]

Southeast Asian developments by the late 1960s actually shared striking parallels with Western Europe's political and economic tendencies in the decade immediately following World War II. As Geir Lundestad argues, Western Europe sought to ward off Soviet aggression and reconstruct its economies after 1945 by drawing a willing United States into an "empire by invitation."[21] On the other side of the world, Southeast Asia's anticommunist elites made analogous choices to forestall the potential of Chinese hegemony with corresponding results.

This invitation to international empire, extended by Southeast Asia's anticommunist nationalists and accepted by U.S. cold warriors, proved effective because of their shared concerns about the region's Chinese diaspora. My book examines Anglo-American views of the Chinese communities in Malaya, in Singapore, and across Southeast Asia to reveal how these regional concerns drove Allied thinking, thereby illuminating yet more important continuities in U.S.–Southeast Asian relations through the global wars of the middle to late twentieth century. Indeed, the domino logic of U.S. policy toward Southeast Asia arose from apocalyptic visions of China and its diaspora repeating Imperial Japan's shocking wartime victories over the colonial powers, the most notable of these Britain's humiliating surrender of Singapore, its "impregnable fortress." At base, U.S. and British leaders feared that the Chinese communities throughout the region would collectively serve as Beijing's fifth column. For once the communist revolution swept China in 1949, Anglo-American leaders began worrying about "Chinese penetration" of the resuscitated colonial order; they pondered with dread the transnational threat of some ten million ethnic Chinese in Southeast Asia, linked by diasporic networks, mobilized for China's expansionist designs.[22]

Scholars have long studied the Chinese diaspora of Southeast Asia in cases of individual countries and colonies, though some have examined the diaspora through a regional lens. These works consider Chinese migration to Southeast Asia over the duration of centuries, underscore the heterogeneous nature of the region's Chinese, and trace their "Southeast-Asianization," the process by which their attenuated affiliations toward China faded against growing attachments to their adopted country.[23] Nevertheless, the misguided presumption that Southeast Asia's Chinese would naturally support Beijing's ambitions for regional dominance was real for U.S. and British cold warriors and shaped their policymaking. This presumption also featured prominently in the nation-building policies of anticommunist leaders in Malaya, Singapore, and other Southeast Asian states, for they amassed political power by intertwining nationalist fervor with popular anti-Chinese prejudice seething within their indigenous communities, prejudices that dated back to the colonial era (and in some countries, before). Southeast Asia's "long-settled creolized" Chinese "elites" had been the targets of local resentment through the centuries, for they had visibly prospered from their effective service as "intermediaries" between colonial authorities, western capital, Chinese labor, and businesses. The anti-Chinese pogroms that now and again flared up in colonial Southeast Asia, the anti-Chinese themes that permeated early-twentieth-century nationalist movements, and the colonial policies that designated "foreign Asians" as "scapegoat[s] for the economic woes" of the Great Depression all returned in spades when anticommunist nationalists unleashed coercive and violent campaigns against their Chinese communities, rich and poor alike.[24] Put simply, anti-Chinese prejudice rallied under new flags. Disciplining the Chinese diaspora, a corollary of resisting China, provided the connective tissue between Southeast Asia's anticommunist nationalism, U.S. containment policy, and British neocolonialism in Malaya and Singapore.

Thus, a chief concern of this book is also the intimate U.S.-British connection in Southeast Asia, the lasting regional impact of Britain's imperial presence being intertwined with the nascent U.S. empire well into the 1970s. There is certainly a wealth of scholarship broadly concerned with Anglo-American relations. Historians have already compared the structure and institutions of British and U.S. empires; considered the worldviews of, and relationship between, their ruling elites; mulled the future of contemporary U.S. power in Britain's shadow; and picked apart popular U.S. denials of its imperial legacy.[25] But they have not considered how the years of Anglo-American predominance in Southeast Asia produced different and more consequential patterns in post-1945 Southeast Asia than the United States' mishandling of France's former colonies. Among other distortions to our analysis, concentrating on U.S.-Vietnam relations overstates the continuity between French colonialism and U.S. policy in Southeast Asia. In Fredrik Logevall's acclaimed *Embers of War*, for example, France's defeat at Dien Bien Phu supposedly "straddles" the "midpoint of the twentieth century," a hinge between the colonial order and the "emergence of the United States as the predominant power in Asian and world affairs."[26] The existence of such a midpoint is doubtful. The colonial order outlived the French Empire. Indeed, Britain's deep political and military ties to Malaya and Singapore saw its influence endure in the region for some two decades following France's withdrawal from Indochina, for almost thirty years after the end of World War II. Britain and its Southeast Asian partners, their rivalry with Indonesia, and diplomatic efforts to forge a regional grouping with other anticommunist states in the wider region were surely more crucial to U.S. policies and prospects in Southeast Asia than the long-departed colonial powers.

To be sure, a few scholars have conducted fine-grained studies of U.S.-British relations in Cold War Southeast Asia. However, these remain limited in scope, tightly focused on the British advisory mission in Vietnam (1961–1965) or the Indonesia-Malaysia rivalry known as the Confrontation (1963–1966).[27] Furthermore, major works on the Malayan Emergency (1948–1960), which U.S. leaders watched closely, have kept the United States at a distance or absent altogether, unless the U.S. experience in Vietnam appears as an object lesson in failed counterinsurgency and nation building.[28] In contrast, *Arc of Containment* examines U.S.-British relations in Southeast Asia over the longer term, from the Pacific War through the Emergency, the war in Vietnam, the Confrontation (or *Konfrontasi*, as the Indonesian leaders called it), and Britain's final military withdrawal from its Singapore bases just as the United States was extricating itself from Indochina. In so doing, this book sheds light on the significant continuities between the British and U.S. empires that shaped the fortunes of the region, among these the woefully under-studied decisions of Malaya and Singapore, as Britain retreated, to shelter under and extend the wing of the United States further into Southeast Asia.

The U.S. war in Vietnam, important without being central, unfolded within this larger regional context. Viewed through this wide-angle lens, the story of U.S. empire in Southeast Asia is different from the one often told by historians of U.S. intervention in Indochina. For, if U.S. leaders were often downcast about Indochina, they were also buoyed by the successful anticommunism of Malaya and Singapore, and the pro-U.S. tilt of Thailand and the Philippines. This did not prevent President Johnson from committing U.S. forces to Vietnam and may have even given him confidence (fragile and false) that he might rescue the tottering Saigon government. More to the point, the region had largely turned in Washington's favor when Johnson Americanized the Vietnam conflict in 1965, ordering U.S. military leaders to take control of the campaign against the Viet Cong. By the middle of that year, virtually all the Southeast Asian allies of Britain and the United States had already triumphed against their socialist rivals at home. U.S. troops deploying to Vietnam therefore entered the embrace of a "wide anti-communist arc," its grip deadly to so many. Tens of thousands of U.S. soldiers, and many more Vietnamese fighters and civilians on either side of the war, would perish while the authoritarian regimes of the arc consolidated their power and tied their fates to U.S. hegemony. The tragedy was that these deaths, numbering in the millions, occurred when the United States had already achieved broad success in the region.

The geostrategic arc of containment would become even more robust at the end of 1965 with the addition of the fifth most populous country in the world: Indonesia. Again, events that transpired outside Vietnam proved more critical to Southeast Asia's rightward course. From the early to mid-1960s, Britain, Malaya, and Singapore mounted diplomatic and covert military offensives against Sukarno, Indonesia's left-leaning leader, making him increasingly vulnerable to right-wing rivals. Indonesia's anticommunist military, led by General Suharto, executed a bloody purge of the Indonesian Communist Party (PKI), ousted Sukarno (who had depended on the PKI's support), broke relations with China (that Sukarno had nurtured), and drove Indonesia deep into the U.S. orbit. U.S. leaders, alert to these developments, moved to consolidate their gains. They did not acquire their empire in a "fit of absence of mind."[29]

While mired in Vietnam, the United States vigorously cultivated politico-military and economic ties with Indonesia as well as the other Southeast Asian nations that constituted the arc of containment.

For their part, the five nations of the anticommunist arc returned the favor. In 1967, they founded the Association of Southeast Asian Nations (ASEAN), and claimed to be nonaligned but fully supported the U.S. military intervention in Vietnam. Some fueled the conflict by volunteering their troops and bases; others took to international forums and broadcast apologetics for U.S. containment policy and the war in Vietnam; yet others provided maintenance services, supplied oil to U.S. military machines, took on military procurements contracts, and more yet (all of which brought generous U.S. support for their regimes). As stable bulwarks open for business to the capitalist world, they also welcomed the U.S. investments that seeded the region's purported economic miracle of the 1980s.

Despite all this, historians have presupposed that the U.S. debacle in Vietnam represents the end of the "short-lived American empire" in Southeast Asia.[30] In fact, Vietnam was anomalous. ASEAN's pro-U.S. diplomacy meant that the United States' failures in Vietnam had by the 1970s become less significant to its Cold War objectives for the region. Scholars have typically downplayed the agency of ASEAN statesmen: one historian of U.S. foreign relations contends that ASEAN's "diplomatic gyrations" affected neither the U.S. war in Indochina nor Sino-U.S. relations.[31] Yet, the United States, standing strong in the arc that overlay the ASEAN states, had prevailed in the larger struggle for the region. Indeed, this book reveals that Beijing and Moscow felt the U.S. strategic advantage acutely—the leaders of both communist giants were thus eager for détente with the United States. This facilitated the end of another arc—the story of U.S. military intervention in Southeast Asia, codified in the Nixon Doctrine announced in July 1969 in Guam. From a position of de facto hegemony in Southeast Asia, President Richard Nixon successfully pursued triangular diplomacy with China and the USSR, withdrew U.S. troops from Vietnam, and ended the confrontational phase of containment policy in that country.

Southeast Asian actors—the dominoes that never fell—had been vital to welding the arc of containment together, not least the Malayans and Singaporeans who have rarely appeared in histories of U.S. foreign policy. In this book, anticommunist nationalists like Malayan prime minister Tunku Abdul Rahman and Singapore's leader Lee Kuan Yew share center stage with the likes of Kennedy and Lyndon Johnson. These "friendly kings" exerted a surprising impact on the worldviews of Eisenhower and Nixon, the policies of Zhou

Enlai and Leonid Brezhnev, and even the opinions of nonaligned leaders such as Gamal Abdel Nasser and Josef Tito. In the vein of Arne Westad's *Global Cold War*, this book explores how Third World elites like the Tunku and Lee intertwined their nation-building aims with the superpower ambitions of the United States, the neocolonial designs of Britain, and the goals of other Southeast Asian anticommunist nationalists (even those with whom they had serious differences).[32] It is in the machinations of these Southeast Asian actors that the Cold War intersected so fatefully with decolonization, "illuminat[ing] historical linkages in the international system running horizontally from East to West, vertically from North to South, [and] transversally across the South itself."[33] The Tunku and Lee waged the global Cold War at home and abroad, the results of which affected the United States, its allies, and antagonists and reverberated back to Malaya, Singapore, and the region as a whole.

Highlighting the agency of Malaya and Singapore's pioneer generation of leaders also decenters the United States. It parallels recent works such as Pierre Asselin's *Hanoi's Road to the Vietnam War*, Jessica Chapman's *Cauldron of Resistance*, Edward Miller's *Misalliance*, and Lien-Hang Nguyen's *Hanoi's War*, all rich and compelling studies of how Vietnamese leaders directly influenced the actions and agendas of the superpowers and, by extension, international history.[34] There is little doubt that Southeast Asian leaders shaped the struggle for the region, since the Cold War powers vied so avidly for collaborators in the decolonizing world.[35] But whereas the careers of Vietnamese leaders in Saigon and Hanoi are increasingly well documented, there is still a poor understanding of how anticommunist nationalists in Malaya and Singapore and their left-wing opponents affected U.S. policy and the global Cold War. *Arc of Containment* is in part an act of archival recovery. Along with U.S. diplomatic archives, it draws on records in Malaysia and Singapore largely untouched by scholars of U.S. foreign relations, and on recently declassified British documents concerned with the empire's cooperation with conservative Southeast Asian allies during its waning years in the region. This multiarchival survey does not aim to recount every detail of Malaya and Singapore's nationalist struggles—its focus remains key moments in the relationships of U.S., British, Malayan, and Singaporean decision makers who from the 1940s through the 1970s shaped imperial transition in Southeast Asia.

The first chapter of this book treats Japan's conquest of Southeast Asia as a window to the longer history of Anglo-American perceptions of Southeast Asia's interconnectedness. Japanese victories fueled what would become the domino logic, entwining race with the struggle for ascendancy in the region and preparing the way for U.S. Cold War fixations with the perceived threat from China and its diaspora to Southeast Asia. Despite the domino theory's significance in U.S. foreign relations, historical studies of its origins remain few and dated. Without exception, these studies maintain that geopolitical lessons far removed from Southeast Asia inspired the domino principle; that Nazi and Soviet aggrandizement in Europe taught U.S. leaders to contain such aggressors rather than appease them; and that failing that, the United States would lose all credibility in the eyes of its allies and, thereafter, see them capitulate to the United States' rivals like falling dominoes.[36] In fact, U.S. policymakers' Cold War visions of Southeast Asia emerged from the Euro-American colonial experience in that region, from the war against Japan for that same region, and from long-standing anxieties about Chinese diasporic links to mainland China. These, far more than the precedents of Nazi and Soviet aggrandizement, underpinned the domino logic of U.S. strategy toward Southeast Asia well into the 1970s.

The next two chapters examine how Britain's apparent success with thwarting the MCP influenced U.S. leaders' views on, and strategy for, the Cold War in Southeast Asia. Chapter 2 shows that as U.S. policymakers cast about for how to deal with the challenges of decolonization and the Cold War in the region, they drew special inspiration from the British nation-building project in Malaya. Britain had cultivated Malaya's anticommunist nationalists, and together they forged a popular multiracial political alliance that undermined the MCP's appeal to several hundred thousands of ethnic Chinese in Malaya. When Malaya gained independence in 1957, its relative stability and leaders' determination to side with the West were received by U.S. leaders as a notch on the belt.

Chapter 3 examines the other half of Britain and Malaya's success story, their counterinsurgency campaign against the MCP guerrillas. It recovers the outsize U.S. fascination with British counterinsurgency, tracing how U.S. policymakers' attempts to cherry-pick lessons from the British campaign in Malaya shaped the United States' regional and global strategies from the 1950s through the 1960s. Certainly, scholars have long discussed the usefulness of British-Malayan counterinsurgency methods to the U.S. effort in Vietnam, or lack thereof.[37] A few lament the British-Malayan tactics (and triumphs) forsaken in Vietnam, while others enumerate the disparities between Malaya and Vietnam to decry the applicability of British-Malayan strategies.[38] But these lines of inquiry, anchored to the U.S. war in Vietnam, remain limited; the value of British-Malayan counterinsurgency to Vietnam is quite beside the point. As this chapter shows, the U.S. preoccupation with British-Malayan counterinsurgency tactics, as well as British and Malayan leaders' attempts to exploit this preoccupation and thereby strengthen their Cold War partnership with the United States, illuminates the larger reality of Britain's critical and enduring influence on U.S. empire building across the global South in the 1960s.

The fourth chapter examines how the creation of Malaysia in 1963 completed a geostrategic arc of anticommunist states in Southeast Asia and undermined Sukarno's left-leaning regime in Indonesia, providing a powerful fillip to U.S. Cold War aims. Malayan leader Tunku Abdul Rahman's efforts to create an indigenous anticommunist alliance with Thailand and the Philippines bore fruit in the early 1960s. Soon after came the formation of Malaysia, which was smoothed by the application of Singapore's internal security apparatus toward the repression of its socialist movement. To date, scholars concerned with the emergence of Malaysia have focused only on the agendas and actions of Britain, Malaya, and Singapore.[39] They pay little heed to U.S. Cold War suspicions that Singapore's Chinese might enable Beijing to expand its power and, consequently, overlook the broader implications of how Malaysia figured in U.S. visions of anticommunist Southeast Asia. This chapter demonstrates that, with Singapore nestled inside pro–West Malaysia and the island's critical naval and air bases still run by British forces in service of Anglo-American interests, the arc of containment began to solidify. Also, Britain and Malaysia's anticommunist offensives against Sukarno would by the mid-1960s severely destabilize the Indonesian government, paving the way for Sukarno's ouster and Indonesia's alignment with the United States against China and the USSR.

The final chapter examines Southeast Asia's passage from Anglo-American predominance to U.S. hegemony between the late 1960s and mid-1970s, a product of British decolonization strategies in Singapore and the growing stability of the arc of containment. As Britain's military pulled out of Singapore, it established the Five Power Defense Arrangement (FPDA), a security framework for Malaysia, Singapore, Australia, and New Zealand. And heretofore, scholars have ignored the FPDA's impact on Soviet policy in Southeast Asia and the broader Cold War rivalry for the region.[40] Indeed, through the FPDA, British neocolonialism's final burst of fire thwarted Soviet hopes of expanding the USSR's regional influence beyond Indochina, persuading Moscow to accommodate to U.S. hegemony in Southeast Asia.

At the same time, Southeast Asia's anticommunist-nationalists, five of whom founded ASEAN in 1967, forged increasingly intimate political, economic, and military ties with the United States, stabilizing their regimes as well as effectively containing Vietnam and China. When the United States pulled its troops from Vietnam, neither China nor the USSR possessed political and military links with the Philippines, Thailand, or Indonesia to the degree that the United States did. Neither communist giant could claim more than trading links with, or embassies in, Malaysia and Singapore. With a substantial strategic advantage over the communist powers in the region, Nixon could retool U.S. containment policy as triangular diplomacy, finding both Beijing and Moscow keen to thaw relations with the predominant superpower. Even the fall of Saigon in 1975 would not shake the arc of containment.

But stare long enough into the fiery ruin of South Vietnam, and the conflagration may be blinding. It can consume our sight with what seems like the failure of U.S. imperial pretensions, a catastrophe borne disproportionately by the peoples of Indochina. Yet ringing the South China Sea, there are other emblems of the United States' grandiose and ignoble endeavor. The "friendly kings" of Southeast Asia rose to power as Indochina teetered toward disaster; they presided over the majority of the region's peoples and resources and stood from year to year as proof that the domino theory was actually running in reverse.

In charting the emergence of Malaya's and Singapore's "friendly kings," this book brings us back to the earliest iterations of the domino principle in the Pacific War, iterations bound tightly to Japan's onslaught against both British-controlled territories and the security guarantees they afforded the other western powers in Southeast Asia. Into this logic of regional interconnectedness, Washington and London would later pour their fears of China's communists and the Chinese diaspora. Here, the domino theory materialized, profoundly shaping the United States' fateful Cold War encounter with Southeast Asia.

But the Cold War crisis also offered the United States opportunities. For while Eisenhower conjured the domino imagery to describe Southeast Asia's vulnerability, he also advocated "build[ing] that row of dominoes so they can stand the fall of one."[41] With British or U.S. assistance (and sometimes both), the "friendly kings" did just that. They won, seized, or clung to power by whipping up a deadly cocktail of anti-Chinese prejudice and anticommunism at home. By right-wing coups, crackdowns, and massacres, they cemented their authority. Many more across Southeast Asia would perish violently like the millions in the Indochina conflicts. And then Malaysia and Singapore, together with their ASEAN counterparts, transformed their row of dominoes into the arc of containment. Regardless of what Beijing or Moscow could claim to have done for their Vietnamese allies against the U.S. war machine, the prospects for communist expansion beyond Indochina were paltry. The arc had coursed through war and strife, across nations and time, and it marked out the formidable shape of U.S. empire.

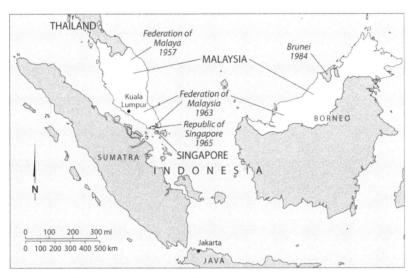

Map 1. Map of Malaysia and Singapore. Malaya, comprising only the peninsula, secured independence from Britain in 1957. In 1963, Malaya merged with Singapore and Britain's Borneo territories (Sabah and Sarawak) to become the independent Federation of Malaysia. Singapore exited the federation to become independent in 1965.

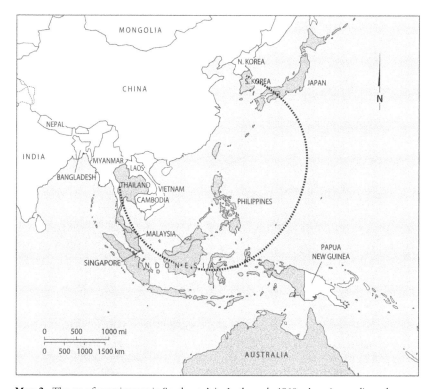

Map 2. The arc of containment in Southeast Asia. In the early 1960s, American policymakers envisioned a geostrategic arc of U.S. allies made up of Thailand, Malaysia, Singapore, and the Philippines. Indonesia's rightward shift in the late 1960s strengthened the arc enclosing the South China Sea. Taken together with Japan and South Korea, U.S. allies completely encircled Vietnam and China.

Chapter 1

Darkest Moment

The Fall of Singapore, "Chinese Penetration,"
and the Domino Theory

Japan's invasion of mainland Southeast Asia was already underway when its forces struck Pearl Harbor. The 25th Imperial Japanese Army had been shelling the northern coast of British Malaya since midnight on December 8, 1941.[1] The United States' day of "infamy" would dawn only some two hours later, Hawaiian time, when Japan attacked the Philippines as well as Pearl Harbor to immobilize the U.S. Fleet in the Eastern Pacific.[2] That same day, the Japanese bombed Singapore, the island that—for its $400 million naval and air bases— British strategists had called the empire's "impregnable fortress" in the Far East.[3] Over the next three days, Japan would hit U.S. bases on Midway and in the Philippines, occupy Guam, and sink the 35,000-ton British battleship *Prince of Wales* and the battle cruiser *Repulse* just off the Malay Peninsula.[4] Japanese tanks, joined by troops deploying from occupied bases and airfields in Vietnam and Thailand, then plowed rapidly southward through the Malayan jungles.[5] In just three weeks, Japan would advance more than three hundred miles into Malaya.[6] As British and Australian forces retreated, Japanese engineers and infantrymen raced on bicycles down Malaya's highways to lay siege to Singapore.[7]

The British had once bragged that Singapore's eighteen-inch guns "outranged anything at sea," that its harbor was large enough to shelter the combined navies of the United States and Britain.[8] They had repeatedly assured other western nations that the island was "unassailable."[9] And they surrendered Singapore after just a week of fighting on February 15, 1942. One hundred thousand troops of the British Empire had capitulated to thirty-four thousand Japanese.[10] Profoundly shaken, Prime Minister Winston Churchill called it "the darkest moment of the war."[11] Japanese leaders, as if to drive the insult home, renamed the island Shonan, the "Light of the South."[12] With control of mainland Southeast Asia, Japan swiftly enclosed the Dutch colonial islands of Sumatra and Java within its "pincers."[13] By May, the Japanese had fully seized the Philippines from the United States and threatened Australia.[14]

From this "darkest moment" came the underpinnings of U.S. policy toward Southeast Asia through the 1970s. Japan had treated spectators and sufferers alike to a brutal preview of how Asian communism, pouring out of China, might bring the region to heel. For U.S. and British policymakers, Japan's campaign had proven vividly that one state's capitulation to an external aggressor undermined the stability of its neighbors. Of course, the Euro-American colonial authorities in Southeast Asia had already assumed before 1941 that anticolonial revolts or budding communist parties in any one of their colonies would excite similar movements throughout the region. And they had cooperated during the interwar years to put brakes on Tokyo's expansionist ambitions, concerned that the burgeoning Asian empire might embolden Southeast Asia's nationalists to rise against the western colonial order. Until 1941, that colonial order seemed able to evolve in step with multiple threats to its power.[15] But Japan's dramatic victories early in the Pacific War were of a different magnitude. The "darkest moment" made the dynamic of regional interconnectedness axiomatic to achieving ascendancy in Southeast Asia; cold warriors with shared memories of the Pacific War built their strategic visions for postcolonial Southeast Asia on this embryonic domino logic. President Dwight Eisenhower's idiosyncratic imagery came much later.[16]

Crucially, Japan's brief supremacy entwined race with the struggle for Southeast Asia thereafter. U.S. officials lamented that the fall of Singapore, in particular, had "lowered immeasurably . . . the prestige of the white race."[17] In turn, *Foreign Affairs* stole glances at the future, sure that "the memory of the surrender of Singapore to Asiatic troops [would] not easily be effaced from the consciousness of Asiatic peoples." The journal predicted that anticolonialism would surge with the knowledge that "white empires" "*can* be defeated . . . by non-whites."[18] Even when Japan was in full retreat by 1945, President Franklin Roosevelt expressed concerns that Tokyo might still rally all of Asia to its side, instantly stirring "1,100,000,000 potential enemies" to action.[19]

But with Japan counted an ally of the United States after World War II, U.S. leaders transitioned to envisioning China in the colors of the Yellow Peril.[20] As the Chinese Revolution crested in 1949, Secretary of State Dean Acheson approved a policy paper on U.S. Cold War approaches toward Southeast Asia that echoed Roosevelt's final fears. The paper, "NSC-51: U.S. Policy toward Southeast Asia," stated that the Chinese communists would exploit the pervasive "anti-white Asiatic zenophobia [sic]" in Southeast Asia and marshal millions of agents in region against the restored but much weakened colonial order. Above all, the paper contended that Southeast Asia's Chinese had become enamored of how the Chinese Communist Party (CCP) "waxed enormously in strength," and that with such advantages "Chinese penetration" of the region would prove "a simple matter."[21]

One historian has suggested that NSC–51 carries an early version of the domino theory but delves no further.[22] In fact, the paper renders the base elements of the domino logic explicitly: fears of Chinese hegemony via its interconnected Southeast Asian diaspora. It was a strategic vision with roots in the colonial powers' anxieties, quickened by the "darkest moment," made visceral after 1945 by the subversive activities and guerrilla warfare of the mostly Chinese Malayan Communist Party (MCP) in Malaya and Singapore. This vision owed much to the influence of British colonial authorities whose assessments of Southeast Asia the United States trusted most. Indeed, Britain nurtured U.S. Cold War prejudices against Southeast Asia's Chinese diaspora and its supposed connection to mainland communists. In the frequent meetings between U.S. officials visiting British colonial administrators in Malaya and Singapore, a domino logic specific to the states of Southeast Asia congealed within U.S. policy toward the region.

Throughout 1941, as Japanese troops entered Indochina (by agreement with Vichy France), the Allies persuaded themselves that Japan planned to capture Singapore. On January 4, U.S. officials in Bangkok informed Secretary of State Cordell Hull that Japan would use Thailand as a "base for operations against Singapore."[23] In February, U.S. ambassador to Japan Joseph Grew sent word to Hull that an attack on Singapore was integral to Japan's southward advance, for "that strategically essential base" was "fundamental" to the "immediate defense" of the British Empire.[24] That same month, Churchill himself wrote Roosevelt that Japan desired Singapore.[25] Even the Dutch government-in-exile warned its allies in August that Japan aimed at Singapore, the most "desirable springboard" for a "thrust" at the East Indies.[26] In November, Britain's ambassador to the United States wrote the State Department that he expected Japan to soon invade Thailand, encroach on the Malay frontier, and level an "obvious threat" at Singapore.[27] Repetition turned these predictions into convictions.

Due to what the Allies assumed of Japanese designs on Singapore, and the mounting stakes they thus placed on defending the island, Singapore's significance to Allied strategy (real and imagined) continued to grow. As one of Roosevelt's closest advisers had insisted in April 1941, Singapore was "key to the Indian Ocean, Australasia and Oceania . . . indispensable to the continuation of Britain's war effort [as well as] Japan's dominance of the East." Roosevelt was thus counseled that the "defense of Singapore should be a cardinal feature of our strategy," that the United States could "effectively tie up"—in a word, contain—Japan by "attacking Japanese shipping and airdromes in Indo-China."[28] The western allies soon came to see Singapore as a symbol of the interconnected security of the colonial order, as the "keystone" of Anglo-American strategy in the "Eastern Theatre."[29]

U.S. reporters also inflated the importance of Singapore. From December 1941 until Singapore fell in February the next year, U.S. journalists claimed repeatedly that British and U.S. military planners considered the island Japan's "key objective."[30] They, too, named Singapore the "gateway to the Far East," the Indian Ocean, India itself, the Dutch East Indies, and Australia.[31] Citing sources in the Anglo-American high command, reporters stated ad nauseam that Singapore was the "keystone of the strategic arch of the democracies of the Far East," the "keystone of the defense structure of the United Nations in the Southwestern Pacific," and the "keystone of all Allied plans for the Pacific War."[32] Few U.S. news reporters ventured that losing Singapore fell "far short of determining ultimate control of the Orient."[33] On the front pages of papers like the *Chicago Daily Tribune*, the *Los Angeles Times*, and the *New York Times*, the battle for Southeast Asia warped around Singapore's fate. Most U.S. newspapers continued to call the island the "Gibraltar of the Orient" or "Key to the Pacific" well into January 1942.[34]

These characterizations of Singapore were not new. A 1938 U.S.-made film travelogue named Singapore the "most strategic point of the British Empire," for it lay at the "crossroads of India and Australia, South Africa and China." The film insisted also that Singapore, as the "military base and home of the combined British Far Eastern Fleet," was "rightly . . . the Gibraltar of the East." In a transparent retort to Japanese incursions into China at the time, as well the distant rumblings of coming war in Europe, the film acclaimed Britain's military might. It mentioned the "regular troops composed of European, Indian and Malay units" garrisoned in Singapore, and dwelled conspicuously long on ranks and ranks of marching Indian soldiers to underscore the size of Britain's forces. Britain owned the "finest and most efficient air force in the Far East" and airdromes "unrivalled in the Orient," or so the narrator said.[35] These taunts at Japan betrayed early U.S. anxieties about the power of the Japanese forces, inscribing Singapore with hope that Britain could repel the Yellow Peril.

Certainly, Britain had fostered such hope as well. Its Ministry of Information, for one, had sponsored a 1941 film by British Movietone News titled *Alert in the East* that lavished praise on the "first class naval and air base[s]" of Singapore. The film placed the island "stronghold" at the "strategic center" of the empire, asserting that its military installations ensured the safety of all Britain's colonial possessions. Singapore's bases apparently meant India was "undistracted by self-defense," enabling Britain to spirit India's "magnificent fighting men" to every corner of its gigantic empire. The film then enumerated Britain's far-flung possessions that relied on Singapore's security guarantee, superimposing their names—Kenya, Egypt, Hong Kong, Fiji, Aden, and Darwin, Australia—on footage of numerous deploying Indian and British troops. For Australian officers in Darwin, the sphere of security projected by Singapore allowed their peaceful relaxation on a patio under a thatched roof, the leisurely reading of newspapers, and the drinking of tea without a care for the unnamed threat "which may arise in the Far East."[36] These boasts were intended as much for Britain's rivals and allies as its own imperial subjects. More and more, it seemed ordained that white imperialism, with Britain its great champion, must make its fateful stand in Singapore against Japan.

The day Singapore surrendered, the *New York Times* carried a depiction of the "aerial pattern of Japan's conquest," demonstrating what Japan had wrought. The graphic featured a map of Southeast Asia's countries enveloped by a chain of overlapping spheres. The Japanese attacks at the epicenter of each sphere radiated crises outward, and each sphere merged with the neighboring spheres that it overlapped. Its meaning was plain: Southeast Asian security was indivisible; the collapse of one was deadly for all.[37] The next day, the *New York Times* reported that Washington had "conceded that Sumatra, too, must inevitably fall."[38] A week later *Time* magazine predicted that once Japan took Sumatra, "very soon [they] would be at Java."[39] Japan's southward drive had defied all the sovereign boundaries in the Euro-American colonial order, stringing the region from Indochina down to the Dutch East Indies in interconnected insecurity. By mid-1942, the Southeast Asian states had, to all appearances, already fallen like dominoes.

Time did attempt to put it differently, sexualizing Singapore's strategic value just days after it had fallen. The magazine called the island the "key" to Britain's "seraglio" of colonies. It portrayed Japan as a man whose "hot hand" had pried the "key" from Britain's dead fingers, whose "gleaming eye" now "ogled bejeweled India . . . peeped up the rippling skirts of the Indian Ocean . . . [and] winked at little Madagascar."[40] *Time*'s writers left no mystery as to what they thought of Japan's intentions. Though the magazine distinguished Japan from

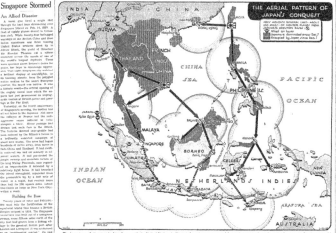

Figure 1. The aerial pattern of Japan's conquest, a graphic from the front page of the *New York Times*, communicated the region's interconnectedness, an embryonic version of the domino theory. From the *New York Times*, February 15, 1942, © 1942 The New York Times. All rights reserved. Used by permission and protected by the copyright laws of the United States. The printing, copying, redistribution, or retransmission of this content without express written permission is prohibited.

the rest of the feminized Orient, endowing it with masculinity enough to defeat the (presumably male) protector of India, it also inscribed the Japanese man with animalistic urges to dehumanize him. In this *Time* was not unique. Jingoism was par for the course in numerous U.S. publications and in government propaganda during the war.[41] More to the point, *Time* also approached Singapore's fate alive to the presumed interconnectedness of Britain's empire.

Little wonder, then, that Britain's leaders remained engrossed throughout World War II with retaking Singapore by force. In 1943, British military planners advocated to their U.S. counterparts the "recapture of Singapore." They said it would shake Japan "psycholog[ically]" and "electrify the Eastern world." They conjured for U.S. officials grandiose visions of driving Japan from Southeast Asia. From Singapore, they argued, Anglo-American forces could threaten Japanese communications to Thailand and Burma, attack Dutch oilfields directly, "flank and undermine the whole Japanese defense structure in Southeast Asia," and then launch operations to retake Hong Kong or Formosa, control the South China Sea, and establish a sea supply route to China.[42] The interconnectedness was all.

Whatever the direction this formative domino effect ran, it burrowed deeper within western strategic thought as the war progressed. Even disagreements between U.S. and British military planners illustrated the Allies' belief in the interconnectedness of Southeast Asia. U.S. military planners agreed with their British allies that retaking Singapore affected all Japanese positions in Southeast Asia; they concurred that from Singapore the Allies could unlock the South China Sea for U.S.-British forces to deploy against the Japanese navy. But Roosevelt and his military planners had by 1943 weaned themselves off obsessing specifically with the island. Because U.S. officials did agree that Singapore possessed strategic advantages, they expected Japan to be deeply entrenched there—the island was not a soft target and any Allied expedition there would become bogged down instead of speedily embarking on other campaigns in the region. Until 1945 U.S. planners rejected all British suggestions to recapture Singapore, preferring to attack perceptibly weaker Japanese positions in Burma so as to connect Allied supply lines to Chiang Kai Shek's armies in China. If via Burma Japan could be battered in China, the ripple effect on Japanese positions throughout Southeast Asia would surely favor the Allies.[43]

For a time, Churchill, unlike his military chiefs, shared the U.S. focus on Burma. But he may have been waiting for an opportune moment to make the case for attacking Singapore. In September 1944, he told Roosevelt that Singapore should be recovered "in battle" not the "peace table." Churchill spoke passionately of "aveng[ing]" the loss of Singapore. Roosevelt disagreed, wishing to strike vulnerable Japanese positions in Bangkok. He reminded Churchill that Japanese forces on Singapore Island would be too strong. Churchill, frustrated, retorted that "undoubtedly [there would] be a large force of Japanese" in Malaya and Singapore, but surely "destroy[ing]" them would boost U.S. operations in the Pacific. Roosevelt sensed a protracted argument about Singapore looming and would not get embroiled. He said nothing and yielded the floor to his military advisers, and the discussion of Allied strategy spun toward other topics.[44] Churchill would be disappointed for almost a year.

Yet both men held to similar strategic visions of Southeast Asia. Both believed that securing one corner of the region could shape the destinies of all its countries; they differed only over the location. The British identified the region's interconnectedness (and their wounded pride) with the fall of Singapore, so they fixed upon the island. Roosevelt viewed Southeast Asia with a capacious sense of U.S. national interests, treating U.S. security as inseparable from the fates of other nations. According to historian Michael Sherry, once Germany invaded Poland in 1939, Roosevelt expressed that "when peace has been broken anywhere, the peace of all countries everywhere is in danger."[45] Indeed, the Pacific War powerfully confirmed what Roosevelt had intuited. And with the fall of Singapore, the *New York Times* echoed the president, treating Pearl Harbor and Singapore as interrelated losses, stating that the Allies fought an "indivisible war" against Japan. As if paraphrasing Roosevelt, the article also insisted "a loss on any front immediately affect[ed] adversely the situation on all other fronts."[46] These formulations of U.S. national security interests lived on in NSC-68, the landmark policy document of 1950 that for decades underpinned U.S. Cold War policy with dictums such as "A defeat of free institutions anywhere is a defeat everywhere."[47] Perhaps this expansive logic of global interconnectedness afforded the United States the latitude to pick choice spots for attacking Japan, latitude not available to the European powers focused on regaining their colonies, latitude the United States would lose in stages as it assumed the burdens of its allies during the Cold War.

Only in July 1945 did Churchill get his wish. With Burma more or less in Allied hands, the combined chiefs directed the supreme allied commander of Southeast Asia, Lord Louis Mountbatten, to "open the Straits of Malacca at the earliest possible moment . . . complete the liberation of Malaya . . . capture key areas of Siam [and] establish bridgeheads in Java and Sumatra." These directives mandated recapturing Singapore as a base for Allied operations.[48] By then, Japan was weak, and Singapore had at last become the soft target that U.S. planners sought. But President Harry Truman's decision to use atomic bombs on Japan in August, and the British returning to Singapore a month later without needing to fight their way in, rendered these plans moot.

Atlantic Echo Chamber

After 1945, U.S. and British policymakers could not but perceive Southeast Asian security through the prism of Japanese imperialism. Even Japan's southward trail left an indelible mark on U.S. and British decision makers. U.S. policymakers could easily imagine that the Chinese communists marched to the martial drumbeat of Japan so recently silenced. In August 1950, State Department officials returned from fact-finding missions to Southeast Asia convinced that the "Japanese had demonstrated the way" the Chinese would invade the region. The military men on these missions concluded alike that if the "Chinese Communists take Indochina . . . Thailand would soon fall," making it easy for Chinese forces to "come down the [Malay] peninsula as the Japs did in the last war."[49] Officials at the U.S. embassy in Indonesia concurred. They too invoked the Japanese invasion as a way to comprehend and express their fears of Chinese communism. The U.S. ambassador in Jakarta reported to the State Department in September 1950 that a communist-controlled Indonesia eased "communist penetration" of the Philippines and the vital bases of Australia, "as was demonstrated when the Japanese mounted their greatest threat" to western interests in the Pacific from the Indonesian islands.[50]

British strategists entertained parallel visions. To be sure, Britain's Office of Foreign Affairs did predict in November 1949 that the CCP would seek chiefly to stimulate "conspiracy against and subversion" of the governments in Southeast Asia, for lacking military prowess comparable to the Japanese in World War II, the CCP remained "unlikely" to pursue military aggression beyond its southern frontier. Yet when these same British officials pondered the details of Chinese foreign policy, they insisted China would replicate the Japanese campaign. They made this disconnected conclusion when nothing in China's use of conspiracy and subversion demanded it must follow a systematic southward course through mainland Southeast Asia. Britain's secretary of state for foreign affairs even informed the cabinet that all in his team "agreed that Indo-China . . . would probably be the immediate objective of Communist action." The British looked first to Japan's original launching pad despite acknowledging Thailand's outstanding "strategic importance," for it bordered Burma, Indochina, and Malaya. They locked onto Indochina even after noting that independent Burma suffered from "chaotic" civil strife that "rendered [it] . . . acutely vulnerable to infiltration and exploitation by the Chinese communists."[51]

The persistence of memory went even further for British officials. After Indochina, they "expected" China to do as the Japanese had done, "overthrow[ing] the existing regimes in Siam and Burma" before turning its attention toward Malaya, Singapore, and eventually, India.[52] Believing that China (like Imperial Japan) wanted Malaya and Singapore most, British strategists drew the Cold War battlefront of Southeast Asia at the French colonies from which the Imperial Japanese had entered Thailand. It was a strategy cast explicitly from the past. In 1952, a full decade after losing Singapore to Japan, Britain's chiefs of staff continued to formulate the empire's "Defense Policy and Global Strategy" with the "darkest moment" in mind. Gesturing at a familiar pattern of expansion, the chiefs calculated that China would first gun for the "fall of Indo-China to Communism," and then "inevitably" (and in sequence) target Thailand, then Burma, before preying on Malaya and Singapore.[53]

Australia, too, figured in this picture of insecurity. During World War II, the danger to Australia had seemed so immediate after the fall of Singapore that British officials subsequently situated Southeast Asia and Australia within the same strategic space. Sir William Strang, undersecretary for foreign affairs, in his March 1949 report on Southeast Asia, reminded his colleagues that Singapore was an "indispensable link in communications with Australia," a link so strong that when Strang visited Singapore earlier that year, he felt himself "there within the sphere of Australian interest."[54] Across the Atlantic, U.S. policymakers held much the same view. NSC-51 (penned by the State Department's policy planning staff at roughly the same time that Strang made his report) stated that if Southeast Asia were ever "swept by communism," this "major political rout" meant a "critically exposed Australia."[55]

Thus, when Truman dispatched three fact-finding missions to Southeast Asia between December 1949 and August 1950, U.S. and British officials encountered each other as though trapped in an echo chamber. Historians Andrew Rotter and Mark Lawrence have already shown that both British and French officials in the late 1940s convinced their U.S. allies to give economic and military aid to the French in Indochina, though U.S. leaders certainly heeded their allies' arguments because they melded easily with U.S. strategic assessments of Southeast Asia after the Chinese revolution.[56] Even so, the records of the Jessup, Griffin, and Melby-Erskine missions (named after their leaders) to Southeast Asia suggest that U.S. officials paid somewhat more attention to British colonial administrators in Malaya and Singapore than the French in Indochina.

Indeed, U.S. officials on all three missions seemed to seek the legitimation of their analyses of the region from British authorities above all. Equally, the British considered these U.S. missions rare opportunities to have their allies see—through British eyes—"the South East Asian picture correctly."[57] Malcolm MacDonald, the loquacious British commissioner-general for Southeast Asia based in Malaya and Singapore, was deeply committed to binding the U.S. view of the region to that of Britain. He shared London's larger objective of building an intimate strategic relationship with the ascendant United States, thereby extending the lifespan of Britain's global influence and slowing the empire's post-1945 decline. And he shared his views so copiously that the records of U.S. officials' meetings with him are thicker than those of their visits elsewhere in the region. U.S. officials were more than ready to meet MacDonald halfway. On March 23, 1950, when Ambassador Philip C. Jessup reported on the first mission's findings to Dean Acheson and Deputy Under Secretary of State Dean Rusk, Jessup stressed his conclusions were "in accord" with those of British officials in Malaya and Singapore. Many of Jessup's insights drew on MacDonald's, whom Jessup referred to affectionately as "McD."[58] Jessup echoed MacDonald's opinion that Indochina was "key to the situation" in Southeast Asia, specifically, the region's "military weakness in meeting Communist guerrillas" in "hot wars" like those raging in Indochina, Malaya, and Burma.[59] According to Jessup, MacDonald believed that "if Indochina or Burma fell to the communists, it would be very easy for them [the communists] to sweep over the Thais who were most unlikely to resist."[60] In paraphrasing and elaborating MacDonald, Jessup recalled in his own expressions how U.S. newspapers during World War II characterized Thailand's collaboration with Japan, claiming that "weak" Thailand (which he qualified was the "British view also") would "not attempt to stand up" against communist aggression.[61]

Likewise, Colonel R. Allen Griffin, leader of the second mission, recalled years later that "you had to talk with the British if you were to understand" the region since "you never found an American who knew anything, in that part of the world." He also sought out MacDonald, for whom he had "great respect," to ascertain how the United States could meet Southeast Asia's security needs.[62] At the time of his fact-finding mission, Griffin had assured Rusk that "the British analyses of the situation in Indochina and in Southeast Asia as a whole were similar to those which he and his mission developed."[63] Griffin's recommendations to the State Department, laced with MacDonald's

Figure 2. Malcolm MacDonald, the United Kingdom's commissioner-general for Southeast Asia (1948 to 1955), departs Singapore in 1955 to take up the position of British high commissioner to India. Photo from the Ministry of Information and the Arts Collection, courtesy of the National Archives of Singapore.

perspectives, were critical to the United States' first steps into Vietnam. Citing the importance of Griffin's reports to Truman's decision, Rusk in April 1950 informed Under Secretary James Webb that the president had reserved $36.5 million for military assistance projects in Indonesia, Indochina, Thailand, and Japan, and sought another $5 million for Indochina as well as other increases in military aid to Indochina from the Mutual Defense Assistance Program.[64] By July 1950, when the third mission led by John Melby arrived at its first stop, Saigon, the belief that Indochina was a gateway for communism's sweep into Southeast Asia had reverberated through the Atlantic echo chamber enough to sound like fact.[65] In August, Melby and Major General Graves B. Erskine, chief of the military group on the mission, opined that it was "almost a commonplace, now, to state that failure in Indochina" to contain communism would "make well-nigh inevitable the over-all and eventual victory of Communism throughout the area."[66]

But the U.S. decision about Indochina, while important, should not cause us to overlook the regional dimensions of Anglo-American thinking. When

Indochina appeared in the exchanges between MacDonald and U.S. officials, its fate was always tied to the other Southeast Asian countries. Here was nothing new. The Allies had used similar expressions during the Pacific War to situate Singapore within the interconnected region. Imperial Japan, too, had been preoccupied with taking Singapore from Britain, and after seizing the island had announced it would serve as the "center" of the southern part of Japan's "East Asian sphere."[67] Emerging from the Atlantic echo chamber, U.S. officials were convinced that Washington must aid the French in Vietnam, that dealing with the Chinese diaspora of Southeast Asia must be central to U.S. Cold War policymaking, central to undergirding western power in the region.

Imperium in Imperio

Race had always been salient to Euro-American dominance in Southeast Asia. The western powers' belief in a racial hierarchy, wherein the inferior Asian populations must be ruled and civilized (through western education, Christianizing, and economic modernization) was vital to legitimating the colonial project. And though the Japanese Empire challenged that racial hierarchy, it barely dimmed the western powers' desire to cling to their colonial possessions after World War II.[68] If anything, the "darkest moment" galvanized Euro-American antipathy toward the particular groups of Asians that (in western eyes) appeared capable of threatening western dominance. As John Dower has written of the Pacific War, in the "race hate [that] fed atrocities" on the battlefield and the "impression of a truly Manichean struggle between completely incompatible antagonists," race was intertwined with the contest for power in the region.[69] In the Atlantic echo chamber, the western powers' race hate for the Japanese segued easily into Euro-American hostility toward communist-controlled China and extant distrust of Southeast Asia's Chinese.

The Chinese diaspora of Southeast Asia numbered more than eight million by 1947.[70] And as Sunil Amrith notes, the "commercial and migratory links" between China and Southeast Asia had existed for centuries. In the early 1400s, the Ming Dynasty's maritime voyages to the region saw small Chinese communities established in its wake. Through the seventeenth and eighteenth centuries, thousands of Chinese settled in European-controlled Southeast Asian cities such as Batavia (now Jakarta), Malacca (in peninsular Malaya), and Manila for commerce with the Europeans, though many also considered themselves sojourners and ultimately returned to the mainland. Until the nineteenth century, the Chinese communities of Southeast Asia grew slowly, occasionally facing persecution or "brutal massacres" (as in Manila and Batavia at the hands of Spanish and Dutch authorities, partly assisted by local forces). Even so, the Chinese frequently intermarried with the indigenous populations over the course of centuries, melding their cultures with that of the locals to form "mixed, or creole, communities" such as the Mestizos of the Philippines and the Peranakans of Malaya and the Dutch East Indies.[71]

Chinese migration to Southeast Asia spiked from the mid-1800s through the early decades of the twentieth century. Britain's imperial policy was one reason, for in expanding the rubber and tin industries of Malaya and establishing Singapore and Penang as trading ports "free" from Dutch and Portuguese monopolies and levies, the British attracted far larger numbers of Chinese laborers and merchants to their territories than had previously ventured to the region. Additionally, the Chinese traveled to Southeast Asia in order to escape a homeland that was in turmoil: a weak Qing government humbled by the British in two Opium Wars (1839–42 and 1856–60), beset by natural disasters and famines in the mid-1800s, and churned by the fallouts of anti-West rebellions in the mid-to-late century that were annihilated by coalitions of western powers. To be clear, Indian migration to the region also occurred on a considerable, though slightly smaller, scale compared with that of the Chinese, and for the most part was limited to British-controlled Malaya, Burma, and Ceylon (now Sri Lanka). In contrast, numerous sophisticated Chinese "migrant networks" that were "rooted in the family and kinship . . . native-place and surname associations" as well as "dialect group and regional associations" facilitated massive flows of Chinese from the mainland to Southeast Asia. These networks conducted Chinese in the millions to the British-ruled territories and other colonies where imperial authorities were growing their primary production and extractive industries. Between 1850 and 1940 some twenty million Chinese migrants traveled to Southeast Asia. Ninety-six percent of the Chinese who arrived in the region from the late 1880s through the 1930s would decide to stay.[72]

Having contributed so significantly to the explosion of Chinese migration to Southeast Asia, Britain simultaneously took the view that Chinese migrants remained "racially, culturally and politically . . . bound to the mother country China." They described the large Chinese populations of Malaya and Singapore as an "'Imperium in Imperio,' a 'State within a State.'"[73] Indeed, the Chinese migrant networks had bestowed on their Southeast Asian communities what Amrith describes as a "dens[e] web of social institutions." Furthermore, the British felt that unlike the Indian migrants (whose movements the British supervised closely), the Chinese networks were more difficult to understand

and manage, which led the British to "allow" them greater economic and social autonomy. At any rate, the Chinese migrant networks also deliberately placed their incoming fellows in sectors of the colonial economy that enabled many to attain greater economic and social mobility (such as Malaya's flourishing tin industry), which in turn saw them range farther from Britain's direct control. On top of all these, strains of Chinese nationalism had trailed the migrants, merchants, and literati to and from Southeast Asia, carrying Chinese ambitions for reform and revolutionary ideologies that had bloomed at the intersection of the Qing government's feebleness and China's semicolonial status after decades of western encroachments. Many overseas Chinese responded with financial contributions to assist the Chinese Nationalists who had toppled the ailing Qing Dynasty in 1911.[74] They readily did so again when China struggled against the Japanese Empire from the late 1930s through World War II.[75] But whether they were recent arrivals to or longtime residents of Southeast Asia, the Chinese pondered constantly what it meant to be a Chinese overseas. Must Chinese loyalties lie with the mainland for even those whose families had lived for generations in Southeast Asia? By the end of the 1940s, British colonial authorities were confronted with more than two million Chinese in Malaya and Singapore and understandably feared whatever influence emanated from the CCP government.

U.S. policymakers also considered the Chinese diaspora of Southeast Asia a major source of regional instability even before the CCP's victory in October 1949. Like Britain, the United States presumed the overseas Chinese could serve as China's fifth column, just as the U.S. government had once suspected that all Japanese-Americans were potential agents for Tokyo.[76] The Central Intelligence Group (precursor to the Central Intelligence Agency, the CIA) in 1946 had deemed the "4,500,000 alien Chinese and millions more persons of part-Chinese blood" as a "potential tool for the extension of China's influence in Southeast Asia," whether that influence was of the CCP or the Nationalist Guomindang (GMD).[77] The fact-finding missions that Truman sent to Southeast Asia produced a chart detailing the distribution of ethnic Chinese across the region, state by state. The descriptions accompanying the chart portrayed the Chinese as an "alien and unassimilated group" in Southeast Asia, an "entering vehicle for infiltration of Communism" into the region.[78] It was critical to know the enemy's numbers and where they lived.

How U.S. policymakers viewed the Chinese in the late 1940s is no surprise. Historians have uncovered a history of white hatred of the Chinese in the United States, Britain, and Australia, hatred evinced by violent local and transnational racist reactions to the Chinese immigrant workers entering these countries in the 1800s. White U.S. citizens, British, and Australians for years before World War II had already designated "Chinamen" as the original Yellow Peril.[79] Rekindling one's first race hate, an older flame, proved easy. NSC-51, for example, described the Chinese of Southeast Asia as a contagion that "afflict[ed] the entire region," a problem made "doubly ominous" by the CCP's presumed role in supporting and guiding the communist movements in Southeast Asia. Indeed, Chinese hegemony over Southeast Asian communism seemed a potentially greater threat to U.S. interests in the region than Soviet influence.[80]

In the same vein, British officials like Strang maintained that the "darker side" of the "Far Eastern picture" was how the communist revolution in China and anticolonial impulses might mobilize the "great Chinese communities" of Southeast Asia against western interests.[81] Britain's troubled relationship with the MCP, composed 95 percent of ethnic Chinese, likely reinforced Strang's distrust of the Chinese diaspora as a whole. During World War II, Britain had roped the MCP into a ragtag anti-Japanese force (the Malayan People's Anti-Japanese Army) and, as a reward for the communists' resistance against Japan's occupying forces, initially allowed them to operate freely within Malaya and Singapore after 1945. The British quickly regretted indulging their former allies. The MCP's formidable capacity for organizing en masse Singapore's Chinese middle school students and trade unions soon had British authorities on the back foot. MCP leaders exploited the fact that Singapore's population (nearly one million by 1947) was 78 percent Chinese, focusing a large measure of their efforts on the territory's young Chinese population through the Chinese middle schools. The MCP in Singapore astutely recognized that workers' unions could play a defining role in the island's political life and plotted accordingly. Singapore was, by British design, a commercial center, and after World War II, its recovering industries demanded manual labor increasingly, which multiplied as well as packed workers' unions.[82]

The consequence: the MCP's affiliates in Singapore honed an urban strategy for revolution that vexed British authorities to no end. On May Day in 1947, British authorities found themselves lacking the confidence and power to forestall an MCP meeting of some 50,000 people, assembled to hear a "Russian female Communist . . . promise that the USSR would fight for the Colonial Peoples." The MCP in Singapore exploited this ethos with aplomb and shifted the gears of this anticolonial May Day meeting into another display of power. Singapore's commissioner of police reported that the meeting then transformed into a mile-long procession through Singapore's streets, led by the MCP's "picket corps . . . [who] controlled and diverted vehicles with a most authoritative air," while all efforts of the police force to assert control "were completely ignored."[83]

Even when the police force detained MCP members, the communists cannily turned its jailed fellows into fallen heroes, glorifying their victimhood under the boot of the colonial authorities. In August 1947, the MCP organized another mass procession in Singapore, this time to lionize one of its members who had died in prison. Anti-British propaganda made its rounds among funeral attendees and onlookers, and again, the police force watched helplessly as the massive procession overturned a taxi that crossed in front of it (the vehicle then caught fire) and assaulted its driver.[84] This all-too-visible commemoration of an MCP martyr flamed with the spectacle of the British Empire's limits. British authorities would concede some years later that the MCP in Singapore possessed such a "strong control of labor, youth and women's movements [that it] was in a position to paralyze the Colony over-night."[85]

Hoping to cut the MCP's Singapore chapter off from its guerrilla faction in Malaya, Britain drew a thickening administrative and political line between these two territories. British officials then blew off questions from locals about uniting the two territories in the future. In fact, the legacy of their colonial rule had created this pretty pass in the first place. For decades, the British had administered the Malay Peninsula from Singapore. Goods and services had always flowed back and forth between Malaya and Singapore as if they were one economy; those who resided in Malaya and Singapore, too, still lived like there was no effective division between the territories (or their families, businesses, and histories on both sides). Despite this stroke of a pen by the British, MCP activities in both territories continued, largely unabated. Meanwhile, the MCP faction in Malaya had taken up sabotage and assassination.

In June 1948, Britain declared the MCP illegal in Malaya and Singapore and a state of emergency in both territories. Chin Peng, the leader of the MCP's guerrilla fighters, led his forces into the Malayan jungles to resume the mode they had employed against Japan until just three years before. The MCP of Singapore adopted a subversive approach, apparently under the tutelage of Chinese communists. British intelligence learned that the CCP wished to lead the "liberation movement of the Chinese people" in Southeast Asia and had dispatched at least twenty agents to Singapore to "assist in the organization and direction" of the guerrilla and urban campaigns.[86] Though Chin would claim in his memoirs that he had received no worthwhile support from China, the MCP in Singapore seemed to have cottoned on quickly how to destabilize British power.[87]

With the emergency regulations in place, Singapore's police force was empowered to arrest and detain any suspected persons, control roads, disperse assemblies, prohibit seditious publications, conduct searches, and impose curfews.[88] But despite the force's aggressive recruitment policy, its increasing size, and its growing effectiveness in ferreting out MCP members and incarcerating them, the Singapore communists remained resilient. The MCP in Singapore even attempted to assassinate Sir Franklin Gimson, the British governor of Singapore. Furthermore, when colonial authorities rounded up suspects in large numbers, they found the communists "proceeded almost unchecked by the detention" of their members. The Singapore communists had discovered that "strikes could still be exploited in spite of the Emergency Regulations" and with "added confidence" they "staged 8 simultaneous incidents in a night" toward the end of 1950 and produced "12 new propaganda publications in a month." The MCP also regularly committed arson, intimidating and killing Europeans and other locals friendly to Britain. The Singapore communists also attacked law enforcement officials. Once, the MCP shot a policeman "in broad daylight in a crowded street [in Singapore] and his arms were removed." The bland language of officialdom, perhaps meant to veil the gruesome dismemberment, only emphasized British desperation to control the narrative while developments in Singapore spun out of their hands. The Special Branch in Singapore, Britain's internal security agency, conceded that the MCP had "cowed" the public and Singapore being "a city of summer patriots . . . [was] a pitiable sight in the face of danger."[89]

The Singapore police force, led by British officers, continued to throw MCP members behind bars, sometimes up to several hundred in a single month.[90] But it was to no avail. The MCP's propaganda machine ensured that communist newsletters continually surfaced and circulated in Singapore—in the Chinese language and later, to Britain's shock, in English too—even though the Special Branch kept shutting down whatever printing operations sprouted.[91] MCP leaders also made quick work of training labor organizers to infiltrate Singapore's trade unions and propel them toward the left, deriding British and other white employers as well as their indigenous (and therefore traitorous) lieutenants so as to whip up anticolonial sentiment.[92]

The MCP exerted perhaps its greatest influence on Singapore's Chinese middle schools, where the organization did aggressive ideological work. The Special Branch frequently caught ethnic Chinese students red-handed with MCP and CCP literature, but (judging by the Branch's conspicuous silence on the matter) failed to make the students give up their sources.[93]

The supply of communist literature, pouring into the schools, seemed inexhaustible. A study commissioned by the Center for International Studies at the Massachusetts Institute of Technology in 1957 explained that the MCP had shrewdly preyed on the fact that "youth, being in school, gather in large groups in specific locations . . . mak[ing] them effective for mass activities." According to the study, Singapore's communists used a "calculated appeal to ideals and emotions," encouraged "an uncomprehending but strong emotional pride in Chinese culture," framed "British attacks against the MCP as racial" persecution, deployed emotive "music and drama" to win young hearts and minds, and created its martyrs from Chinese students arrested or killed by the police while protesting the colonial government's policies. The author of the study, Grace Kennan (daughter of George F. Kennan), argued that the MCP had turned the Singapore Chinese Middle School Students' Union into something of a "religious cult." At its peak in 1956, the union roll boasted 9,293 of the roughly 10,000 students who attended Chinese middle schools, as well as thousands more graduates.[94]

Thanks to the CIA, U.S. leaders were by the late 1940s already apprised of Britain's distress.[95] Jessup's meetings with MacDonald merely confirmed what U.S. intelligence had surmised. In his report to the State Department, Jessup reiterated what the Allies believed in common, that the "overseas Chinese communities form[ed] one of the most important elements in the strength of the Communists in Asia," that they would power Chinese expansionism.[96] Jessup concluded that countries with strong local Chinese communities were as threatened as those sharing "common borders" with China.[97]

Jessup's assessment illustrates how race profoundly influenced U.S. and British approaches to the Cold War in Asia. The abiding suspicions that U.S. and British policymakers directed against the overseas Chinese reinforced the idea of interconnectedness core to the domino logic; they explain why the United States often treated the Southeast Asian countries as strategically indistinguishable from each other. For U.S. leaders at least, what real differences existed between Southeast Asian countries ultimately paled in significance, and offered little obstruction, should China exploit the millions of overseas Chinese to their advantage. No wonder Jessup believed a country's large Chinese community, like that of Singapore, though physically distant from the mainland, was tantamount to sharing a common (and porous) border with China.

Such suspicions survived well into the 1950s. And with good reason. Beijing did court ethnic Chinese in Indonesia throughout the 1950s to win them away from the GMD in Taiwan. In particular, the CCP targeted the Indonesian

Chinese whose families had more recently immigrated to the archipelago, those who (unlike the Peranakans) had yet to adopt local customs and languages or intermarry with indigenous communities. The CCP's modus operandi in Indonesia mirrored the MCP's political operations in Singapore, not least its efforts to pump the Indonesian republic's Chinese-language schools with pro-Beijing propaganda. The CCP even organized tours for Indonesian Chinese to the mainland, hoping to galvanize their existing linguistic, cultural, and familial ties to China. The results spoke for themselves. Many Indonesian Chinese refused to take up Indonesian citizenship or assimilate into Indonesian society. Graduates of Indonesia's Chinese-language schools even entered the Chinese civil service in considerable numbers, becoming CCP cadres and diplomats. Such developments easily fed the western powers' visions of Chinese expansionism through its diasporic networks. In truth, the CCP's goals were less grand, and bent mostly toward convincing Indonesian Chinese that the People's Republic, not Taiwan, was the true, legitimate China. Beijing regularly reassured Jakarta that it had no plans to raise a fifth column in the archipelago (though Indonesian leaders were never fully persuaded and sporadically lashed out with discriminatory policies and violent acts against noncitizen Chinese in the country).[98] Indeed, the Indonesian leaders were not so different from their western counterparts, for they all harbored deep misgivings about the presence of the Chinese diaspora in Southeast Asia; they all viewed with anxiety its potential to drag the region into Beijing's sphere of influence.

Fredrik Logevall has argued in *Embers of War* that the domino theory "egregiously" approached the countries of Southeast Asia as if they "had no individuality, no history of their own, no unique circumstances in social, political and economic life that differentiated them from their neighbors." But these were not merely simplifications arising from what Logevall calls the "apocalyptic anti-Communism" that had infected the Truman administration thanks to Senator Joseph McCarthy.[99] These Cold War fears did not work alone. Rather, they united powerfully with U.S. and British anxieties about race—their lasting dread of the original Yellow Peril—overwhelming their recognition of each country's differences. U.S. and British policymakers did not ignore these distinctions as much as hold that race trumped sovereignty, a lesson they had learned from the "darkest moment." The specter of colonial collapse in the face of an Asian power still haunted Anglo-American strategic thinking. If the smaller outfits that had served as Japan's fifth column had combined to wreak such havoc, U.S. and British leaders could easily imagine large masses of Chinese intimately linked across (and despite) the borders of distinct Southeast Asian states. If the overseas Chinese locked arms with each other and the mainland, their sheer numbers could pull the western powers asunder.

On the day that Jessup delivered his recommendations to State, Griffin had just completed his weeklong discussions with MacDonald in Malaya and Singapore.[100] Griffin's mission had been to ascertain what "emergency economic and technical assistance" the United States could provide its allies in Southeast Asia, but his analyses often concerned the latent dangers posed by the Chinese diaspora. MacDonald knew to amplify these concerns, and Griffin to heed them.[101]

So, while the absolute numbers of ethnic Chinese residing in Thailand and Indonesia were higher than that of Malaya and Singapore combined, it was the proportion of Chinese in the British territories that unnerved Griffin. From its first sentence, his report about Malaya and Singapore counted both as a single unit and focused on how "almost half" of its population was Chinese. Like the British, Griffin held that the Chinese diaspora pledged "deep underlying" and "primary loyalty . . . to China." Worse, Griffin reported, the MCP's "campaign of violence" aimed to "drive Europeans away and disrupt the government and economic activities" in both Malaya and Singapore. He emphasized the international implications of the MCP's attacks on European civilians as well as British rubber and tin plantations in Malaya, reminding the State Department that Malaya was Britain's largest net dollar earner, generating 45 percent of the world's natural rubber and 34 percent of the world's tin. Should the "sinister and effective" MCP derail Malayan production of rubber and tin, two items high on the U.S. strategic commodity list, Britain would struggle to contribute to the Cold War effort not only in Asia but in Europe as well.[102]

Moreover, Griffin believed the MCP's efforts in Malaya remained on the uptick despite British forces' suppression operations. This was to be expected, he surmised, because Malaya and Singapore with their large Chinese populations were "peculiarly inviting target[s]" for communist aggression "either from within or without." In Griffin's opinion, should the Chinese communists assault Malaya directly, or Malaya's Chinese join with Beijing, this outpost of the British Empire must "fall to the Communists." With that outcome, Chinese communists abroad and locally would control the major British military bases in Singapore, which meant thereafter "Burma, Thailand and Indonesia would face greatly increased Communist pressure."[103]

To be clear, the MCP's guerrilla faction in the Malay Peninsula did at times seem to enjoy an advantage over British authorities. When Japan surrendered in September 1945, the MCP was able to assert control over large swathes of

Malaya while British soldiers returned in trickles from campaigns all over the region. For a time, the MCP was the de facto law of the land in Malaya and its fighters gloried in admiration from Malaya's Chinese community—many of Malaya's Chinese flew the MCP's red flag from their homes and feted MCP forces with whatever food, supplies, and shelter they could spare.

After listening to MacDonald worry aloud about the Chinese populations of Malaya and Singapore, Griffin viewed Burma, Thailand, and Indonesia through the perceived Chinese threat, preoccupied with an invasion by the "mother country," subversion by Chinese from within, or both in combination.[104] Griffin's reports demonstrate the imaginative work U.S. officials performed in acknowledging the unique conditions of each Southeast Asian country while diminishing those distinctive features. For example, Griffin noted that Burma faced a spectrum of problems unrelated to the Chinese threat: its largest minority group—the Karens—struggled against the government for an autonomous state. Moreover, the size of Burma's Chinese population was small compared with that of Malaya and Singapore. Then again, Griffin focused on a Chinese invasion. He argued that Burma's "proximity with Communist China" constituted the "principal factor" in the country's foreign relations, in particular its "undefined and frequently disputed border" with China. Griffin considered Burma an "attractive goal for Chinese expansion," a "pathway . . . from Southern Yunnan province to Thailand and Indo-china."[105] From Thailand and Indochina, the Chinese could then follow the path Japan had already worn into mainland Southeast Asia.

And Griffin certainly had Japanese imperialism in mind. When it came to Thailand, Griffin deplored the Thai "record of World War II," specifically its accommodation with the rising power in the region based on its "estimate of who is likely to win." This "precedent" meant the Thais would collaborate with China and, like they once did for Japan, facilitate Chinese incursions into Southeast Asia.[106] A week after speaking with MacDonald, Griffin cabled Acheson from Bangkok that Thailand "like rest [of] SEA [Southeast Asia] threatened by Communist imperialism controlled from China, which makes no secret [of its] designs [on] SEA." Griffin eyed warily Thailand's "large Chinese minority [of] about 3 million . . . susceptible [to] use" by a China "already exerting pressure."[107] With mounting anxiety he described Thailand's "well-organized Chinese Communist Party" and the successful cooperation in propaganda and subversion between the Chinese and Thai converts to communism.[108]

Indonesia was not safe from the Chinese either. According to Griffin, Indonesia's coastal areas remained "susceptible to easy Communist penetration from the mainland." His analyses distorted by a racial lens, Griffin knew but skated past the unique characteristics of Indonesia. Though Indonesia had a population of almost eighty million in 1950, Griffin zeroed in on the country's Chinese "minority of nearly two million," which he believed an internal communist threat if utilized by China.[109] His treatment of Indonesia aptly illustrates the overpowering assumptions that U.S. policymakers harbored with regard to the region's Chinese. It mattered less that Indonesian Chinese did not control the national government or that they were vastly outnumbered by native Javanese and Sumatrans. Griffin could not but zero in on the new republic's Chinese population while casting his mind toward how Malaya and Singapore's Chinese posed a potential menace to British authority.

A Row of Dominoes Set Up

The third U.S. fact-finding mission to Southeast Asia, the Melby-Erskine team, did not simply reiterate the conclusions of Jessup and Griffin. Melby's records reveal that in August 1950 he and Erskine took away from discussions with MacDonald and other British officials the most developed enunciation of the early domino logic, nodding at its origins in the "darkest moment" and the critical importance of race in its vision of the communist threat to Southeast Asia. Crucially, the Melby-Erskine team's conclusions rested on its leaders' substantial military and diplomatic expertise in Asia. Erskine had led the war campaigns against Japan at Saipan and Iwo Jima, to name only two. Melby had served as a diplomat in China from 1944 through 1948, and was the principal author of the *China White Paper* in 1949 that recounted the past century of U.S. policy toward China. His insights into Chinese relations with Southeast Asia carried weight in the State Department and with Rusk especially, to whom he was special assistant.

Until Melby and Erskine met MacDonald, the domino logic had appeared only piecemeal in U.S. and British officials' assessments of Southeast Asia. But on August 8, when Melby invited MacDonald to offer his "views on [the] situation" in the region, the British official launched into his most developed portrayal of the communist threat to Southeast Asia. To begin, he referred to the ongoing Korean War, suggesting two months before the fact that China would intervene there. When neither Melby nor Erskine objected to this prediction, MacDonald talked about China threatening Southeast Asia in turn. He stated that if in Korea China's expansionist "design is successful . . . Indo-China is next." Even if China chose not to use force, MacDonald reasoned that it could destroy western power "by proxy, linking up with the local fifth column" that operated "in every one of these countries—Burma, Indo-China, Siam and Malaya," a fifth column driven by "first, all the communists, and secondly, all the Chinese community." He quickly explained that the Chinese would strike Indochina first because "as a result of the colonial rule continuing there, there is a very powerful nationalist movement, a large part of which is under the control of the communists."[110] Within a few minutes, MacDonald had rhetorically (if awkwardly) linked the possibility of Chinese invasion with the importance of Indochina, his description of China's fifth column conflating communists with overseas Chinese.

MacDonald was not done. He next focused on China's potential aggression toward Malaya, the country he called the "great prize" of the region because of its tin and rubber. He expected members of the Melby-Erskine team to recall Japan's pursuit of Malaya's natural resources, to remember how Malaya fell to Japan. For China to conquer Malaya, he argued, Indo-China would be the "place of attack . . . the highway to the rest of South East Asia," for "if Indo-China falls Siam would be easier to pick up." Siam (Thailand), he contended, "wouldn't resist at all." Shared memories would have finished the job: after Siam, Malaya, then Singapore. But to be sure, MacDonald harked back to how the Thais had once yielded to the Japanese and would again do so when the Chinese were at their gates.[111]

This statement had the desired effect. State Department officials reported later that they agreed with MacDonald that "Thai officials and the Thai public would be apt to seek some accommodation with communism" if the West appeared "unable to counter-act" China's advance. They concurred that Thailand's "record *vis-à-vis* the Japanese in World War II [was] a precedent" of great relevance to the Cold War.[112]

Transcripts of the Malaya conference indicate that Melby and Erskine continued to let MacDonald have free run of the floor. And MacDonald seized the chance to hammer home his view: "Indo-China is the place where Communists . . . would want to conquer in their plans for South East Asia. If Indo-China holds, all holds. Indo-China is top priority . . . and we should give it first place in all our considerations." He then made quick work of detailing the difficulties France faced with the Viet Minh before getting back on track, declaring "the Communists are working very hard to make war this autumn . . . training large numbers of Vietminh troops in China." Once again, he stated: the "route through Indo-China and Siam is the route. We expect trouble in October or November."[113]

Figure 3. John F. Melby, U.S. diplomat and leader of the third U.S. fact-finding mission to Southeast Asia in 1950. Melby returned from discussions with Malcolm MacDonald convinced that Southeast Asia's Chinese diaspora would be central to Beijing's expansionist ambitions. From the Collections of the University of Pennsylvania Archives.

At this point, Melby and Erskine signaled their assent with more than silence. Melby shared that intelligence gathered in Hong Kong indicated October 1 was "the invasion date" and that the United States knew that thirty thousand Viet Minh had already been trained and organized in China. Erskine pitched in, underscoring the weaknesses of the French defenses. He believed the French "are not in a good position," that "if the Chinese make any movement southward . . . the northern [French] force (in Tonkin) would be practically annihilated."[114] Melby and Erskine knew the rout for the western powers that must follow the obliteration of their French ally. The U.S. officials had found in MacDonald the great communicator of all they wanted to hear.

In the days that followed the conference in Malaya, Melby would increasingly frame Indochina's problems and their impact on Malaya in the terms that MacDonald had presented. On August 10, Melby told the *Malay Mail* that "should Indochina fall to the communists, followed by Burma and Siam, Malaya's position would be critical indeed."[115] The *Singapore Standard* reported that same day that Melby expected the "Chinese Communists will march over the borders" into Indochina.[116] Even Singapore's leftist Chinese newspaper, the *Nan Chiao Jit Pao*, recorded Melby saying that "Indo-China was under the threat of New China's troops" but commented that it was "laughable" how the American was "unable to quote any evidence" to support his statements.[117]

In hindsight, it seems that MacDonald's vivid portrayals of Southeast Asian insecurity had provided all the evidence that Melby needed. Indeed, before the *Nan Chiao Jit Pao* confronted him, Melby had asked MacDonald and General Sir John Harding, British commander-in-chief of Far East land forces, for "any evidence" that the MCP was benefiting from "political guidance" outside of Malaya. Harding had confirmed that the Malayan communists received "guidance from Peking." But MacDonald with his proclivity for graphic detail gave Harding's statement motion and substance. He described Chinese messengers traveling throughout Southeast Asia, communicating with the MCP not by radio (for that image would seem too remote) but in person in "Bangkok, Hong Kong, much through the USSR Embassy in Bangkok." A letter that Melby sent weeks later to his personal friend in the State Department best expresses MacDonald's influence: "Malaya has been the most stimulating experience and Malcolm MacDonald the most constructive man I have talked with."[118]

The reports submitted by members of the Melby-Erskine team recalled MacDonald's views again and again. State Department officers on the mission pondered the possibility of China mounting an "overland invasion of Malaya" explicitly using the example of Japan, and amplified MacDonald's hints and suggestions. They anticipated this invasion would come by Malaya's "northern frontier" as with the "last war," and that Malaya would fall if the Chinese southward drive had, like Japan, already forced "one or more other Southeast Asian countries . . . [to] succumb."[119] The U.S. Navy echoed. They used the "Japs" campaign to visualize China's path to power and cited MacDonald to assert that Chinese "enemy land forces" would first conquer Indochina, causing Thailand to fall, bringing the danger "right across the border" to Malaya.[120] If the idea of interconnected insecurity among Southeast Asian states had previously been a free-floating concept for U.S. officials, it rapidly gained mass when their British counterparts reiterated it with choice words.

And so, with Melby and Erskine the domino logic returned to the United States fully formed, awaiting only the specific metaphor that Eisenhower later provided. Subsequent enunciations of the domino logic by U.S., British, or French leaders following the Melby-Erskine-MacDonald encounter rehashed the principles and imagery that had already congealed for U.S. policymakers. Logevall, though, invests a fair amount of significance in French high commissioner of Indochina, General Jean de Lattre de Tassigny's declaration in August 1951 that "Tonkin is the keystone of the defense of Southeast Asia" and that "if Tonkin falls, Siam falls with Burma and Malaya is dangerously compromised."[121] In fact, de Lattre picked up this formulation two months earlier from discussions in Singapore with British officials like MacDonald and Harding. Attendees of this Singapore Conference later confided in Dean Rusk that the Frenchman took at "full value" the recommendations of his British counterparts that stated: "Tonkin is the key to all of Southeast Asia and were it to fall to the communists the area as a whole would be lost."[122]

In any case, in October 1950, months before de Lattre even convened with MacDonald and Harding in Singapore, the CIA had already built upon the findings of the Melby-Erskine mission and installed the domino principle in its strategic vision of Cold War Southeast Asia: "The fall of Indochina would provide the Communists with a staging area in addition to China for military operations against the rest of mainland Southeast Asia, and this threat might well inspire accommodation in both Thailand and Burma. Assuming Thailand's loss, the already considerable difficulty faced by the British in maintaining security in Malaya would be greatly aggravated."[123] Within days of the CIA's appraisal of mainland Southeast Asia's prospects in the face of communist domination, China intervened on behalf of North Korea against the U.S.-led forces of the United Nations. The UN coalition (composed primarily of U.S. and British troops) and South Korean forces had by then crossed the Yalu River at the border of North Korea and China, surging, as the Truman administration hoped, toward reunifying Korea under pro-U.S. Syngman Rhee. The Chinese leadership, perceiving a direct threat to its sovereignty, tried both to acquire assistance from Soviet leader Josef Stalin and to hurl the People's Liberation Army into battle. Chinese forces, with tremendous numbers and at great human cost, drove the United States and the United Nations deep into South Korea, seizing Seoul in January 1951. For a time, the western allies were reeling. It was not difficult for U.S. and British leaders to see a replay of Japanese imperialism in Southeast Asia on the Korean Peninsula.

China's entry into the Korean conflict, and the prestige it won from fending off U.S. forces, also intensified U.S. fears that the Chinese would mobilize both its diaspora in Southeast Asia and all the militant nationalists throughout Asia in a global war against the western allies. The "darkest moment" seemed due for a second coming. It was all the worse because after World War II, the European powers' empires in Asia were dissolving earliest, most rapidly, and in the most tortured ways. Between 1947 and 1948, Britain had yielded to the nationalist demands of India, Pakistan, Ceylon, and Burma, granting independence or dominion status to all. The Netherlands retreated from Indonesia in 1949 (under pressure from the United States), having failed to crush the militant Indonesian nationalists, though it was not for lack of trying or considerable bloodshed.[124] And this was not to mention the MCP's campaigns in Malaya and Singapore, or the Viet Minh's war against the French.

The white empires were under siege throughout Asia. The CIA had already surmised in 1948 that the fundamental challenge for the United States in Southeast Asia was "racial antagonism between white and native peoples," which Imperial Japan had once rallied under the banner of "Asia for Asiatics" against "white oppression."[125] The phrase for this in NSC-51 had been "white-colored polarization," underscoring the potential for the Soviets and the Chinese to borrow pages from Imperial Japan's playbook, to harness the "deep-seated racial hostility of native populations toward their white overlords."[126] If China ever struck south through the Chinese diaspora at the hobbled colonial order in Southeast Asia, it could also commandeer all the Chinese along the way, as well as the nationalists and their anticolonial angst, eviscerating the white empires' already narrow bases of power and legitimacy.

In January 1953, the imagery Eisenhower employed in his inaugural address seemed just a step away from the domino metaphor he would coin the following April. Not halfway into his inaugural speech, he proclaimed common cause with the United States' French and British allies. He spoke of the "common dignity" of European and U.S. soldiers who fought the Cold War in Asia, soldiers who fell one by one to unseen Asian enemies. In this vein, "the French soldier who dies in Indo-China, the British soldier killed in Malaya, the American life given in Korea" whom he described were all linked, and in more ways than one.[127] The order in which Eisenhower chose to refer to these fighting men, their deaths occurring from north to south in mainland Southeast Asia before encroaching on U.S. interests in the broader region, reveals how intensely Eisenhower believed in the interconnected vulnerability of western interests. Eisenhower's row of soldiers, protectors of the colonial order, vividly performed the dynamic of falling dominoes, the first knocked over in Indochina making certain the last would go over very quickly. By the time he was asked to explain the "strategic importance of Indochina to the free world" in April 1954, the "falling domino" principle he offered was only the latest rendition of ideas that had been circulating since the "darkest moment of the war."

Chapter 2

Patriot Games

How British Nation-Building Colonialism
Inspired the United States

U.S. diplomat John Melby and Major General Grave Erskine's fact-finding mission to Southeast Asia had been traveling through the region since mid-July 1950. It was the third such team that President Harry Truman had dispatched to Asia since the Chinese Communist Party (CCP) swept to power in China eleven months earlier; its objective: to learn how the United States could assist its allies' military efforts against communism. Of late the situation seemed increasingly desperate. The Soviets and Chinese had backed North Korea's invasion of the pro-U.S. South in June 1950, presaging the communist powers' possible incursions into Southeast Asia. Worse, Washington suspected that Moscow and Beijing were abetting the most dangerous Southeast Asian communist groups of the moment, the Viet Minh and the Malayan Communist Party (MCP). Both Southeast Asian groups had cannily exploited antiwhite resentment in the colonies, rode high on claims that they were patriots, and threatened to hijack their country's nationalist movement.[1] On August 20, 1950, Melby and Erskine sent Washington a report stating that Malaya faced challenges "as serious and as menacing" as any Southeast Asian country "torn [by] a world-wide ideological fight." Yet with all they had seen in the region, both men contended that Malaya also presented the "brightest and certainly the most optimistic prospect of any of the countries concerned."[2]

According to Melby and Erskine, "what distinguishe[d] Malaya" from other Southeast Asian countries was its "enlightened colonial administration." In their view, Britain had begun to "enlist the cooperation of the majority" of Malaya's people, including many of its Chinese, in a multiracial coalition against the

MCP which "for all practical purposes [was] entirely Chinese."[3] Malcolm MacDonald, Britain's commissioner-general for Southeast Asia, had recently described London's policy toward Malaya as "progressive evolution" toward "self-government" in "cooperation with the local peoples."[4] In practice, however, Britain (like the MCP) strove to bend nationalist strivings within Malaya toward its agenda. On the ground, MacDonald and colonial officials thus recruited suitable collaborators from among Malaya's would-be nationalists—self-styled patriots (also like the MCP)—to steer the country's decolonization in a pro-British, anticommunist direction. London's actual policy was, in a word, neocolonial. Its self-evident goal was to preserve Britain's imperial influence by ensuring that the leaders of independent Malaya remained firmly aligned with London.

For their part, anticommunist Malayans.desiring a hand in the country's destiny tied their aspirations to Britain's neocolonialism and struggle against the MCP. Among them were conservative Malays and Chinese hoping to safeguard their wealth and status from the MCP's socialist revolution; Malays who constituted about half the country's population and despised the MCP; Chinese (as well as Indians) of various social classes who banked (cagily) on Britain's guarantees that independent Malaya would be a tolerant, multiracial state that protected the rights of minorities like themselves. As such, men like Malaya's first prime minister, Tunku Abdul Rahman, a pro-British Malay prince and popular leader of the United Malays National Organization (UMNO); and Tan Cheng Lock, an Anglophile, successful businessman, and founder of the anticommunist Malayan Chinese Association (MCA), were the type of patriot that Britain sought. These anticommunist nationalists, their self-interests entwined with Britain's, swiftly cobbled together a popular Malay-Chinese alliance against the MCP. It was no mean feat given the preexisting Sino-Malay antagonism, exacerbated by the MCP's lethal reprisals against those (mostly Malay) it had accused of collaborating with the Japanese.[5] When months later Melby tried to distill lessons from his visit to Malaya, he concluded that "it is time we learnt the trick of at least having Asians fight Asian battles . . . where necessary, yellow men will be killed by yellow men rather than by white men alone."[6]

By the mid-1950s, Malaya's anticommunist nationalists had triumphed at the ballot box, seemingly outmaneuvered the MCP, and stood (to Britain's satisfaction) ready for self-government. As Malaya rose to independence in 1957, U.S. officials remarked with admiration that Britain had "relinquish[ed] control in a manner which would ensure them continuing influence and goodwill."[7] In essence, Britain and its Malayan collaborators had come together in "nation-building colonialism," a term that historian Paul Kramer has used to theorize how an empire might "pursue 'external' power through the cultivation, sponsorship, and ordering of other people's nations."[8] U.S. leaders studied British nation-building colonialism in Malaya closely because U.S. policy toward post-1945 Southeast Asia was basically the same project: ushering the region from formal colonialism to an order of stable, independent anticommunist nations ensconced in the western orbit. In fact, Washington perceived in Malaya's anticommunist nationalism promises that the domino logic could be reversed to favor the western allies, that the Chinese diaspora could be turned away from Beijing and coaxed into aiding anticommunist operations directed chiefly at members of their own ethnic community. From this auspicious beginning, British neocolonialism in Southeast Asia would deeply influence the fate of U.S. empire in the wider region.

Collaborators for Empire

Secretary of State Dean Acheson approved NSC-51 in July 1949, endorsing the paper's broad vision for U.S. policy toward Southeast Asia.[9] The core premise of NSC-51 was that "19th century imperialism is no longer a practicable system in SEA [Southeast Asia]" and that the western allies must accept that reanimating the prewar colonial order was an "anti-historical act." The paper acknowledged that Imperial Japan had enabled "militant nationalism" to become the "most potent idea" among the peoples of the region. And it contended, too, that the white empires were fast dissolving across Asia in bloody revolutions. These paroxysms of decolonization were inextricably bound up with the Cold War. Acheson, State Department planners, and U.S. intelligence officials were all certain that the USSR and the CCP were feeding the racial antagonism that underpinned Asian anticolonialism as well as exhorting noncommunists to forge united fronts with homegrown communists in a global struggle against the western powers.[10]

However, it was not simply a case of Moscow and Beijing manipulating their Southeast Asian proxies. Communist leaders like Ho Chi Minh and the MCP's Chin Peng saw their local revolutions as inseparable from the anticolonial logic of international communism. They also wished to make their calls for united fronts welcoming to noncommunists, and they tried to nest their left-wing causes in the hearts and minds of their fellow nationalists by touting that they were all patriots on the same side, the right side of history.

In light of this, U.S. officials understood that to wage the Cold War while decolonization proceeded apace, while the collapse of the Japanese Empire and the moribund colonial order produced a "vacuum of power" in Southeast Asia, they must co-opt the anticolonial cause into the fight against communism.[11] Acheson, fresh from consolidating the western alliance in Europe with NATO, seems to have pondered a similar structure in post-1945 Southeast Asia. NSC-51 certainly proposed that Washington keep Southeast Asia friendly to trade with the United States and the West, resisting Soviet access to its resources and Chinese influence over its diaspora. Most importantly, the paper also carried hopes that the region's indigenous nationalists would willingly join a U.S.-led security framework. Because NSC-51 held that the United States and the colonial powers must "satisfy the militant nationalism" as the "first essential requirement" for containing communism, the word of choice throughout the paper was "collaboration." Memories of Vichy France and its collaboration with the Nazis seemed not to perturb Acheson when he approved the paper. Indeed, NSC-51 recommended that the United States "in collaboration with like-minded nations" establish a "multilateral collaboration" that employed "sympathetic western influence" to enlist Southeast Asian "collaboration" against the USSR and China. To this end, the paper suggested, the United States must press the colonial powers to mobilize anticommunist Asian nationalists to defeat homegrown communists and win the loyalty of—or else pacify—the Chinese diaspora. This order of anticommunist nation-states would impede the transnational flows of communist (especially Chinese) influence with bright sovereign lines upheld by nationalist fervor. Per NSC-51, the United States meant for the "SEA [Southeast Asian] region [to become] an integral part of that great crescent formed by the Indian Peninsula, Australia and Japan."[12] Put another way, the Southeast Asian countries would become part of a wide geostrategic arc.[13]

Washington had recently taken action in Southeast Asia along these lines. The Truman administration granted the Philippines independence in 1946 but tethered that nation to itself with trade agreements and support for Filipino political elites that U.S. officials had carefully nurtured. The United States also retained its air and naval bases on Philippine soil to project U.S. military power into Southeast Asia.[14] Writing of the U.S. empire in the Philippines, journalist Stanley Karnow described this condition as "dependent independence."[15] It was nation-building colonialism by another name. And NSC-51 in principle advocated a region-wide elaboration of such "dependent independence" to establish a sphere of influence from the tenuous fusion of western dominance and the sovereign consent of Southeast Asians.[16]

This conservative U.S. impulse explains the variance in the Truman administration's approach to Southeast Asian nationalism over the course of 1949.

On the one hand, Truman compelled the Dutch to leave Indonesia and championed the country's militant nationalists (for they appeared anticommunist and might be made collaborators in the Cold War). On the other, Washington warily accepted France's tokenistic "Bao Dai solution," whereby France installed the former Annamese emperor as head of state in Vietnam but granted the country only nominal independence within a French imperial structure (known as the French Union) as well as retained control over Vietnam's diplomatic, economic, and military policy.[17] Washington preferred the predictability of cooperating with the "like-minded" anticommunist French. When France fell to defeat at the hands of the Viet Minh in 1954, Truman's successors cast about for a new collaborator and ultimately threw their weight behind the anticommunist South Vietnamese leader Ngo Dinh Diem.[18]

U.S. leaders had always sought collaborators for their imperial projects, even prior to World War II.[19] And they were not exceptional in this. All the great powers to some degree employed local collaborators through which to exercise imperial control. In colonial Southeast Asia, for decades before the Pacific War, small numbers of Euro-American officials nurtured a class of pliant indigenous allies so as to wield authority over large Asian populations. Collaboration also underpinned the Axis sphere of influence that connected Vichy France to Japanese-controlled Indochina. Japan's Greater East Asia Co-Prosperity Sphere, stretched thin through the region, also relied heavily on Indonesian, Filipino, and Burmese collaborators who, in turn, leveraged their relationships with the occupying power for their own benefit.[20] In the fearsome new world of the Cold War, Acheson advised that the United States must play the game of patriots, must compete with the communists for collaborators. It was the wave of the future, a current as old as empire.

Anti-Chinese Anticommunism

Britain's nation-building colonialism in Malaya paralleled and advanced the U.S. Cold War project for Southeast Asia. Like their U.S. counterparts, British officials acknowledged that Japan had "hastened the development of these Nationalist movements" by proving "an oriental race could defeat Europeans" and "deliberately fostering nationalist movements" in ways that "increas[ed] the difficulty of re-occupation by the Colonial powers."[21] Even so, Britain wanted to protect its investments in Malaya's rubber industry. Malaya remained the world's largest rubber supplier and Britain's biggest dollar earner, and kept the United States its most important customer. These were vital to Britain's postwar economic reconstruction. Moreover, following the decolonization of India, Pakistan, and Sri Lanka (formerly Ceylon), Britain had shifted the strategic center of its Asian empire to the military bases of Singapore at Malaya's southern tip.[22] To maintain influence in Southeast Asia and still stake a claim to world power status, British leaders pursued a compact with the nationalists in Malaya and Singapore "with which they could hope to live subsequently."[23] The empire would endure in a new form, so its leaders thought, by building nation-states from its colonies that of their sovereign volition linked themselves to Britain.

But Britain's first experiment with nation-building colonialism in Malaya foundered on the explosive rise of ethnic Malay nationalism and its anti-Chinese tendencies. The Malays roundly rejected British plans for a new administrative system, the Malayan Union, which had been designed to centralize the administration of the nine Malayan states of the peninsula and create a unified, multiracial Malayan nation. In the first place, centralizing the Malayan government overturned the decades-long British practice of governing each Malayan state separately with the blessings of its sultan. Over the nineteenth century these blessings had been exchanged for British protection of each sultan's special privileges, such as rights to vast tracts of land and recognition as a temporal head of the Muslim religion. Thus, Malays vigorously objected to the union's proposal to substantially reduce the power and status of the Malay royalty, which to Malays certainly represented a blow to their community's social standing. Worse, the union's instruments would offer non-Malay immigrants like the Chinese easy access to Malayan citizenship, a move to integrate the Chinese into this new nation and thereby dilute their transnational affiliations to either the Guomindang (GMD) or the CCP. For Malays across the political spectrum, this constituted another attempt to undermine their community. At base, Malays considered their ethnic community *bumiputra* (sons of the soil), the country's true indigenes, and the union an unacceptable affront. But Britain fueled Malay resentment further by foisting the proposal upon the sultans (often arm-twisting them into agreement using allegations that they had supported the Japanese Occupation).[24]

British officials could not simply ignore Malay opposition to the union. Malays accounted for about 48 percent of the population. Also, UMNO (the United Malays National Organization) emerged as the most effective of all the communal political groups, protesting against the union with well-organized and popular civil disobedience demonstrations. UMNO vocalized what many Malays believed, that the Chinese minority had thrived in the commercial world under British benevolence at the Malays' expense, or else powered the

MCP and its anti-Malay reprisals after World War II. Malay antipathy toward the Chinese at the time seemed formidable. Britain, recalling the ethnic strife of recent years, bowed to UMNO's pressure and abolished the union in January 1948. Pragmatism dictated that Britain draw close to UMNO—the organization seemed the most moderate of all groups in the country, the most predisposed to entering a political bargain with colonial authorities. To replace the Malayan Union, Britain established the Federation of Malaya that acceded to Malay demands for restrictions against Chinese immigrants seeking Malayan citizenship, preserved the privileges of the Malay royals, and enshrined the Malays as *bumiputra*. Not that the Malayan Union would have ever worked, but Britain's decision to placate the Malay nationalists ensured that whatever Malayan nationalism emerged thereafter must favor the Malay community's status over any visions of multiracial equality.

As the federation agreement supplanted the Malayan Union in 1948, the MCP began to ramp up its anti-British guerrilla campaign. There were predictable ideological reasons for the MCP's decision connected to the Cold War. The Soviets and the Chinese—and supposedly one Ho Chi Minh—had helped to set up the MCP in 1930, so the organization was from its inception tied to the conflict against capitalist empires of the West. The MCP's literature bears this out, stating that the organization's raison d'être was derived from the Comintern's "irreconcilable opposition [to] . . . the free democracies" and woven into the fabric of its broadly anticolonial, specifically anti-British, pretensions to Malayan patriotism. Thus, the MCP may have expediently joined with Britain against Japan during World War II but returned to its ideological roots when that crisis had passed. According to captured MCP documents, in particular "An open letter to compatriots on the realization of the People's Democratic Republic [*sic*]," the MCP aspired to create the "Malayan Peoples' Democratic Republic." Named in the familiar style of other communist republics, this involved the "amalgamating [of] Singapore and Malaya" after "the British Imperialists have been driven out of Malaya and their military, political and economic influence has been thoroughly eliminated."[25] The MCP also situated its "war of liberation of the Malayan people" within the worldwide Marxist-Leninist revolution, framing its patriotic war against the "British Imperialists" as one part of the "'angry roiling wave' of emancipation sweeping across China, Vietnam, the Philippines, Indonesia, Burma, India and Greece."[26] MCP anthems of the late 1940s and early 1950s such as "Fighting Youth Song" communicated the same global vision. Its lyrics declared the MCP had "brothers and sisters all over the world," "Comrades in Greece, Africa and Spain," and that China watched the MCP "as friend and brother" while the USSR "shows the way."[27] Such texts easily confirmed the suspicions of those U.S. and British leaders who believed, somewhat uncritically, that groups like the MCP (and the Viet Minh, too) were but manifestations of the transnational communist threat, guided by Moscow and Beijing.

But there were other reasons for the MCP's resort to war that complicate the picture, specifically the dissolution of Britain's abortive effort to integrate Malaya's Chinese population into the ill-fated Malayan Union. Indeed, when the Malayan Emergency began in June 1948, the MCP enjoyed the support (some tentative, others full-throated) of nearly a million alien Chinese in the peninsula now ineligible for Malayan citizenship due to the instruments of the federation. For such aliens, the MCP's political manifesto promised finer things. For though its ranks brimmed with ethnic Chinese, the MCP had for years advocated a "principle of racial equality." MCP policy promised that the people of "all races [would] have the right to establish schools and cultural organs" with the assistance of the communist government. In stark contrast to the citizenship restrictions of the Malayan federation, the MCP pledged to accord "reasonable treatment and legal protection" for "people of all races who look upon Malaya as their home and object of loyalty." The MCP seemed ready to reward such loyalty, regardless of race, language, or religion, with Malayan citizenship. In doctrine at least, the MCP sought to install its own version of multiracial harmony in Malaya and Singapore. Every component of this utopian vision also guaranteed women "equal pay" for their labor and that "all color prejudice will be eliminated."[28] We can never know what chance this utopia had, and how far the MCP would honor it. By launching its armed revolt against Britain and failing, the MCP ensured its vision would never be tested.

In any case, the MCP's gesture at multiracial harmony appears out of step with not only the Malay-dominated nationalism in the peninsula but also the prevailing anti-Chinese sentiment that indigenous Southeast Asian elites had marshaled before and after World War II to underpin their nation-building projects. When nationalists in Siam had sought in the 1930s to craft a national identity based on the Thai ethnicity, they whipped up anti-Chinese prejudice reminiscent of King Vajiravudh's "notorious 1914 tract calling the Chinese the 'Jews of the East'" and in addition to arresting and deporting GMD activists executed a "Thai-ification" program to replace Chinese with ethnic Thai in major industrial and labor sectors of the economy. In Indonesia, the nascent indigenous nationalists of the 1910s targeted Chinese as "capitalists, as infidels, as aliens, and as collaborators of the hated" Dutch, and such antipathy boiled over into ferocious attacks on local Chinese businesses in the 1930s. This anti-

Chinese sentiment endured in independent Indonesia, feeding off widespread suspicions that even "long-settled" Chinese would power Beijing's expansionist ambitions, a view not so different from that of the Anglo-American powers. Indonesian president Sukarno responded to the mounting antipathy against the local Chinese community in the 1950s by restricting their economic activities (which the Philippine government also did to its Chinese community at much the same time). Some one hundred thousand ethnic Chinese fled Indonesia, fearing Jakarta's moves portended new pogroms against their community.[29]

To be sure, many of Malaya's Chinese believed the MCP fighters were the true patriots of the peninsula well into the 1950s, not least because the communists had continued to fight Japanese forces (in truth, sparingly) after Britain's surrender and until the war's end. Recently released British intelligence reports on the MCP judged the organization more Malayan in outlook than oriented toward the CCP or Marxism-Leninism (though the MCP did intermittently refer to China as its homeland). British intelligence admitted, too, that the principal leaders of the MCP were not foreign agents but Malayan born, educated in Malaya and Singapore's Chinese-language schools (some even in Singapore's English-language schools). British and U.S. intelligence officials knew that the CCP had dispatched agents to assist the MCP. But there was no clear evidence that Beijing had offered more than rhetorical support, even though the MCP's operations in Singapore bore some resemblance to the CCP's efforts in Indonesia (see chapter 1). Nonetheless, Anglo-American intelligence shied away from deeming the MCP a legitimate nationalist movement. At the same time, Britain at least seemed prepared (or complacent enough) in the immediate aftermath of World War II to tolerate the MCP's part in Malayan political life. Britain had even honored several MCP soldiers like Chin Peng (who during the Emergency would be damned as public enemy number one). Indeed, until the MCP began attacking Europeans in Malaya in 1948, British authorities had allowed the party to operate freely in the country so long as they had laid down their arms.[30] This peaceful coexistence did not last. As the MCP's violent activities mounted in mid-1948, London declared the crisis an "Emergency," and simultaneously applied the label to Singapore where Britain faced MCP affiliates who had ostensibly seized control of the trade unions and held sway over Chinese cultural organizations and middle schools.

The MCP, having secreted away large caches of Japanese and British weapons, was ready for war in Malaya. The jungle covering four-fifths of the Malay Peninsula provided impenetrable cover for the MCP's bases, allowing the guerrillas to attack Europeans and their local allies and evade capture by melt-ing back into the forest.

Soon, the exigencies of guerrilla war appeared to overtake the MCP's loft-ier aspirations of winning the hearts and minds of Malayans, let alone fellow Chinese. The MCP sustained itself mostly by taking advantage of some half a million ethnic Chinese who, displaced by World War II, lived in makeshift settlements on the edges of Malaya's jungles. British colonial authorities rush-ing to rebuild Malaya's infrastructure called them "squatters" and for a time could do little to address the problem. The MCP made the squatters its re-source, extorting from them food (since many squatters raised subsistence crops the MCP could seize by force or intimidation) and press-ganged its youths, male and female, into its ranks. The MCP also obtained financial support from the wealthy and working-class Chinese of Malaya and Singapore that feared the organization's "killer squads."[31] All these decisions had the effect of build-ing up resentment of the MCP within even the community most inclined to support the organization.

Additionally, the MCP remained but for a few high-ranking, multilingual Malays, mostly ethnic Chinese. MCP leaders knew this limited the organ-ization's claim to represent the multiracial reality of Malaya but had little success with recruiting more Malays.[32] With Britain's declaration of the Emergency, the MCP tried unsuccessfully to entice the all-Malay political group, the Ma-lay Nationalist Party, into a plot against British authorities.[33] Malays and other non-Chinese were often repulsed because the MCP seemed no more than a Chinese-dominated movement. That the MCP persisted in wringing support from the squatters and other Chinese only hardened this perception.

British leaders, having failed to build a unified Malayan identity through the union proposal, now discerned a way of dovetailing their nation-building colonialism with their efforts to suppress the MCP. Originally, Britain's "Chi-nese problem" had revolved around fears that the Chinese diaspora, suppos-edly in league with the CCP, might endanger western interests in Southeast Asia.[34] However, with mounting evidence that the MCP's campaign relied entirely on Malaya's Chinese, the "Chinese problem" had changed. As newly declassified British records show, officials like Malcolm MacDonald, British high commissioner for Malaya Sir Henry Gurney, and Governor of Singapore Sir Franklin Gimson agreed in 1949 that their common goal was "pushing the Chinese . . . into an anti-Communist position."[35] It is probable that all three had this scheme in mind well before they learned their views were in concert. More to the point, if large numbers of Malaya's Chinese could be made to join with British, Malays, and Indians in a campaign directed chiefly at (communist) members of their own community, a multiracial Malayan national identity might still emerge, albeit founded narrowly on anticommunism and (paradoxically) anti-Chinese sentiment.

To this end, MacDonald mounted his anti-MCP propaganda efforts through Radio Malaya.[36] His goal was to rhetorically brand the MCP a foreign movement, to ensure the communists never monopolized the title of Malayan patriots, and to discursively craft a Malayan patriotism that valorized signs and acts of the Chinese community's prejudice against the MCP. Studies of Britain's Emergency policies usually credit the colonial administration's use of economic uplift and security guarantees for winning the confidence of the Malayan populace in general and the Chinese to some degree.[37] The crucial ideological work undertaken by officials such as MacDonald receives far less attention.[38] Yet the very implausibility of a Sino-Malay political alliance following the interethnic conflict of 1945 and 1946, coupled with the polarizing fact that the MCP was mostly Chinese, suggests that Britain employed other strategies that compelled Malaya's Chinese to take action against their fellows in the MCP, actions that repudiated their historical affinities for those likely connected to them through a complex "web of social institutions" and "migrant networks."[39] Little wonder, then, that U.S. officials who studied Britain's use of Radio Malaya during the early Cold War judged it an indispensable and effective tool for winning the hearts and minds of people in Malaya and Singapore. Compared with the rest of Southeast Asia, a high proportion of both countries' populations actually owned radios.[40] Via the airwaves, MacDonald would become a frequent visitor to many Malayan and Singaporean households in those early days of the Emergency, furnishing his ethnic Chinese listeners with reasons to turn on the MCP.

In his radio broadcasts, MacDonald asserted a binary opposition: the MCP as invading "enemies" against Malayan patriots defending their "homes," the image of "homes" plainly standing in for Malaya.[41] He stated repeatedly that the MCP was an "alien movement," staffed by "petty tyrants," its "murderers . . . [the] agents of foreign interests and powers."[42] His words invoked precisely the kind of anti-Chinese sentiments that seethed in other Southeast Asian nations, the designation of ethnic Chinese throughout the region as perpetual foreigners, untrustworthy interlopers. Indeed, MacDonald invested so heavily in this idea of the MCP's foreignness that at one point he conflated the organization with the communists of Eastern Europe, insisting that the MCP employed the "same tactics" as the communists of Poland, Romania, Czechoslovakia, and "other enslaved countries." Crucially, he warned his listeners that, like the communists of distant Europe, the MCP would "pose as their champions" so as to "infiltrate" every sector of Malayan life, especially the "homes of their intended dupes and victims."[43]

Above all, MacDonald wanted his Chinese listeners to believe that it was patriotic to betray fellow Chinese who had joined the MCP, fellow Chinese who in comparison had "no patriotic love" for Malaya. Indeed, he lionized such betrayals. On October 6, 1948, MacDonald praised the sacrifices made by Malaya's Chinese—they had accounted for the "greatest number of assassinations" since the start of the Emergency, murdered by the MCP for siding with the British. Even so, MacDonald promised that there was safety in numbers. He made it easy to imagine, even see, Malaya's Chinese thronging the ranks that had been mobilized to pursue, subdue, and destroy the MCP.[44] With deliberate phrasing, he vividly planted Chinese faces within every conceivable effort directed against the MCP: "Large numbers of our detectives are *Chinese*. The interpreters attached to our squads of jungle fighters are *Chinese*. Most of the villagers who bring information enabling the police, soldiers and airmen to assault terrorist hide-outs are *Chinese*. . . . *Thousands* of others are assisting as auxiliary policemen and in similar ways. The *overwhelming majority* in the Chinese community are on the side of law and order [*sic*]."[45] Did it work? The response of the Malay vernacular press, ever suspicious of the Chinese, attests to the growing visibility of Chinese in the anti-MCP campaign. In reference to the rising numbers of Chinese recruits in the Malayan Special Constabulary, the Malay-language presses warned of "foxes in fowls' skins."[46] On the other hand, the MCP's propaganda materials increasingly denounced all Chinese members of Malayan auxiliary force, signaling that the communists had begun to feel the pinch of Malaya's Chinese turning toward the British.[47] If Malaya's Chinese harbored any revulsion for supporting the colonial authorities' anti-Chinese anticommunist campaign, it was dwindling.

MacDonald also compared the valor of Malaya's Chinese volunteers against the squatters who continued to supply the MCP out of "no higher motive" than fear. He calculated that the squatters remained at the time beyond the reach of British reconstruction and his broadcasts; he might as well use them rhetorically. He depicted the squatters as "mostly immigrant Chinese" with "no patriotic love for Malaya." Some of these squatters "care[d] not a straw for any movement for Malayan freedom," and others felt they had no choice but to support the MCP's "alien" cause. All this served the "concerted plan" (so MacDonald said) of the communists also "on the war path" in China, Indochina, Indonesia, and Burma. MacDonald argued that Malaya and Singapore's Chinese must not be passive, must abjure the simple self-preservation practiced by the squatters, for that helped the "petty tyrants." It was a veritable call-to-arms, and it bound ever tighter the language of patriotism with the binary of insiders (Malayan patriots) versus outsiders (the MCP).[48]

In all this, MacDonald calculated that most of Malaya's Chinese yearned to be treated as equal citizens; that they were keen to refocus Malay hatred and distrust exclusively on the MCP as long as they could deflect such antagonism from themselves. He crafted his speeches to exploit not only this desperation on the part of Malaya's Chinese but also the pervasive anti-Chinese prejudice in Malayan society. Thereby, MacDonald upheld Britain's most important strategic objectives in the postcolonial era. These objectives were less about winning the Cold War than using the Cold War's imperatives to preserve the British Empire. Above all, MacDonald's speeches were meant to create a broad-based Malayan patriotism that, on account of its anticommunist stance, became reliably pro-British.

True Chinese, Good Malayans

MacDonald did not just talk. He also assembled the most prominent pro-British Malayan nationalists from each major ethnic community to anchor the country's transition toward self-government. The goal was to give multiracialism in Malaya another go, despite the Malayan Union having foundered upon Sino-Malay tensions, despite the fact that intercommunal strife due to anti-Chinese prejudice troubled almost all Southeast Asian societies. From mid-1948, MacDonald personally cajoled influential Chinese from Malaya and Singapore toward cooperating with UMNO. And he primed these men, as well as senior UMNO officials, with the understanding that Britain would not grant Malaya independence without a durable political accord between the races. Of course, Britain was not merely interested in peace between Malaya's two largest ethnic groups, the Chinese and the Malays, which together made up almost 90 percent of the population. For its neocolonial project to survive, Britain needed the leading Chinese of Malaya to buy into multiracialism, to believe it was attainable (and their Malay counterparts trustworthy), and to fight for it by converting even more of Malaya's Chinese to anticommunism. A year into the Emergency, MacDonald's nation-building efforts finally paid off. In September 1949, several leaders of Malaya and Singapore's Chinese and Indian communities convened what came to be known as the Communities Liaison Committee with UMNO leader Dato Onn bin Jaafar at Onn's home.

With MacDonald serving as an arbitrator at the committee's request, the leaders of Malaya's different ethnic communities temporarily shelved their mutual antipathy. Perhaps MacDonald's presence had them on their best behavior. Then again, they surely understood that only British sponsorship could underwrite this political bargain and guarantee their interests were upheld if and when Malaya attained independence. Since the specter of the MCP hung above all their heads, the incentives for these Malayans to cooperate were just right at that precise moment. The agreed principles of this committee enabled the emergence of the multiparty, multiracial Alliance coalition in 1951 that would later lead Malaya into independence. At Onn's house in 1949, the attendees agreed that they all sought a racially tolerant and independent Malaya, all hoped for the inhabitants of Malaya to "psychological[ly]" adopt a "Malayan mind" that transcended their communal loyalties, and all aspired to meld Malaya's different races into a united nation in the successful way they believed the United States had done.[49]

Given that *Voice of America* radio programs broadcasted regularly on Malayan and Singaporean radios and that the program's promotion of an idealized United States enjoyed a warm local reception, the committee's resolution is no surprise.[50] In fact, the attendees expressed at length their admiration for the United States. Or, more accurately, their desire to emulate a romanticized version of the United States, one in which school-going children every day saluted the U.S. flag and sang the national anthem, in which recent immigrants and their descendants may "still maintain their own national customs . . . and frequently speak their own national languages in their own homes . . . [but] are whole-heartedly American." The Communities Liaison Committee published its communiqué, and its intention to draw from the "carefully planned psychological methods" used by the U.S. government to inculcate its citizens, especially the young, with the knowledge and imperatives of their duties and rights as U.S. citizens.[51]

If one gets the impression from these events that British officials like MacDonald were pulling all the strings, we must remember that the British nation-building project could not succeed without collaborators. Nothing could be achieved unless all the would-be collaborators concurred that Britain's agenda served their interests. Onn, for one, would justify the committee's agreed principles to the UMNO General Assembly with the themes that MacDonald had given currency—Malayan patriotism and multiracialism. Onn had apparently taken ownership of these themes, for he contended that the cause of Malayan independence mandated "establishing a common sense of patriotism to the country amongst its peoples, transcending communal barriers."[52]

Likewise, Britain's Chinese allies in Malaya would circulate and elaborate the committee's themes with increasing reach and impact. Tan Cheng Lock, whom MacDonald invited in December 1948 to play a "leading part" in winning over Malaya's Chinese, would powerfully endorse the value of multiracialism to his fellow Chinese. MacDonald held that Tan, renowned for his success in business, would prove an invaluable Chinese collaborator against the MCP. Tan might draw to Britain's side the wealthy Chinese of Malaya and Singapore, especially those who had been intimidated into financing the MCP. Perhaps, MacDonald expressed in a letter, Tan could even shepherd other leaders of Malaya's Chinese toward an accord with their Malay counterparts.[53] MacDonald believed that Tan understood the urgency of this endeavor; that Tan also worried about Sino-Malay animosity in the country, animosity that the MCP's campaign could only intensify.[54]

Tan's history of advocating Malayan unity suggested MacDonald had picked the right man for the job. Tan had from the 1920s insisted that colonial officials "foster and creat[e] a true Malayan spirit" so as to "eliminat[e] . . . racial and communal feeling."[55] He continued to do this publicly after World War II, prompting many Chinese in Malaya, China, and even Britain and the United States to send him letters of encouragement, urging him to lead Malaya's Chinese and "struggle for Unity, Liberty and Equality among the different races living in Malaya."[56] While MacDonald persuaded Malay leaders to make peace with the Chinese, he needed Tan to guide the Chinese toward amity with the Malays.[57]

Co-opting Tan held another benefit for the British cause. In Tan, MacDonald had an individual somewhat impervious to criticisms of being Britain's imperial stooge. In 1947, Tan had hogged Malaya's limelight by leading huge sections of the country's moderate and extreme Chinese in peaceful but disruptive *hartals* (strikes). Tan had got Chinese business-owners and workers, as well as a number of Malays and Indians, to stop work on designated days in September and October that year. These *hartals*, protesting Britain's decision to adopt the instruments of the Federation of Malaya, brought Malaya to a standstill. In goading the Chinese to stage strikes, Tan had publicly decried British policy as a "negation of the principles of democracy," and proclaimed that "we asked for bread and to our deep dismay we have been given stone."[58]

Many British leaders were concerned that Tan, while not himself a communist, had knowingly organized the *hartals* in concert with several MCP representatives. They concluded that either Tan had allowed himself to be used by the communists or, worse, he knew no better than to trust the MCP. Whatever the truth, many British policymakers prepared to blackball Tan on the premise that the Malayan communists had corrupted the political front that Tan had helped to assemble, the All-Malaya Council for Joint Action.[59]

MacDonald did not judge Tan as harshly, though he confided in Sir Henry Gurney that he did not think Tan "outstandingly wise." But MacDonald saw in Tan a deep longing to play a role in Malaya's struggle for independence, potential in the fact that Tan "command[ed] high respect amongst many of the Chinese" in both Malaya and Singapore. MacDonald considered it bad strategy to exclude Tan from Britain's nation-building project when he wielded such "extraordinary influence," influence that according to Malaya's other Chinese leaders could make all the country's Chinese "fall into line." Mac-Donald's plan was to pluck Tan from premature obscurity, let him play the part of a man who had rejected the communists who had gathered expediently at his coattails, a man who had converted to the British worldview though he had once opposed it. MacDonald wanted a Chinese man to win the Chinese over and urged Gurney to give Tan time and space to prove his worth to Britain.[60] MacDonald also made sure Onn included Tan in the meetings of the Communities Liaison Committee in September 1949. Although Gurney remained convinced that Tan was not "capable of any great things," he nonetheless took MacDonald's recommendation seriously and began involving Tan in Britain's prosecution of the Emergency.[61]

Tan, meanwhile, did not step into fray just because MacDonald asked. He also sought a bargain with the Malays and the other races and pursued this to protect his own interests—to forestall the emergence of a Malaya dominated by either the Malays or the Chinese in league with the MCP. He had grown up an Anglophile who did not even speak Chinese.[62] Because he had been an out-and-out capitalist, thriving in British Malaya, he did not expect a triumphant MCP to long remain sentimental about their heady days organizing *hartals* together—in a communist Malaya Tan knew that his days (and likely those of his family and closest friends) would be numbered.

In February 1949, three months after receiving MacDonald's letter and encouragement from Gurney, Tan formally established the Malayan Chinese Association (MCA) and assumed leadership of the organization as its president. He approached the task with remarkable energy despite his sixty-six years. As MacDonald hoped, Tan declared at the MCA's inaugural meeting that its "twin fundamental objectives [were] bringing about cohesion and unity among the Malayan Chinese . . . and promoting inter-racial goodwill, harmony and cooperation." He emphasized, as MacDonald's letter had, the "supreme significance" of building "inter-communal understanding . . . between the Malays and Chinese." With even greater force, and on even more occasions than MacDonald, he asserted that Malaya's races could be "welded into one nationality" in the style of nearly every "multi-national" state in Europe.[63]

Crucially, Tan urged his Chinese listeners to unite with Malaya's other races for reasons besides collective resistance to the MCP. He acknowledged publicly that the "relative prosperity" of the Chinese in Malaya had "induced [in the other races] some feeling of resentment."[64] As a corrective, Tan wanted Malaya's Chinese to treat the other races to a charm offensive. He advised the wealthy Chinese at the MCA inaugural in Kuala Lumpur to invest in the "economic uplift and advancement of the mass of the Malay people," to prove by this their "loyalty, love and devotion" to Malaya and so gain the trust of the Malays.[65] Tan and his closest colleagues in the MCA also agreed with British authorities that they must block GMD officials who tried to join the MCA—they concurred that the GMD's "China-ward outlook" risked undermining the MCA's mission of "educat[ing] local Chinese . . . [to] identify themselves with Malaya and Malaya alone."[66] In line with this mission, Tan publicly chided the ambitious Chinese who chased political influence in Malaya by playing exclusively to the Chinese gallery and the "China bias" being stoked at the time by the GMD and MCP. "Wake up and unite . . . with the Malays and other Communities," Tan thundered in one speech, give the other races no grounds to "blame the Chinese as a whole" for the Emergency.[67]

Gradually, more British officials came to see that Tan's calls for the Chinese to "make Malaya their permanent home" served Britain's nation-building and Cold War objectives well, that Tan might really rob the MCP of Chinese support in Malaya.[68] In any case, China's consulates in Malaya that had for decades worked to protect the civil rights of overseas Chinese had fallen into disarray just as the MCA emerged. China had been wracked by a long and destructive civil war, and the CCP had risen to power only to become locked in the Korean conflict. Furthermore, Beijing continued in the 1950s to compete against Taipei in various other arenas, including propaganda operations to win influence over Chinese Indonesians. Thus, the CCP had limited resources to support the work of its consulates in Malaya and seemed never to make them a priority, allowing the MCA to fill the vacuum. Malayan Chinese, increasingly disappointed by the ineffectual Chinese consulates, also turned their attention increasingly toward winning political rights in the Malayan federation, toward Tan and the MCA.[69]

Furthermore, Tan's speeches to Malaya's Chinese often appealed to the better angels of Chinese chauvinism. Tan had convinced himself that the nationalist cause rested entirely on the shoulders of Malaya's Chinese. According to historian Tim Harper, the "intellectual foundations" of Tan's charm offensive were laced with Chinese chauvinism and Social Darwinism. In October 1949, Tan had told MCA members that "inferior races are raised by living in political

Figure 4. Tan Cheng Lock, founder of the Malayan Chinese Association (MCA), helped Britain win Malayan Chinese away from the Malayan Communist Party (MCP), no mean feat given the MCP was composed mostly of ethnic Chinese. This image of Tan was taken in 1953, featuring his local and international honors, including his knighthood of the British Empire. The Tan Cheng Lock Private Papers Collection, courtesy of the ISEAS Library, ISEAS–Yusof Ishak Institute, Singapore.

union with races intellectually superior." Tan could not reconcile himself to the vision of interracial unity unless he could state that Malaya's Chinese were bearing a glorious burden, the uplift of the country's "exhausted and decaying races," in particular the Malays.[70]

In one speech, Tan argued, gesturing at Confucianism, that the very fundamentals of Chinese culture demanded loyalty to one's adopted country, that being true Chinese in Malaya meant becoming good Malayans. Tan would go on to ply numerous Chinese audiences with this theme, stating that "the noblest ideals of our race," the things that "make us good Chinese," remain our "old moral standards . . . Loyalty and Filial Devotion."[71] He flattered Chinese pride with references to "numberless brilliant examples of loyal citizens who chose to die rather than . . . dishonor . . . their country." Believing this shored up his credibility as a true Chinese (despite not speaking the language), he "express[ed] the fervent hope that you [Chinese], my friends . . . become staunchly loyal and good citizens of Malaya." Tan insisted that "loyal service" to Malaya made it "incumbent" on the Chinese to become "completely at one" with the other ethnic communities, to forge a "Malayan consciousness and Malayan patriotism."[72] In reality, Tan did not expect the Malays to come naturally to multiracialism unless driven by "contact [with] a younger vitality," by the leadership of Malaya's Chinese.[73]

At the same time, though, Tan intoned that there was "no other alternative open" to Malaya's Chinese. If multiracialism failed in Malaya, he believed that the Chinese—at less than 40 percent of the country—could never expect "justice in all things without discrimination."[74] He advocated multiracialism for self-preservation. It was the pragmatic route.

And Tan was certainly pragmatic about his political future. At first, he had been so dedicated to the idea of multiracialism that he offered to bring the MCA into a partnership with Dato Onn's new political party, the Independence for Malaya Party (IMP). Onn had resigned from UMNO in 1951 when the party rejected his proposals to allow non-Malays to become members. He had formed the IMP in 1951 as a retort, continued to call for multiracialism in Malaya, and invited members of all races to join. Perhaps expecting their relationship to follow on famously from the Communities Liaison Committee, Tan had promised Onn the MCA's support. However, Onn's "abrasive personality" finally turned away Tan, Onn's close friends, and potential supporters.[75] Though Tan judged the IMP nonviable, he understood the MCA could not promote its message of multiracialism alone, not least because MCA leaders adamantly refused to accept non-Chinese associate members.[76] Thus, in 1952, Tan entered a partnership with UMNO that became known as the Alliance.[77] The Alliance coalition sated the desire of both UMNO and the MCA to keep their respective parties racially pure while also enabling both to pursue (to all appearances) the multiracial accord that Britain had made a prerequisite for Malaya's progress toward independence.

For Tan this was far from ideal. But UMNO remained the most popular of all political parties among the Malays and could constrain the anti-Chinese sentiment that still seethed in the larger Malay community. At least UMNO elites agreed that working with the MCA offered both parties their best chance of dealing with the MCP. In Tan's heart of hearts, though, he believed that no possible compact with the Malays would allow Chinese commerce and industry—the sources of Malay resentment—to truly flourish. In one moment of such despair, Tan even blurted what British officials thought a "virulently communal remark" that the Malays survived competition with the Chinese only by Britain's mollycoddling.[78] In public, however, Tan stumped for the Alliance with such fervor that none could guess how he privately agonized over the potential fallout of shaking hands with UMNO.

Whatever he did for the cause, Tan could not please everyone. As MCA leader, he won such fame that some Malay royals indulged exaggerated fears of a local groundswell against the monarchical system, replete with the nightmarish prospect (for them) of Tan being "elected President of the Republic of Malaya in the immediate future."[79] Even the British worried at times about the rapid surge in Tan and the MCA's influence, and colonial authorities in 1953 complained about the MCA's "evident monopoly" of the Chinese community's "contact with the government."[80] Malays in the civil service distrusted the MCA also, though they understood that Britain's transparent "object" in encouraging Tan was to "get the cooperation of the Chinese to smash the Communists in Malaya." Even so, these Malay civil servants told British officials that "the more the Chinese get together the stronger the Communists will be," warning that the more support Britain gave the MCA, the more it risked "losing the confidence of the Malays."[81]

Even so, British officials learned that most Malays "generally welcomed" the creation of the MCA.[82] The organization's widely publicized "first duty . . . to cooperate with the other communities and to find ways and means of helping the Government" defeat the MCP seemed to improve Sino-Malay relations.[83] As Tan's efforts produced more MCA chapters across the country, the MCP deduced he was a threat. The communists labeled Tan the "Number One Big Dog of the British Imperialists."[84] On April 11, 1949, an MCP member lobbed two grenades at Tan as he spoke at a new MCA chapter in Ipoh and fled. Tan survived the attempt on his life.[85] Gurney visited Tan in the hospital four days later, on Good Friday, to give him an "oral message of sympathy." But, in a telegram to the Colonial Office, Gurney expressed that Tan had been making a speech "considerably off the rails" when the grenades sailed his way. Gurney's words were drenched with relief that Tan had been attacked at that precise moment. Seeking other silver linings, Gurney informed the Colonial Office that the MCP attack "may be helpful," for it stirred up sufficient "outrage" on Tan's behalf and unexpectedly steeled the will of other MCA leaders. Better yet, Gurney wrote, MCP propaganda had veered into the counterintuitive, attributing the grenade attack to the British. Gurney felt sure this was an indication that the communists had become desperate, that they had belatedly "recognized as a mistake" their move against Tan.[86]

Tan, nursing grenade splinters in his shoulder, was galvanized to further the case for Malayan multiracialism. There was no going back for him now. British authorities now saw it fit to deploy him, an almost-martyr for their cause, toward "penetrating" the Chinese squatters.[87] In July 1949, British officials wrote to Tan requesting that the MCA set up liaisons with squatters and begin using the MCA's personal contacts to dissuade the squatters from supplying goods and paying protection money to the MCP. The MCA was also tasked with acquiring information about the communists from the squatters and, with British guarantees, could reward squatters for valuable intelligence.[88] By this time, reconstruction in Malaya had begun speeding up. As part of British counter-insurgency strategy against the MCP guerrillas, the squatters were being reset-tled into so-called New Villages, away from the edge of the Malayan jungle, sepa-rated and protected from the communists. Director of operations from 1950 to 1952, Major General Harold R. Briggs reasoned that above all the Chinese squatters must not remain vulnerable and susceptible to the communists. The resettlement scheme was the keystone of the Briggs Plan (see chapter 3).

Tan swung into action, encouraging MCA members to visit and engage the squatters as well as partially finance the resettlement programs. As the MCA's efforts progressed into 1950, Tan made radio broadcasts to remind MCA members to plow their monies into the "welfare and well-being" of the squat-ters as well as persuade other Chinese to "win [the squatters] over to our side eventually to form a bulwark against Communism."[89] All these measures fell in step with Tan's conviction that the squatters would be made "Communist-proof" should they attain a "standard of living . . . under which the siren voice of Communism [lost] its dangerously alluring attraction."[90] By early 1951, Tan had pressed the wealthy Chinese of the MCA long and hard enough to ensure that thousands of squatters, resettled now in multiple New Villages, were self-supporting and could even build schools for their children.[91] In 1952, Britain judged that while the Emergency might grind on for several more years to whittle down the MCP's numbers, the tide had turned against the "Chinese problem." That year, along with retired Lieutenant-General Harold Briggs, Tan received his knighthood from King George VI.[92]

Most Optimistic Prospect

When John Melby visited Malaya in 1950, British officials presented their U.S. counterparts a memorandum that Tan had written for Britain's secretaries of state for the colonies and war. Tan's ten-page memorandum detailed the "compromise achieved by leading men of good will" in the multiracial Communities Liaison Committee, the work of the MCA with the squatters, and the progress (albeit checkered) toward easing non-Malay claims to citizenship in the federation. This last was a policy Tan considered most appropriate for "securing Chinese cooperation in suppressing the Communist revolt in Malaya," for "weaning" Malaya's Chinese off the MCP and "Chinese national politics" and "transfer[ing] such affections to the land of their adoption." Tan had embraced British strategy as his own, the principle that the "best man to catch the Chinese bandit, Communist rebel or agent is the Chinese policeman, detective or soldier."[93] The Melby team concluded that "given the temper and determination of the British program there are reasonable prospects of success."[94]

At first blush, Melby and Erskine's optimism seems misplaced. Few would dare prophesy in 1950 that Malaya would gain independence just seven years on, much less that the Emergency would ever end. Moreover, Melby's team had come face to face with local skepticism regarding Britain's staying power and capacity to overcome the MCP. But U.S. leaders had also required that its fact-finding missions rank the troubles of Southeast Asia's countries to prioritize the allocation of U.S. aid. According to the Army officers accompanying Melby, the list ran thus: Indochina's severe problems with communism and the failing Bao Dai solution saw it clinch the top spot; Melby had called Indochina the "powder keg" of Southeast Asia.[95] Thailand's proximity to that "powder keg" and supposed penchant for accommodating northern invaders made its problems the second most pressing. The Philippines, reeling from the Hukbalahap peasant rebellion and escalating economic problems, was next. Fourth was Indonesia, for its independent government at least behaved like it was anticommunist. Malaya was dead last.[96]

Therein lay the hope. Developments in postwar Malaya signaled it was possible to reverse the domino logic in the interconnected region. Melby and Erskine believed that the "more rapid success is in Malaya, the more persuasive will be the Anglo-American example in other and admittedly more difficult areas of Southeast Asia." Thus, the Melby team extolled Malaya's achievements, however humble. U.S. military and civilian officers on the mission all agreed that the British were well ahead of other governments in the region when it came to military preparations.[97] In time the United States would try adapting British and Malayan antiguerrilla tactics for use in Vietnam. Based on later correspondence between Melby and MacDonald, U.S. officials were also enthused by British methods of reeducating captured MCP members to reject communism, and sought British reports about their reeducation camp to help the Philippine government deal with its local communists.[98] U.S. officials had begun to hope that Malaya's success might be replicated elsewhere.

Malaya also likely shone brighter because of U.S. officials' gathering unease about developments in the Philippines. After evaluating Manila side by side with Kuala Lumpur and Singapore, Melby labeled President Elpido Quirino "ineffectual, dilatory and disturbingly corrupt." Melby contended that if the Philippines served as "the American show window" of U.S. benevolence and enlightened world leadership, then Quirino's floundering amid the country's internal crises presented only an ugly picture. By mid-1949, the Truman administration had already begun comparing the weaknesses of the Quirino government to those of the declining GMD regime in China.[99] As such, Melby strove to boost British morale, eager for Malayan achievements to shape developments in the region. In the local press he paid tribute to Malaya's progress. To the *Malay Mail* on August 15, Melby stated that "Malaya presents an example by which other nations might well benefit." In the *Malaya Tribune* that same day, he elaborated that Britain possessed "experience that can be helpful to other countries."[100] He then told the *Straits Times* that "the most impressive thing about Malaya is that the Government"—by which he meant colonial officials and their local allies—"knows its problems and is tackling them." Malaya, he continued, had "many lessons to teach other countries."[101]

Most importantly for U.S. Cold War objectives, the British appeared to have successfully aligned themselves with Malayan nationalism and looked to be turning the country against the MCP. In his final report to the U.S. government in December 1950, Melby contended that the West could defeat communism in Southeast Asia only if it was able to "identify itself with nationalism."[102] NSC-51 had articulated this goal; the British seemed on the verge of realizing it. In Melby's opinion, British policies had diminished among the Malayan people that "sullen anti-colonial, anti-white, anti-Western world attitude" rampant in Southeast Asia.[103] Given time, the British might even deliver the free world a new, independent ally in Malaya, one decidedly anticommunist in worldview.

The British Empire had changed in the course of its nation-building project. While the metropole's controls over its former colony seemed looser, its influence remained considerable. One might visualize it this way: in the empire's postcolonial guise, Malayan collaborators now upheld the British sphere of influence in Southeast Asia by lashing their new nation to their former rulers diplomatically, economically, and culturally. Inside Malaya too, Britain and its collaborators bound the new Malayans together so as to draw them away from their old transnational affiliations. The United States had tried this with the Philippines, and until the early1950s it was not going as well as hoped. Thus, Malaya inspired Melby and Erskine. Over the ensuing decades, the United States would carefully watch the British experiment, admiring (and even envious of) its progress, eager to learn and adapt whatever the British had done well in Malaya for the region and beyond. Melby even wrote a letter to MacDonald at the end of August 1950 hinting at this special relationship. He thanked MacDonald for the "genuine pleasure of our time in Malaya" and expressed "trust that it is only the beginning of a long and friendly association."[104]

Sir Henry Gurney was less sanguine. On October 4, 1951, he wrote to Tan expressing his frustration with Malaya's Chinese community. Gurney believed that the MCP was "trying hard to penetrate" the New Villages and, "unopposed by any Chinese effort," appeared close to "succeeding." He predicted the whole Chinese rural population of the New Villages would "soon come under Communist domination" and complained that Malaya's Chinese had "done absolutely nothing to help their own people resist communism." He warned Tan that Britain would not keep "protecting people who are completely unwilling to do anything to help themselves."[105] His tone was impatient, angry. Perhaps Gurney meant to spur Tan to further action. But Tan never got the chance to respond. Gurney was assassinated two days later.

MCP guerrillas had ambushed Gurney and his wife as they traveled north of Kuala Lumpur to a government resort. The front page of the *New York Times* on October 7, 1951, told of Gurney "defying a hail of bullets until he fell" dead. His car had become a sitting duck after the guerrillas' first volley of machine-gun fire killed his driver. Gurney reportedly pushed his wife to the floor of his Rolls Royce and staggered out, killed as he drew fire away from the car. The attackers engaged in a brief gunfight with Gurney's bodyguards before fleeing the scene. Lady Gurney was found without injury, her husband's bullet-riddled dead body some distance from the car. Over the past three decades, Gurney had served the empire in imperial outposts like Kenya and the Gold Coast. In 1946, Jewish terrorists had failed to kill him by dynamiting the King David Hotel in Jerusalem.[106] He had arrived in Malaya, his final destination, in September 1948 after two years in the British Mandate for Palestine. He had survived just over a thousand days in Malaya.

The Prince

The patriot games went on. By 1955, British authorities felt confident enough to allow Malaya's first general elections. They had held municipal elections in various states in 1952 and 1953, in which the UMNO-MCA Alliance had scored impressive victories; in Kuala Lumpur, the Alliance had taken nine of eleven seats. By the end of 1953, Alliance candidates had won more than two-thirds of the 124 municipal positions up for contest. To the eyes of most British policymakers, their chosen patriots in the Alliance coalition had weathered the skepticism of observers at home and abroad, beaten off political competitors, and stemmed the undercurrent of Sino-Malay rivalry. The UMNO-MCA partnership already catered to about 90 percent of the country's population. By 1954, UMNO and the MCA had picked up another partner, the Malayan Indian Congress, a political party formed to represent the country's ethnic Indians. With the growth and ostensible stability of the multiparty Alliance, Britain's experiment with multiracialism appeared to gain a life of its own. Most importantly, the Alliance won the 1955 elections by a landslide while advocating "inter-racial unity," a vision of an inclusive multiracial Malaya that Tunku Abdul Rahman, the man who replaced Dato Onn, had coaxed the all-Malay members of UMNO to accept.[107]

The Tunku—a Malay word for prince—actually became UMNO's leader because he was at first an "exclusionary Malay nationalist." He had fiercely opposed Onn's proposals to open UMNO's membership to non-Malays and personally hurled criticisms at Onn. His outspokenness on this issue won him a following among UMNO's Malay chauvinists and quickly propelled him into the presidency of the organization. Moreover, the Tunku's inaugural speech as UMNO president in August 1951 rattled British authorities: he questioned the usefulness of the word "Malayan" since the British imperialists had "received [the country] from the Malays and to the Malays it ought to be returned." The Tunku had been focused on a policy of "Malaya for the Malays" until the municipal elections of 1952. Then, in an expedient turnabout, the Tunku campaigned for "inter-racial unity"—an echo of Tan's gospel of "Malayan unity"—to outflank Onn's Independence for Malaya Party (IMP), entice the MCA, and prevent Onn and Tan from combining their efforts.[108]

Soon afterward, the Tunku's expediency morphed into a personal conviction that an independent, multiracial Malaya could not but be inclusive. Years later, he would explain that Malaya's numbers simply could not justify an exclusionary pro-Malay position.[109] Perhaps the surprising popularity of "inter-racial unity" in Malaya during the early 1950s, demonstrated by the Alliance's re-sounding electoral triumphs, sealed the deal for him. Just as likely, the Tunku within a few months as UMNO leader probably lighted upon an epiphany similar to Onn's, recognizing that effective multiracialism in Malaya would fore-stall Sino-Malay conflict and keep the MCP off-balance. The Tunku and his closest colleagues ultimately came to echo "their predecessors [and sought] to reconcile the burgeoning demands" of Malay chauvinism with the "*Realpoli-tik* of inter-racial accommodation."[110] At any rate, it was good politics.

Not everyone believed the Tunku's advocacy for multiracialism was sin-cere. British officials like Sir Donald MacGillivray, Britain's last high commis-sioner for Malaya (1954–1957), felt that the Tunku was "reluctant to make major concessions to the Chinese and the Indians which would undermine the commanding position held by the Malays in the political field."[111] The Tunku had, after all, presided over the promulgation of UMNO's "Memo-randum on the Economic Position of the Malays" in 1953, which argued (in hostile tones) that British rule had combined with the "inhuman industry and skill of the Chinese and to a lesser extent . . . the Indians" to preclude for decades any Malay participation in the modern economic life of the country. The memorandum demanded that the future government of independent Malaya make "every attempt . . . to place suitable Malays in every branch of economic life," that the government should "have recourse to legislation should these attempts fail," indeed that "legislation should be introduced to compel private undertakings to take in Malay apprentices." The memorandum revealed the deep anxiety of the Malay community over falling further behind economically at the exact moment when self-government might redistribute political power to the other races.[112] In many respects, it tapped the same pools of anti-Chinese resentment that produced the economic "Thai-ification" pro-gram of the 1930s and the Indonesian government's policies that empowered indigenous merchants to seize Chinese-owned businesses.[113]

In places, UMNO's memorandum read like a screed. It stated that "the Ma-lay is sick and tired of being told his weaknesses and his disabilities in the economic sphere where these weaknesses and disabilities have been caused by factors largely not of his own making." And it concluded that the Malay had "begun to suspect there is a deliberate attempt to create the impression, both in Malaya and abroad, that his people have no place in the modern economic system because of their allegedly inherent laziness and incapacity."[114]

The Tunku, in allowing the memorandum to be drafted, may have been talking from both sides of his mouth. He was likely playing for time, absorb-ing the force of UMNO members' pro-Malay advocacy, placating them with the promulgation of the memorandum (looking the part of a Malay national-ist), and hoping he might altogether avoid or just partially fulfill the memo-randum's strident "revolutionary character."[115] Several UMNO members sensed he had abandoned his older pro-Malay stance and apparently shared their frustrations with British officials. By 1956, Britain's Far Eastern Department worriedly reported "dissatisfaction . . . at all levels" of UMNO with the Tunku, its members bitter that his "dictatorial" pursuit of interracial unity and "concessions to other Malayan races . . . neglect[ed] the true interest of the Malays."[116]

Certainly, the Tunku had been too single-minded about Malaya's indepen-dence to recognize how intensely Malay resentment had begun to burn against him. After all, the British government had time and again reminded him and his partners in the Alliance that Malaya's independence must be preceded by a "durable accord between the country's races."[117] As MacGillivray informed the Colonial Office, the Tunku "will resort to virtually any device [to] estab-lish to the satisfaction" of Britain that the "various communities in Malaya are united and that the country will be ready for independence."[118] Thus, the Tunku busied himself with making the best representation of the Malayan people's common ideals and unity to British leaders. He led the Alliance in persuading the Malayan royalty to embrace the coalition's concept of inter-racial unity.[119] He also proposed that a commission tasked with drafting inde-pendent Malaya's constitution must be composed of constitutional experts from elsewhere in the British Commonwealth, that Malayans must not be involved, not even himself. On the face of it, the Tunku argued that "persons with spe-cialized knowledge of constitutions of federal government" remained best suited to perform the task, as opposed to unqualified Malayans.[120] In this way, he shrewdly prevented Malayans of any race derailing the drafting of Malaya's constitution with their competing communal demands, whether it was Chi-nese and Indians insisting on Malayan citizenship by birth (which Malays op-posed) or Malays demanding permanent special privileges in public service jobs, educational scholarships, or Malay reservations of land. The resulting Malayan constitution, drafted in large measure by Sir Ivor Jennings—a veteran of drafting the postcolonial constitutions of India and Sri Lanka and the Tunku's contemporary at Cambridge University in the 1920s—performed a precarious balancing of these competing communal demands.[121] The consti-tution guaranteed citizenship to Malaya's Chinese and Indians through birth, various legal avenues, and naturalization and mandated that the special privileges established for Malays in 1957 would be reviewed in fifteen years with the goal of phasing them out.[122]

For years, Malaya's multiracialism seemed to work so well that during his visit to the United States in 1960, the Tunku proudly hailed his country as "living proof that different races can live and work together." It was, in his words, a retort to "many a Clever Dick" who had predicted the country would slide quickly into interracial strife soon after independence.[123] The State Department's briefing booklet for the Tunku's official visit bought into this, stating that Malaya's "vitality" arose from its many races, all of which lived in "peace and harmony."[124] The *Washington Post* too reported that the Tunku walked his talk, for he had adopted a Chinese girl, firm that the minority ethnic Chinese community should enjoy "equal rights."[125] Almost a decade after, in January 1969, a Harvard study continued to praise the nation's multiracial harmony, going so far as to hint that its example carried useful lessons for the United States given that U.S. race relations had descended into such violence in 1968.[126]

In May 1969, though, all the bitterness over the Tunku's fixation with interracial unity returned in spades. Poorer, rural Malays envied the economic success of the Chinese and Indians, and the Tunku's enemies within UMNO refashioned this envy into accusations that he had pandered to the Chinese. His critics in the Malay community derogated him as "anti-Malay" and called him the pro-Chinese "high priest of inter-racial harmony." For their part, Chinese and Indians resented the privileges for Malays that had been written into the constitution. In particular, the Chinese blamed the MCA for selling them out to the Malays and withdrew much of their support from the party. The "durable accord" unraveled chaotically over two months of brutal racial riots. Malay student groups burned effigies of the Tunku. Believing he had been sapped of all moral authority, the Tunku stepped down as prime minister in September 1970, recalling later that he heard a "shout of joy from the back of the hall" as he left the General Meeting of UMNO for the last time. In response, he admonished all present, "Listen to the voices of the merchants of evil." Few of his former colleagues bid him goodbye.[127]

Could any have foreseen such a denouement when in 1955 the Alliance had swept all but one of the seats available in the elections?[128] Perhaps the British did. They had conducted their postcolonial experiment in Malaya in the shadow of India and Pakistan's vicious interethnic and religious strife (not to mention their bloody quarrel over Kashmir), which had erupted following the subcontinent's "tryst with destiny." And they had knowingly recruited allies from Malaya's pro-British elites, hoping to rely on "great men" to bag the support of all Malayans. For the moment, men like Tan and the Tunku remained popular with Malayans. But what happened when the glow of their prestige faded, when the opposition to the Tunku's inclusivity within UMNO bloomed, when MCA members leery of Tan's campaign against their fellow Chinese in the MCP finally rejected him? No wonder, then, that at Malaya's independence celebrations in 1957, some British officials could barely stifle their reservations, whispering to visiting U.S. undersecretary of state Christian Herter that they expected the Tunku's government to eventually abandon its moderate course in race relations.[129]

These British anxieties begin to explain why, even when British authorities were relieved that the Tunku had broken bread with the MCA in 1952, they still proceeded with caution. The nationwide elections of July 1955, for all the hype, meant only to select Malaya's Federal Legislative Council—Britain deferred the granting of formal independence. For the Tunku, as leader of the Alliance, the electoral triumph conferred on him the office of Malaya's chief minister, a title that only reminded of how near and yet so far he remained from becoming prime minister of independent Malaya. With the MCP's armed struggle still ongoing, Britain remained in control of Malaya's internal security and national defense, parallel to what France had deigned to grant the Bao Dai government in 1949.[130] The great difference between the French and British nation-building experiments appears to be the fact that Britain had picked its local champions correctly (or by plain luck), finding men like the Tunku and Tan who actually commanded widespread respect among the majority of Malayans. These collaborators were driven in their pursuit of independence in ways that Bao Dai was not. More to the point, the final hurdle for the Alliance coalition was to, with Britain's assistance, bring the Emergency to an end. The patriot games now turned on peacemaking.

Peacemakers

Britain's deferral of independence for Malaya had enabled MCP propagandists to assert that the British planned to cling to Malaya forever. The communists still hoped to be thought Malayan patriots by the population, and continually burnished their anticolonial credentials by arguing that they alone fought for Malayan nationalism and freedom from British imperialism.[131] At the same time, because the MCP had come to realize its military campaign might never score a decisive win, it adopted peacemaking as a new plank of its message. In June 1954, the MCP publicized its "peace offer" to the Alliance and the British authorities in the Chinese language newspapers in Malaya sympathetic to its cause. The gist of the MCP's peace offer was that the Emergency could end once Britain and its local allies welcomed the MCP back into the Malayan nation, honored its loyal sacrifice during the Japanese Occupation, granted it equal political status, and allowed the party to participate in the nation-building project.[132] MCP leader Chin Peng calculated that Malaya's population was so exhausted by the Emergency that even the trappings of self-government in the multiple municipal elections could not assuage how the conflict had dragged on without clear resolution. Rashid Maidin, a Malay member of the MCP, would recall in his memoir that the party's Central Committee also resolved to "talk peace" because the alternative was allowing Britain to continue painting them as "bogeymen" to the masses of Malaya.[133]

To one-up the MCP, the Tunku played peacemaker too. British officials learned in January 1955 that he planned to "go into the jungle to discuss an amnesty" with the MCP "with a view to bringing the emergency to an end."[134] The Tunku had explained his strategy to Indian prime minister Jawaharlal Nehru at the start of the year. Confident that the Alliance would sweep to overwhelming victory in Malaya's general elections that July (which it did), he told Nehru that the validation of his coalition of anticommunist nationalists at the ballot box must surely void all the MCP's claims that they were "fighting against imperialism." If the MCP recognized this and accepted the amnesty offer, the fighting could end. But, the Tunku shared with Nehru, "if they do not accept . . . then we would go all out, [and] everybody would be mobilized to fight them."[135] Indeed, the Tunku informed British officials he had "not thought . . . [there] any substantial hope" the MCP would accept an amnesty, and to some degree relished the public's "full co-operation" for "full mobilization" to eradicate the communists. Nehru's response is not recorded, though British authorities upon discovering the Tunku's plans were concerned that he had brought an amateur's worldview to the prosecution of the Emergency.[136] Even so, British officials found the Tunku's mandate from the July elections so "complete and overwhelming," and the man himself so stubbornly fixed on pursuing (and very publicly advertising) his amnesty initiative, that they grudgingly supported his plans.[137] Britain's nation-building colonialism had fruited in its own obstinate way. Now that their Malayan collaborators rode a tide of popular legitimacy and plotted their own path, their former colonial rulers judged it prudent not to break with them.[138]

On September 8, 1955, the Tunku offered amnesty to the MCP and Chin Peng. In the main, the amnesty allowed MCP members who had committed acts of terrorism to surrender and "go back to China," while those "without criminal records" who wished to stay in Malaya were required to "undergo rehabilitation."[139] The Tunku also clarified that he would meet Chin not to negotiate the terms of the amnesty but merely to explain them and hear the MCP's responses.[140] In November, Chin, whom none but his MCP comrades had seen since the start of the Emergency, responded through a letter his emissary read publicly in a town to the north of Kuala Lumpur. Chin's letter suggests he was convinced that the MCP was still in the game; that the party could at a minimum share credit in the peacemaking. He wrote that the MCP, as one of the "patriotic parties" standing with the "people of Malaya," had long been "fighting for peace, democracy and independence" and therefore also sought "peace talks." He claimed to speak for the "masses" and that he, far more than the Alliance, would treat any peace talks with "sincerity, conciliation and compromise." Chin's insinuations incensed the Tunku, but the chief minister still wanted to use the amnesty offer to arrange face-to-face talks. He continued to use backchannels to bring Chin to the table, as if welcoming the climactic encounter. It almost did not happen. For whatever reason, the MCP launched an attack on a New Village that November, enabling the Tunku to remind the public of the "unreliability of Chin Peng's assertions that he was a Malayan patriot," and that furthermore the MCP evidently would not "renounce the armed struggle" or "join the peaceful march . . . toward democratic independence."[141] Ultimately, it seems that in a mix of despair, optimism, and even naïveté, Chin also desired a public confrontation of words with the Tunku. These back-and-forth verbal snipes would not prevent the talks.

The Baling Talks of December 28 and 29, 1955, as they came to be called, brought Chin out of hiding. The prospect of glimpsing Chin proved a powerful draw for the local and international press. News reporters eagerly sought invitations to Baling, a town near the Thai-Malay border. In his memoirs, Chin recalled how those reporters crowded the conference room for the five minutes granted by Malayan and British officials, conducting their "frenetic business" of "intermittently taking notes" amid their "clicking, whirring cameras [and] flashing bulbs."[142] According to Rashid Maidin, one of the two MCP members who accompanied Chin to Baling, "tens of thousands of people had gathered" at Baling, many of them shouting "*Merdeka*" (the Malay word for freedom and independence) to affirm the MCP's cause.[143] The press was not permitted to speak to Chin, though he remembers wanting to say that traveling to Baling carried considerable risk to his life, that he did not take lightly the decision to trust in the British soldiers' guarantees of safe passage as they conveyed him to the talks.[144]

When the talks began, Chin was surprised that the Tunku did not immediately come out swinging. Chin even found the Tunku's initial stance "moderate to the point of being mild," for he remembers the Tunku politely thanked

Figure 5. MCP representatives (from left) Rashid Maidin, Chin Peng, and Chen Tian at the Baling Talks in December 1955. The MCP, as the backbone of the anti-Japanese resistance during World War II, had for some years been popular with Malaya and Singapore's large Chinese populations. Photo courtesy of the Imperial War Museums.

Chin for agreeing to the talks and insisted that he did not come to "judge" the MCP. In reality, the Tunku played a wilier game. He was accompanied by Singapore's chief minister (for the British had been managing the colony's transition to self-government too), a former lawyer named David Marshall well known for his histrionics both in court and in political speeches. Whereas Marshall came bruising for a fight, the Tunku would appear that much more reasonable. Chin's memoirs suggest that he often sidestepped Marshall during the talks, wary of getting embroiled with the "pugnacious" Singaporean in "aimless verbal jousting."[145] Likewise, Rashid's memoirs make special note of how the "Jewish" Marshall "kept repeatedly attacking us like a feral boar" as though by this he "would be trusted and loved by his masters, the British."[146]

Also with the Tunku and Marshall was Tan Cheng Lock, by then seventy-two and, judging by the transcript of the Baling Talks, beyond his years of vigorous oratory. Chin remembers that Tan sat there "quietly, passive."[147] What little Tan said at Baling was a looping argument that Chin must acknowledge that his actions had harmed Malaya's Chinese most of all. Ailing, Tan was by then a spent force—he would live to see Malaya gain independence but died within a few years of it. Perhaps, when finally facing the MCP, he pulled his punches, mindful that many in the MCA harbored misgivings about his all-out efforts against their fellow Chinese. The Tunku, comparatively spritely at twenty years Tan's junior, impressed the British (and even U.S. leaders), looking every bit the leader of an independent Malaya.

In the months running up to the Baling Talks, British leaders had actually feared that the Tunku would capitulate to anything Chin demanded. Senior officials even beset the Tunku with tutors before the Baling Talks, trying to instruct him on how to justify the Alliance government's "retention of existing powers of arrest, detention and control" as well as its refusal to recognize the MCP "without detentions, and deportation of the hard core."[148] They need not have worried.

Though the talks failed to end the Emergency, records of the proceedings reveal the Tunku ably outflanking the communists. Chin had wanted the Alliance government to recognize the MCP as a legal political entity. He believed this, in one move, could end the Emergency and ensure the survival of Malayan communism (with his party as its vehicle).[149] The Tunku countered that Malayans would not recognize the MCP so that it could then "disperse throughout the country to organize communist activities." He then relied on Marshall to drum up the drama, which the Singaporean did without prompting. Marshall roared that Chin and the MCP had brought only "hot hatred . . . violence" and "misery for the people."[150] The Tunku then returned to his amnesty offer, requesting the MCP surrender to Malaya's elected leaders, which he knew forced Chin to acknowledge the legitimacy of the Alliance government. Sensing that the MCP faced an existential threat if deprived of its arms, Chin refused to surrender the organization's weapons unless the party was recognized.[151] U.S. officials took special note of the Tunku's counter: "There must be surrender because your ideology of violence is in conflict with our ideology of peace. We cannot accept the Communist Party to have equal status with us. What is happening in China, what is happening in Korea and what is happening in Viet-Nam will happen to us and I think that Malaya is too small to be divided into warring factions."[152]

The Tunku had fused peacemaking with the MCP's surrender. Chin could not say he cared for the former without acceding to the latter. After all, he had come to Baling crowing his patriotic desire for peace in Malaya. What U.S. officials most appreciated about the Tunku's response was that Chin, there and then, could not call himself a Malayan patriot without surrendering to the

Figure 6. Tan Cheng Lock, Tunku Abdul Rahman (chief minister of Malaya), and David Saul
Marshall (chief minister of Singapore) at the Baling Talks with MCP representatives in
December 1955. To British and U.S. officials, the Tunku performed splendidly in the talks.
Photo courtesy of the Imperial War Museums.

Alliance government. The Tunku had locked Chin into tacit admission that
by refusing to lay down its arms, the MCP sought the division of Malaya (like
Viet-Nam) and war without victory (like in Korea). The Tunku told Chin
that if the MCP did not surrender, "we would rather not accept you in our
society"—peace in Malaya demanded "one side must give in."[153]

The records of the Baling Talks reveal that the Tunku (with Marshall as a
foil) cornered Chin at every turn. At one point, Chin spoke abstractly about
citizens enjoying "freedom of thought" in a fair and independent Malaya. The
Tunku responded that he had "no doubt whatsoever" that in free elections
the Malayan people would "choose our system" rather than communism. Chin
had answered, "Yes, I know that too," but argued that the larger principle of
free choice remained at stake, so the MCP fought for the "dignity of man."
Marshall, with reliable bluster, snorted that using "violence to enforce [your]
views on a population . . . was hardly compatible with the dignity of man."
Chin, dodging Marshall, stated "they were not prepared to argue" the point

further.[154] Marshall's verbal attacks had the effect of abruptly truncating discussions and silencing whatever deeper reasoning Chin had to share. And for all Chin's attempts six decades later to lucidly recount his state of mind at Baling to interested historians, he made little headway against both chief ministers, and came across in 1955 as little more than an obdurate (and intellectually disappointing) ideologue.

According to Rashid, the talks demonstrated only that Britain was using the Tunku as a "political weapon" against the MCP. He derogated the Tunku as a British "puppet," lacking the power to make substantive decisions about the Emergency as long as Britain "held strategic control over the army, police and economy." Rashid also recalled that he and Chen Tian, a third MCP representative selected for the Baling Talks, discovered a "white officer" in the room adjoining the one in which the Tunku, Marshall, and Tan had met Chin Peng. Rashid and Chen, thinking themselves "wise in these matters," had immediately "surmised" this officer was "controlling Tunku." They confronted the Tunku about the "white man in the next room" and remembered the Tunku was evasive. Rashid quickly concluded that the Baling Talks were "bound to fail." He, like Chin, thought the British were manipulating the proceedings through the Tunku, that Britain fully intended "to continue the war" against the MCP regardless of what passed between the Tunku and the MCP.[155] British records, of course, contain no evidence of the "white man in the next room" at Baling. True, the British once had serious qualms about the Tunku's ability but found that he did not yield easily to their advice and influence. More importantly, in the two years between Baling and *Merdeka*, British leaders began to see the Tunku as a capable and shrewd statesman.

Indeed, the Baling Talks made the Tunku's negotiations for formal independence in London a virtual nonevent. The Tunku and Marshall had out-talked Chin in ways that revealed the MCP's basic motivation rested entirely on Britain withholding independence from Malaya. Chin had argued with some confidence that while Marshall and the Tunku were popularly elected, Malaya was still not independent, possessing no "self-determination in matters concerning internal security and national defense." Chin had stated that "as soon as" Malaya gained these "then we can stop the war immediately." Now the Tunku pounced. He demanded if Chin had just made a "promise," because "when I come back from England that [independence] is the thing that I am bringing with me." Confident that the Tunku's negotiations with the British government would fail, Chin repeated that the MCP would "straightaway stop our hostilities and also disband our armed units." Marshall almost leaped to read from a note he had just scribbled for the MCP representatives to initial

(Chin did label him "theatrical"). The note pinned Chin, stating: "As soon as the Federation [of Malaya] obtains control of internal security and local armed forces, we will end hostilities, lay down our arms and disband our forces."[156]

Only then did Chin see that he had been outfoxed. He became cagey, saying he would accept Marshall's formulation but not "surrender" as the Tunku's amnesty offer mandated. Chin then deflected any discussion of the slender difference between "surrender" and the "laying down of arms and disbanding forces," swerving instead toward quibbling with other terms of the amnesty offer in the final minutes of the talks.[157] The Baling Talks clarified for Britain that, in the Tunku's words at the negotiations in London in 1956, "the only real alternative to Communism is nationalism . . . [so] Her Majesty's Government . . . must be prepared either to foster the growth of genuine nationalism, or hand over this country to the Malayan Communist Party."[158] As U.S. officials noted after the Tunku's performance at Baling, Sir Donald MacGillivray "no longer regarded the shooting war as a deterrent to the granting of independence," and his blessing followed the Malayan delegation to London and back.[159] True to what he promised Chin he would do, the Tunku returned from London armed with Malayan control of internal security and national defense, with a scheduled date for the country's independence, August 31, 1957. According to British reports, "The persistent rain did little to dampen the warmth of the welcome with which Abdul Rahman was received on his return to Malaya. It was apparent to all that the *Merdeka* Mission had been successful, so much so that one senses in some quarters a feeling of bewilderment that so much was achieved against so little opposition."[160] On the face of it, the "Chinese problem" had been solved. MacDonald and Tan had worked to rally Malaya's Chinese to become Malayans and war against the Chinese-dominated MCP. The Tunku's peacemaking—ironically, without achieving peace at all—appeared to complete the task, largely within the framework of British nation-building colonialism. President Eisenhower's officials certainly saw things in this light, reporting to the U.S. Congress that "on balance, the prospects for the new country [were] favorable, given the present responsible, anti-communist character of the elected government."[161] Again and again in their analyses, U.S. officials chose to see in Malaya's independence "grounds for cautious optimism."[162]

The night before *Merdeka* Day, patriotic songs like "Kekal Lah Malaya Merdeka" (Federation of Malaya—God Bless Her) played on Radio Malaya, sung in English, Chinese, Malay, and Tamil by the fifty-strong Mandarin choir of the Yan Keng Benevolent Association.[163] Kuala Lumpur was festooned like a "fairy-land of glittering lights and brilliant colors."[164] At midnight on

August 31, 1957, "thousands of Malayans of all races stood in darkness for two minutes" in Kuala Lumpur's main square to mark the end of seventy-one years of British rule in their country. The Tunku delivered a speech as prime minister–elect, describing *Merdeka* as "the greatest moment in the life of the Malayan people."[165] And though it rained throughout the young nation on its independence day, the *Straits Times* reported widespread "*Merdeka* rejoicing," "formal ceremonies . . . gay cocktail parties, grand parades and solemn prayers."[166] The Union Jack was lowered and the Malayan flag raised, its horizontal stripes alternating red and white, with a blue field in the canton (featuring a yellow crescent and an eleven-point star), bearing an unmistakable resemblance to the United States' Old Glory. The Tunku had personally chosen this design.[167] The "Stripes of Glory"—as Malaya's flag was named—went up as the Tunku, his arm raised to the sky, led the tens of thousands in seven thunderous shouts of "*Merdeka*."[168] Even as Malaya joined the British Commonwealth, the young nation's flag signaled that it would draw close to the United States.

Within hours of independence, the Tunku broadcasted "greetings to America" on behalf of Malaya. While his speech conceded that Malaya still struggled against an "enemy within our boundaries," he stated that the country would "triumph" by "binding up its destiny with the democratic world." Within the orbit of the United States, the Tunku continued, Malaya was determined to "show the world the contribution" it could make to global "peace and economic stability."[169] In reality, he could thank the United States for little more than its "moral support" in Malaya's rise to independence. Prior to 1957, the British government had obstructed Malayan nationalists trying to forge political connections with the United States while the Eisenhower administration for its part had held that Malaya was primarily a British responsibility.[170] The Tunku could cite only that "America [had] been foremost among nations" outside the British Commonwealth with "sympathetic regard for [Malaya's] aspirations."[171] But he hoped the United States would see "a new star had risen in the eastern sky—a star of freedom for yet another Asian people."[172]

Chapter 3

Manifest Fantasies

British-Malayan Counterinsurgency and Nation Building in U.S. Strategy

U.S. leaders certainly took note of Malaya's rise to independence; they were most encouraged by how Britain and its Malayan allies had triumphed over the guerrilla fighters of the Malayan Communist Party (MCP). When Secretary of State Christian Herter learned on July 25, 1960, that Kuala Lumpur was days from declaring an official end to Malaya's twelve-year-long Emergency, he urged President Dwight Eisenhower to acknowledge Malaya's achievement.[1] Eisenhower sent hearty congratulations to Malaya the very next day, framing the "termination of the Emergency" as a "victory" against "Communism in all its forms."[2] Britain and Malaya's achievement buoyed Eisenhower's optimism about the West's struggle for Southeast Asia. And when Malayan prime minister Tunku Abdul Rahman visited the United States a few months later, Eisenhower welcomed him with an effusive toast. He declared the Tunku one of the United States' "staunchest friends," a "staunch defender of freedom in the world," a "partner" that Washington "value[d] highly" in the Cold War.[3] In private, Eisenhower told the Tunku that Malaya "could exert terrific force" to "counter expanding Communist influence" in Southeast Asia.[4] Little wonder that in the final months of Eisenhower's presidency, the U.S. Army's new *Handbook for the Suppression of Communist Guerrilla/Terrorist Operations* looked to the Malayan Emergency for proven "practical measures successfully utilized" against guerrilla activities.[5] The U.S. Army's *Handbook* represents just one point in a longer U.S. preoccupation with Britain's solution to the "Chinese problem" that shaped the contours of U.S. Cold War strategy and empire in Southeast Asia and beyond.

Figure 7. President Dwight Eisenhower receives Malayan prime minister Tunku Abdul Rahman on October 26, 1960. Eisenhower privately told the Tunku that Malaya could "exert terrific force" to counter communism in Asia. National Park Service photo, courtesy of the Dwight D. Eisenhower Presidential Library and Museum.

There is no exaggerating U.S. leaders' fascination with British–Malayan counterinsurgency. From the mid-1950s through the 1960s, this fascination flourished and influenced—even infected—the United States' policies toward Vietnam, wider Southeast Asia, and its client governments outside the region. It had begun in the early 1950s when U.S. policymakers became enamored of Britain's nation-building project in Malaya. As Malaya's Emergency came to an end, it seemed that Britain's counterinsurgency tactics had succeeded as well. Thus, with growing intensity into the 1960s, U.S. officials nurtured a fantasy that Britain possessed a magic bullet to kill revolutionary communism; that, with conscientious study, the United States could appropriate it for Vietnam, the rest of the interconnected region, and elsewhere. British and Malayan leaders fed this U.S. fantasy to make themselves indispensable to the United States as well as forestall any MCP resurgence inspired by the Vietnamese communists. To this end, British and Malayan officials promoted the virtues of their counterinsurgency model and touted the brilliance of their experts to their U.S. ally, as well as purposefully massaged or withheld information about the Emergency to burnish their record. They captured the imagination of U.S. leaders who, equally, hankered after any imperial know-how possessed by the allies they most admired.

But the United States was not a mere neophyte at Britain's knee, innocent of having wielded this instrument of imperial control. The U.S. military had ample experience in counterinsurgency. From the first days of the Republic through the 1930s, U.S. soldiers had repeatedly conducted early versions of counterinsurgency that leading military officials came to describe as "small wars."[6] The U.S. Marine Corps' *Small Wars Manual* of 1940, for example, featured the antiguerrilla tactics the corps used to wage its so-called Banana Wars in Nicaragua and Haiti in the early twentieth century.[7] Likewise, the U.S. Army boasted a long history of pacification and irregular warfare campaigns as part of the United States' westward expansion, its colonizing of the Philippines, and more. In these "small wars," the Army often used punitive measures against defiant civilian populations that had succored local guerrillas who opposed the United States, measures that included forcible resettlement, taking hostages, destroying their food and property, and subjecting them to arrest, trial, and execution. Between the two world wars, the U.S. Army also studied France's suppression of Moroccan irregulars during the 1920s and 1930s to hone its own basic combat manual, *Field Manual 100–5 (Field Service Regulations, Operations)*.[8] Furthermore, the United States used its Philippine colony as a testing site for its counterinsurgency against indigenous rebels. With these experiments, the United States refined its colonial surveillance techniques, covert operations, and tools of repression, all of which would be imported back to the United States and redeployed to later imperial adventures after 1945.[9]

Why then the U.S. interest in the British methods employed in Malaya? Because U.S. military leaders—officials of the Army in particular—had entered the 1950s anxious to fill a perceived "doctrinal void" in U.S. counterinsurgency strategy for the Cold War era. The U.S. Army had carried out so few counterguerrilla campaigns during World War II that in the decade following 1939, its *Field Manual 100–5* saw virtually no revisions. With the Chinese communists' victory in 1949, which Mao Zedong had won by intertwining guerrilla tactics with a peasant-based movement, U.S. military planners sought a thoroughgoing update of their "small wars" methods, one that had to be undertaken swiftly since Mao's theories of revolutionary warfare had started to spread to communist factions across the decolonizing world. U.S.-assisted efforts in the Philippines against the left-wing Hukbalahap rebels (known also as the Huks) and Britain's campaign against the MCP quickly became the two most studied campaigns for practices the United States might emulate. No doubt, British-Malayan and U.S.-Philippine records being in English ensured their "overwhelming popularity" with U.S. planners.[10]

Then again, Britain's example held particular appeal for the United States. Alone of the European colonial powers in Southeast Asia, Britain had effectively co-opted anticommunist Malayan nationalists in a campaign to, quite literally, exterminate the MCP. In contrast, the Netherlands had been unable to suppress Indonesia's revolutionary nationalists and retreated from the region in 1949; France fell to defeat at the hands of the Viet Minh in 1954 and completed its withdrawal from Southeast Asia the next year. U.S. policymakers thus pored over British strategies because that fading empire seemed otherwise tenacious, crushing a homegrown communist guerrilla movement that, like the Viet Minh, had once been popular for resisting Japan's occupying forces.

Recently declassified British records show how eagerly the United States sought to transplant Britain and Malaya's counterinsurgency strategy to U.S. clients in Southeast Asia and across the global South. The U.S. Army would call this project its "transmission belt" of "tactical . . . know-how and experience"; Kennedy officials dubbed it the U.S. Overseas Internal Defense Policy.[11] These projects created an imperial network across the world to equip U.S. allies with the specs of an extermination campaign for their domestic rivals, establishing a "limited-liability empire" upheld by non-U.S. allies so that U.S. soldiers could remain safely out of the fray.[12] But this fantasy also became a gateway to deeper U.S. involvement, particularly in trouble spots such as Vietnam. U.S. leaders' faith in this fantasy undergirded their commitment to any South Vietnamese policy that resembled British-Malayan counterinsurgency, and to a doomed misalliance with President Ngo Dinh Diem. The very notion that a magic bullet for Vietnam's problems lay within the reach of the United States would influence even President Lyndon Johnson's views about Americanizing the Vietnam conflict.

Swatting Mosquitoes in Malaya

In October 1950, U.S. secretary of state Dean Acheson wrote with concern about "communist-controlled guerrilla warfare . . . on a world-wide basis." He urged the NSC to study how the United States might "collaborate with friendly governments on exchange of information" to "develop and perfect techniques, strategy and tactics" to defeat communist guerrillas. Soon, the Truman administration was officially resolved to "obtain and assemble all possible information on counter-guerrilla warfare . . . [and] develop a program for making available to our friends and allies a common fund of knowledge" for fighting "Soviet and communistic inspired guerrilla activities."[13]

Britain's struggle with the MCP guerrillas, still touch and go in the early 1950s, was one of several conflicts that U.S. officials watched closely.[14] But as early as 1951, the U.S. Army's foremost expert in psychological warfare, Major Paul Linebarger, insisted that British operations in Malaya offered "one of our most valuable codes of military training and doctrine."[15] In 1952, a few months after the MCP assassinated Sir Henry Gurney, British high commissioner for Malaya, U.S. Army officers stationed in Singapore began in earnest to scrutinize British military training, organization, and methods in Malaya.[16] U.S. officials placed high stakes in Britain's campaign against the MCP. The NSC, for one, was convinced that due to the "interrelation of the countries" of Southeast Asia, the loss of Malaya to the MCP would see the entire region "passing into the communist orbit."[17] In April 1954, Eisenhower had used the image of "falling dominoes" to portray the interconnected region.[18]

But the Malayan domino stood firm. In late 1954, the Eisenhower administration abruptly discerned that the Emergency had turned a corner (though there had been some signs of this by 1952).[19] Thereafter, any positive developments in Malaya's situation seemed more dramatic. By 1955, U.S. officials reported that British and Malayan forces had killed or captured over eight thousand MCP guerrillas, "more than the original number" that had actually started the armed struggle in 1948. The Emergency had become a "one-sided war" in the opinion of U.S. policymakers, which to them explained why MCP leader Chin Peng sought (without success) a truce with the Malayan government.[20] When Chin's negotiations for peace with the Tunku collapsed in December 1955, British-Malayan forces resumed their efforts to wipe out the MCP (see chapter 2).

The counterinsurgency campaign against the MCP, the baser half of Britain's solution to the "Chinese problem," was nothing less than one of coercion and extermination.[21] As Lieutenant-General Sir Harold Briggs, Britain's director of Malayan operations from 1950 to 1952, explained to *Time*: "You can't deal with a plague of mosquitoes by swatting each individual insect. You find and disinfect their breeding grounds. Then the mosquitoes are finished."[22] The Briggs Plan—for which the general was later knighted—called for the immediate relocation of half a million Chinese "squatters" from the edges of Malaya's dense tropical forest where the MCP (operating from jungle bases) was strongest, where the guerrillas had been able to obtain supplies and recruits from squatters by intimidation or the appeal of their cause. Per the Briggs Plan, British security personnel would surround squatter settlements in surprise "dawn raids" and evict the squatters from their makeshift homes (which British troops then torched), before transporting whole communities by truckloads to "forced, concentrated settlements" known as the New Villages.[23]

The New Villages were essentially military camps, replete with sentries, barbed-wire fences, and curfews for the residents. Well aware of this, British officials tried to stem any comparisons to the Nazis' reviled concentration camps at home and across postwar Europe by using the term "New Village" instead of "camp." This bald "semantic shift" actually dampened the criticism of British policies in Malaya that emanated from the metropolitan publics of western nations. Britain's euphemism was, after all, bolstered by some "functional" realities. London held up the New Villages—the schools, infirmaries, and sanitary facilities therein—as "model sites for accelerated modernization," appealing to western publics' lingering attachments to the "civilizing missions" of their colonial past and current fondness for the latest iterations of those worldviews, a "modernizing mission" inspired by supposedly liberal principles.[24]

It is true that the New Villages' facilities offered squatters a vast improvement on their prior living conditions. But as David French points out, Britain's counterinsurgency victories in Malaya and its diminishing world empire were secured not by "winning [the] hearts and minds" of the people but "by being nasty" to them.[25] Within the New Villages, Malayan Chinese were expected to take the carrots of "forced modernization" funded partly by the pro-British Malayan Chinese Association (MCA) and thereby serve as informants, join in the hunt for the MCP, and support the Alliance party that negotiated with, rather than fought, Britain for self-determination.[26] If not, the former squatters must endure the stick of British military officers' reprisals and "unofficial acts of brutality" to squeeze from them intelligence about the MCP.[27] The Emergency Regulations allowed General Sir Gerald Templer (Briggs's successor from early 1952) to treat New Villagers to "collective punishment." Long curfews and severe food restrictions were commonplace. In one New Village where the MCP killed an ethnic Chinese resettlement officer, sixty-two residents were accused of abetting the communists and detained; the entire village was then demolished and all the inhabitants relocated.[28] Another New Village was subjected to a twenty-two-hour curfew and thirteen days of deep cuts to its rice rations, meant to break the villagers' silence about suspected MCP hideouts in the vicinity. *Time* magazine extolled Templer's "toughness."[29]

Figure 8. The view from one of the fifteen watchtowers surrounding the New Village of Tanjong Malim, northwest Malaysia (undated, likely early 1950s). British authorities forcibly relocated half a million Malayan Chinese into such New Villages to cut them off from the MCP. Photo courtesy of the Imperial War Museums.

In late 1953, Eisenhower wrote Templer a personal letter expressing his "admiration . . . for the magnificent job" Templer was doing.[30]

Crucially, the New Villages aided Britain's lethal campaign against the MCP, a veritable "swatting of mosquitoes" writ large. The forced resettlement of Malaya's ethnic Chinese squatters, accompanied by the detention and deportation of some forty thousand suspected communist sympathizers, hived Malaya's civilians off from the MCP, choked the communist guerrillas' supply lines, and provided the British sufficient intelligence to better wage their counterinsurgency campaign.[31] In effect, the Emergency had enabled a ferocious expansion of state power, a process that combined with the political maneuvers of UMNO, the MCA, and their British patrons (see chapter 2) to create a Malayan nation–state that simply did not exist before the 1940s.

State making in Southeast Asia after World War II had typically proceeded in this way, with one local faction rising to dominance by incorporating, policing, ousting, or eradicating its opponents. The ascent of Malaya's pro-British, anticommunist government was akin to that of Philippine president Ramon Magsaysay's U.S.-friendly leadership, which crushed the Huk uprising by the mid-1950s; and that of Thailand's pro-U.S. military elites, who consolidated their authority via crackdowns on their civilian rivals.[32] These assertions of sovereignty, these efforts to extend state power to the very limits of their respective territories, were, at base, imperial projects.

As British decolonization occurred in tandem with the imperial tendencies of Malaya's state making, extermination of the MCP remained high on the agenda. In 1956, the British director of Malayan operations, to prove that Malaya was safe and ready for independence, submitted a *Review of the Emergency Situation* to the Foreign and Commonwealth Office in London that fixated on the number of MCP fighters "eliminated" per month compared with civilians and security forces "killed." According to the review, that ratio was two to one in 1952, which amounted to more than thirty MCP fighters mowed down each week for twelve months.[33] Clearly, British officials used the word "eliminate" in place of "kill" intending to produce a "semantic shift" akin to when they eschewed "camps" in favor of "New Villages."

London's wordplay never concealed the bloodlust of its forces in Malaya. In April and May 1952, the *Daily Worker*, newspaper of the British Communist Party, printed damning photographs: one featured a Royal Marine commando holding the severed head of an MCP guerrilla (when located by British authorities, the Marine in question admitted the photo was genuine); another showed a different Marine brandishing two decapitated heads of MCP guerrillas, a female and a male. Privately, senior members of the British government acknowledged that such acts might constitute "war crimes"; publicly, they parried the *Daily Worker*'s exposé with panache. British colonial secretary Oliver Lyttleton confronted the scandal in parliamentary discussions, insisting that decapitation served identification purposes (one could not ferry so many dead bodies out of the jungle while a war raged), and besides, these heads had been taken by the Dayak headhunters of Borneo that Britain had deployed for jungle warfare in the Malay Peninsula.[34] Though Lyttleton had admitted to widespread decapitation as standard procedure, the story died anyway. British dailies, perhaps under pressure from the government, largely ignored the gruesome decapitation story. Collective Anglo-American anxiety over aggressive Chinese forces in the ongoing Korean conflict may have enhanced Lyttleton's public relations spin, drowning popular aversion to beheading communists with yellow faces.

At any rate, the British-Malayan campaign against the mostly Chinese MCP was not unique. It was entwined with preexisting local antipathy toward the

Chinese diaspora like other nation-building projects across Southeast Asia. Throughout the 1950s, the Thai, Indonesian, and Philippine governments had exploited the pervasive indigenous hatred of their Chinese communities. They had crafted their national identities from popular hostility toward this perceived alien minority (though many Chinese families in Southeast Asia had long assimilated into the dominant culture) and nurtured nationalist fervor from native resentment of the economically successful Chinese (though not all the Chinese were wealthy). Sino-Malay antagonism was a kissing cousin to these, as were the Malay leaders' demands for more economic opportunities (see chapter 2) analogous to the Thai, Indonesian, and Philippine programs to force ethnic Chinese from vital sectors of the economy.[35]

In all these countries, anti-Chinese sentiment intersected easily with anti-communist nationalism, underpinned by widespread local suspicions that Southeast Asia's Chinese would naturally support the CCP. The key difference in Malaya, however, was that its population was almost 40 percent ethnic Chinese. Unlike in Thailand or Indonesia where the Chinese communities were proportionally much smaller, Britain and its local Malayan allies had to aggressively recruit ethnic Chinese collaborators to entice their fellows toward executing the anti-MCP campaign. Because Britain actually accomplished this, Malaya's Emergency unfolded with much in common to the anti-Chinese policies of its regional neighbors. Indeed, the extermination of the MCP, prosecuted by the pro-British nationalists of Malaya, was of a piece with the programs that Jakarta directed against its own Chinese communities. This potent combination of anticommunist nationalism and anti-Chinese prejudice animated the Indonesian and Malayan policies that banished thousands of Chinese to China, even though many of these Chinese lacked any real ties to the mainland.

Energized by anti-Chinese prejudice, Britain and Malaya's campaign against the MCP would not be derailed. By 1953, the number of MCP guerrillas "eliminated" each month was seven times that of civilians and security forces killed. By 1955, the ratio had jumped to more than ten MCP fighters dispatched for each civilian life the guerrillas claimed.[36] The hobbled MCP continued to launch raids and assassinate British and Malayan civilians, but they fought a losing battle. Between 1956 and 1957, with *Merdeka* Day within touching distance, MCP fighters were still being killed at a rate of twenty or more a month.[37] The British, supported by a growing stable of Malayan military and police officers, were waging a war of attrition, their looming victory scored by a body count the MCP could not sustain.

Figure 9. A wounded MCP guerrilla fighter held at gunpoint after his capture (undated, likely early 1950s). During the twelve-year Malayan Emergency, Britain and its allies killed more MCP fighters than had originally started the communists' armed revolt against the British in 1948. Photo courtesy of the Imperial War Museums.

Civic Action and the Bloodless Counterinsurgency

While executing their counterinsurgency campaign in Malaya, the British also strove to manage their U.S. ally's knowledge about the Emergency. Britain's Colonial Office, for one, was determined to keep from the CIA and other U.S. officials any report on Malaya that had been composed in "complete frankness and without any inhibitions." Such documents must not go to "third parties," least of all the United States. Because London sought the "fullest political and strategic cooperation" from Washington, British officials fed their U.S. counterparts "specially prepared" reports that highlighted the success of their policies in Malaya while exuding calculated anxiety so as to compel the United States to deepen its commitment to the region.[38] Nearly seventy years would pass before the British government released records such as its yearly *Review of the Emergency Situation.*

On the other hand, Britain never withheld the truth of how much money it was pouring into the Emergency. *Time* reported in 1952 that it cost Britain about "$150,000 a day" to conduct its anti-MCP campaigns.[39] By 1957, U.S. officials knew that Britain spent "the equivalent of three million American dollars weekly" on military operations in the Malayan jungles, thrice the cost of running the basic administrative functions of the Malayan government.[40] It appears that British officials were most concerned with shielding their U.S. allies from the grisly statistics of its monthly MCP death toll. Furthermore, the Colonial Office in London concurrently pursued an even broader policy of forgetting: either refusing to document or burning the records of their counterinsurgency campaigns the world over.[41] These measures helped to bury the atrocities that Britain and its collaborators perpetrated in the late colonial period, from the wholesale massacres of innocent villagers in the Malayan jungles to the torture of Kenyans involved in the anticolonial Mau Mau movement of the 1950s.[42] Apparently, this worked. There is scant evidence that Eisenhower's officials ever set eyes on Britain's monthly reports about the Emergency.

But should the British have worried that the United States would be squeamish about bloodletting? It is unlikely that Britain's kill-ratio for the MCP would have alarmed U.S. military or civilian strategists. U.S. forces at war—in colonizing the Philippines and fighting Japan—evinced few qualms about annihilating their Asian enemies. Indeed, U.S. leaders in the early 1900s had belatedly legitimized U.S. soldiers' ongoing barbaric treatment of Filipino insurgents, and in the Pacific War they chose to target Japanese forces as well as civilian populations with conventional and nuclear weapons. Historian John Dower has determined that U.S. strategists were all too adept at the "psychological distancing that facilitates killing."[43]

If so, then a variant of "psychological distancing" was in play for U.S. officials analyzing the Emergency for ways to augment U.S. counterinsurgency: the British had labored to convince the United States that the British nation-building project in Malaya—specifically, their socioeconomic modernization programs—and not their military campaigns, represented the definitive ways of addressing the roots of communist insurgency; U.S. receptiveness to such notions enabled the British to gradually elide their violent record in Malaya. Put simply, Britain wanted to make counterinsurgency look bloodless; the United States wanted to believe it.

Such belief did not come easily, however. There was no question that the British and their Malayan allies were killing MCP fighters. But U.S. officials,

both intentionally and not, frequently lighted on ways of obscuring and diminishing the reality or trained their focus elsewhere. Records of the Eisenhower administration, for example, suggest that its officials cared for grand totals rather than subtotals, for cumulative figures such as the British and Malayan forces' total record of MCP personnel killed (6,200), surrendered (1,800), and captured (900) between 1948 and 1955.[44] By their nature, such balance sheets diffused the everyday savagery of the Emergency. When comforted that Malaya was making progress by 1955, Eisenhower's officials pivoted their distress toward other trouble spots like Singapore where they perceived the "marked acceleration of Communist-inspired and directed activities."[45] Moreover, Eisenhower's strategists, their attention divided during the 1950s between covert action in Iran and Guatemala, repeated Chinese aggression against Taiwan, the crises in the Suez, and Diem's struggles in South Vietnam, spared curiosity for only the lessons of the successful Malayan Emergency.

The single-minded U.S. pursuit of lessons from Malaya was simpatico with British authorities' attempts to make their policies appealing and palatable to Washington. When U.S. citizens like political scientist and China specialist Lucian Pye traveled to Malaya to study the Emergency in the 1950s, British officials carefully chaperoned them through a sanitized narrative. Pye, whom the State Department and the NSC frequently consulted, visited Malaya at least twice in the early 1950s to investigate the draw of the MCP for Malaya's Chinese. Both times he relied exclusively on British officials to assist him in his research. After all, only British authorities could grant him interviews with captured and surrendered MCP personnel (whom the British would have preselected to cast themselves in the best light).[46] British officials even put Pye's manuscript *The Appeal of Communism in Asia: The Case of the Chinese in Malaya* through a meticulous sentence-by-sentence critique in order to "modify" Pye's narrative to their advantage. As John Watson, British ambassador to the United States, noted: "Pye holds a respected position in Princeton" and "exercises influence not only in American Government circles, but indirectly on responsible public opinion." Pye for his part willingly submitted his manuscript to British vetting, likely taking the pragmatic scholar's view that he must not offend those who could facilitate his fieldwork in Malaya.[47]

Pye later funneled his research in Malaya into a 1957 publication entitled *Lessons from the Malayan Struggle against Communism*. The slim volume, at just sixty-one pages, contained what he thought were "lessons [that] can be learned which may be of general value in meeting the problem of Communist subversion in underdeveloped countries." Though Pye's prose tiptoed cautiously around forecasting the MCP's final defeat (the Emergency would not end for another three years), his conviction that Britain would win seeped through. He implied that he had delved into the Emergency and found the tenets for a general U.S. counterinsurgency doctrine. The "most important single lesson" from the Emergency, he wrote, remained that the Malayan government had achieved a "very fine balance" between "destroying" the MCP and "creating a stable political process in the society."[48]

Yet Pye's work remains patently imbalanced. British officials had contrived to shield him from any of the "destroying" he mentioned in *Lessons* (in passing, at that). Consequently, his study of the Malayan Emergency implied that the relocation of Malayan Chinese squatters into the New Villages primarily served the socioeconomic goals of nation building, not so much Britain's military campaign against the MCP. Though Pye noted that the New Villages severely cut the MCP's food supply and (like Chin Peng's memoirs attest) prevented the guerrillas from dictating the timing and location of their raids on British and Malayan civilians, such observations seemed no more than afterthoughts. In reality, the New Villages had always been central to the military campaign—MCP guerrillas attempting to score aid from the residents of New Villages unwittingly exposed the paths to their hideouts, leaving them vulnerable to ambushes by British and Malayan forces.[49] But Pye's analysis instead underscored that Britain's pursuit of socioeconomic modernization was indispensable and perhaps even structurally prior to the effective functioning of the Briggs Plan. In effect, his *Lessons* reinscribed what *Time* in 1952 had called Templer's "unsoldierly" yet "main occupation": establishing Malaya's "social services," taming the country's jungles by "getting more doctors and nurses into rural areas," and jump-starting the country's "rural industrial development."[50] It bears repeating that Briggs himself had said this of his plan: "You find and disinfect their breeding grounds. Then the mosquitoes are finished."[51] (He chose not to say that until complete disinfection there remained much swatting to do.) And it was this particular lesson from the Emergency that enabled U.S. leaders to willfully marginalize even their limited acknowledgement of Britain's brutality in Malaya.

Briggs's glib portrayals of the Emergency, amplified by Pye, underpinned the "psychological distancing" core to U.S. strategy as more and more U.S. officials studied British-Malayan tactics in the early 1960s. One such study was the U.S. Army's *Handbook for the Suppression of Communist Guerrilla/Terrorist Operations*, which was completed in December 1960. The *Handbook* grimly noted that "nearly 700 million people and 5 million square miles, about one tenth of the total land area of the world and about one quarter of its population, have been brought under the control of communist regimes." The communist powers, the *Handbook* continued, "employ[ed] indigenous communist party cadres" throughout the global South, facilitating "civil war, revolution, terrorism and guerrilla warfare" to subvert governments or groups friendly to the "Free World." Counterinsurgency thus seemed wholly germane for U.S. Cold War objectives. And the *Handbook* contained proposals for action, sampling from "five years of civil war in Russia (1918–23), twenty-five years of conflict in China (1924–49) and the continuing conflict in Indo-China and Malaya since 1945." In the *Handbook*'s historical survey of "Revolutionary Warfare" up to 1960, the communists had prevailed everywhere but Malaya. The British in Malaya, or so the *Handbook* suggested, presented the United States with successful tactics to defeat guerrilla communism.[52]

Thus, the *Handbook*'s pacification plan blended preexisting U.S. antiguerrilla tactics with lessons drawn chiefly from Britain's decimation of the MCP. Crucially, the first phase of the *Handbook*'s program paired its recommended military and police operations with initiatives for economic recovery, initiatives to be implemented from the very beginning of the entire counterinsurgency campaign.[53] Here, the Malayan example was central to what the *Handbook* called its "conceptual approach." Guerrilla movements, the *Handbook* insisted, were "a result not the cause of the problem." And nation building was "essential," indeed the very "foundation" for ultimate and swifter "military victory" over communist guerrillas. As such, while the *Handbook* predictably called for the U.S. military to provide allied governments with tactical advice and preparation in antiguerrilla warfare, it emphasized that U.S. military and civil personnel must simultaneously provide its allies with "material relief in the form of food, medical supplies, construction materials and equipment" to accelerate their "rehabilitation and reconstruction." Only these contributions to socioeconomic reform could "eliminate the causes of dissension and revolt" and the "economic destitution" and instability that communist factions worldwide exploited to enlarge their influence and ranks.[54] The echoes of Pye's work and Briggs's mosquito metaphor were unmistakable.

In fact, the *Handbook*'s conclusions, aided by its reading of the Malayan example, did not break new ground so much as reinforce U.S. leaders' prior convictions. From the end of World War II, U.S. policymakers had presumed that communism could not thrive in a country once that country's socioeconomic hardships had been adequately addressed. Such views animated the Marshall Plan for European economic recovery in the late 1940s. Through the next decade, many U.S. military planners made similar assumptions about the anti-Huk campaign in the Philippines, persuaded by U.S. Air Force colonel Edward Lansdale that "civic action" (a term Lansdale coined)—the military's involvement in social, political, and economic reforms—had obliterated the Huk rebellion's raison d'être. Actually, the surrender of Huk general Luis Taruc and many of his troops in the mid-1950s had more to do with Magsaysay's effective military campaigns. Lansdale's "civic action," which championed military-led nation building from the village level upward, had done little to address the Philippines' ongoing economic woes. But the United States and even its Filipino allies had bought their own hype about "civic action," regardless of whether it proceeded downward from the upper echelons of government and its experts (like Pye) to the villages, or welled up from the grassroots.[55] The *Handbook* nourished this fantasy. With a little help from their British friends, Washington officials consistently sanitized the violence that had cemented the Tunku's hold in Malaya. The killing of guerrillas occurred offstage, out of sight and mind; front and center, "civic action" in service of nation building promised that guerrillas might never breed at all.

The luster of British nation building would further brighten during the Kennedy administration, producing the paradoxical condition of U.S. leaders energetically extolling and promoting antiguerrilla warfare to their client governments while fantasizing that U.S. military-led "civic action" might preclude the need for warfare in the first place. In December 1961, the Kennedy administration issued National Security Action Memorandum 119, to embed "civic action" within U.S. counterinsurgency strategy. The memorandum recommended deploying "military forces on projects useful to the populace" of "less developed countries" in "such fields as training, public works, agriculture, transportation, communication, health, sanitation, and others helpful to economic development."[56] A month later, the U.S. Army had made this vision of "nation-building" a critical part of its policy for assisting indigenous military forces of client states against communist guerrillas.[57] Of course, U.S. leaders were by no means averse to the violence that came with the exercise of U.S. military power. But the lessons from the Malayan example that U.S. leaders took to heart made it easier to pretend that it might never come to that, and that should antiguerrilla warfare ever occur, it might be as bloodless as the British had made the Emergency appear.

To be sure, not all the branches of the U.S. Armed Forces were so taken with the Malayan Emergency. The Marine Corps had produced its own counterinsurgency manual for instructing its recruits by September 1960, and it contained no mention of Malaya. In February 1961, the corps' chief of staff, Wallace M. Greene Jr., forwarded the manual to the naval aide of President John F. Kennedy, boasting of the Marines' rich and varied knowledge of "small unit operations" honed since its first "successful hit and run" tactics in the

Revolutionary War. Greene insisted the Marines had employed techniques "essentially the same as those required in guerrilla and anti-guerrilla warfare" for hundreds of years. The manual, he confidently wrote, rested on the corps' experience of fighting the "Banana Wars" in Panama, Cuba, and Haiti prior to World War II; its engagement of supposed "communist-inspired forces" in China and Korea after 1945; and its use of Nicaragua in the 1920s as a "vast field testing laboratory" for the Marines' "guerrilla and anti-guerrilla type" operations.[58]

It remains unclear what purchase the Marines' manual secured in the Kennedy administration. President Kennedy and his advisers, just three weeks in office when the manual arrived in the White House, may not have carefully perused it. The fates appear to have led the newly minted attorney general Robert F. Kennedy to the U.S. Army's *Handbook*. And Robert Kennedy reacted as if he had chanced upon some compendium of arcane knowledge that would solve the world's problems. Perhaps it was due to the eye-catching cover art of the Army's *Handbook*. Under the *Handbook*'s title was an amateurish drawing of a guerrilla fighter (his face a desiccated skull) with a military cap emblazoned with a five-pointed communist star. To make the *Handbook*'s purpose explicit, the guerrilla's face had been emphatically crossed out. Robert Kennedy enthusiastically forwarded the Army's *Handbook* to the president in May 1961 with the recommendation that "this is the report which I spoke to you about. I hope that you get a chance to look at it. It is well worthwhile." In this note, he also complained that there were no equivalents of this *Handbook* for dealing with Central and South America, and that reports penned for similar objectives with respect to Iran were sorely lacking. The United States, Robert Kennedy maintained, should conduct "this kind of study" of other trouble spots if it was to "handle violence, insurrection and guerrillas" and all the "matters which are usually at the core of revolutionary movements."[59] Robert Kennedy's zeal for the U.S. Army's *Handbook* may have helped ensure the Malayan Emergency's hallowed place in the imagination of President Kennedy and his policymakers. A fascination for British-Malayan counterinsurgency would soon encroach on the young president's New Frontier.

A Strategic Concept for the World

To be sure, counterinsurgency was only one of several strategies for expanding U.S. global influence that swirled within the Kennedy administration's one thousand days. Kennedy arguably enjoyed a wider range of options for acting on the world than his predecessors since the United States, at the dawn of the 1960s, was wealthier than at any time in its history and, indeed, far more prosperous than any other nation. Furthermore, Kennedy, unlike Eisenhower, was keen to engage the Third World's aspirations for political recognition, social reform, and economic development. As a junior senator, Kennedy had traveled to the Middle East and Asia, met with leaders such as Indian prime minister Jawaharlal Nehru, and quickly determined that Third World nationalism in many countries was genuine and not simply subject to communist control. The surge in African decolonization that erupted in the mid-1950s reinforced Kennedy's worldview. In 1960 alone, as he campaigned for the presidency, seventeen African nations gained their independence. The Third World bloc in the United Nations expanded substantially, as did the nascent nonaligned movement that many Third World leaders—leery of their former colonial rulers and the superpowers—were determined to join. Kennedy believed the Cold War must from then on take place in the Third World. Strategically if not morally, Kennedy hoped to outdo the Soviets and the Chinese by satisfying, and thereby harnessing, Third World nationalism. His approach in many respects elaborated that of former secretary of state Dean Acheson toward Southeast Asia. In 1949, Acheson had approved NSC-51's recommendation that the United States satisfy militant Asian nationalism so as to win collaborators over to its side (see chapter 2). In like vein, Kennedy used personal diplomacy to court African nationalism; tried to engage the leaders of nonaligned Asian, African, and Middle Eastern nations (such as Ghana's Kwame Nkrumah, Indonesia's Sukarno, and Egypt's Gamal Abdel Nasser); and had his New Frontiersmen design a raft of economic aid programs for Third World development.[60]

President Kennedy's fundamental aim in undertaking all these interventions was to transform the domestic institutions of Third World nations. He believed that newly independent governments so recently freed from colonialism—their people facing poverty and strife, their leaders tempted by autocracy—remained susceptible to communism. His Cold War policies therefore centered on changing Third World nations from within, which often required persuading their leaders of the United States' good intentions and then using economic aid to modernize their economies and social institutions, thereby inoculating them against communist insurgency. But Kennedy remained as much fascinated with the cure for communist insurgency as with the prevention. As political scientist Elizabeth Saunders has noted, Kennedy's bent toward "deep involvement in local institutions" also manifested consistently in programs to

MANIFEST FANTASIES   99

tutor Third World military and police forces in the "transformative elements" of counterinsurgency.[61]

Thus, counterinsurgency radiated tremendous appeal for President Kennedy and his closest advisers, since it fell in step with the administration's "flexible response" strategy, a strategy meant to address the perceived shortcomings of Eisenhower's "new look" defense policy. Throughout the 1950s, Kennedy had disparaged Eisenhower's "new look" for its substantial cuts to U.S. conventional forces and overreliance on nuclear deterrence. In Eisenhower's final year in office, Kennedy argued in the Senate that the "new look" saddled Washington with "the hopeless dilemma of choosing between launching a nuclear attack and watching aggressors make piece-meal conquests." By simply threatening to use nuclear weapons, he contended, the United States could neither prevent "Communist aggression which [was] too limited to justify atomic war" nor "Communist takeover [of nations] using local or guerrilla forces."[62] Indeed, according to several of those present, Kennedy's first question to his cabinet following his inauguration was, "What are we doing about guerrilla warfare?"[63]

For Kennedy, counterinsurgency promised a smorgasbord of choices to deal with guerrilla warfare. Counterinsurgency was less a strategy than an "array of tactics" that included nation-building colonialism (and where necessary, "propping up corrupt, unpopular, and quasi-colonial governments" friendly to Washington); "population control," which included the "corralling of populations into government-controlled zones, and control of food"; and "forced silence" by antiguerrilla operations or "detention and torture."[64] Charles Maechling Jr., a lawyer called to serve on Kennedy's Special Group on Counterinsurgency, recalls that the president's preoccupation with overcoming guerrilla warfare gained even more urgency when Soviet leader Nikita Khrushchev declared in 1961, as Mao Zedong had twelve years earlier, that the USSR would also support "wars of national liberation" throughout the global South. In these wars, anticolonial forces typically employed guerrilla tactics—many culled from Maoist teachings—to frustrate the modern, mechanized militaries of their colonial rulers.[65]

Thus, in the records of the Kennedy administration, counterinsurgency is a category unto itself. Discussions and studies of counterinsurgency methods crowd the files of the Military Assistance Advisory Group (MAAG) in Vietnam, turn up with great frequency in Department of Defense reports about U.S. involvement in Latin America, dominate Deputy National Security Adviser Walt Rostow's reams of staff memoranda, and fill the papers of both NSC mainstay Robert Komer and Roger Hilsman, the director of the Bureau of Intelligence and Research. According to Maechling, President Kennedy's team of "Cold War zealots" (which included Robert Kennedy and Defense Secretary Robert McNamara) harbored such an "obsession with subliminal warfare" that counterinsurgency ascended precipitously to top the national security agenda.[66] Komer in early 1961 had nothing but praise for counterinsurgency's effectiveness. "Effective use" was also Komer's favorite phrase when he described how such tactics allowed the "effective use . . . of covert propaganda" as well as "effective use of third country nationals" in the "effective use of trained 'Hunter-Killer' teams" to defeat guerrilla insurgents.[67] Again, counterinsurgency offered U.S. policymakers a means of further "psychological distancing"—U.S. soldiers might never need to personally do any hunting and killing; "third country nationals" could perform the task (with some American training); just leave the U.S. Army to perform the munificence of the United States through "civic action."

Most in Kennedy's team then accepted General Maxwell D. Taylor's dictum that the best practices of counterinsurgencies must be, as Maechling remembers, "simplified." Taylor insisted that the simplification process would "serve as an underlying basis" for drafting U.S. military doctrine in order to "assure uniformity of tactics."[68] The challenge now facing the Kennedy administration was to formulate that general counterinsurgency doctrine for the United States, a program with explicable, practicable, and replicable methods for the troubled world.

Kennedy's team cast a wide net to cherry-pick from the antiguerrilla campaigns of the recent past. It peered abroad as far as the Greek guerrilla war of the late 1940s and the contemporary French-Algerian war, close to home in the anti-Huk campaign, as well as examined how the National Liberation Front (NLF) of South Vietnam conducted its operations.[69] In April 1961, the Office of the Chief of Staff proposed that "contact be established" with the British and French officers with "experiences in counter-guerrilla warfare in Malaya and Algeria to further allied agreement regarding doctrine of unconventional warfare."[70] In turn, the Department of State concluded that "the postwar histories of Malaya and the Philippines prove that Chinese Communist-style rebellions can be quelled." The United States' "success in preventing or defeating them [communist rebellions] elsewhere," the State Department argued, depended on U.S. leaders "understanding the nature of the threat and on our drawing from its nature, as well as from past victories and defeats, the relevant lessons."[71] For the next three or so years, following the example of the U.S. Army's *Handbook*, Kennedy's officials would churn out study after study of counterinsurgency campaigns in various parts of the world, striving to distill these campaigns into the perfect formula. Over time, the case studies of Algeria (because France withdrew despite military success over the Algerian guerrillas) and the Philippines (its main booster, Lansdale, grated on the Joint Chiefs of Staff) lost some sheen in the eyes of U.S. leaders. The Malayan Emergency, however, remained a constant in the formulation of U.S. counterinsurgency doctrine.

As the White House's clarion calls sounded Kennedy's desire for counterinsurgency studies, U.S. officials, civilian and military, as well as U.S. think tanks raced to get their treatises to the president. However, a few leading U.S. Army officers did not share President Kennedy's enthusiasm for counterinsurgency in the Third World. These military men opposed the president's goal of dedicating the Army to quashing communist guerrillas in the global South, insisting that the United States should remain focused on Europe. (The careers of these once prominent officers subsequently hit a wall; their colleagues would assume Kennedy had a hand in it.) Civilian agencies, for their part, balked at what they considered a militarization of foreign policy under Kennedy, a gateway to the unwelcome expansion of military influence over the U.S. government.[72] Such resistance was futile. Many other U.S. officials readily bought into the young president's vision, sought his favor, and were raring to serve faithfully. The Kennedy administration was swiftly buried under an absurd number of counterinsurgency studies, all spinning out similar conclusions extracted from the same case studies. These were giddy days of work produced in duplicate, triplicate, and more.

Here are but a few. In March 1961, Walt Rostow received a "useful little study" from the Policy Planning Council of the State Department that unearthed "relevant lessons" applicable to Vietnam and Latin America in the "postwar histories of Malaya and the Philippines."[73] At more or less the same time, military officers of MAAG-Vietnam produced their own study of *Tactics and Techniques of Counter-Insurgent Operations*, citing the "British experience in Malaya" as one campaign (the other being the anti-Huk operation) from which the MAAG picked up strategies now "tailored to fit the situation in Vietnam."[74] MAAG-Vietnam's study featured several portions borrowed directly from the British manual titled *Conduct of Anti-Terrorist Operations in Malaya* (*ATOM*, as the British military called it). *ATOM* drew from the syllabus of the Malayan Jungle Warfare Training School and one British commander's successful operations against the MCP in the early 1950s. The manual "included a history of Malaya and of the Organization and Armed Forces of the MCP, the Emergency Regulations, Methods of Searching, Platoon Organization and

Equipment, Patrolling and Ambushing; and Intelligence and Training."[75] By 1960, the year the Tunku declared the Emergency was over, the U.S. Army had distributed copies of *ATOM* to all its service schools for the formulation of doctrine.[76]

In November 1961, National Security Advisor McGeorge Bundy pressed his NSC team to produce a memorandum "enumerating the major factors contributing to success" in Malaya, the Philippines, and Greece.[77] Bundy was in a hurry. The month before, on behalf of President Kennedy, he had had to issue National Security Action Memorandum 104, requiring the secretary of state, the defense secretary, and the CIA director to "initiate guerrilla ground action" in South Vietnam and begin deploying U.S. advisers where the need arose.[78] Bundy needed a study of appropriate guerrilla tactics quickly. In five weeks, Under Secretary for Political Affairs George McGhee and Edward– "civic action"–Lansdale met Bundy's directive, asserting that while the Philippines "warrant[ed] the closest study for lessons which may be applied to South Vietnam," the military tactics of the British in Malaya "deserve[d] special attention."[79] McGhee and Lansdale attributed Britain's "pin-point counterinsurgency" to "systematic intelligence," facilitated in turn by Britain's shrewd alignment with Malayan nationalism and "control of the population through food rations, curfews, [and] travel restrictions."[80] McGhee and Lansdale's report landed in the White House just a day after Roger Hilsman's Bureau of Intelligence and Research produced its own study, titled *Internal Warfare and the Security of Underdeveloped States.*[81]

It was never enough. After President Kennedy created the Special Group for Counterinsurgency at the beginning of 1962, his officials worked on drafting U.S. counterinsurgency doctrine while constantly stealing glances at Britain's record in Malaya. Hilsman penned *A Strategic Concept for South Vietnam* in January 1962 detailing that "the basic approach followed in this plan was developed by Mr. R. [Robert] G.K. Thompson, who played a major role in directing counter-insurgency operations in Malaya and who is now a Special Advisor attached to the British Embassy in Saigon."[82] A few months later, the U.S. Army—though it already possessed *ATOM*—reported with anticipation that the British Commonwealth Brigade in Terendak, Malaya, would soon produce yet another counterinsurgency manual about the Emergency for the United States to study.[83] In October that year, the U.S. Army invited Malaya's head of the Psychological Warfare section, Too Chee Chew, to share his expertise with the U.S. Army Command and General Staff College at Fort Leavenworth, Kansas.[84] The balance of U.S. fascination tilted ever more toward the Malayan Emergency. For, even though U.S. officials continued to study their nation's apparent success against the Huks, the joint chiefs had begun to judge that campaign's renowned veteran, Lansdale, too brazen, obnoxious, and nettlesome.[85]

Before the joint chiefs bogged Lansdale down in CIA operations, including plots to assassinate Fidel Castro, Lansdale's last starring role as McNamara's counterinsurgency specialist may have been at a symposium RAND Corporation convened in April 1962. The Kennedy administration had charged RAND with "distill[ing] lessons and insights" from past insurgent conflicts to "inform and shape" U.S. involvement in Vietnam. As the chair of the symposium, RAND analyst Stephen T. Hosmer, recalls, he had invited U.S. and allied military men as well as civilian officials with "expertise and a proven record of success" in guerrilla or counterinsurgency warfare to the five-day conference.[86] Of the eight non–U.S. citizens at the symposium, four were British Army officers who had served in Malaya as well as Kenya and the Middle East. Two other participants were Australian military officers; one had been invited because he had fought the MCP. Rounding out the foreign experts was a veteran of the Algerian war from the French marine corps and a Filipino colonel. Hosmer in an interview decades later expressed frustration that despite his having "papered Washington" with the symposium's findings, RAND's efforts were given "short shrift" and the report seemed to have "dropped into a bottomless pit."[87] He seemed unaware that shortly after the 1962 symposium, the assistant secretary of defense for international security affairs tasked another RAND analyst with producing five new and highly detailed studies of the Malayan Emergency, studies that saw the analyst holed up in the British archives with access to previously classified materials, studies that would be completed only in September 1964, the month after the fateful Gulf of Tonkin Resolution had authorized President Lyndon Johnson to wage war in Vietnam.[88]

Even as Hosmer convened the RAND symposium, the Malayan Emergency received increasing attention in U.S. society beyond policymaking circles. In May 1962, no less than William J. Lederer, coauthor of *The Ugly American*, had gushed in *Reader's Digest* about Malaya's "brilliantly executed 13-year war" against the MCP. He wrote that "in communist-threatened Southeast Asia there shines one bright spot . . . the happy land of Malaya."[89] Lederer's article about the "guerrilla war the reds lost" in Malaya had first appeared in the *New Leader* in April, before gaining even wider readership in *Reader's Digest* the next month. Similar to many on Kennedy's team, Lederer was enthused by British counterinsurgency. He praised the Briggs Plan for destroying the "swarm of poisonous insects" that was the MCP (the mosquito metaphor had morphed, barely). He also hailed the "shrewdest, toughest experts from throughout the British Empire" who had converged on Malaya, spoke in glowing terms of how "all races" in Malaya "began working as a team" to fight the communists, and called the "squatter-resettlement program . . . one of the wonders of the war."[90]

In August 1962, President Kennedy's Special Group for Counterinsurgency, inundated with stacks of studies to sample from, finally promulgated its own doctrine. Charles Maechling, years after participating in writing up the doctrine, titled "U.S. Overseas Internal Defense Policy" (OIDP), believed it read like "boiler-plate" thanks in part to Maxwell Taylor's bent toward simplifying for uniformity.[91] There was precious little to distinguish the OIDP from other manuals that had been parceled around Washington in the first two years of Kennedy's presidency. Like all the other studies, the OIDP echoed that the "post-war examples of Greece, Malaya, and the Philippines" proved communist guerrilla warfare was "not invariably successful." Against these examples, the Special Group concluded that the "protracted" Algerian War had gone the way of the Algerian guerrilla nationalists despite the French military's "superior material resources" and numbers.[92] And like the U.S. Army's *Handbook* of 1960, indeed, like Pye's *Lessons* from 1957 and the gist of *Time*'s feature on Templer in 1952, the OIDP blandly rehashed the same principles: effective counterinsurgency mandated population control through some iteration of Malaya's New Villages, nation building that pacified—in both senses of the word—the restive population, culling intelligence from reliable collaborators, and a range of antiguerrilla tactics.[93]

Also, by combining "overseas" and "internal defense" into a baffling oxymoronic phrase, Kennedy's Special Group betrayed the tensions at the heart of the emergent U.S. empire. For one, the Special Group penned its policy paper chary of the United States appearing to be a unilateral and intrusive superpower. The phrase "internal defense" was meant to shroud the OIDP in the trappings of upholding the norms of national sovereignty. Since the Kennedy administration planned to share its counterinsurgency program with client governments, those allies must be framed as legitimate and sovereign, as "defending" their country from "internal" threats, their local rivals, the guerrillas of revolutionary communism. As with state making in postcolonial Southeast Asia mentioned above, imperial impulses were core to U.S. support of "internal defense" and clearly meant to enlarge the state power of U.S. clients in various corners of the world. This supposed "internally focused view" was completely in tune with Kennedy's determination to transform the domestic conditions of Third World nations, if not by injections of aid, then by solutions of a military nature.[94] At base, the United States sought to adapt and elaborate Britain's nation-building colonialism and counterinsurgency methods for the world. The Special Group's awkward pairing of "internal defense" with "overseas" reveals precisely the policy's international dimensions and ambitions. Ever in search of communist monsters to imagine and slay, the U.S. imperial project ventured further abroad.

At last with an "approved national doctrine," the Joint Chiefs of Staff issued their *Status of Military Counterinsurgency Program* report in August 1963, touting a "concept for exploitation of U.S. military capabilities in the counterinsurgency field." The annotated bibliography of this manual clarifies yet again that the United States drew most heavily from Britain's campaign in Malaya, attending to as many aspects of it as it could. The bibliography included Pye's work, of course, along with numerous reports, books, and articles about how the Royal Air Force (RAF), in particular its helicopter squadron, waged war against the MCP; how resettlement measures and the New Villages were "established to control civilians"; the training at Malaya's Jungle Warfare School; the tactics used by the Royal Marine Commandos against the MCP; how Malay Scouts bombed the MCP's night encampments; how the Sino-Malay rivalry affected Britain's prosecution of the Emergency; how the construction of roads and other infrastructure overcame the MCP guerrillas; what were the "the civil ramifications of the Emergency"; how the RAF and British army units "combined air-ground action" in the Malayan jungles; several "revealing interviews" with captured MCP personnel; psywar tactics in Malaya; and even the "everyday life" of a medical officer attached to Britain's counterinsurgency operations.[95]

The U.S. preoccupation with British-Malayan counterinsurgency did not only affect U.S. policy toward Vietnam. The deluge of studies surged toward transforming British methods into a strategy for all U.S. client states across the global South that faced alleged communist insurgencies. Vietnam was but one of numerous countries, interconnected by U.S. design, through Washington's international program for training its allies in anticommunist counterinsurgency. After all, the United States was not like Britain, for which declining fortunes and power after 1945 narrowed its leaders' strategic focus. Instead, with a preponderance of power and faced with revolutions against its allies that veered toward the Chinese or Soviet orbits, U.S. policymakers could not but think and operate in epic scale. Washington officials imagined their nation's security—or lack thereof—was mapped onto an unstable world. The U.S. empire was not one diminishing into points but an unfolding and expanding terrain mired in communist insurgencies. And the United States had a doctrine, a strategic concept, for them all. Bearing the talisman of British triumph in Malaya, the U.S. became engagé globally.

Furthermore, the U.S. Army refused to wait for the OIDP. In January 1961, having taken for granted that "our problem world-wide is one of dealing with insurgency," and already equipped with its own *Handbook* from December 1960, the U.S. Army initiated planning for "all [its] combat and combat support units" to be "used to combat insurgency operations . . . [even] under primitive conditions until the task is accomplished." The Army's 7th Special Forces Group had also started training detachments for "missions to assist indigenous governments in combating insurgencies in Southeast Asia, the Caribbean, the Middle East and Africa," and informed the White House that, to date, the U.S. Army had trained "fourteen thousand foreign personnel" in antiguerrilla tactics from countries such as Laos, Korea, Taiwan, and Thailand. Additionally, the U.S. Army proposed to use its "on-the-ground capability"— twenty-three MAAGs, nineteen Army Missions, and twenty-four Attaches with Military Assistance Program missions (in sixty-six nations by 1961)—to train the forces of client governments in "combating [the] extension of insurgency world-wide."[96] In reality, it was the U.S. empire of counterinsurgency knowledge that was extending worldwide.

In early 1962, much to President Kennedy's delight, the U.S. Army barreled ahead with establishing "a course in counterguerrilla tactics and techniques" for its commander-in-chief in the Caribbean, alongside the "expansion of current training activities" to include similar counterinsurgency courses for the U.S. commander-in-chief in Europe and in the Pacific.[97] In addition, the chairman of the Joint Chiefs of Staff also compiled a list of "friendly or neutral foreign countries which might request" U.S. "advice and assistance on short notice" for counterinsurgency expertise. The list included Burma, Ceylon, Laos, South Vietnam, Indonesia, and South Korea (and many more in Latin America, Africa, and the Middle East).[98] There was an undisguised eagerness to enlarge the U.S. imperial network. It was (to use Komer's words) the "effective use of third country nationals" to consolidate the U.S. position and allies in the Cold War. In May of that year, the U.S. Army's Special Warfare Center proposed to its chief of staff that the United States "capitalize on U.K. Counterinsurgency Experience" in Southeast Asia. British skills, Special Warfare officials argued, "should be passed on to appropriate free world forces now engaged in operations in Southeast Asia." For example, Army officials continued, the U.S. government should send U.S.-friendly "indigenous hill tribesmen" from Laos, Vietnam, and Thailand (accompanied by U.S. servicemen) to train in the British Jungle Warfare School in Ulu Tiram, Malaya.[99] By the start of 1962, the Tunku's government, on its own initiative, had already provided jungle warfare training to some twelve hundred South Vietnamese.[100]

Britain and Malaya's example undergirded the expanding U.S. imperium. A February 1962 status report submitted by the Department of Defense to McNamara and Kennedy called this "expanding program" of "tours" a "transmission belt" of "tactical . . . know-how and experience."[101] In Asia, this belt, an arc, ran through MAAGs or similar U.S. military missions or installations in Japan and Taiwan (like daggers into the heart of China) and extended south to Korea and the Philippines before sweeping up through pro-West Malaya and landing squarely on Thailand and South Vietnam, a veritable beachhead in mainland Southeast Asia for the struggle against the NLF and its patrons. Within and beyond the region, U.S. military and civilian officials had begun deploying through these lengthening circuits of the U.S. empire.

No Exit

The vain fantasy of borrowing glory from Britain's defeat of the MCP became a bright shining reason for Washington to persist in its commitment to Saigon, hurling its treasure at any South Vietnamese policy that resembled British counterinsurgency. Britain and Malaya always helped this fantasy along. In May 1961, the British government offered its U.S. ally the services of Sir Robert Thompson, their foremost counterinsurgency expert from the Malayan Emergency, to assist South Vietnam in its campaign against the NLF. In fact, the Tunku had suggested such an arrangement to President Ngo Dinh Diem well before the British overture and found him keen.[102] Like British and U.S. policymakers, the Tunku entertained thoughts of exporting Malaya's success northward, and soon after ending the Emergency funneled to Saigon war materiel that Malaya no longer needed: 55,475 shotguns, 346 pistols, 450 browning automatic pistols, 836 carbines, 45,707 rifles, and more than 10,000 other small arms, 346 armored vehicles, 241 scout cars, and 205 armored weapon carriers.[103]

When Kennedy and his advisers learned that Thompson would lead the mission (known as BRIAM, the British Advisory Mission), they came on board readily. Thompson was well known for executing the Briggs Plan and for his close work with Templer. The U.S. journalist Richard Critchfield had recently described Thompson as the "world's greatest counterinsurgency expert."[104] So with the Tunku's blessing, Thompson left his post as Malaya's secretary of defense to assemble his team of British military officers (all then serving the Malayan government) for Saigon. As BRIAM prepared to travel north, British foreign secretary Lord Alec Home whetted the appetite of U.S. policymakers by stating that there was "nothing that Thompson doesn't know about counterinsurgency methods."[105] British officials certainly bought into their own propaganda. Up to early 1963, British reports about BRIAM's progress carried hopes that South Vietnam might see the "history of Malaya . . . repeated," and the NLF "gradually fragment" over about a decade.[106]

Whatever the value of Thompson's expertise to South Vietnam, the fact remains that the British-Malayan model was never actually applied there. As historian Peter Busch shows, Diem's government stubbornly resisted Thompson's advice. Moreover, Diem and his brother Ngo Dinh Nhu's Strategic Hamlets Program (which Hilsman had attributed to Thompson) was not even based on the New Villages of Malaya. The British government knew this but remained loath to disclaim the Hamlets, hoping through BRIAM to shape U.S. policy in Vietnam and Southeast Asia.[107] Edward Miller's study of the Ngo brothers' approach to counterinsurgency underscores that Diem and Nhu thought little of the British model. Also, the Ngos guarded their independence fiercely, wishing to chart their own way against the NLF instead of leaning too much and too publicly on assistance from Britain and the United States. Nhu, as chief administrator of the Hamlets Program, favored French counterinsurgency theories that had been utilized in Algeria, in particular the ideas of Roger Trinquier, who coined the term "*hameaux stratégiques*." Trinquier, not Thompson, was the proper source of the ideas that Nhu eventually incorporated into his Strategic Hamlets Program.[108]

Of course, Thompson did try his best to influence the Hamlets Program. He attempted flattery, praising the program to gain Diem's confidence and ear before making proposals.[109] The Tunku, too, while on a trip to Saigon on behalf of the Malayan Football Association, counseled Diem to listen to Thompson. Instead of complimenting Diem, though, the Tunku "warned he would never win [the] fight" without learning from the Emergency. The efforts of Thompson and the Tunku went nowhere. But Diem recognized, given that U.S. officials were watching his exchanges with the Tunku, that he must appear "impressed" and amenable to the Tunku's guidance. Diem calculated that, by acting like he accepted external advice, U.S. officials would convince themselves that they could also influence him and, most importantly, continue to support his regime. Hence, he embraced the Tunku's offer of ten more Malayan experts in police and intelligence activities, though he never intended to let these Malayans prevail over him or Nhu.[110] Likewise, Diem welcomed

Thompson's recommendations outwardly but otherwise kept his close counsel with just Nhu. Thompson would meet Nhu only once.[111]

Though Thompson held no stock with the Ngos, he was most persuasive when it came to U.S. officials. Throughout his tenure with BRIAM, Thompson never disabused men like Hilsman of the illusion that he had inspired Nhu's Strategic Hamlets. Indeed, Thompson extolled the program liberally whenever he encountered U.S. decision makers, including President Kennedy.[112] Indeed, for the ill-fated president, Hilsman, and other Thompson devotees in Washington, Thompson's stamp of approval for the Hamlets, the imprimatur of a British expert, shaped reality.[113] As long as Thompson sounded optimistic about the Hamlets—to get his advice in edgewise to Diem—Kennedy's advisers pricked up their ears and copiously furnished South Vietnam with military aid to see the program through. Kennedy himself came away from meeting Thompson in April 1963 quite convinced by the latter's confidence in the Strategic Hamlets. Thompson's aura and his message that "we are winning" in Vietnam continued to challenge the pessimism that loomed over Washington's commitment to Saigon.[114]

Thompson understood that his bullish forecasts could keep BRIAM relevant to the U.S. officials and, if Diem desperately needed U.S. aid, might even force the South Vietnamese leader to listen to BRIAM. Thompson's deception was characteristic of Britain's efforts to foster its special relationship with the United States after 1945, to keep Britain important to the dominant world power, to ensure Britain remained proximate to the hub of U.S. Cold War policymaking. His force of personality sustained U.S. leaders' fantasy that some germ of the British triumph in Malaya was being brought to bear on the NLF. U.S. officials were so enamored of Thompson that in April 1963, RAND Corporation on behalf of the U.S. government entreated him to leave BRIAM to assist the think-tank in penning a study of guerrilla warfare, a "take-over bid" (as Thompson later called it) which he spurned.[115] His persistence in Vietnam would not save the Hamlets Program or the Ngos.

In November 1963, South Vietnamese general Duong Van Minh led a coup (which Washington subtly encouraged) that removed Diem and Nhu from the equation—the brothers were assassinated. Nevertheless, Diem's dictatorial rule had taken its toll on the stability of the South Vietnamese state. The British government concluded that the Ngos' repressive policies in the name of anticommunism, the brothers' disastrous anti-Buddhist stance (in a majority Buddhist country), and their stonewalling of Thompson had handed the NLF the advantage. By early 1964, British officials learned that the NLF had overrun or destroyed a large number of hamlets. Thompson tried to explain that the

Hamlets Program had faltered because the Ngos had "pushed [it] forward far too fast, into areas where hamlets could not be properly defended." The result, he argued, was that the NLF easily "penetrat[ed]" the "deplorably weak" hamlets.[116] He also decried how South Vietnam's new leaders, the Military Revolutionary Council, had merely renamed all surviving hamlets the "centers of the new rural life" and displayed "lack of urgency" in salvaging what good was left of the Strategic Hamlets for the fight.[117] In the midst of these unfavorable turns, Britain's ambassador in Saigon, Gordon Etherington-Smith, gloomily wrote the assistant under-secretary for Southeast Asia, Edward Peck, "We are not in Malaya."[118]

Never mind British officials' pessimism; U.S. officials seemed to still believe that the magic bullet for the NLF—perfected during the Malayan Emergency—was attainable. Former vice president Richard M. Nixon, from outside of the White House looking in, helped keep the notion popular. In an August 1964 issue of *Reader's Digest*, Nixon (who had visited with Templer in Malaya a decade earlier) wrote that "the same tactics that were used successfully to clean out the guerrillas in the Philippines and in Malaya can be used effectively in South Vietnam." The United States, he implied, need only remember these victories, redeploy these tactics, and forge into South Vietnam with "confidence."[119]

By then, Washington's counterinsurgency fantasy had seeped into U.S. silver screens. In September 1964, United Artists released *The 7th Dawn*, a film starring William Holden as a U.S. World War II veteran caught up in the Malayan Emergency.[120] With no gestures at historical accuracy, Holden's character, Major Ferris, is portrayed as a formidable jungle and guerrilla warfare expert who had fought alongside the MCP during the Japanese occupation of Malaya. No such thing had happened. In Australian journalist Michael Keon's 1960 novel *The Durian Tree*, on which the film is based, Ferris is an Australian.[121] In the context of escalating U.S. involvement in Vietnam, however, Holden's Ferris represents an optimistic appropriation and Americanization of Britain's counterinsurgency methods. The film depicts British colonial authorities seeking Ferris's help in flushing out the MCP leader Ng, a dashing substitute for Chin Peng. It emphasizes how much the British military needed the U.S. war veteran's expertise. Ferris's familiarity with the jungle (though he is dwarfed by its towering trees), the ease with which he locates the hidden MCP headquarters, all before the British forces manage to, are played up. The movie, filmed on location in Malaysia, forecasts and aspires to U.S. success in the Vietnamese jungles. Late in the film, Ferris floors the MCP leader Ng in a fistfight, repudiating his opponent's declaration that the Emergency "is not [merely] a local war in Malaya. It is sweeping all Asia. It will sweep Africa, South America, the world." In Ferris's triumph, the film envisions the dominoes falling in favor of the United States. Then, at the last minute of the Ferris-Ng brawl, the young daughter of the British high commissioner for Malaya grabs a pistol off the ground and shoots Ng dead. The awkward and perhaps predictable takeaway: a third-country national had done the deed; the American's hands remained clean.

The 7th Dawn mirrored the kind of fantasy still stirring Washington officials and the RAND Corporation. The film hit U.S. theaters the same month that RAND finally completed the five reports on the Malayan Emergency requested by Kennedy's assistant secretary in 1962. The RAND analyst who penned these studies, one Riley Sunderland, expressed in the introduction to his first report how he was "indebted to the War Office and other British government archives where . . . he was generously given access to records of the Emergency."[122] Several of the British documents Sunderland cited concerning the MCP, including the monthly count of MCP fighters killed, would not be released in whole or part to the public by the British government for decades.[123] Also, Sunderland cited the "authoritative British manual" ATOM repeatedly.[124] In more than six hundred pages, these RAND reports delved into army operations in Malaya, how Britain organized counterinsurgency, antiguerrilla intelligence, resettlement, and food control and won the hearts and minds of the people.[125] The main objective of these RAND studies was obvious and stated again and again: scrutinize Britain's "victory," learn how it achieved "mastery" of the "tactics and techniques" that "enabled the ground forces of the Commonwealth to defeat the insurgents."[126]

As the Johnson administration Americanized the Vietnam conflict, it appeared most desperate to replicate the British experience in Malaya. In December 1964, with more than twenty thousand U.S. advisers and auxiliary staff stationed in South Vietnam, Washington still sought "increased British assistance to their effort," and in particular requested more "British advisers" like Robert Thompson to work within what BRIAM officials remarked was an already "enormous American advisory machine."[127]

While South Vietnam's prospects grew bleaker, the United States' manifest fantasies about British counterinsurgency in Malaya burned bright. And if Thompson's stint in Saigon failed to influence the former, he had doubtlessly contributed a great deal to the latter. In March 1965, his resignation from BRIAM to "devote more time to personal affairs" and write a book on counterinsurgency excited more fictions in the minds of U.S. policymakers and social scientists.[128] What secrets to defeating the Vietnamese communists did

Thompson take with him? Had Diem, Nhu, and U.S. officials in Saigon not paid sufficient heed to Thompson's counsel? Maybe Nhu did drive the Hamlets "forward far too fast" (as Thompson claimed) and might have routed the NLF had he made the Hamlets in the image of the Briggs Plan. Once Thompson was gone, Britain's under-secretary of state, Sir Harold Caccia, learned from U.S. officials that Thompson had left a "deep impression on the Americans," that U.S. officials "now more than ever, are prepared to admit that if they and the Vietnamese had been able to put into effect the ideas M. Thompson had been recommending over the last 3 years, the situation might not be so perilous as it is."[129] With U.S. combat troops deploying in the thousands to accompany the "Rolling Thunder" bombing campaign in Vietnam, U.S. military officials continued to produce studies of the British-Malayan example. In November 1965, the U.S. Army Command and General Staff College assembled "historical accounts of how Communist-supported insurgency was defeated in Malaya" into a "reference book" titled *Counterinsurgency Case History: Malaya 1948–1960*. The first page of the "reference book" pointed out that the "application of population and resources control, the intelligence operations, and the political reforms that culminated in Malayan independence in 1957 are classical examples of counterinsurgency."[130]

In the meantime, Thompson at last pulled from the ether the counterinsurgency manual he had declined to write for RAND. His memoir, *Defeating Communist Insurgency: Experiences from Malaya and Vietnam*, arrived in 1966 to sustain the U.S. fantasy of a British-Malayan magic bullet.[131] In turn, the *American Political Science Review* celebrated Thompson's "devastating critique of American ineptness in Viet Nam," calling it an instant "classic" by a "soldier-administrator," penned in the "carefully understated" register of an "English gentleman." In many parts fawning, the review described Thompson's "knowledge [as] so vast, so detailed, and so incisive," a knowledge drawn from being a "twenty-three-year veteran of the Malayan Civil Service in which he played a major role in the defeat of the Malayan Communist's terrorist campaign." While admitting that Thompson's work fell short in discussing "political action" against communist guerrillas' ideological appeal, the review contended that *Defeating Communist Insurgency* represented the "first study with a political sophistication approaching" the "major Communist theories" of Mao and "two brilliant Vietnamese, Vo Nguyen Giap and Truong Chinh." The reviewer, a political scientist at Princeton University, concluded with the "hope" that Thompson's book would "be as pervasive as it is profound and that its influence will soon be manifested in policies in Viet Nam."[132]

Following the publication of Thompson's second book, *No Exit from Vietnam*, in 1969, the Nixon and Ford administrations welcomed him as a consultant on the U.S. war in Indochina, continuing to solicit his advice even as U.S. involvement widened to Cambodia in 1970 and transitioned from counterinsurgency toward conventional warfare. At one point, Nixon even credited Thompson with directly influencing U.S. policy in Vietnam. Nixon was taken by Thompson's performance as "booster rather than critic," and his "buoyant analysis" of U.S. and South Vietnamese war efforts (as with his BRIAM days and encounters with Kennedy) produced a similar and enduring impact on U.S. leaders. Ultimately, though, Nixon could not abide Thompson's insistence that the United States should exercise "strategic patience" and commit to more decades of war in Vietnam in order to win.[133]

But Nixon and Kissinger's willingness to negotiate with Hanoi and determination to withdraw U.S. troops from Vietnam only enhanced the glow of Thompson's ideas, ensuring U.S. fantasies about British counterinsurgency would become both pervasive and profound, a glittering myth of lost opportunities. No less than Robert Komer waxed nostalgic in 1972 about the Malayan Emergency in a report he prepared for the Department of Defense. He expressed yearning for a second chance to diligently study British methods, to forestall the United States' "costly and dubious experience in Vietnam." The British campaign in Malaya, Komer wrote, "seems even more relevant" for having "quite successfully" crushed a "serious insurgency." In his preface, Komer quoted from Thompson's *No Exit from Vietnam*: "As Sir Robert Thompson aptly said: 'Many Americans made studies of the British experience in Malaya, but these were largely superficial . . . never comprehended as a whole.'"[134] Invoking Thompson's name, Komer rebuked his colleagues, himself, and those who succeeded him for not learning properly from the British model. In truth, U.S. officials had by the early 1960s thoroughly combed through every last detail of the Emergency. U.S. policymakers' desire to emulate Britain's success in Malaya would continue to haunt U.S. military adventures into the twenty-first century.[135]

Chapter 4

The Best Hope

Malaysia in the "Wide Anti-Communist Arc"
of Southeast Asia

On February 14, 1963, President John F. Kennedy lauded the imminent formation of Malaysia, which he called "the best hope of security" for Southeast Asia, that "very vital part of the world."[1] For two years, the president's advisers had invested high stakes in the emergence of this new nation, the product of Malaya absorbing Singapore and the British territories of Sabah and Sarawak into an enlarged federation. They were convinced that Malaysia would energize anticommunist efforts across Southeast Asia and bring a "stabilizing influence" to the "former Indo-Chinese colonies now in such turmoil."[2] After all, Britain and Malaya's triumph over the Malayan Communist Party (MCP) had inspired Washington officials from the late 1950s. And the extension of Malaya's internal security apparatus—just one aspect of its counterinsurgency repertoire—to strategically important Singapore promised to obliterate the island's socialist movement for good.[3] With these considerations in mind, Roger Hilsman, President Kennedy's director of intelligence and research, envisioned Malaysia "would complete a wide anti-communist arc enclosing the entire South China Sea."[4] The *New York Times* echoed in April 1963, anticipating that this "potential giant . . . [this] strong bulwark against communism" would establish a "1,600-mile arc . . . from the border of Thailand to the Philippine archipelago."[5]

The "wide anticommunist arc" significantly advanced broader U.S. strategic interests in Southeast Asia even as U.S. policy toward Vietnam foundered. From the late 1950s through the mid-1960s, the personal agendas of Malaya's and Singapore's anticommunist leaders intertwined with British neocolonial-ism to create Malaysia, lay the foundations for a pro-West regional organization, and undermine Sukarno's left-leaning, pro-China regime in Indonesia. From Malaya, Prime Minister Tunku Abdul Rahman declared common cause with the Saigon government and forged an anticommunist grouping with Thai and Filipino leaders to brace his regime against political tremors produced by the ongoing Vietnamese revolution. The Tunku also supported Britain and the United States' abortive plot of 1958 to topple Sukarno, an operation that served the Tunku's own regional ambitions (which to Sukarno's cost the Tunku would keep very much alive).

The onetime leftist Lee Kuan Yew of Singapore adopted an anticommu-nist stance once he assumed office as prime minister in 1959 and thereafter sought British and Malayan assistance in suppressing his socialist rivals, men who had once been his political allies. Lee's success in this endeavor made it possible for Singapore to join the Malaysian federation in 1963 and thereby gain formal independence from Britain. Ironically, this arrangement also ful-filled Britain's neocolonial designs because its military would retain full con-trol of Singapore's air and naval installations, enabling the British to uphold their commitments to the Southeast Asia Treaty Organization (SEATO) alliance.

Britain and Malaysia would take a second stab at Sukarno in the early 1960s. Their forces waged a clandestine war against Indonesian troops in Borneo while Lee led diplomatic offensives that turned many Afro-Asian nations against Indonesia. All these efforts eviscerated Sukarno's influence overseas and au-thority at home, paving the way for the Indonesian army's right-wing elites to oust him by coup d'état in 1965. Jakarta's new authoritarian anticommunist leaders quickly wiped out the Indonesian Communist Party (PKI), set their foreign policy against China (the PKI's patron), and brought their nation—the fifth most populous in the world—into the "wide anticommunist arc" with Malaysia, Singapore, Thailand, and the Philippines. For British leaders, though, the expensive triumph over Indonesia (after twelve costly years of the Malayan Emergency) persuaded them to at last end their neocolonial tenure in Singapore and permanently withdraw their military from Southeast Asia. The Tunku, and Lee in turn, would lean increasingly toward the United States. These key changes in Southeast Asian politics contain a crucial irony about U.S. involvement in Vietnam: that at the very moment when President Lyndon Johnson Americanized the Vietnam conflict, developments in wider Southeast Asia had already begun to substantially favor the United States.

Figure 10. President John F. Kennedy exchanges gifts with deputy prime minister of Malaya Tun Abdul Razak Hussein during a meeting in the Oval Office on April 24, 1963. Two months earlier, Kennedy had declared Malaysia "the best hope for security" in Southeast Asia. Photo by Robert Knudsen, White House Photographs, John F. Kennedy Presidential Library.

Dedicated to the Same Principles

The first state capital that the Tunku visited was Saigon in 1958. As the Emergency ground into its tenth year, the Tunku had grown more convinced that Malaya's and South Vietnam's struggles against communism were interlinked. Throughout the early 1950s, any news of Viet Minh triumphs had been accompanied by sudden drops in the number of MCP fighters surrendering to British and Malayan forces. Thus, when the Tunku met President Ngo Dinh Diem for the first time, he declared that Malaya stood with Vietnam "at the frontline of the defense of the Free World."[6] When Diem repaid the visit in February 1960, the Tunku committed to helping Diem against his communist enemies and stated that Malaya planned to "share" its successful anticommunism with its "neighbors."[7] When the Emergency ended a few months later, the Tunku channeled generous amounts of military equipment to South Vietnam and attempted to recommend British-Malayan counterinsurgency expertise to Diem (see chapter 3).[8]

The Tunku also engaged Diem to get the attention of U.S. leaders. He knew that senior U.S. officials at the time believed Diem their "miracle man" in Southeast Asia.[9] And since the Tunku held that the United States was in ascendancy, he wished to bind Malaya up with Diem's and the United States' Cold War campaigns to preserve both his position and Malay political dominance against the remnants of the mostly Chinese MCP. For while the Tunku had brokered the Anglo-Malayan Defense Agreement (AMDA) that committed the British to defending Malaya until 1963 and felt confident that Britain would in any case protect its investments in Malaya's rubber and tin industries, the tenacious British Empire was nonetheless in decline.

For the same reason, the Tunku began modifying his portrayals of the Emergency to match what he presumed of the United States' anticommunist rhetoric and strategic vision for Southeast Asia. He strove increasingly to situate Malaya within the global Cold War struggle. Thus, while his *Merdeka* broadcast to the United States in 1957 had called the MCP an "enemy within our boundaries" and allowed that the Emergency might actually have been a civil war, he soon shifted to asserting that the MCP was but one node in a worldwide network of communists. In a 1958 session of the Malayan parliament, he stated that "there are no such things as local communists," that the MCP served "an international organization which aim[ed] for world domination" by using the "sons of [every] country" in the "overthrow [of] democracy." He insisted there was "no question whatsoever of our adopting a neutral policy," for "Malaya is at war with the Communists."[10]

The Tunku knew well that such bald professions of anticommunism were politically risky at home. He had in the recent past encountered fierce local opposition to his decision to align with the West. Malaya's Tamil Association and many Chinese groups had deplored any formal security ties with the western powers, wary of being dragged into Cold War battles such as those that ravaged Korea and Vietnam. Likewise, members of the United Malays National Organization (UMNO) had on the cusp of Malaya's independence rejected any possibility of their country joining SEATO. They exhorted the Tunku to defer to India and Indonesia, the Asian giants of nonalignment that were vocally opposed to SEATO.[11] The Tunku thus eschewed SEATO membership but found his opponents and several colleagues remained on his case. Now, they pilloried AMDA because it permitted Britain to maintain military bases in the federation and use these installations in direct support of SEATO. The UMNO Youth Wing, for example, energetically decried this glaring link to SEATO.[12] Several Malayan officials even saw through the Tunku's thinly veiled agenda in welcoming Australia and New Zealand's participation in a Commonwealth Strategic Reserve that would operate in tandem with AMDA.[13] Since the ANZUS Pact (Australia, New Zealand, United States Security Treaty) of 1951 tied the security interests of its three signatories together, the Tunku clearly sought an informal security relationship with the United States at the intersection of ANZUS and AMDA.

As the Tunku's conspicuous pro-U.S. gestures drew increasing criticism at home, he resolved to confront charges that AMDA and its connection to SEATO compromised Malaya's sovereignty. A month following *Merdeka* Day in 1957, he reminded both his domestic allies and rivals in parliament that Malaya had "an army of less than one division . . . no air force, not even a single plane . . . no navy . . . not even a sea-going craft." Malaya's sovereignty in the short term, he argued, rested entirely on the continued presence of the British military. To decisively quell the rumblings, he gambled on his popularity, stating that a rejection of AMDA constituted a vote of no confidence in him. Certain that Malayan society held him in great esteem, that he was at the height of his prestige for securing Malaya's independence, the Tunku volunteered to "make way for some other clever 'Dicks' to run the country." For the moment, the taunt cowed the Tunku's opponents, and they grudgingly accepted AMDA coming into force.[14]

Perhaps these little victories made the Tunku careless in later defenses of AMDA. In December 1958, when his political opponents resumed their criticism of the defense agreement, the Tunku stumbled into clumsy equivocations. He asserted that "we are not in SEATO [and] not committed" to any war fought by SEATO countries. But, he qualified, "if Britain entered the war" or if British territories like Singapore or Borneo were attacked, then Malaya was "treaty bound to fight." He seemed to suddenly realize he was backpedaling but could not stop, blurting that Britain being "tied up with" Malaya's defense certainly "tied us up" with Britain's SEATO commitments. Unable to escape the entanglement, the Tunku bulldozed ahead with "we are not in SEATO" but "indirectly connected with SEATO."[15] These poor explanations, which in the ensuing years the Tunku never tried to express with more care, would soon make him, Britain, and the plan to

create Malaysia easy targets for Sukarno's allegations of a British neocolonial plot to destroy Indonesia.

Sukarno's criticism of the Tunku was not without substance. The Tunku had attempted to expand Malaya's influence in Southeast Asia by supporting the United States and Britain's subversive operations against Sukarno's government in the late 1950s.[16] The Eisenhower administration had noted with alarm in 1956 that Sukarno had welcomed the PKI (and its vaunted social networks and tools for mass mobilization) into his government, though it was done mostly to fend off challenges from the right-wing elements of the Indonesian army. In addition, the PKI was the third largest communist party after that of the Soviets and Chinese. So, when procommunist politicians in 1957 won a major proportion of the popular vote in Javanese provincial elections, Eisenhower and his national security team decided to overthrow Sukarno by covertly supporting anti-Javanese separatists in Sumatra and Sulawesi. The British, keen to nurture the Anglo-American partnership and contain communism in Java (a threat much closer than Vietnam), assisted readily.[17] The rebels of Sumatra and Sulawesi were particularly appealing proxies for the Anglo-American move against Sukarno because they were non-Javanese (unlike Sukarno and his closest political allies) and suitably pro-western in their outlook. In Sumatra, the dissident politicians and military officers formed the PRRI (Revolutionary Government of the Republic of Indonesia) in February 1958. They opposed the Jakarta government's accumulation of resources at Sumatra's expense, Sukarno's embrace of the PKI, and cultivation of relations with the Soviet Union. In Sulawesi, the military-based political movement, named *Permesta* (Universal Struggle Charter), revolted in March 1957 against Jakarta's efforts to dissolve Sulawesi's semiautonomous regional military units and assert Javanese domination.[18]

The Tunku was aware that U.S. and British leaders had hatched a plan to unseat Sukarno. Officially, he denounced any external intervention on behalf of the Indonesian rebels. Privately, though, he was sympathetic to the Sumatran rebels, who by virtue of culture and ethnicity shared stronger bonds with the peninsular Malays than with the Javanese. Malayan leaders like the Tunku even considered Sumatra "an integral part of the *Semananjung Melayu* (the Malay Peninsula)." Many in the Tunku's cabinet were outright pro-Sumatran. The Sumatran rebels for their part supported the principle of seceding from Indonesia to join the Malayan federation and had assured government officials of the Netherlands that should the PKI ever seize control of Java, Sumatra would immediately declare independence, and by extension, alignment with the West.[19]

The Tunku's pro-Sumatran and anticommunist outlook prompted him to back the Indonesian separatists. These regional developments also presented him an opportunity to win his domestic political opponents over, for he could now meld the Sumatran cause with his support for the United States. Equally, he appreciated that the *Permesta* and PRRI rebellions might permit him to enlarge the Malayan federation by removing Sukarno and weakening Javanese control over Sumatra and Sulawesi. Scholars have rarely portrayed the Tunku as an ambitious statesman bent on regional expansionism, but evidence suggests otherwise. He enabled arms purchased in Singapore to be smuggled to the Indonesian rebels through Malaya, allowed the PRRI to visit Malaya and publicize their cause and utilize Malaya's military facilities for their operations, and smiled upon Malayans who privately raised funds for the Sumatran dissidents.[20] The Tunku could not have wanted the rebels to succeed without expecting to benefit, without remotely desiring that Malaya become the suzerain of Sumatra and Sulawesi.

Britain's Secret Intelligence Service also sought a rebel victory, believing this could constrain the PKI, which appeared strongest in Java. British leaders calculated that any developments at Sukarno's expense and to Malaya's advantage would likely augment London's influence in Southeast Asia. To this end, British Secret Intelligence Service arranged for the CIA's supply planes to use Singapore's air bases for deploying to drop zones in Sumatra. Throughout the rebellion, Britain also allowed U.S. military personnel to operate out of, and U.S. naval vessels to dock at, Singapore's military installations.[21]

Like the Tunku, British leaders hoped to keep their cooperation with the United States under wraps. However, Jakarta unearthed the connections easily and protested ferociously. The Javanese-dominated military also choked the separatist movement in Sumatra by April 1958 and afterward destroyed the Sulawesi rebellion. When a U.S. pilot was shot down over Ambon, Washington abruptly ended its support for the rebels. Malayan and Anglo-American hopes of regime change in Indonesia folded swiftly, leaving Sukarno embittered by the Tunku's complicity with the United States and Britain as well as more dogged about courting the communist powers.[22] In April 1959, though, the governments of Malaya and Indonesia, bowing to popular domestic pressure, would grudgingly ink a friendship treaty to signal that the *Permesta* and PRRI rebellions were behind them.[23]

Four years later, the two governments came to blows again. Sukarno would declare his opposition to the formation of Malaysia, for it provided the Tunku yet another ploy to expand Malaya's influence by incorporating the British territories of Sabah and Sarawak, a move that brought the Tunku's proven record of aggression against Sukarno right to the Indonesian border in Borneo.[24] Indonesian officials would confide in U.S. ambassador Howard Jones in 1963 that the Tunku with "outside support," by which they meant the sinister hand of Britain, would enable Malaysia to "recreate" the destabilizing forces of the *Permesta* and PRRI rebellions and tear Indonesia asunder.[25]

By then, the Tunku's strident anticommunism, his support of the U.S. plot against Sukarno, and Malaya's victory over the MCP had brought Kuala Lumpur even closer to Washington. When the Tunku visited the United States for the first time in October 1960, he seized the chance to publicize his anticommunist convictions further. He may not have realized that every word he uttered about the Cold War had already gone some distance to reassure U.S. citizens in and beyond policymaking circles that he was a staunch anticommunist ally. Members of the World Affairs Council and the Asia Foundation were gratified just to hear the Tunku emphasize that in a world "divided into two power blocs" there could be "nothing neutral at all" about Malaya's foreign policy, for the "choice between democracy and communism [was] between what is good for us and what is not."[26] And though the Tunku had been tongue-tied in distinguishing AMDA from SEATO at home, people in the United States thought him eloquent at speaking engagements throughout the United States, and were elated to "discover" that he spoke "excellent English" (like Malaya's colonizer), played golf (like Eisenhower), rose early each day (unlike the president), authored plays and movie scripts (in English as well as Malay), raised orchids, drove outboard motor boats, and was a "delightful dinner companion with many Western interests."[27] He was the very model of a modern major Asian leader (or, a recognizably westernized one), and U.S. policymakers were prepared to trust him in ways they felt increasingly unable when it came to Diem.

The U.S. response to the Tunku's ten-day visit in 1960 reveals how eagerly U.S. leaders sought an Asian partner who could articulate the tenets of the United States' ideological positions as though they were his own. Washington's last favorite son of Southeast Asia, Philippine president Ramon Magsaysay, had died in a plane crash in 1957, the same year that Malaya gained independence. The Tunku was therefore precious to the United States. If anything, his speeches assured those in the United States of the universal appeal of their cause in the decolonizing world and promised through the efforts of able junior partners like Malaya to extend the reach of the United States.

During the official luncheon held in the Tunku's honor, Eisenhower himself was preoccupied with endorsing the Malayan leader's anticommunism and its positive impact on other countries. He extolled how the Tunku had sent an armed Malayan contingent to join the United Nations in the Congo to "prevent communism from taking it over."[28] Most importantly, Eisenhower directed the attention of his listeners to the words that the Tunku had spoken to his troops before they left for Africa. The president had read the Tunku's speech only hours before meeting him but was so "deeply impressed" that he had the State Department make copies for distribution to "all the high officials of the American government."[29] Eisenhower had warmed specifically to the Tunku's "statesmanlike definition of colonialism" in the speech, especially the bright line that he had drawn between European colonialism (happily, the Tunku said, in retreat) and communism, which pretended to "champion the cause of the colonial and enslaved people" but actually "imposed the worst kind of slavery on mankind."[30]

Though the Tunku was unlikely to have read it, his language appeared to have been plucked straight from NSC-68, the landmark National Security Council document that had served as the blueprint for U.S. Cold War policy since 1950. That the Tunku and U.S. policy seemed in harmony impressed Eisenhower the most. NSC-68's author, Paul Nitze, had written that communism "compounded . . . the well-known ills of colonialism," and sought to establish and preserve "slavery under the grim oligarchy of the Kremlin."[31] Likewise, the Tunku had referenced the Soviet invasion of Hungary in 1956 and China's annexation of Tibet in 1959 to depict communism as "a novel but more sinister type of colonialism and imperialism." Eisenhower was especially cheered that the Tunku's speech warned "all democratic and freedom-loving leaders of Asia and Africa" to remain vigilant against the threat posed by communism.[32] Indeed, he stated explicitly that the Tunku's warning and comparison of colonialism and communism would prove all the more helpful to U.S. strategy in Asia since it came not from the mouths of U.S. officials but from an authentic "Asian leader."[33] In his toast to the Tunku, Eisenhower did not doubt that Malaya's government was "dedicated to the same principles" as the United States.[34]

In confidence, Eisenhower also affirmed the Tunku's attempts to drum up support for a defense treaty organization for Southeast Asia that remained separate from, and untainted by, the western influence that pervaded SEATO.[35] U.S. officials took to heart the Tunku's explanation that Southeast Asian countries needed "an organization which satisfied regional aspirations" and appeared "aloof" of the Cold War without succumbing like the "Afro-Asian Bandung groupings" to communist "exploitation." Though Sukarno was not named, the Tunku and U.S. officials were probably thinking of the Indonesian leader, his intimate ties to Moscow, and budding relations with

Beijing. Because the Eisenhower administration perceived the long-term potential of the Tunku's efforts, it resolved to encourage the Malayan leader, but from afar, else the stamp of U.S. approval and suspicions of neocolonialism foul his strivings.[36]

On July 31, 1961, the Tunku's efforts bore fruit. Malaya, the Philippines, and Thailand formed the Association of Southeast Asia (ASA). Predictably, ASA drew immediate criticism from Indonesia and China, both of which declared that the Philippines' ties to SEATO and the United States and Malaya's ties to AMDA and Britain meant neither was "really independent" and their project of indigenous regionalism inauthentic.[37] Then again, ASA formalized, however loosely, a framework within which the anticommunist nations of Southeast Asia could collaborate. It was a framework dedicated solely to the subregion (unlike SEATO, which included Pakistan, Britain, Australia, and New Zealand), one that had never before existed for the independent nations of this once heavily colonized space. ASA thus laid the foundation for the future emergence of the anticommunist, if not pro-West, Association of Southeast Asian Nations (ASEAN) in 1967, a larger grouping indigenous to the region that would also include Indonesia and Singapore. The Tunku's pro-West foreign policy and efforts at establishing ASA had made visible a nascent geostrategic arc of anticommunist nations in Southeast Asia.

Another Cuba

However, until September 1963, the "wide anti-communist arc" remained incomplete. The missing link was Singapore, between the westernmost point of the Philippine archipelago and the southern tip of the Malay Peninsula. Since the early Cold War, U.S. policymakers had maintained that Singapore was the "only major naval operating base between Cape Town and Sydney or Yokosuka" and that "its loss would compel [the] withdrawal of [western] naval forces in . . . Southeast Asia to less desirable peripheral bases" such as the United States' Subic installation in the Philippines.[38] By the late 1950s, U.S. officials had come to believe that the prospect of losing Singapore to an "internal takeover by [local] Communists or . . . extreme leftists" was very real.[39] From Washington's view, the problem was, and had always been, Singapore's Chinese. Indeed, the political allegiance of Singapore's Chinese—constituting 75 percent of the country's 1¾ million people—was perpetually suspect given long-standing U.S. convictions that Beijing possessed a "built-in subversive potential in the 12,000,000 overseas Chinese" of Southeast Asia.[40]

William Maddox, former U.S. consul-general to Singapore, spoke directly to Washington's mounting anxieties with a *Foreign Affairs* article he published in April 1962. Maddox warned of the "pro-Communist . . . Chinese chauvinists and extreme leftists" in Singapore, underscoring that their "cultural proclivities" accentuated the "expediency of accepting control from Peking." Worse, every move the British had made to accommodate local political aspirations in Singapore—moves entirely in step with British policy toward Malaya—only seemed to strengthen the hand of those that Maddox described as the "Singapore Reds."[41] In turn, U.S. intelligence officers warily predicted that the "rapid growth of leftist influence in Singapore," if left to seethe "on the doorstep of Malaya," could undermine even the federation's security.[42]

The Tunku certainly had Singapore's Chinese in mind whenever he called the island a "Cuba in his Malayan backyard."[43] And if the Tunku's allusion to Cuba seemed strained, the fact is that Britain had deployed atomic bombs to Singapore's Tengah airbase in 1962 for its plans to attack China, a move meant chiefly to elicit a U.S. invitation to jointly formulate nuclear strike policy.[44] What if Britain's bases and these nuclear weapons fell into the hands of the "Singapore Reds?" The Cuban Missile Crisis later that year made vivid any similar scenarios involving Singapore.

As such, U.S. officials had always treated the formation of Malaysia as a way to quash the so-called Singapore Reds. According to the CIA, Malaysia was "designed for the primary purpose of checking" the "influential and energetic" Barisan Sosialis (Malay for Socialist Front), the political party that purportedly led Singapore's "extreme leftists." The Barisan had been established in July 1961 by defectors from Lee Kuan Yew's People's Action Party (PAP). And with formidable support from Singapore's mostly Chinese-educated population, the trade unions, and the Chinese middle schools, the Barisan seemed poised to eclipse the PAP. Creating Malaysia, the CIA asserted, would therefore empower the fervently anticommunist Tunku to subdue the Barisan, the one thing tantamount to a "Communist threat" in Singapore. This would leave Lee politically dominant in Singapore and inoculate the "preferred political position of the Malays" in Malaya against Singapore's left-wing Chinese.[45] Likewise, U.S. ambassador to Malaya Charles F. Baldwin wrote Undersecretary of State Chester Bowles in November 1961 that even if Malaysia could "become a valuable activating element in plans . . . for creating greater Asian regional organization and solidarity," its immediate future "will almost certainly be . . . to contain the growth of Communism in Singapore."[46] On this issue, U.S. official thought was consistent. In September 1962, Roger Hilsman also concluded that Malaysia was an "artificial political unit . . . lack[ing] the inner dynamism of independence forged out of demands of indigenous peoples" but "no better alternative" existed to help Britain get "rid of the steadily deteriorating situation in Singapore."[47]

Had British nation building in Singapore truly fallen so short? If Britain's aim had been, like in Malaya, for pro-West and anticommunist indigenous leaders to gain control of the country through a phased democratization process, yes. Britain had allowed general elections in Singapore in 1959 despite widespread resentment against Chief Minister Lim Yew Hock's anticommunist crackdown on the Chinese schools and cultural organizations three years earlier; indeed, despite the surging popularity of the PAP (at the time supposedly dominated by the leftists who would later form the Barisan).[48] With Malaya already two years independent, British leaders judged it impossible to hold Singapore from the precipice much longer. Nevertheless, London attempted to erect some safeguards. British officials would control Singapore's foreign policy and military even after the 1959 elections, protracting the decolonization of Singapore and buying time to somehow shepherd the country into alignment with the West. To placate the Singaporeans, British officials gave this political condition a name, "internal self-rule," and allowed that the leader of this elected legislative assembly (not yet a sovereign government) could assume the title of prime minister. This British move paralleled France's "Bao Dai solution," which the French had hatched a decade earlier to defuse the aggressive Vietnamese nationalism roiling within Indochina.

The 1959 elections in Singapore saw a whopping 92.9 percent voter turnout that went almost entirely with the PAP. Lee's party took forty-three of the fifty-one seats available, and Lee became Singapore's first prime minister. Chief Minister Lim Yew Hock stepped down and, after some time, out of Singapore politics. The CIA, alarmed by the PAP's rising star, excoriated Britain for allowing the "Communist-infiltrated" PAP to win "an overwhelming majority."[49] The Eisenhower administration pondered military action against Singapore's communists, though it is unclear how committed U.S. leaders were to this extreme option given the PAP had secured power through free elections.[50] Then again, Eisenhower had betrayed few qualms about launching covert operations against the democratically elected, left-leaning leaders of Guatemala and Iran.

At any rate, Lee's mindset began to parallel that of U.S. officials. The PAP's thumping electoral wins in 1959 had made him reflect on how far his party depended on the labors and sociocultural networks of colleagues like Lim Chin Siong and Fong Swee Suan, men Lee had recruited because they seemed so attuned to the aspirations of Singapore's Chinese-educated community. Lee and his western-educated allies in the PAP had from the party's founding in 1954 sought to harness what he called the "vitality [and] dynamism" of Singapore's "Chinese-educated world," its rich experience with organizing trade unions and the Chinese-educated grassroots, skills gleaned from consorting with the MCP's Singapore chapter.[51] British records confirm that Lee (in his own words) thought himself "handicapped by being English-educated," unable to fathom "the peculiar workings of the Chinese mind." Thus, he and his closest associates invited left-leaning, Chinese-educated individuals like Lim and Fong into the PAP, striving to better communicate with Singapore's "Chinese-speaking mass" and plug "openings [that could be] exploited by the Communists."[52]

Lee had told British officials he was "aware of the danger that, by doing this, [he would] facilitate the extremists' challenge to his position."[53] From the time he drew them into the PAP, Lee already believed that his compatriots were communists, and that "should the communists succeed in their aims [for Malaya or Singapore], he and his kind would leave the country since they could anticipate no mercy from that quarter."[54] The MCP in Malaya, by then crippled by the British and Malayan forces, seemed to understand this too, and exulted over how recent "patriotic" graduates of Singapore's Chinese middle schools—like Lim and Fong—now packed the ranks of the PAP.[55] This explains why British officials found Lee sinking repeatedly into "pessimistic moods" a month after his 1959 electoral victory, harping an "old theme" that the communists recruited "able young Chinese from the Chinese schools" at a ratio of "ten . . . to every one that the PAP could find."[56] Even when men like Lim and Fong languished behind bars (due to Lim Yew Hock's above-mentioned crackdown on Chinese schools, organizations, and suspected communists in 1956), PAP supporters spoke their names with awe. Newly declassified documents of the British intelligence services held that the considerable political influence of Lim Chin Siong and his cohort rested on a "combination of extreme left and Chinese chauvinist elements," which Lim had ably used to build a "pro-communist" network on the island.[57] Britain's deputy high commissioner to Singapore, Philip Moore, later concluded that even if Lim did not take instruction from China, "we accept that Lim is a communist."[58] In desperate tones, Lee told British officials that he must strangle the communists' supply of recruits by "quietly . . . increas[ing] the number of English-speaking schools."[59] At the time, the new prime minister possessed no better ideas.

Then, in what seemed a perplexing turn to U.S. observers, Lee secured the release of Lim, Fong, and others who had been imprisoned since 1956.

One U.S. official guessed that Lee might be "trying to buy insurance" for the day that Lim and his ilk seized control of the PAP. Or, the official ventured, Lee may have hoped to exert some influence over the detainees, having got them out of jail.[60] Whichever it was, Lee soon held that he had inadvertently ushered Singapore's communists to the threshold of political dominance in the country. Now, he cast around frantically for solutions to his "Chinese problem." For one, Lee pressured Lim, Fong, and other detainees, as a condition for their release, to "sign an undertaking of loyalty to the PAP doctrine and program." He believed vainly that this licensed him to take "swift measures of discipline should Lim in any way deviate from the party line."[61]

For another, Lee looked northward with hope—as did U.S. officials—to the Tunku and Malaya. To entice the Tunku into a political union between Malaya and Singapore, Lee played the race card. In November 1959, Lee warned the Tunku that the communists would take Singapore through its Chinese; that they would "inevitably subvert" Malaya through its Chinese population too.[62] He hoped this prospect would scare the Tunku into enlarging Malaya's sphere of anticommunism, ridding Lee of those who had helped him and his party to power. For the moment, the Tunku seemed unfazed.

Then in 1961 came Lee and the PAP's *annus horribilis*. Lim Chin Siong had distrusted Lee all along and finally acted against him. Lee's overtures to the Tunku had been no secret; Lim and his allies knew that Lee wanted to suppress them and interpreted any talk of merging with Malaya in this spirit. As their suspicions deepened over the first half of 1961, Lim, Fong, and other Chinese-educated PAP members gradually withdrew from the PAP their support and sway over the trade unions and other Chinese-dominated organizations.[63] These moves caused the PAP to lose two seats in humiliating by-election defeats in April that year. The defeats did not unseat the PAP as the ruling party but exposed the PAP's grave weakness once bereft of the popularity its Chinese-educated colleagues brought to the table.

In response, the Tunku called Singapore "another Cuba," having lost all patience with Lee's inability to scotch those whom the Tunku considered Chinese chauvinists and communists. Soon after, U.S. State Department official George Ball echoed the Tunku's assessment of Lee, calling him a "weak and not very attractive or dependable reed upon which to rely."[64] The Tunku and his government now accepted that one solution to Singapore's "Chinese problem" was to absorb the island, take over its internal security operations, and decapitate its communist movement.[65] On May 27, 1961, the Tunku announced at a Foreign Correspondents Association luncheon in Singapore that he was intent on bringing Malaya, Singapore, Sabah, Sarawak, and Brunei "closer together" within some kind of political and economic union.[66] The Tunku would recall that once he had uttered these words, "suddenly everyone was sitting bolt upright. . . . The atmosphere was electrifying."[67] The die was cast. Lim, Fong, and many others immediately glimpsed the dire threat to their political future now that the Tunku and Lee alike pursued a merger of Malaya and Singapore.

In July 1961, Lim finally led his allies in a devastating defection from the PAP to create the Barisan, which historian Tim Harper calls an "almost fatal blow" to Lee's party. The split cost the PAP nearly 80 percent of its members.[68] In addition, the rise of the Barisan reduced Lee's party to just twenty-six seats in the fifty-one-seat assembly, "vulnerable to motions of no confidence and further parliamentary defections." To most eyes in Singapore, and abroad in Britain and the United States, the Barisan looked strong enough to win an outright majority in the next general election that Britain had scheduled for some time prior to 1964.[69]

Lim and the Barisan were wildly popular. Thousands flocked to Barisan rallies to hear Lim, secretary-general of the party, denounce the merger with Malaya. Wise to the Tunku and Lee's agenda, Lim and his colleagues lambasted Malaya's Internal Security Act, insisting that it was merely a rebranding of the repressive extrajudicial Emergency powers, that Singaporeans must beware its shadow encroaching on the island.[70] In the photographs taken of Lim from this period, he strides through Singapore's streets with a self-assured grin, surrounded by hundreds of supporters wearing serious looks. In other pictures, he addresses massive crowds under a huge banner with the Barisan logo, a blue ring with a red five-pointed socialist star atop. In a televised interview from late 1961, Lim stated with his reedy voice through a smile: "We are quite confident, if there's a general election, we can beat the government [the PAP]. . . . I'm sure the government will be defeated." Pausing, he smiled again, saying: "I am confident of that. We can wait for that."[71]

By that time, the Tunku's mind had become so set on the merger, on a move against the Barisan, that he spoke of Malaysia almost exclusively in Cold War terms. In November 1961, the Tunku insisted during a televised interview for the British ITN network that the formation of Malaysia was to ensure communists had "no opportunity to work against Britain and the Americans." When asked if he sought a "non-communist or anticommunist Malaysia," the Tunku answered without reservation: "Malaya is anticommunist. . . . That means that Malaysia, as a country, as a nation, is anticommunist." With the Tunku expressing the basis for creating Malaysia so bluntly, to hear his perfunctory nod at how creating Malaysia "would . . . uh . . . end colonialism in this part of the world" signaled that the decolonization of Singapore was merely an afterthought for him, a convenient cover for solving the "Chinese problem" in Singapore.[72]

Equally, the creation of Malaysia served the Tunku's expansionist ambitions. His support for the *Permesta* and PRRI rebels had foreshadowed this moment. He had contemplated a "grand federation of Malaya and the British colonies in North Borneo" well before Malaya's independence in 1957, though there was no occasion at the time to justify it. In 1959, perhaps due to Lee's nettling, the Tunku privately told British officials of his interest in Singapore joining such a political union, though he remained wary of Singapore's Chinese teaming with their fellows in the peninsula against the Malays. With their numbers combined, the Chinese of Malaya and Singapore would swell to become the majority race in a federation composed of only these two territories. Now, with the merger already in the cards, the Tunku's imagination and ambition were fired by the idea of also incorporating into Malaysia all the "indigenous races of the Borneo Territories [that the Tunku thought of] as almost Malays."[73] He was game, too, for the oil-rich Brunei to fall under Kuala Lumpur's control. In this Greater Malaysia, the Chinese would remain (safely) in the minority. Britain, keen to sweeten the deal for the Tunku so he could help them forestall "another Cuba," was prepared to talk about letting their Borneo territories go.

Cold Store

The course of creating Malaysia never did run smoothly. The Tunku and Lee, their trusted lieutenants, and British officials, had to iron out devilish details about the status of British bases in Singapore (could Britain still use them for SEATO purposes?); containing the Barisan (how would Malaya's internal security regime work in Singapore?); Singapore's political autonomy (did the federation have room for two prime ministers?); and the incorporation of Britain's Borneo territories (Brunei's ambitious sultan, unwilling to cede his personal power, ultimately refused to join the union).[74] Along with these points of contention, Singapore's hankering after a Malaysian common market, Lee's vying with the Malayan Chinese Association (MCA) for Chinese support in the peninsula, and an ensuing PAP-UMNO rivalry for Malay political loyalties would eventually tear Malaysia apart.[75]

These issues were so contentious that U.S. officials like David Bruce, ambassador to Britain, often found his British counterparts "reluctant to discuss . . .

details of thinking on Malaysia" until the new federation came into being. Bruce reasoned that this was "probably because [of] disagreements" within Her Majesty's Government "not yet resolved and considered basically [a] family matter."[76] As British records show, Lee also kept details about his negotiations with the Tunku and Britain secret from the Singapore parliament. This made it easy for the Barisan, which was not privy to the negotiations, to deplore Malaysia as a "device to halt constitutional advance" for Singapore, a way of "getting the Federation Government [of Malaya] to police British interests in Singapore" with the same old counterinsurgency tools—"security laws and powers [that would be] primarily used against labor—the working people and their trade unions."[77]

Still, with some probing U.S. officials learned separately from the Tunku, Lee, and any British official willing to talk, that despite obstacles the formation of Malaysia was on track. Throughout, the United States remained deeply invested in the outcome of the merger negotiations. As Charles Baldwin pointed out informally to British high commissioner to Malaya Sir Geofroy Tory and Malayan permanent secretary for external affairs Ghazali Shafie, British bases in Singapore were of "great interest" to the United States, for they "related to over-all defense against Communist expansion [in] SEA."[78] U.S. leaders should not have worried. The Tunku's anticommunist tilt was ever reliable. He had "repeatedly stated he would offer no objection" to Britain's continued use of the Singapore bases for Commonwealth purposes, and implied that as long as the name of SEATO was not invoked, the bases could certainly serve the organization's objectives.[79] Likewise, British officials reminded Lee in May 1962 that Britain "intended to maintain and strengthen our position in this most important base [Singapore]," and to ensure Malaysia hewed to a "foreign and defense policy that would be anticommunist and based on a military alliance with Britain."[80] Lee for his part relentlessly pursued the merger for a common market for Singapore's industrial exports as well as to have the Tunku's government "tak[e] responsibility for any unpopular repressive action that might have to be taken against the [Singapore] Communists or their sympathizers."[81] To the general satisfaction of the Kennedy administration, therefore, the issues of greatest importance to the United States' Cold War aims were going its way.

In Singapore, though, the battle for merger would wend through still more complicated turns. To take the sting out of the Barisan's ongoing criticisms of the Malaysia Plan, Lee and the PAP sought to prove that the majority of Singapore's population desired the merger. The PAP thus held a national referendum in September 1962 that offered Singaporeans three ways of integrating with Malaysia, each with different levels of autonomy. The ballot contained no option to reject the merger. Determined to manage the results to the smallest detail, the PAP also stipulated that all blank ballots would be counted as votes in favor of the merger option that guaranteed Singapore the greatest political autonomy within the Malaysian federation. Lee and his men had contrived this proviso to outflank the Barisan's call for voters to cast blank ballots as objections to the merger. Ultimately, while some 70 percent of voters felt resigned that there was probably no way out of Malaysia and picked the merger option with most autonomy, blank ballots still counted for one-quarter of all votes cast. The referendum therefore returned almost 96 percent in favor of the first merger option.[82] By contriving the plebiscite such that the merger could not be protested or escaped, the PAP's machinations rivaled that of Vietnamese leader Ngo Dinh Diem. In 1955, Diem had wrested leadership of South Vietnam by structuring a referendum as a choice for or against the already unpopular Bao Dai, France's choice to head its former colony.[83] The Barisan were not wrong to declare that the referendum had been rigged, and with popular acclaim kept launching tirades at the merger, ensuring Lee's position remained precarious even as the coming of Malaysia seemed imminent.[84]

Ironically, while the fundamental cause for creating Malaysia was to have the Tunku's government crush the Barisan, Lee's fragile authority in Singapore abruptly placed the cart before the horse. In November 1962, the Tunku confided in British officials that he "no longer consider[ed] the PAP capable of maintaining political control in Singapore," and demanded that Lee and the British crack down on the Barisan as a precondition for merger.[85] British leaders simultaneously learned that Lee, too, had "come to the view that some repressive action was necessary before Malaysia" and regretted not doing so directly after the referendum.[86] Right or wrong, Lee believed that he could have shored up the legitimacy of the referendum had he prevented the Barisan from immediately criticizing the result. There seemed now, in Lee's mind, no way to secure his legacy in Singapore's history without employing the tools of repression against his tenacious rivals.

But British authorities were leery of using Singapore's internal security regulations, holdovers from the Emergency, to incarcerate Lim and his cohort without irrefutable evidence. And they certainly did not want Lee and the Tunku to force their hands when, to all eyes, the Barisan was operating well within legal limits. At the time, Britain's brutal suppression of anticolonial groups in Kenya and Nyasaland (in echoes of the Malayan Emergency) had only recently come to light. Any callous and ill-timed use of the power to arrest and detain would fuel the anticolonial ethos in Singapore and probably deliver the country to the Barisan.[87]

In any case, December 1962 saw Lee and the Tunku find a fitting justifica-
tion for the "repressive action" both wanted to rain upon the Barisan. In
Brunei, a popular uprising led by A. M. Azahari's Party Rak'yat (People's
Party) against joining Malaysia had erupted. In a fatal miscalculation on the
part of the Barisan, the party's members publicly expressed sympathy for Azahari's rebels while Lim himself met Azahari in Singapore just days ahead of
the rebellion. Lee told Philip Moore that these Barisan blunders represented a
"heaven-sent opportunity" to end them. Now, the Barisan could be condemned by trumped-up charges of sedition or other convenient reasons. For
London, the specifics did not seem to matter anymore; now, its approval for
action against the Barisan came easily.[88]

Only vaguely aware of the forces moving against him, Lim in January 1963
"warned of the turning point in the political development of Malaya leading
to the establishment of a Fascist and military dictatorship." He derided the
"police terror" that persisted within the internal security tools of both Malaya
and Singapore. He asserted, too, that "the Malaysia Federation [could only]
be imposed by force and deceit."[89] A month later, he was removed from Singapore politics. On February 2, the operation to arrest "communists, communist sympathizers, suspected communists and fellow travelers" in Singapore
took place. It was named Operation Cold Store. Lim, labeled "Ser. No. A1"
in the list of "Hard Core Organizers of the Communist Conspiracy," was
among 169 persons targeted for detention by Singapore's internal security
council before the formation of Malaysia. The Tunku did not even need to
lift a finger. For compelling evidence, Lee, his colleagues, and British officials
assembled Lim's "brief summary of security record," detailing his involvement
in communist activities as a member of the "Little Devil Corps" of the MCP
in 1948, his training in The Chinese High School where he became a "cell
leader" of the Anti-British League, his infiltration of trade unions and the PAP,
and his leadership of "Communist open front workers . . . Communist controlled Trade Unions and . . . [the] Communist United Front" in Singapore.[90]
Every name on this list carried a damning citation, ready proof for the purge.[91]
Lim would emerge from detention six years later a broken man, never again a
danger to the PAP.

Along with Lim, twenty-three other Barisan members were arrested for allegedly collaborating with Azahari in the Brunei revolt, and further, for planning to transform Singapore into the Tunku's version of Cuba, a base from
which to subvert the rest of Southeast Asia. With the Barisan's brightest and
best out of the picture, Lee dissolved the legislative assembly on September 3
and scheduled general elections for the independent state of Singapore after

the formation of Malaysia on September 16. It was a patently cynical move, and everything proceeded as Lee had foreseen: the Barisan was in disarray and unable to reignite its demoralized supporters at the last minute; the PAP had freedom of play in the mass media and toured its constituencies across the country (while its remaining opponents mounted ragtag rallies); the PAP asserted that it had brought Singapore independence through Malaysia, an independence already manifest. All these handed Lee's party thirty-seven seats out of the assembly's fifty-one. Had the Barisan ever commanded the kind of influence that the Tunku and U.S. officials feared, it was no longer a factor. Lim's party took just thirteen seats at the 1963 election and continued to decline over the ensuing decades as Lee, arresting yet more members of the Barisan, including elected representatives on various charges, cemented his hold over Singapore.[92]

Hours after learning about Operation Cold Store, U.S. officials in Singapore wrote Secretary of State Dean Rusk. They informed him that the "arrests of Singapore extreme leftists and communists took place early this morning . . . [and] virtually all important Barisan leaders such as Lim Chin Siong, Fong Swee Suan, Sandrasegaran Woodhull, and Dominic Puthucheary, have been detained."[93] It should have become obvious to U.S. leaders in Washington that not all of Lim's key officials were ethnic Chinese (Woodhull and Puthucheary were ethnic Indians), that perhaps developments in Singapore could not be neatly categorized as the so-called Chinese problem, that Cold Store was as much Lee's power grab as an anticommunist maneuver.

Disappointingly, there exists no evidence that U.S. policymakers reflected further on this. Compared with the heavily documented U.S. fixation with the struggle for merging Malaya and Singapore, the conspicuous absence of discussions about Cold Store in U.S. records signals that U.S. leaders were chiefly concerned with the end result, the definitive shift of Singapore toward anticommunism. U.S. officials seemed untroubled by the fact that Singapore's internal security regime (with British assistance) had done the deed, without any direct Malayan intervention, thus voiding the very reason for the merger in the first place![94] The U.S. officials may have had no patience for this twist in the tale. It was more important to Washington that Singapore was communist free and acceptable to the Tunku, more important that the zone of Malaya's anticommunism could expand. Now, Malaysia loomed on the horizon, and with it the anticommunist arc.

Twelve days after Operation Cold Store, President Kennedy called Malaysia Southeast Asia's "best hope." Thus, when Malaya's deputy prime minister Tun Abdul Razak remarked to Kennedy a few months later that Singapore remained "a sort of Cuba," it is unlikely to have worried Kennedy.[95] Indeed, the president probably conjured a nebulous vision of Malaya figuratively absorbing Singapore, reeling the island—shorn of its left wing—into itself, into the U.S. sphere of influence.

Nekolim

On September 16, 1963, five thousand Indonesians marched on the British and Malayan embassies in Jakarta to proclaim their opposition to the creation of Malaysia. The protesters stoned the Malayan embassy and called the Tunku a "British puppet." They reserved even more rage for the alleged puppeteers, raiding the British embassy, shattering windows, pulling down an iron grill fence, burning the ambassador's car, and shredding the British flag.[96] More than a thousand Malaysians retaliated the next day, hurling stones and firecrackers at the Indonesian embassy in Kuala Lumpur. Malaysian men broke through a police cordon around the Indonesian consular offices to destroy furniture and torch the hedge while women yanked plants from the garden and smashed bricks for the men to throw at the building. They burned photographs of Sukarno, shouting "Malaysia forever!"[97]

What goes around comes around. The day after, thousands of Indonesians stormed the British embassy again, this time to set it on fire. Amidst the chaos, British ambassador Andrew Gilchrist sent London three telegrams, the last one—"Building on fire. Got to leave now. Va . . ."—incomplete.[98] Indonesian authorities finally arrived to spirit Gilchrist and his staff to the offices and homes of the New Zealand and U.S. diplomatic corps. The protesters then worked as if from a prepared list of British subjects in Jakarta, invading and vandalizing their homes with slogans like "Kill the English" and "The End of Malaysia."[99]

Such mutual antagonism riddled the three or so years that Indonesia pursued *Konfrontasi*, its political, economic, and military campaign to "crush Malaysia" along with the vestiges of the British Empire in Southeast Asia. In addition to severing trade and communications with Malaysia, Sukarno authorized guerrilla warfare and subversion in Sabah and Sarawak. Indonesian bomber aircraft had been taunting the RAF from February 1963, flying so close to Singapore that the British had to repeatedly scramble their interceptor jets. In 1964, Indonesian forces raided parts of Johore, the southernmost state of Peninsular Malaysia, and attacked Singapore's offshore island petroleum bunkering station. Additionally, Indonesian gunboats seized Singaporean fishing vessels, and Indonesian saboteurs bombed several locations in Singapore. Of course, Britain, Malaysia, Singapore, and their Australian and New Zealand allies responded in kind, with more than a quarter of the Royal Navy called to action, and almost sixty thousand British military personnel mobilized for conflict by the time *Konfrontasi* ended in 1966. To project British military power into the Far East on such a scale, Britain had to draw from its combat units in Germany, troop deployments meant to support NATO.[100]

Konfrontasi was driven by what Sukarno had long believed: that both Malaya and Singapore's self-determination were shams; that the Tunku, Lee, and like-minded imperial stooges in both countries had sustained the British Empire in some insidious form; that all three—Britain, Malaya, and Singapore—had it in for him. If their attempts to help *Permesta* and the PRRI in 1958 were not proof enough, Sukarno was convinced that creating Malaysia presaged a new assault on his country. He described British policy with a portmanteau, *nekolim*, that he had coined some years earlier to express the pernicious new embodiments of colonialism and imperialism.[101] The Chinese, with whom Sukarno and the PKI were nurturing intimate ties, sympathized with Indonesia, deeming Malaysia a "neocolonial scheme" put together by Britain and United States.[102]

Since Sukarno basked in the afterglow of the 1955 Bandung Conference as a founding father and towering figure of the nonaligned movement, most nonaligned nations to a degree sympathized with what one historian has called Sukarno's "deep antipathy [toward] Western neocolonial schemes."[103] And, mindful that nonaligned countries constituted the majority of UN members, Sukarno and his officials thus shrewdly proclaimed in the UN General Assembly that Malaysia was neither "truly independent [nor] sovereign" but instead a "British neo-colonial plot" to encircle Indonesia and cling on to power in Southeast Asia.[104] Sukarno's most scathing attack, formalized in the official explanation for *Konfrontasi* his government sent to the White House, had been that Malaysia's independence was a farce so long as British military installations remained in Singapore.[105]

The "best hope" had touched off a new war in Southeast Asia. U.S. leaders already fretting over U.S. involvement in Vietnam now worried that their ANZUS and SEATO commitments, which the Tunku had been binding to AMDA and ASA, could drag them into *Konfrontasi* as well. Southeast Asia would go up in flames—Indonesia commanded almost half a million combat troops, was bruising to take on Malaysia, Britain and its Australian and New

Figure 11. Malayan prime minister Tunku Abdul Rahman (left) and Indonesian president Sukarno share a lighthearted moment in Tokyo, Japan, between May 31 and June 1, 1963, while discussing Indonesia's objection to the creation of Malaysia. Behind the smiles and laughter, their rivalry seethed. Photo from the Ministry of Information and the Arts Collection, courtesy of the National Archives of Singapore.

Zealand allies, and wielded military equipment acquired from the Soviet Union, the United States, and China (by turns, all had wooed Sukarno). Meetings between the Tunku and Sukarno in Japan and the Philippines between May and June 1963 to defuse the crisis came to nothing once Malaysia's component parts officially joined together in September. Furthermore, Philippine president Diosdado Macapagal had clambered aboard *Konfrontasi* with Sukarno to some degree, testing how vulnerable Malaysia might be to Philippine claims to Sabah. (Macapagal never did press *Konfrontasi* as intensely as Sukarno and was less a feature in this regional rivalry.)

Beijing for its part emboldened Sukarno's pursuit of *Konfrontasi*. The same month that Malaysia was formed, Chinese premier Zhou Enlai met with the communist leaders of Vietnam, Laos, and Indonesia (the PKI's secretary-general Dipa Nusantara Aidit) and proclaimed Southeast Asia was the chief arena for the struggle against the imperial powers. Zhou promised to back all of Beijing's allies in the region, inherently encouraging Aidit to support Sukarno's *Konfrontasi* against Britain's neocolonial presence in Malaysia. Over the course of 1963 and 1964, Beijing promised several times to defend Indonesia should the Anglo-American powers attack.[106]

However, Chinese security guarantees to Indonesia could not prevent Malaysian diplomats from colluding with Britain to legitimize Malaysia in the eyes of nonaligned leaders and turn many of these leaders against Sukarno. Studies of *Konfrontasi* have glossed over the work of Malaysian diplomats within the nonaligned world, concerned instead with the low-grade military conflict between the Commonwealth allies and Indonesia, the fall of Sukarno, Indonesia's subsequent shift toward the United States, as well as Washington's turn from accommodating Sukarno toward siding with Britain and Malaysia (a change coterminous with Lyndon Johnson's assumption of the presidency).[107] Paying close attention to Malaysian diplomatic offensives against Indonesia reveals how regional rivalries intertwined with British neocolonial ambitions and the Cold War to power the rise of a pro-U.S. order. By mid-1964, Malaysian diplomacy had left Sukarno and his country isolated. The leading lights of the nonaligned world, including Egypt, India, and Yugoslavia, had declared that they were for Malaysia. Other nonaligned leaders decried Sukarno's *Konfrontasi* campaign; all in fact accepted that Malaysia represented not neocolonialism but the legitimate fulfillment of its peoples' strivings for self-determination. With the endorsement of various nonaligned leaders, and in the face of Indonesia's hapless protests, Malaysia in January 1965 even assumed a nonpermanent spot in the UN Security Council, prompting Sukarno to withdraw Indonesia from the United Nations into further international isolation.[108]

The *New York Times*, in celebrating how Malaysia completed a "1,600-mile arc" through Southeast Asia, may have foretold Sukarno's downfall as early as April 1963. The *Times* had described Malaysia as a "great counterweight . . . to the vague threats of Indonesian expansion from the south."[109] Indeed, Britain worked closely with Malaysian diplomats on strategies to outflank Sukarno on the issue of British bases in Singapore. London's enduring relations with many of its former colonies in Asia and Africa enabled Malaysian diplomatic missions to reach further and gain greater purchase, while Sukarno's communist patrons offered negligible guidance to Indonesia's inexperienced diplomatic cadre. Months before Indonesian foreign minister Subandrio could officially promulgate the "Crush Malaysia" policy in January 1963, Lee Kuan Yew had already visited Burmese leader Ne Win, Indian prime minister Jawaharlal Nehru, Egyptian president Gamal Abdel Nasser, and Marshal Josef Tito of Yugoslavia, to make the case for Malaysia and turn these prominent nonaligned leaders against Sukarno. Speaking over Radio Singapore when he had returned from these travels, Lee stated that he had visited these men to explain the facts about Malaysia. Detailing his strategy, Lee explained that since Indonesia had tried to whip up world opinion against Malaysia in the Afro-Asian nations and isolate Malaysia by alleging it was Britain's lackey, then Malaysia must return the favor in similar ways.[110]

According to Alex Josey, the British journalist who produced anticommunist propaganda for British authorities in Malaya in the 1950s and later became Lee's co-speechwriter, Lee wanted to burnish his own reputation as a "reasonable nationalist, basically a neutralist."[111] Josey's private papers suggest that he and Lee strategized incessantly in 1962 about how to persuade Ne Win, Nehru, Nasser, and Tito to embrace him as a "junior member of the Afro-Asian leadership," one who genuinely spoke for Malaysia, "on behalf of a couple of million Asians anxious to throw off the last remnants of colonialism." To do so, Lee had to prove that "he was no colonial stooge, and that Malaysia [was] no British imperialist plot."[112]

Yet Lee plotted to undermine Sukarno's reputation among the non-aligned nations with none other than the British. After all, neither Lee nor British leaders, not to mention the Tunku, wanted to end Britain's military presence in Singapore, even though it was the very substance of Sukarno's case against Malaysia. In 1962, British officials had reminded Lee that regardless of Singapore's formal independence, Britain still expected "unrestricted use of the Singapore base" and would utilize these bases to keep Malaysia firmly anticommunist. Lee, too, wished for Britain to maintain the bases, and sought assurance that Britain would "continue to employ the same number of local civilians in Singapore after merger" with Malaya.[113] According to a 1967 CIA report, more than thirty thousand Singaporeans worked at the British bases, which accounted for about 20 percent of the country's national income.[114] In fact, recent estimates suggest that up to one hundred and fifty thousand Singaporeans' livelihoods were connected to, and sustained by, the activities of these bases.[115] Britain did not complete its military withdrawal from Singapore until 1971 and only relinquished its last base on the island in 1976.

Lee concluded that his best, if disingenuous, response to Sukarno was that the British bases remained in Singapore only at the pleasure of Singaporeans, that as prime minister he had full authority to make Britain vacate them at any time. During his visits to Egypt, India, Burma, and Yugoslavia in 1962, he trotted out this response, employing it most deliberately to reassure both Nehru and Tito that he "would not allow [British] base[s] in Singapore to continue very long."[116] It was a vapid and unverifiable assertion. Yet both Nehru and Tito, as we shall see, gave their blessing to Lee and the plan to create Malaysia.[117]

THE BEST HOPE   139

Perhaps Lee's charisma carried the day? Just as probable, leaders like Nehru and Tito reasoned that the bases in Singapore served Britain's purposes as much as Lee's and that, at its worst, this mutual relationship did not amount to neo-colonialism. The rise of Malaysia at least guaranteed that formal British control of Singapore would radically shrink—full independence could still be earned in stages. Additionally, unspoken rivalries within the nonaligned movement and even an undercurrent of distaste for Sukarno's egomania and theatrics may have contributed to Lee's success. All the same, British officials believed that Lee had hatched a winning argument. When he embarked on a similar mission to plead Malaysia's case in Africa two years later, British officials subtly hinted he recycle his claim. Lee appreciated the encouragement. He wrote enthusiastically about this ploy to Philip Moore, now British high commissioner to Singapore: "Once we get [the nonaligned nations] over this antipathy for foreign troops and bases, we can effectively isolate the Indonesians."[118]

By Josey's account, Lee's diplomatic efforts in 1962 produced the desired effect. In Rangoon, Ne Win and his advisers gave Lee sympathy and room enough to explain that Malaysia represented the "solution of the survival of small states" and stood for neutrality.[119] In New Delhi, Nehru, who had been supportive of Malaya and the Tunku, also "got on very well" with Lee.[120] At a press conference on April 25, 1962, Lee declared that Nehru agreed that the formation of Malaysia was a "logical way of liquidating the British Empire in South-East Asia."[121] It is likely that Nehru was also worried about the mounting Sino-Indian antagonism since China's annexation of Tibet in 1959 and India's granting of asylum to Tibetan leader Dalai Lama. And Nehru was not far off the mark when it came to Beijing's malign intentions. Chairman Mao Zedong in 1961 had actually tried to turn Sukarno against Nehru by suggesting that Nehru planned to overshadow him as the vanguard of anti-imperialism.[122] Even if Nehru was not privy to China's intrigues against him, he must have thought Britain's continued military presence in Singapore benign in comparison to the prospect of Chinese expansionism in Southeast Asia.

In Cairo, Lee and his retinue were greeted by an Egyptian honor guard and escorted to Nasser's palace by "twelve outriders, horns blazing." Josey remarked later that it brought "lumps to throats and all that sort of crap." But if somewhat blasé, Josey was still impressed by Nasser's eagerness to "impress upon us Egypt's friendship." Nasser told Lee to "count me among your personal friends" as he signed a joint statement expressing Egypt's support for the formation of Malaysia.[123] When Lee visited Egypt again in 1964, he found Nasser "quite prepared to help us gather support among Afro-Asian nations in bringing Indonesia to a reasonable line."[124] Though there is scant evidence beyond Josey's

Figure 12. Indian prime minister Jawaharlal Nehru meets with Singapore prime minister Lee Kuan Yew in New Delhi in April 1962. Lee visited Nehru and other prominent nonaligned leaders to make the case for creating Malaysia, a federation that would include Singapore. Photo courtesy of the *Hindu Times*.

papers that clarifies why Nasser so readily embraced Lee and Malaysia, leaders of middle powers like Nasser and Ne Win were probably keen to increase their influence over the newly independent nation, influence that Nehru already possessed given his good relations with Malaya, influence that came at Sukarno's expense.

Lee did meet some resistance in Belgrade. British ambassador to Yugoslavia Michael Creswell sensed the "omens . . . not particularly favorable" since the Yugoslav government had for the past year been "hostile to the Greater Malaysia scheme," which they had denounced as an "artificial creation of colonialism." Creswell had learned that Yugoslav officials obtained their impressions of Southeast Asian politics largely from the views of the Indonesian government.[125] However, after an hour with Lee, Tito unexpectedly promised to "modify the Yugoslav line." Furthermore, when the next day *Komunist*, the government's official weekly, carried a hostile article labeling Malaysia a "typical neo-colonialist act," senior Yugoslav officials scrambled to assure Lee and his party in private and public that the "Yugoslav Press could no longer be relied upon to report the Government's views correctly" and that, following this bungle, the editor of *Komunist* was "on the mat." The author of the article also apologized to the Singaporeans (with Josey present), admitting he had never even visited the Far East and "got most of his facts from *The Economist*." After Lee and his team departed Yugoslavia, Josey's contacts in Belgrade informed him that a Yugoslav government spokesman had once more denounced *Komunist* and added that Marshal Tito had received Lee's explanation about Malaysia "with understanding."[126]

Throughout *Konfrontasi*, Indonesian officials never mounted any diplomatic campaigns equal to that of the Malaysians. Of course, they knew well enough to present their complaints against Malaysia in the United Nations. And the Indonesian embassy in Washington, D.C., certainly tried to win U.S. sympathy for Indonesia's cause.[127] But these efforts were striking for their limitations. Most of all, they paled beside Lee's thirty-four-day mission in the early months of 1964 to seventeen African nations, accompanied by Malayan, Sabahan, and Sarawakian officials (some of whom complained later that Lee was "hogging the limelight").[128] Sukarno probably believed that *Konfrontasi* turned entirely on his relationship with the Tunku and British leaders. Lee, only a few years a prime minister at the time, may have seemed to Sukarno a minor player. But who can fault Sukarno for thinking this way? No less than Robert Kennedy had been dispatched by President Lyndon Baines Johnson in January 1964 to mediate between Sukarno and the Tunku. Johnson may have intended to exploit the prestige of the late president by sending his younger brother to resolve *Konfrontasi*, but this inadvertently flattered Sukarno, puffing him up further. Thus, while the Indonesian leader would have been aware that Lee was on a whirlwind tour of Africa to win support for Malaysia, he probably dismissed the effort as insignificant compared with his own dealings with Robert Kennedy.

While tied up in futile negotiations with the Tunku and Robert Kennedy, Sukarno ignored Lee at his own peril, for Lee and his team did well to make Malaysia appear the victim of Sukarno's belligerence. Sympathy flowed from virtually all the leaders of the African nations Lee visited. *Konfrontasi* had made the British bases in Singapore seem essential for Malaysia's security. No wonder Malagasy (now Madagascar) and Ethiopia offered "explicit support for Malaysia's reliance on Britain" in light of Indonesian aggression.[129] Most of the African leaders, including these two, had no idea that Britain and Malaysia pursued an especially hostile campaign against Indonesia. In echoes of the *Permesta* and PRRI rebellions, Britain and Malaysia covertly aided secessionist movements in Indonesia in order to undermine Sukarno's government.[130] British troops conducted clandestine cross-border raids well into Indonesian Borneo to keep the Indonesian military on the defensive.[131] Even British counterinsurgency expert Robert Thompson took a break from his advisory mission in Saigon to visit Borneo and suggest how antiguerrilla maneuvers might be employed against the Indonesians.[132]

Meanwhile, Lee raced through Africa in early 1964, finding himself on a roll. He easily convinced the leaders of Nigeria, Liberia, and Tanganyika (now part of Tanzania) to endorse or else withdraw their criticism of the British bases or troops in Singapore. President Camille Alliale of the Ivory Coast expressed "grave disapproval of the Indonesians" and promised, like Kenyan prime minister Jomo Kenyatta, to support Malaysia's candidacy in the UN Security Council.[133] Gathering endorsements for a seat in the Security Council was a key objective, for Lee, the Tunku, and their British allies reasoned that with the embrace of the United Nations, Malaysia would lock in a massive diplomatic advantage over Indonesia. Lee had anticipated that several African nations, as former British colonies, would at least be predisposed to his arguments since they too retained similar defense ties with their former rulers.[134] But many African leaders agreed, too, that the creation of Malaysia ended British colonialism in Southeast Asia, and that Sukarno's patent intimacy with China undermined his claims to genuine nonalignment.

Indeed, the deepening ties between Jakarta and Beijing were in plain sight. Sukarno was inspired by Mao's radical left turn toward supporting aggressive revolution and anti-imperialism across the Third World, and in 1960 took China's side in the Sino-Soviet conflict, spurning the USSR's pragmatic "peaceful co-existence" with the West. The Chinese supported Indonesian claims to West Irian in 1961 that ultimately (under the United Nations' aegis) saw that territory pass into Indonesian control. And a year into *Konfrontasi*, China initiated plans to furnish Sukarno with military aid, encouraged and supported the creation of a "Fifth Force" (a militia of armed peasants and workers to reinforce the army, navy, air force, and police), and even considered assisting Indonesia in the acquisition of atomic weapons. Simultaneously, the Chinese Communist Party (CCP) enthusiastically engaged Aidit and the PKI, anticipating that he and the Indonesian communists would be China's gateway into directly influencing Jakarta. Chinese leaders saw *Konfrontasi*, in conjunction with the conflict in Vietnam that so vexed the United States, within a "magnificent wave of anti-imperialist struggles," washing the Anglo-American presence from Southeast Asia.[135] Sukarno's commitment to nonalignment was therefore tenuous at best and his credibility among the nonaligned African leaders in sharp decline.

At the same time, Lee's tour of Africa, more than he or British leaders expected, struck a thick artery of disdain for Sukarno. Ethiopian emperor Haile Selassie told Lee that expansionist behavior like Sukarno's "had happened in history before . . . referring to Hitler."[136] Ghana's president Kwame Nkrumah took Malaysia's side and explicitly called Sukarno a "Hitler."[137]

Not all the African leaders that Lee visited were persuaded, though. Some discerned signatures of *nekolim* by the British that they could not dismiss. After all, several members of the Tunku's government, the ones who had always opposed AMDA, had declared publicly in 1962 that Britain should not be allowed to use the Singapore bases for SEATO purposes once Malaysia was formed. When these same government officials abruptly walked back their statements after sounding off, it was clear that they had been censured. British protests made "confidentially" had forced these Malayan politicians to "adopt [the] much more helpful line . . . that Britain legally could use the [Singapore] Base without Malaysia's consent, and for SEATO purposes." The Malayan politicians' best retort to this was merely that Britain should make a public show of obtaining that consent, while knowing that "it would not be refused."[138]

Nevertheless, bullying uncooperative Malayan politicians was hard for Britain to conceal. Thus, while President Habib Bourguiba of Tunisia endorsed the creation of Malaysia and deplored Sukarno's aggression, he warned Lee that the British bases in Singapore remained an "embarrassment vis-à-vis world opinion." Likewise, Mali president Modibo Keita's "doctrinaire opposition to foreign bases" was greater than his sympathy for Lee's mission.[139] Keita insisted that nonalignment "meant [being] against foreign bases of any kind."[140]

Still, Keita, like the Algerian president, Ben Bella, and Guinea's president, Sekou Toure, concurred with Lee that on balance creating Malaysia accomplished self-determination for its peoples and constituted "no neo-colonialist device."[141] When Lee returned to Southeast Asia weeks after Robert Kennedy had departed, the tide of African opinion appeared to be substantially on Malaysia's side. To be sure, the Soviets did attempt to defend Sukarno's "crush Malaysia" campaign at the United Nations, vetoing a Norwegian resolution for peaceful negotiations between Kuala Lumpur and Jakarta, and insisting (in echoes of Sukarno) that the creation of Malaysia was simply Britain's "rotten colonial system . . . obstinately trying to cling" to power in Southeast Asia.[142] The Russian effort was feeble. In October 1964, Afro-Asian delegates at the nonaligned conference in Egypt roundly condemned Sukarno's *Konfrontasi*.[143]

By early 1965, Malaysia's diplomats, with British help, had gutted the international bases of Sukarno's influence as well as the legitimacy of *Konfrontasi*. Malaysia then swept into the Security Council, endorsed by various nonaligned nations and opposed by none but Indonesia. At last, Sukarno saw that he had been outplayed. The Soviets were unwilling to get embroiled in an extra Southeast Asian war besides the Vietnam conflict. China offered cold comfort, much of it rhetorical. Zhou had promised Sukarno that China would not stand idly by if the western powers invaded Indonesia (but Beijing did nothing about repeated British military forays into Indonesian Borneo). At that point, Chinese leaders had actually become more concerned that the Indonesian army's right-wing elites planned to seize power, destroy the PKI's rising influence, and upend Sukarno's turn to China. Mao never broached the topic with Sukarno, however, and in August 1965 talked contingencies with Aidit instead.[144]

Unaware of Beijing's anxieties and in despair, Sukarno confided in President Hastings Banda of Malawi that "the acceptance of Malaysia as a member of the Security Council was the culminating point" of his hopeless struggle against the "tool[s] of neo-colonialism."[145] In his autobiography, Sukarno claimed to have "prayed our walkout" of the United Nations might "catalyze" its reform, but his supplications came to naught. In this round at least, he had been overcome. He lamented that "colonialism wasn't retreating in my backyard, just changing shape."[146] He was right.

"The First Falling Domino"

But the year contained still more twists. Within months of Indonesia's ignominious exit from the United Nations, Sukarno and his advisers suddenly found themselves celebrating. On August 7, 1965, the Tunku and Lee with select cabinet ministers concluded an agreement that would formally remove Singapore from the Malaysian federation.[147] Malaysia's representative at the United Nations only learned the news of the separation from a radio report on the morning of August 9. "Visibly shaken," he told the press that it had come as "a stunning shock."[148] The Malaysians had even kept the British government in the dark until the agreement was a fait accompli.[149] On Malaysian national television, the Tunku described Singapore's departure as the "most painful and heartbreaking news" that he had the "misfortune" to announce. However, he claimed it had been "completely impossible" to work with Lee and the PAP for the "common good of Malaysia."[150] Lee, in a separate press conference that same day, portrayed the separation as his personal "moment of anguish." His voice faltered when he said that "the whole of [his] adult life," he had believed in the unity of Malaya and Singapore. With the camera trained on his face, Lee wept.[151]

Malaysia had not been an unstinting success. Sino-Malay riots exploded in Singapore in July 1964, emerging from a PAP-UMNO rivalry present at the conception of the new federation. As the ruling party of a majority Chinese country, the PAP could never stomach UMNO's determination to favor Malays over Chinese and deplored the MCA for accepting this condition just to share power in the Alliance coalition (see chapter 2). Lee, bursting with confidence from his diplomatic mission to Africa, led the PAP in challenging the UMNO-MCA bargain that held up the pro-Malay policy in the peninsula, hoping to win Malaya's urban Chinese from the MCA in the federal elections of April 1964.[152] However, the PAP failed to supplant the MCA (earning that party's lasting ire) and, worse, prompted UMNO's hard-line pro-Malay members, the so-called ultras, to incite Singapore's Malays against the PAP on the premise that the party discriminated against them.[153] Indonesia saw an opportunity and stirred the brew.[154]

All these produced the 1964 racial riots in Singapore, during which five hundred persons were injured and twenty-two perished. The wounds refused to heal. The Tunku could barely tamp down the ultras' insistence that he incarcerate Lee (the ultras would turn on the Tunku five years later). Lee, for his part, grew even more strident in his calls for a "Malaysian Malaysia," one in which all the races enjoyed equal privileges of citizenship.[155] His pitch to Malaysians faintly echoed the MCP's older exhortations for multiracial harmony in Malaya and Singapore. It was just as incompatible with the conditions on the ground in Malaya and could not defeat the cause of the ultras. The Tunku expected the ambitious Lee to eventually gun for the office of Malaysian prime minister. He saw more Sino-Malay clashes on the horizon. By the summer of 1965, he decided that Singapore had to go.

Sukarno's closest colleagues hailed the breakup of Malaysia as a "victory" for *Konfrontasi*.[156] Subandrio declared that it proved Malaysia was all along "artificial . . . exploited by the British to undermine Indonesia and protract their domination over Asia." He predicted that Sabah and Sarawak would quickly secede.[157] Chinese officials in Jakarta that same week to celebrate the twentieth anniversary of Indonesia's independence proclamation were jubilant too. The Chinese told *Antara*, Indonesia's national newspaper, that the failed merger was a "joyful present . . . a victory for all of us" against neocolonialism.[158] His spirits soaring, Sukarno declared, "We are now fostering an anti-imperial axis—the Jakarta-Phnom Penh-Hanoi-Peking-Pyongyang axis."[159]

Popular U.S. opinion offered a gloomy contrast. The *Boston Globe* stated that the Malaysian federation "proclaimed under British aegis less than two years ago with pageantry and hope—[now] appears as good as dead."[160] U.S.

journalist Andrew Kopkind wrote in the *New Statesman* that Singapore was "the first falling domino" of the U.S. "muddle" against the "overseas Chinese and the Indonesians."[161]

Not so. Malaysia did not fragment further. Leading officials of Sabah and Sarawak expressed little desire to follow Singapore's example, admitting, however, that they preferred London to Kuala Lumpur managing their affairs. (The territories remain part of the federation today).[162] Instead, Sukarno, his trusted officials, and the PKI, all the advocates of *Konfrontasi*, lost political power or their lives—and sometimes both—just two months after Singapore gained independence by ejection.

Sukarno's botched campaign to eradicate *nekolim* had squandered his prestige overseas and left the brittle Indonesian economy in freefall. His Chinese patrons even came to think that he had mounted *Konfrontasi* as a grandiose distraction for his people, to make them overlook the country's economic troubles.[163] To Sukarno's opponents at home, particularly the anticommunist army officers who had long opposed the links he was forging with China, Sukarno appeared ripe for supplanting. However, there was no compelling pretext to launch a coup against him. It was ironically Aidit who delivered that pretext on a silver platter. On October 1, 1965, he abruptly activated the contingency plan he had shared with Mao. With a small team of PKI members, and aided by sympathetic pro-Sukarno air force officers, Aidit tried to seize control of parts of Indonesia. His goals were to protect Sukarno from the army's right-wingers and then establish a revolutionary military committee that bolstered Sukarno's authority, reinforced his left-leaning tendencies, and augmented the PKI's power. *Konfrontasi*, British military operations in Borneo, and Malaysian diplomatic offensives had so destabilized the Sukarno regime that Aidit likely believed he must preempt an army-led coup.[164]

Aidit's precipitous decision caught Beijing off-guard, but the Indonesian army was more than ready. It had been preparing for this moment for years, and with U.S. assistance throughout. For, soon after the United States' bungled operation to overthrow Sukarno in 1958, Washington switched its tack toward cultivating the Indonesian army, training, equipping, and funding its officers (just as the Soviets plied Sukarno's regime more generally with economic and military aid). Moscow ultimately lost Jakarta to Beijing because Sukarno became enamored of China's radical anti-imperialism. Meanwhile, U.S. designs for the Indonesian army went much further than either communist power, creating what one historian has called a "government-in-waiting."[165]

Major General Suharto of the army swiftly accused the PKI of organizing a movement against Sukarno. Supported by a robust propaganda machine that exploited deep-seated anti-Chinese prejudice in Indonesian society as well as stoked fears of a Chinese fifth column, Suharto alleged that the CCP was also in on the act.[166] Newly declassified U.S. records show that the CIA readily aided Suharto with communications equipment to broadcast the false reports far and wide.[167] It was almost too easy. The last spate of anti-Chinese violence had occurred only in May 1963. Sukarno himself had in the recent past enacted discriminatory laws against Chinese residents in Indonesia, one of which empowered officials to evict Indonesian Chinese from their homes on the premise that they were security threats. No matter that Aidit had not involved the rank and file of the PKI in his plans, or that most PKI members were non-Chinese. Suharto and the army effectively rallied the multitudes toward a bloody purge of the PKI that intersected with popular anti-Chinese sentiment. Within a few months, more than half a million Indonesians, thousands of them ethnic Chinese (and some of them communists), were massacred.[168]

When the slaughter began, U.S. officials knew well that most of the victims were innocent. But the U.S. embassy in Jakarta assisted Suharto covertly in various ways, offering inaccurate evidence of the PKI's "guilt and treachery" to egg the Indonesian army on, as well as attempting to suppress media coverage of the bloodshed.[169] In December, Suharto's troops located and killed Aidit. Eager to eradicate any roots from which Beijing might again grow its influence, the army also coerced Chinese Indonesians to leave the country altogether. An estimated two hundred thousand Chinese fled the archipelago and resettled in China, ferried by Chinese ships to a country they did not know.[170]

With the PKI annihilated, so went Sukarno's power base. Suharto could easily sideline Sukarno and gravitate toward the United States. In Indonesian society, anti-Chinese hatred mixed with anticommunism and continued to burn—right-wing students and the army attacked the Chinese Embassy in 1966. Jakarta officially broke diplomatic relations with Beijing the next year.[171]

The wide anticommunist arc now absorbed the world's fifth most populous nation, likely the most important transformation within Southeast Asia during the tumultuous 1960s. Much more had transpired, and with far greater consequence, than anything Kennedy might have foreseen when he called Malaysia "the best hope." A broader pattern in U.S.–Southeast Asian relations was unfolding around the troubles of Indochina, unfolding as U.S. combat troops arrived to Americanize the conflict in Vietnam. In fact, Indonesia had become the first left-leaning domino to fall in U.S. favor.

Also, Singapore's separation from Malaysia catalyzed one historic shift; it convinced Britain to completely disengage from the Asian mainland. The British military presence in Singapore, endorsed by much of the nonaligned world

and the UN Security Council thanks to Lee's charm offensive, had been justi-
fied almost entirely upon defending the country from Indonesia. When Singapore broke with Malaysia in August 1965, Indonesian officials had quickly
dangled an official recognition of Lee's government, promising to cease hostilities on the condition that Britain leave its Singapore bases.[172] Most British
politicians welcomed this chance to end their nation's costly obligation to
Singapore, convinced that *Konfrontasi* must be their nation's last extravagant
adventure in the Far East. Throughout the conflict with Indonesia, Britain's
military chiefs had bemoaned how the British army was overstretched, unable
to cope with any other major crisis. Significant factions of the ruling Labor
Party held that British defense policy must end its sprawling commitments.
Prime Minister Harold Wilson and Defense Minister Denis Healey, on the
other hand, were determined to maintain Britain's presence east of Suez and
hoped that an extensive defense review begun in 1964 would vindicate their
plans.[173] By June 1965, the review had concluded the opposite; that the nation's
economy could not sustain its global military presence; that Britain had to
end its expensive war with Indonesia; that it must vacate all its air and naval
complexes in Singapore and the few that remained in Malaysia. At almost
$200 million annually, the cost of maintaining these installations had out-
stripped any earnings from British holdings in either country.[174] By the last
days of *Konfrontasi* in 1966, the bill for Britain's Singapore bases—integral to
moving more than two hundred thousand troops to and from combat zones
in Borneo—had ballooned to some $700 million.[175]

   Though Wilson and Healey remained deeply reluctant, their colleagues began working out how to withdraw from east of Suez by the mid-1970s.[176]
When Suharto abandoned *Konfrontasi* in 1966, British leaders only stepped up
the execution of their exit strategy despite stern opposition from Malaysia and
Singapore as well as the governments of New Zealand, Australia, and the
United States. With Britain's determination to fold up its neocolonial presence speedily, the European colonial order in Southeast Asia was finally (and
to an extent voluntarily) entering its grave. Protecting Malaysia, the federation that was to be Britain's best hope of extending its tenure in the region
had instead bled the empire out. Now, the anticommunist arc would be left
alone with the United States.

Chapter 5

The Friendly Kings

Southeast Asia's Transition from Anglo-American
Predominance to U.S. Hegemony

More than two decades after its "darkest moment," the British Empire prepared to leave Singapore again. There would be no returning this time. When
British foreign secretary George Brown met his U.S. counterpart, Dean Rusk,
in January 1968, it was to explain that Britain planned to bring forward its
military withdrawal from Singapore to March 1971.[1] Rusk was livid. London
had promised only months before to keep its forces in Southeast Asia until
1975, by which time Washington expected to be winding down its involvement in Vietnam.[2] When Rusk could not persuade Brown to consider changes
to Britain's timetable, he remarked that Brown's visit carried the "acrid aroma
of a *fait-accompli*"; that Britain was abandoning an ally in its time of need; and
that the United States would never "fill the vacuum" left by the "withdrawal
of the UK from world affairs."[3]

Brown would later recall that Rusk had been "bloody unpleasant," that at
one point Rusk had barked: "For God's sake, act like Britain!"[4] The outburst
made no difference. And President Lyndon Johnson could only write Prime
Minister Harold Wilson afterward with "dismay," lamenting that the United
States must now "man the ramparts all alone" in Southeast Asia.[5] Per plan,
Britain withdrew nearly all its forces from Singapore by 1971, a process one
historian has called its "humiliating scuttle" from imperium.[6] Two years on,
U.S. troops would retreat from Vietnam in their own haze of humiliation.

Yet as the United States lost Vietnam, it gained hegemony in Southeast Asia.
From the late 1960s through the fall of Saigon in 1975, the anticommunist arc
of U.S. allies in the region effectively contained Soviet and Chinese power

within Indochina. This broad, regional pattern comes into focus once we pivot from the Vietnam War to U.S. relations with Britain, Malaysia, and Singapore.[7] This arc of containment had arisen in the 1960s with the creation of Malaysia and the rightward shift of Indonesia. And by the early 1970s, it became even more robust as British neocolonialism's last exertions in Malaysia and Singapore combined with the pro-U.S. policies of Southeast Asia's anticommunist states, reinforcing U.S. influence in the region.

As Britain pulled out of its Singapore bases, it contrived the Five Power Defense Arrangement (FPDA) that tied the defense systems of Malaysia and Singapore with that of Australia, New Zealand, and itself, albeit in a reduced role. Though British forces were leaving Southeast Asia for good, the FPDA unexpectedly foiled Soviet leaders' designs on the Singapore bases, diminished their prospects for courting Malaysia, and dashed their hopes of supplanting the Anglo-American security umbrella in Southeast Asia with a Soviet-led system. In essence, Soviet officials were stunned by the massive scale of the FPDA's first joint exercise in 1970. The Kremlin thereafter held that Britain's military would persist in Southeast Asia to augment U.S. power in the region, or that Malaysia and Singapore would naturally shift from Britain's orbit to that of the United States. In either scenario, Moscow calculated that its plans to draw Southeast Asia's noncommunist regimes into its sphere of influence had become untenable. With Beijing having long monopolized the loyalties of Southeast Asia's communist parties (except for that of Vietnam), the Kremlin's severely curtailed opportunities in the region left its leaders eager for détente with Washington.[8]

Beijing, too, made few inroads into wider Southeast Asia because the regimes of the arc of containment had cast their lot with Washington. In August 1967, the five states of the arc—Indonesia, Malaysia, the Philippines, Singapore, and Thailand—founded the Association of Southeast Asian Nations (ASEAN) and cultivated increasingly intimate politico-military relations with the United States to shore up their own power and reap the rewards of intertwining their developing economies with that of the world's wealthiest nation. The ASEAN states also embedded themselves within a sprawling pro-U.S. network of crisscrossing bilateral and multilateral compacts within and beyond Asia.[9] Crucially, Singapore followed Malaysia's example and in the late 1960s rushed to replace its declining British patron. Singapore's overtures to Washington, joining its decidedly pro-U.S. counterparts in ASEAN, conclusively transitioned the region from Anglo-American predominance to U.S. hegemony. For its part, the United States met its ASEAN allies halfway, raring to consolidate influence over the interconnected region. Less than two years from the creation of ASEAN, Chinese premier Zhou Enlai openly expressed frustration that China "found itself 'encircled'" and "isolated on most key policy issues."[10] Zhou, who was directly responsible for Chinese foreign policy, would later confide in U.S. national security adviser Henry Kissinger his belief that "the institutions for [containing China] in Southeast Asia are more numerous than in any other area in the world."[11]

When Richard Nixon assumed the presidency in 1969, it seemed that the United States faced serious challenges to its global predominance.[12] But in Southeast Asia, where the United States seemed weakest, where its war machine appeared unable to subdue Vietnam's communists, the region's overall pro-U.S. trajectory had grown more pronounced over time. Moscow and Beijing had by then come to see that their political influence in Southeast Asia paled beyond Indochina, that the United States enjoyed de facto hegemony in the region despite its failures in Vietnam. Indeed, the communist powers had grown anxious to thaw relations with the United States; China to mitigate its isolation from regional affairs owing to the arc of containment; the USSR to blunt the threat posed by China and the United States potentially joining forces due to Sino-U.S. detente.[13] Nixon's successful rapprochement with Beijing and Moscow in the early 1970s enabled him to withdraw U.S. troops from Vietnam with the arc of containment entrenched in Southeast Asia, so entrenched that it could not be dislodged though all of Indochina went communist in 1975.

In effect, the arc of containment underpinned a veritable U.S. empire in Southeast Asia. It was an empire composed, in Charles Maier's words, of a "congeries of client states (or 'friendly kings')." These "friendly kings" had consolidated their political authority at home with the assistance of the Anglo-American powers during the early Cold War, entwining their anticommunist nationalism with local antipathy toward China and, in most cases, the Chinese populations in their countries. "Out of constraint, convenience or conviction," they had all determined to uphold U.S. power in Southeast Asia, to "enlist against common enemies," and thereby acquire U.S. aid, trade, and security guarantees.[14] Indochina's slide toward communism only saw ASEAN leaders and their U.S. ally bind their fates tighter. The "friendly kings" had not cast off the colonial order. Instead, they established a new imperial system in collaboration with the United States to preserve—and voluntarily circumscribe—their existing or newfound independence. Their efforts saw U.S. hegemony arise at the intersection of the Cold War and decolonization in Southeast Asia.

Figure 13. Founding members of the Association of Southeast Asian Nations (ASEAN) in Bangkok, Thailand, August 8, 1967. From left: Foreign Ministers Thanat Khoman of Thailand, Narciso R. Ramos of the Philippines, Sinnathamby Rajaratnam of Singapore, Tun Abdul Razak of Malaysia, and Adam Malik of Indonesia. The ASEAN states were firmly ensconced in the U.S. orbit. Photo from the Ministry of Information and the Arts Collection, courtesy of the National Archives of Singapore.

"Act like Britain!"

Britain had not been the colossus that Rusk and Johnson wanted for at least the preceding two decades. Since relinquishing India, Pakistan, Burma, and Ceylon (now Sri Lanka) in just seven months between 1947 and 1948, Britain had focused on managing its decline. And while Britain's tenacity in Malaya and Singapore betrayed vestigial ambitions for world power, British leaders knew their nation's strength was fading, felt bound by their concessions to the tides of decolonization, and had tried to reinvent rather than reanimate the empire. British neocolonialism thus bent toward making Britain indispensable to the U.S. Cold War, toward maintaining its imperial presence in Southeast Asia by ushering pro-West anticommunists into political leadership in Malaya and Singapore as both countries gained independence. London also inked security agreements with these new nations to project British military power into Asia, rebranding these relationships as familial networks within the British Commonwealth.

Such networks were cheaper than formal empire, though British neocolonialism in Southeast Asia finally became too costly due to *Konfrontasi*. The British pound had also weakened significantly in the latter 1960s. By both design and contingency, then, Britain had turned into a shadow of its imperial self. More than Rusk cared to admit, to "act like Britain" after 1945 entailed precisely a constant retreat coupled with the building of loose political, economic, and military partnerships, along with accommodation to U.S. power.

Thus, even as Britain prepared to withdraw from Singapore, it hoped to preserve the tenuous ties it had to Southeast Asia, Australia, and New Zealand, to "reassur[e] its allies that it [was] not leaving the area defenseless." To this end, the Wilson government promised Malaysia and Singapore an air defense system, including two large radar installations previously in place, about one hundred military technicians to aid in their operation, Rapier surface-to-air missiles, and training for Singapore's pilots and airbase technicians. Britain also planned to cushion its former colonies (particularly Singapore) with their regular share of the British foreign aid budget until the rundown was complete.[15]

In addition, Britain sought to replace its military sphere of influence in Asia and Oceania with the FPDA. This was a taller order. Britain's military bases in Singapore had been central to the empire's claim to great power status after 1945. Hosting more than thirty thousand British troops, these bases constituted a deployment second in magnitude to only the British Army on the Rhine, the fifty thousand soldiers Britain had committed to NATO.[16] Britain's defense cuts in Southeast Asia would instantly abrogate the Anglo-Malaysian Defense Agreement (AMDA), which since Malaya's independence had obligated the British military to defend Malaysia and Singapore in the event of an external attack. In Washington's view, Britain's withdrawal from Singapore also undid its SEATO commitments. U.S. officials judged that Britain's staging facilities on Masirah and Gan, islands in the Persian Gulf and the Indian Ocean, were too distant for the British military to make a sustained impact on Southeast Asian affairs.[17] Australian prime minister Harold Holt was less restrained. British military capability in Southeast Asia had for decades been a "cornerstone" of Australian defense policy. So when Holt first heard of British withdrawal plans, he reportedly exclaimed that Britain had just told "the world East of Suez" to "go to hell."[18]

Left with little choice, Malaysia, Singapore, Australia, and New Zealand agreed to discuss and form the FPDA. According to U.S. intelligence, Britain's four allies had approached the matter with "fatalistic resignation."[19] Nevertheless, they all agreed that Britain's departure mandated they strive to reinforce their existing mutual defense links.[20] With memories of *Konfrontasi* still fresh,

Australia and New Zealand believed strong military ties with Malaysia and Singapore would deter any possible Indonesian belligerence. Also, Australian concerns about the war in Vietnam meant Malaysia and Singapore offered key "forward defense" positions in the region.[21] Malaysian prime minister Tunku Abdul Rahman and Singapore's prime minister Lee Kuan Yew had distrusted each other since their nations' failed merger, but both concurred that the security of their countries was indivisible. Moreover, Lee and the Tunku agreed that with Britain's withdrawal, their measly naval and air defenses needed the FPDA. In June 1968, officials from the four nations convened with their British counterparts in Kuala Lumpur to knit their defenses into a security framework.[22]

U.S. officials reported that the FPDA meeting "went off reasonably well." To U.S. observers, all the "high-level representatives" appeared forthcoming and eager to cooperate: Malaysia and Singapore agreed to the joint use of each other's air defense facilities to better coordinate operations; Australia and New Zealand agreed to maintain forces in both Peninsular Malaysia and Singapore at least until 1971. The conference lasted just two days, so there was no detailed planning, but all parties agreed to meet in Canberra in 1969 to hammer out specifics.[23] The five nations also agreed to stage a major military exercise in 1970, later named *Bersatu Padu* (Malay for "Complete Unity"), to test their joint capabilities without British forces.[24]

Sufficient agreement between the five nations saw the FPDA come into force in November 1971. However, calling the FPDA an arrangement between five powers was a misnomer; it served Britain's exit strategy, to leave four behind. Moreover, it was a stretch to think of Malaysia and Singapore as "powers." Neither had air defense capabilities without Britain. Their navies were in worse shape—Singapore could not even provide a single ship for *Bersatu Padu*.[25]

The FPDA would never match up to the AMDA. The arrangement provided only for its members to consult each other on the appropriate action required should Malaysia or Singapore face external aggression. Worse, Britain's formal commitment to the FPDA was negligible, whereas the AMDA had compelled the British to defend both countries. Britain had to coax Australia and New Zealand to fill its shoes, to station large numbers of troops in Singapore and Malaysia even though the FPDA on paper made no such demand. At the time, Britain's ebbing authority over both still intersected with Australia and New Zealand's self-interests.[26] Just as important, since the Australian government also looked to Washington's view of the FPDA and valued the ANZUS alliance in place since 1951, the Johnson administration managed to prod the Australians to "assume a larger role" in the security of Malaysia and

Singapore, to "take the lead" with their commonwealth partners. U.S. leaders also convinced New Zealand to "work toward the establishment of a joint defense plan embracing both Singapore and Malaysian forces."[27] The tortured process of creating the FPDA made plain that Britain was a far cry from even the power that had thwarted Sukarno's *Konfrontasi*.

Yet through the FPDA, the ghost of Britain's dead empire stalked abroad full of sound and fury. A favorable turn in British politics, at least to the other FPDA members, coincided with the unfolding of *Bersatu Padu* between April and June 1970 in Malaysia's jungles and the South China Sea. The British Conservative Party led by Edward Heath replaced the Wilson government and promised a modest military presence in the Far East. Heath was none too concerned with Malaysia and Singapore and merely wished to reinforce Britain's relationships with Australia and New Zealand.[28] Regardless, Britain's belated military supplements suddenly turned *Bersatu Padu* into a giant. By its conclusion, the FPDA's maiden exercise involved fifty warships, two hundred aircraft, and twenty-five thousand military personnel from the five nations, more than half of which were British troops, deployed directly to Southeast Asia from the United Kingdom in under a day. It was Britain's largest peacetime airlift.[29]

To be sure, the FPDA's innate frailties troubled its members to no end. The joint exercise was expensive. British officials recorded that their part alone ran upward of $3 million, but likely volunteered this misleading figure for the record, since it excluded the tremendous cost of British equipment as well as food and pay for British soldiers. Furthermore, *Bersatu Padu* required overseas troops to undergo six weeks of acclimatization, as well as the advance establishment of a brigade headquarters, all of which cast doubt on the efficacy of such long-range emergency deployments. Knowing Britain was determined to pull its military from the region, some Malaysian officials sneered that the FPDA was simply a public relations exercise.[30]

Soviet leaders, though, took *Bersatu Padu* very seriously. In the years prior to the exercise, Russian officials had already let slip their anxieties at being unable to profit from Britain's and the United States' imminent military withdrawals from Southeast Asia. In March 1968, *Izvestiya*, the Soviet government's national publication, protested that Malaysia and Singapore, once the nodes of Britain's military network, would simply enter the U.S. sphere of influence in Southeast Asia.[31] The Russians were not wide of the mark. Singapore's factories had been churning out military equipment for U.S. combat troops, and the country's bases were open to U.S. naval vessels en route to the Vietnam conflict. The Tunku had, for his part, long allowed SEATO allies of the United States to deploy combat aircraft to staging grounds in Thailand via the Malayan peninsula, and since 1964 Malaysia had trained more than three thousand Vietnamese military and police personnel in counterinsurgency.[32]

In early 1969, as official news broke that Britain planned to create the FPDA, *Pravda*—the official organ of the Communist Party of the Soviet Union—complained that the arrangement would see Britain remain in Southeast Asia to reinforce U.S. military power.[33] The next year, *Bersatu Padu* further unnerved the Soviets. While the exercise was underway, Russian officials continually lambasted the FPDA as a "blood relative" of NATO and SEATO.[34] Indeed, *Bersatu Padu* left such a deep impression that months after it ended, *Izvestiya* commentaries still carped that Britain's "imperialist" impulses shone through the FPDA.[35] Even a year later, Russian writer I. Shatalov in the Soviet journal *International Affairs* recounted the exercise with dread and awe. He described how Britain had deployed "two battalions with engineers, gunners and a signal service, as well as 200 armored carriers, artillery, 20 helicopters and several thousands of tons of military equipment" across "eight thousand miles" to Malaysia and the South China Sea in just "twenty hours." The scale and speed of the operations had convinced Shatalov that the FPDA was a full-blown "British-sponsored military bloc," one that offered the western "imperialist powers" a "springboard" into Southeast Asia.[36]

These official Soviet statements arose from the Kremlin's recognition of its weak toehold in the wider Southeast Asian region. By the mid-1960s, Chinese leader Mao Zedong's ideological predilection toward armed revolution and readiness to support insurgencies (contrasting Moscow's more cautious stance) had won most Southeast Asian communist parties away from the USSR.[37] Even then, most of these Southeast Asian communist groups—excepting the Democratic Republic of Vietnam and its southern ally, the National Liberation Front—had been crippled by the region's conservative governments by the late 1960s with U.S. or British support. Notably, Suharto's coup d'état saw to the massacre of the Indonesian communists (PKI) in 1965 and 1966, the third largest communist party in the world, decisively tilting the ideological balance in the region toward the West. By November 1968, U.S. intelligence officials concluded that "Communist parties in Southeast Asia [had] fared poorly," that communist insurgency now posed "less a threat in Malaysia, Singapore, Indonesia and the Philippines" than in the 1940s.[38] Moscow knew this well.

The USSR had pragmatically vied for the loyalty of the Vietnamese communists and, unlike China, courted the noncommunist Southeast Asian states. Generous Soviet aid to Hanoi, bolstering the resilience of the Vietnamese communists in the face of U.S. military might, did give the Kremlin something to crow about. Hanoi did lean more toward Moscow than Beijing. But the Vietnamese revolution did not spread beyond Indochina. And in 1969, Soviet leader Leonid Brezhnev set about trying to win ASEAN states' acceptance of a Soviet-led collective security system, hoping they might be receptive given the anticipated British and U.S. retrenchment and the potential of China filling the vacuum. From June of that year, Brezhnev and his lieutenants carried his proposal to the ASEAN states. These overtures fell flat.[39] Indonesia remained dead set against friendlier relations with the USSR and cleaved instead to the United States.[40] The pro-U.S. Thai government, apart from inking a trade agreement with the USSR at the end of 1970, never warmed to the Soviet proposal and continued to host U.S. military bases and troops. The Philippines would not even establish relations with the USSR until 1976.[41] Malaysian leaders cautiously opened diplomatic relations with the USSR in the late 1960s to hedge against U.S. withdrawal from Vietnam but spurned Brezhnev's scheme.[42] In fact, the Malaysians increasingly sought U.S. military equipment for their national defense system.[43]

For Russian officials disappointed by the foundering of their collective security proposal, the FPDA seemed to close even Singapore and its naval installations off from the USSR's fleet. To Shatalov, the FPDA had drawn a "gigantic military triangle" in Southeast Asia "in conjunction with the U.S.," a triangle served by Masirah, British bases in Singapore, and U.S. military facilities in Diego Garcia. He warned that Lockheed, which repaired military aircraft being used in Vietnam, was "anxiously waiting for the British to leave" so it could establish in Singapore the "largest commercial aircraft repair center in Southeast Asia." Other U.S. companies in the military industry were, he noted, making similar plans. He believed the "American military umbrella [would soon] open up over Singapore," so the USSR could expect little from courting this former stronghold of the British Empire.[44]

Shatalov was not wrong. As the Nixon administration refined its policy toward Asia in the "post-Vietnam" era, Secretary of Defense Melvin Laird reminded the president that the U.S. military had made "extensive use of Singapore's naval logistical support facilities" in the preceding decades and that all signals from the Singapore government suggested this practice would continue.[45] Singapore would shift from the British sphere to that of the United States as the Russians had feared. Kremlin anxieties about the FPDA coalesced into a self-fulfilling prophecy. Still reeling from *Bersatu Padu* months after the fact, *Izvestiya* grumbled that the FPDA had "knocked together a military bloc"—a "mini-NATO"—that preserved British interests in Southeast Asia and ensured Singapore's military facilities served the United States.[46]

These hyperbolic responses, given Brezhnev's failure to sell his security proposal to ASEAN, reveal Soviet officials' abiding sense of inadequacy when
competing against the Anglo-American powers and China for influence in
Southeast Asia. During a moment of weakness in late 1968, Russian officials
even shared with U.S. diplomats that U.S. predominance in Southeast Asia provided a "desirable" check against China, their "common enemy" in the region.[47] Moscow had gradually been reconciling itself to U.S. hegemony in
Southeast Asia when the FPDA undermined new Soviet ambitions for the region. Thus, from the time of *Bersatu Padu* through the fall of Saigon, Soviet
officials could only broadcast regular (and ineffectual) condemnations of the
ASEAN states as intimate U.S. allies, inadvertently disclosing the USSR's paltry
impact on wider Southeast Asia.[48]

On March 27, 1971, British defense correspondent Henry Stanhope wrote
in wistful tones about the British military retreat from Southeast Asia in the
Times of London. Nine months earlier, *Bersatu Padu* had allowed the empire's
shadow to strut and fret with great force. Soon, it would be heard no more. As
the Union Jack came down during a military parade at one of the Singapore
bases, Stanhope mourned how "another link in the long chain of British associations with Singapore [was being] ceremoniously broken." In those final
days of the British military presence on the island, he concluded that the "new
Singapore" belonged to the United States, within the "new industrial Raj."[49]
Soviet leaders had come to think the same. When Nixon announced a few
months later that he planned to visit China, the USSR was ready to accommodate to the hegemon of Southeast Asia, ready for rapprochement with the
United States.[50]

"Look beyond Vietnam"

ASEAN's pro-U.S. trajectory thwarted Beijing's expansionism in ways that paralleled the FPDA's impact upon Moscow. To the Johnson administration, it was
clear that ASEAN—formed in August 1967 with a big push from Indonesia's
foreign minister Adam Malik—succeeded the pro-West Association of Southeast Asia (ASA) that had comprised Malaya, Thailand, and the Philippines.[51] A
month after ASEAN's creation, Johnson, in an address to elected U.S. representatives in San Antonio, Texas, decided "to call the roll" of the U.S.-friendly
nations in the "great arc of Asia and [the] Pacific." He paid close attention to
the ASEAN states, quoting verbatim their calls on U.S. "leadership" to help
ensure the "Red Chinese" did not "gobble up all of Asia."[52] Clearly, Johnson

officials worked from the premise that Southeast Asians harbored a "traditional fear of China [and] distrust of communism as an antinationalist and pro-Chinese movement."[53] U.S. containment policy had all along approached Southeast Asia with this broad, regional focus; the policy had never been Vietnam-centric. So, while Johnson Americanized the Vietnam conflict to prevent the Southeast Asian dominoes from falling, he simultaneously plowed the United States' immense economic and military capacity toward underwriting the authoritarian, rightward tendencies of the ASEAN regimes that impeded Chinese influence.

Presidential aspirant Richard Nixon had also discerned the arc of containment while he traveled through Southeast Asia in April 1967. He published his analysis in the October issue of *Foreign Affairs*, contending that the "rest of Asia" presented an "extraordinary set of opportunities for a U.S. policy which must begin to *look beyond Viet Nam.*" The piece, following hot on the heels of Johnson's speech in San Antonio, was supposed to showcase Nixon's transformative vision of U.S. policy. It opened with his statement that the Vietnam War had too "long dominated our field of vision" and "distorted our picture of Asia." This "small country," Nixon wrote, "does not fill the map." But while Nixon's prose sounded bold, his approach largely paralleled that of the Johnson administration. Echoing Johnson, Nixon pointed to how "Asian regionalism" had emerged to resist China, how "all around the rim of China," nations were "becoming Western without ceasing to be Asian." Nixon had presumed, like Johnson officials, that most Asian nations perceived the United States "not as an oppressor but a protector." Thus, Nixon argued, China was surrounded by U.S. allies; by the "3,000-mile arc of islands" that made up Indonesia; by the long belt of noncommunist states that stretched "from Japan to India"; and by "occidental Australia and New Zealand."[54] Johnson had said as much in his "roll call" of the "arc of Asian and Pacific nations."

Of course, Nixon's triangular diplomacy did overturn two decades of U.S. nonrecognition of the People's Republic of China, ostensibly charting new directions for U.S. Cold War strategy. Yet, the fundamental basis of Nixon's foreign policy turn was the arc of containment that Johnson had identified and endeavored to fortify, and which Nixon intended to use against China.[55] Nixon believed the arc would "become so strong" that China's leaders must seek "dialogue" with the United States, whereupon he would subject Beijing to "containment without isolation," to the irresistible offer of rapprochement given China's dim prospects in Southeast Asia.[56] As president, Nixon enunciated essentially the same principles when he spoke off-the-cuff in Guam in July 1969 (reporters later termed his remarks the Nixon Doctrine). By then, Kissinger had already initiated the first moves of triangular diplomacy.[57]

From the Johnson administration through the Nixon years, therefore, the intensifying U.S.-ASEAN relationship augmented the arc of containment that encircled Vietnam and China. This entrenched the "ideological polarization" of the region.[58] More importantly, this arc outlasted U.S. military withdrawal from Vietnam in 1973 and withstood the subsequent fall of Saigon. Though the Vietnam War remains historically significant, the U.S.-ASEAN collaboration to contain China and establish U.S. predominance is more characteristic of Southeast Asia's history from 1945 through the Cold War.

Of course, not all the "friendly kings" were like the Philippine, Thai, and Malayan leaders who readily embraced the United States between the late 1940s and 1950s. Lee Kuan Yew kept Singapore straddling between its British patron and the United States in the early to mid-1960s. He even publicly denounced U.S. culture, psychology, and foreign policy in late 1965, which U.S. officials surmised was meant to "intimidate" the British military into remaining in Singapore. Still, the U.S. State Department anticipated (as did the Russians) that Lee would inevitably tilt toward Washington. U.S. analysts noted how Lee conscientiously "avoided virulent criticism" of the war in Vietnam because he saw "no present alternative" that preoccupied the Chinese communists and left the majority Chinese Singapore state unmolested.[59]

U.S. officials did not need to wait long. Within months of Singapore's independence, Lee aligned his government with Washington, supporting the U.S. military effort in Vietnam even before Britain formally announced its plans to withdraw from Singapore. In March 1966, Lee met U.S. diplomats to commence "a new era" in relations with the United States. Singapore soon welcomed U.S. troops from Vietnam for R&R (rest and recreation), bringing a minor U.S. spending boom to the country. Lee followed this with public statements in favor of the U.S. military intervention in Vietnam.[60] Concurrently, he and his colleagues facilitated a "growing volume of U.S. military procurement for Vietnam," which by 1967 accounted for 15 percent of Singapore's national income. The British bases in Singapore, which annually pumped some $200 million into the economy, brought in slightly more at 20 percent (and shrank thereafter). Moreover, as the regional petroleum-refining center, Singapore was critical to the U.S. war machine. Lee's turn to Washington was a transparent attempt to substitute for the British Empire. For Singapore, one of the richest Asian states, the conflict in Vietnam was good business.[61]

The left-wing politicians and labor unionists whom Lee had persecuted since the early 1960s were predictably up in arms over the presence of U.S. troops in Singapore. They portrayed Lee and his political party—the People's Action Party (PAP)—as a "puppet regime" complicit with the U.S.-British imperialist campaign in Indochina.[62] They also circulated a cartoon depicting Johnson and Lee, arms around each other, the U.S. leader cradling Lee's face as if to kiss his pursed lips, while wounded U.S. soldiers hobbled through Johnson's comically spread legs toward their "holiday in Singapore" (*dao xing du jia*).[63] But Lee and the PAP were determined to maintain the revenue streams flowing from the Vietnam War and prevented local newspapers from publicizing Singapore's R&R and military procurement programs without approval, trying to deprive their left-wing opponents of material in order to critique Lee's pro-U.S. stance. Apart from deploying the police to crack down on anti–Vietnam War protesters, Lee led the PAP in August 1966 to pass a capacious bill against vandalism that criminalized—in Lee's own words—the act of "shouting and carrying anti-American . . . and pro-Vietcong slogans."[64]

Siding with the United States undergirded Lee's authoritarian rule in other ways. In October 1967, the CIA studied the "significant bearing" that Singapore's handsome profits from the Vietnam War had upon the PAP's expanding political and social authority. Essentially, the PAP leveraged its impressive economic record to legitimate its ideal of a "tightly knit society," warning its citizens that only an orderly and stable society could attract the world's high-rolling investors. CIA analysts, of course, knew that "tightly knit" translated into "increasing the government's control over the political life of the country." As the dominant political party, the PAP easily passed a Societies Ordinance in 1966 that in the CIA's view gave the PAP "almost unlimited power to control, approve, or outlaw" any organization comprising as few as ten persons. Furthermore, the PAP banned public utilities strikes and "outlaw[ed] political and sympathy strikes" to permanently strangle activism within Singapore's unions.[65]

Johnson was unfazed by the PAP's tightening vise. He gladly welcomed Singapore into the U.S. sphere of influence, most pleased that Lee wrote him a personal letter in late 1967 to emphasize Singapore's "unequivocal" backing of U.S. Cold War policy. Lee pledged to use every opportunity to persuade U.S. opinion-makers that Asian leaders like himself supported the United States. He also encouraged the president to show "indomitable determination, infinite patience" because "ancient peoples"—meaning the Chinese—were currently "without power to match" U.S. military might, which "gives us time" to "consolidate our positions." Johnson's national security adviser Walt Rostow had also used this argument, that the United States was buying time for Southeast Asia. As Lee repeatedly deployed it (and more besides), he quickly became one of the foremost apologists for the Vietnam War.[66]

Lee also cultivated relations with the Nixon administration in this way. Through Kissinger, he proposed to Nixon that a "statement by an Asian neutral

Figure 14. Singapore prime minister Lee Kuan Yew visits with President Lyndon Baines Johnson in Washington, D.C., on October 17, 1967. Lee pledged his "unequivocal support" for the U.S. war in Vietnam and argued fiercely to this effect to western audiences on behalf of Johnson and his successor, Richard Nixon. Photo courtesy of the White House Photo Office Collection, Lyndon Baines Johnson Presidential Library.

leader, such as himself"—though not neutral in practice—"urging the American public not to 'sell out' [Saigon] might reduce domestic pressures" to withdraw from Vietnam.[67] Nixon warmly received Lee's offer to make it "clear to the American public that he wants a continued U.S. presence."[68] Singapore's friendliness to U.S. capital and Cold War aims would more than compensate for Britain's departure, and rapidly at that. In 1971, U.S. officials noted that U.S. private investment was pouring into Singapore, renowned for its political and economic stability, at an "astounding rate."[69] The State Department estimated that U.S. private investments in Singapore had totaled $250 million by 1970 and were "growing at a phenomenal $100 million per year!"[70]

Indonesia, the largest state in the arc of containment, cleaved toward Washington at much the same time as Singapore. But whereas Lee appeared initially hesitant to slough off old affiliations to Britain, Suharto's New Order swiftly eviscerated Sukarno's pro-China legacy. In October 1967, Indonesian leaders suspended diplomatic relations with China, withdrew their personnel from Beijing, and sent Chinese ambassadorial staff in Jakarta packing. Foreign

Minister Malik also informed U.S. officials that Indonesia was solidly behind the U.S. effort in Vietnam, though Jakarta might occasionally voice muted criticisms of U.S. policy for the sake of appearing neutral.[71]

U.S. leaders were so taken with Indonesia's titanic shift toward anticommunism that each one of Suharto's further moves to the right of the Cold War divide turned a profit for him. After all, President Johnson wished to make Indonesia a "showcase for all the world." In a baffling turn of phrase, he told the NSC that he wanted the United States' "ambitious plans which haven't been working in other countries [to be] put . . . into action in Indonesia."[72] Whatever Johnson really meant, the United States was already on the job. Caltex and Stanvac had already arrived in Indonesia to boost oil production and integrate the newly West-friendly nation into the world market.[73] By 1970, the expanding private investment pouring into Indonesia, along with lavish loans from the International Monetary Fund and the World Bank, came mostly from U.S. businessmen or the U.S. government.[74]

Like Lee, Suharto entwined his consolidation of power at home with staunch support for the U.S. Cold War agenda. When Suharto met Nixon and Kissinger in 1970, he said explicitly that Indonesia's "will and capacity to resist ideological [and] political" attacks rested on the United States making his rule "strong economically, socially, and militarily." To emphasize his regime's present strength, and hint at what more U.S. aid might do, Suharto bragged that he had "nullified" Indonesia's revolutionary communists, and that "tens of thousands of these have been interrogated and placed in detention." He explained that Indonesian students had also "received indoctrination" that snuffed out any support for communism.[75] Nixon heartily agreed with Suharto that Indonesia "must be strong enough."[76] To this end, the Nixon administration tripled the U.S. Military Assistance Program to Indonesia.[77]

In addition, Suharto's ambitions to lead ASEAN and gain more rewards from the United States saw him willingly heed Nixon's call to "play a big role in Southeast Asia."[78] Suharto believed this meant, among other things, openly supporting the anticommunist government of General Lon Nol of Cambodia, with which Suharto and his military elites had always sympathized. Suharto had previously, in secret, welcomed his Cambodian allies to Indonesia in November 1969 and January 1970 to study how the Indonesian army had executed its coup d'état. In March 1970, once Lon Nol seized power from the neutralist (but essentially pro-China) Prince Norodom Sihanouk, an Indonesian mission came to his aid.[79]

Thus, in July 1970, inspired by Nixon's talk of Indonesia's "big role," Suharto considerably expanded his support for Lon Nol. Suharto directed the

Figure 15. President Richard Nixon receives Indonesian president Suharto in May 1970. Suharto had broken diplomatic relations with China in October 1967 and further advanced the anticommunist cause in Southeast Asia by assisting the right-wing Cambodian military's power grab in early 1970. Photo courtesy of the White House Photo Office Collection, Richard Nixon Presidential Library and Museum.

Indonesian army to reinforce Cambodia's efforts against a North Vietnamese invasion that had been launched with Chinese assistance, furnishing Cambodia with twenty-five thousand AK-47 rifles and antiguerrilla training programs for Cambodian troops. Indonesia also maintained a brigade of forces to be "projected into trouble-spots" on the Asian mainland with U.S. air and amphibious support.[80] True, the communist factions in Cambodia, Vietnam, and Laos would ultimately triumph in 1975. But the firm U.S.-Indonesian alliance continued to deepen, strengthening the "friendly king" at the center of the arc of containment.

Like the leaders of Indonesia and Singapore, Field Marshal Thanom Kittikachorn, Thailand's military dictator from 1963 through 1973, firmly committed his government to the Vietnam War. Thanom's predecessors had since 1950 taken up the American anticommunist cause, convinced that allying with the United States would ward off the perceived threat of Chinese communism to Thai security. As the war in Vietnam escalated, Thanom calculated that he must hold the United States even closer, not least because Thailand's borders ran alongside Laos and Cambodia, through which the Ho Chi Minh trail snaked. By 1968, the CIA concluded that Thai leaders had "limited options" for trying out a new patron "because of [Thailand's] longstanding and unequivocal commitment to military alliance with the U.S.," an alliance that the Thai elites admitted to U.S. officials remained "indispensable" to counter any "threat from China." On Thanom's watch, Thai troops joined U.S. soldiers in the Vietnamese jungles while U.S. B-52 bombers flew sorties out of U-Tapao, a Thai airbase near the Gulf of Siam, to pulverize Vietnam from 1965 through the early 1970s.[81] Over that period, U.S. military intervention in Vietnam pumped some $3.5 billion in military and economic aid into Thailand, increasing Thailand's economic reliance on the United States and its government's determination to remain aligned to Washington.[82]

Even Philippine president Ferdinand Marcos's attempts to exploit the Vietnam War for his own political ends tied his fate to U.S. support, ensuring the Philippine archipelago at the eastern end of the arc of containment remained within the U.S. orbit. Ever alert to how he might milk U.S. involvement in Southeast Asia for personal benefit, Marcos sensed how desperately Johnson wanted the Philippines to back the war effort in Vietnam. According to journalist Stanley Karnow, Marcos delayed committing Philippine troops to Vietnam until September 1966—a year after U.S. forces had been deployed, when he thought Johnson most vulnerable. Marcos then promised to raise ten Philippine battalions (on the U.S. dollar) for Vietnam as long as he could retain large numbers of them for his own protection. Johnson caved, funneling an additional $80 million to Marcos beyond the military subsidy, doing so even though Marcos sent just a token force to Vietnam.[83] Yet Marcos's machinations also made his regime, like Thanom's, more dependent on U.S. backing. This state of affairs would only intensify in the early 1970s when Marcos—desperate to retain power as his legitimacy dwindled at home—acquired U.S. sanction for his ascension to dictatorship. U.S. leaders, determined to maintain access to U.S. bases in the Philippines, would prop up Marcos for decades, all the while closing their eyes to the profligacy and violent excesses of his regime.[84]

Even nonaligned Burma (now Myanmar) under its isolationist junta entered a testy but ongoing relationship with the United States, underpinned by U.S. provision of economic and military aid. U.S. policy toward Burmese leaders paralleled U.S. relations with all of ASEAN's authoritarians, enabling them to crush their domestic rivals and amass political power. When Burmese leader General Ne Win turned increasingly dictatorial in the 1960s, the United States accommodated itself to his repressive excesses and preserved its "delicate" ties with Burma throughout the Vietnam War. In contrast, the Yangon-Beijing relationship frayed in the late 1960s. Ne Win, suspicious of China's attempts to incorporate Burma into its sphere of influence, had reportedly described Zhou Enlai as a "bastard" in 1965 for presuming that Ne Win was "at his beck and call." Though Burma could not be counted fully on the U.S. side, it was by no means part of the Chinese camp.[85]

By January 1969, the State Department cautiously posited that "on the whole," the U.S. "record in Asia has been good." Once U.S. officials started looking beyond Vietnam, it became easy to see how ASEAN and other regional groups' "multilateral undertakings" had "further strengthen[ed] the fabric of non-communist Asia." With mounting optimism, they detailed the intersecting organizations that had incorporated ASEAN into an extensive network of pro-U.S. and anticommunist countries. Here are but two from the State Department's longer list: Formed in 1965, the Japanese-led Asian Parliamentarians Union plugged ASEAN into cooperation with Taiwan, Korea, Laos, Australia, India, and New Zealand. According to the State Department, this organization pooled these countries' resources for "Free World causes in Southeast Asia"—in effect, U.S. Cold War objectives in the region. The stridently anticommunist Asian and Pacific Council (ASPAC), formed in 1966, brought together Australia, Taiwan, Japan, Malaysia, New Zealand, the Philippines, South Korea, South Vietnam, and Thailand. ASPAC's membership intertwined it with ANZUS, ASEAN, the Asian Parliamentarians Union, the FPDA, and SEATO.[86]

State Department officials predictably sought consolations in Southeast Asia for their report wherever they could. But there was no denying ASEAN's pro-U.S. bent. As State's report acknowledged, the "bonds between us and the East Asian nations [for their analysis included South Korea and Japan] have been strengthened by a variety of contacts." Of course, the report omitted how U.S. assistance had enabled the authoritarian, pro-U.S. governments of the wider region to seize and hold power. Instead, it rehashed a well-worn narrative—one that Lee, Rostow, and Johnson himself had often served to journalists—that the U.S. troops battling in Vietnam had managed to "buy time" for U.S. allies in Asia to "build foundations for stability, democracy and economic growth."[87]

"Domino Theory in Reverse"

Did the "friendly kings" truly need more time? Most of them had routed their socialist and communist opponents at home when Johnson Americanized the conflict in Vietnam (or would, speaking of Suharto, soon seize power).

At base, the argument for "buying time" that U.S. and ASEAN leaders preached to their skeptical citizens and the international press was a rhetorical strategy to valorize the unpopular U.S. war in Vietnam which, in turn, rationalized the volume of U.S. resources poured into strengthening the emergent arc of containment. For Johnson, who chose war in Vietnam to preserve his personal credibility as a tough cold warrior, a broader regional project connected to his ill-fated intervention swiftly became apparent, that of consolidating U.S. hegemony through the "friendly kings" of Southeast Asia.[88] In essence, he moved to capitalize on what Kennedy officials had envisioned from the early 1960s: "a wide anticommunist arc" of allies "enclosing the entire South China Sea."[89] Just two years into the Vietnam War, with Jakarta's anti-China stance and hardening against Hanoi, Johnson boasted that the U.S. presence in Vietnam had put the "domino theory in reverse." U.S. "firmness in Asia," he argued, had "quickened" its allies, seeing them "band together in regional institutions" (such as ASEAN) to resist the "menace of China." Johnson also drew explicit parallels between Western Europe seeking the U.S. "shield of protection" against the USSR and the United States' "protective shield" for "new Asia" that was "building" up "on the periphery of the Orient."[90] NATO and ASEAN were oceans apart but, in common, both organizations upheld informal U.S. empires by invitation and collaboration.

Regardless, actually "buying time" demanded more than simply portraying the war in Vietnam as a grand endeavor to preserve the noncommunist states of Southeast Asia. Opposition to the war roiled within and outside the United States and mercilessly pilloried Johnson and Nixon after him. Furthermore, U.S. leaders did despair over the progress of war, the resilience of the communists, and the weakness of the Saigon government. In the eyes of ASEAN leaders, Washington balked too easily at the mounting U.S. casualties in Vietnam and each year seemed to totter closer to abandoning Saigon and withdrawing from the region altogether.[91]

Nonetheless, the last U.S. troops would not pull out of Vietnam until 1973, more than half a decade after U.S. policymakers began to weary of the war. On the face of it, U.S. leaders had persisted in Vietnam to obtain a settlement with the Vietnamese communists favorable to Saigon. Johnson and Nixon had been loath to yank U.S. troops from the conflict without grounds to assert that the South had been saved from northern aggression. Thus, Johnson opened the way to peace negotiations with Hanoi after the Tet Offensive in 1968 but still sent an additional thirty thousand U.S. soldiers to battle, making for the bloodiest year of fighting for all sides. Nixon made promises to end the war but left the complete withdrawal of U.S. forces until after his reelection. Hanoi, too, protracted the struggle by fiercely waging its military campaign to reduce the sting of any U.S. military gains at the negotiating table, for which the communists paid dearly in blood.[92]

But not all the reasons for Washington's costly foot-dragging in Indochina arose from the dynamics of the U.S.-Vietnam relationship, or even the United States' Cold War rivalry with the USSR and China, for the U.S. agendas of securing a suitable peace from Hanoi and consolidating the arc of containment, both of which required that the United States persevere in Vietnam, converged with ASEAN's determination to bolster U.S. commitment to the region. However sensitive Johnson and Nixon were to domestic and international attacks on their prosecution of the Vietnam War—whether they saw their critics as formidable opponents or nuisances to swat away—the "friendly kings" helpfully presented Washington with usable defenses of the U.S. military campaign in their own words. The ASEAN leaders used the domino logic of interconnected insecurity to justify the U.S. presence in Southeast Asia, which U.S. leaders gamely redeployed to both fend off anti–Vietnam War critics and rationalize even stronger U.S.-ASEAN relations. In effect, U.S. and ASEAN leaders engaged each other as though in an echo chamber, a throwback to the fateful encounters between British officials and the U.S. fact-finding missions that President Harry Truman had dispatched to the region in 1949 and 1950 (see chapter 1). It mattered less whether U.S. and ASEAN leaders truly believed in the domino theory, more that the allies spoke in one voice about their interconnected fates and together deflected international and local opposition to the Vietnam War while firmly lodging the arc of containment within the U.S. empire.

As one of the more eloquent champions of U.S. Cold War aims, the Tunku enjoyed the Johnson administration's high regard, especially when Johnson's "More Flags" campaign failed to collect many other allies' declaration of support for, and commitment to, Americanizing the Vietnam conflict.[93] To all intents and purposes, the Tunku did believe that, absent U.S. forces in Vietnam, "Chinese pressures" and communist victories would galvanize the depleted Malayan Communist Party (MCP).[94] In any case, the United States was Malaysia's second largest export market after Singapore, so the Tunku had good reasons to reinforce the already warm U.S.-Malaysian ties.[95] Most everything the Tunku said or wrote about the Vietnam War would prove handy to Washington. In July 1965, the Tunku addressed all the U.S. foreign policy cognoscenti that might oppose Johnson's decision to intervene in Vietnam, publishing an article in *Foreign Affairs* that underscored how Malaysia "look[ed] northward" with "anxiety," for Beijing and Hanoi threatened Saigon by "infiltration, subversion and open aggression." He stated that "we in Malaysia fully support Washington's actions" in Vietnam.[96] U.S. officials were cheered by this. They appreciated how, in the ensuing years, the Tunku repeatedly affirmed South Vietnam's "right to defend their territorial integrity" with U.S. assistance. Indeed, U.S. policymakers must have savored when the Tunku thundered at the 1967 Commonwealth Prime Ministers' Conference in London that "those who criticize the Americans for their assistance to South Vietnam should not be blind to the intervention of Communist powers in the war in Vietnam."[97]

Lee and his colleagues' public diplomacy hit similar notes. In a March 1965 speech in Christchurch, New Zealand, Lee conjured images of Vietnam scythed by communist forces, followed by Cambodia and Thailand, with Malaysia next. At the UN General Assembly that October, Singapore's permanent representative stated flatly that losing South Vietnam to the communists condemned "neighboring countries" to the same fate.[98] At the Institute for Strategic Studies in London in mid-1967, Lee delivered what U.S. officials called an "exciting *tour de force*" in which he chided British Labor Party members for their "naiveté . . . about Asian power realities and the significance of Vietnam." Lee told his audience firmly that he was a "believer in the domino theory," that "if American power were withdrawn, there could only be a Communist Chinese solution to Asia's problems."[99] In October 1967, on the NBC (National Broadcasting Company) program *Meet the Press*, Lee insisted that U.S. "failure in Vietnam" would see the Thais make "adjustments" to Chinese power, endangering Malaysia and Singapore. "And then . . ." he remarked sardonically, "they've got me by the throat."[100] He had a dramatic flair and a compelling (if studied) presence on screen.

ASEAN leaders also conveyed these views to U.S. decision makers in private. In 1966, Suharto reminded "wise man" Averell Harriman that U.S. troops in Vietnam were "essential to protect South Vietnam" and halt the "Chicom [Chinese communist] advance in Southeast Asia."[101] Likewise, the Tunku and Thanom hounded Vice President Hubert Humphrey in late 1967 on "the big question" of whether the United States was "going to stick it out" in Vietnam; both insisted "there is not one scintilla of hope for anybody if we fail."[102]

Johnson and Nixon eagerly used these ASEAN justifications of U.S. Cold War policy to admonish detractors of U.S. intervention in Vietnam. Both presidents stated ad nauseam that the Southeast Asians proximate to Vietnam knew better than anyone from the United States what were their security needs. In December 1967, soon after Lee's televised description of communist expansionism over NBC, Johnson lashed out at critics of the domino theory at a foreign policy conference, saying, "Communist domination is not a matter of theory for Asians. . . . Communist domination for Asians is a matter of life and death." He declared that it was "clear to Asian leaders that our presence in Vietnam is vital, is necessary, is a must to Asia's tomorrow." Because Asians occupied front row seats in the Cold War for their region, Johnson implied, their insights were beyond reproach.[103]

With the dominoes proclaiming repeatedly to the international press and other world leaders that they lived the domino theory, the Nixon administration, too, had ample ammunition to parry naysayers at home. Suharto's men had used the familiar themes of interconnected insecurity, explaining to Kissinger on July 1, 1970, that they expected the fall of South Vietnam to send other ASEAN leaders (except the stalwart Indonesians) scrambling to accommodate Chinese hegemony.[104] And so, in an interview aired on that same day on U.S. television, Nixon averred with an authoritative air that ASEAN supported the Vietnam War. In a retort to those who said that the domino theory was "obsolete," Nixon fired back that his critics "haven't talked to the dominoes . . . to the Thais, to the Malaysians, to the Singaporans [sic], to the Indonesians, to the Filipinos." He namechecked Lee, the Tunku, Suharto, and Thanom, added Japanese prime minister Eisaku Sato for good measure, and stated that he (unlike his critics) had been "talking to every one of the Asian leaders," and that "every one of them to a man recognizes" the fall of South Vietnam meant that they "might be next."[105]

Certainly, invoking the words of ASEAN leaders did not enable Washington to actually overturn the groundswell of domestic and international opposition to the Vietnam War. There was nothing that ASEAN statesmen could say, which Johnson or Nixon could quote or paraphrase, that dispelled U.S. citizens' shock at the Tet Offensive, brought back the dead and missing U.S. soldiers, or rehabilitated the heinous deeds of U.S. troops in the My Lai Massacre. But Johnson and Nixon were not exactly bent on converting their detractors. Both seemed content to dismiss their opponents with bald statements that the dominoes' testimonies were unassailable, and therefore the U.S. war in Vietnam a just cause. The "friendly kings" were instrumental here. And it seems their verbal support did also buttress U.S. leaders' persistence in Vietnam. Johnson, for one, penned a personal letter to Lee, confiding that Lee's "counsel" steeled his will to "keep on a steady course in Vietnam."[106] As Kissinger shared with Nixon in early 1969, "the efforts of the Southeast Asian countries will influence our policies more than they sometimes realize."[107]

This domino diplomacy (for want of a better phrase) could not go on indefinitely. What meager time it may have bought, the United States and its

ASEAN allies used well. They moved with great speed to fuse their fates. More U.S. money in terms of economic and military aid flowed into the rest of Southeast Asia during the U.S. war effort in Vietnam than ever before, and the amount rose steadily even as U.S. forces pulled out of Indochina.[108]

For their part, the ASEAN leaders made quick work of transforming their regional interconnectedness into a source of strength where once it had brought mutual insecurity. Malaysian foreign minister Muhammad Ghazali bin Shafie may have stated it best in the *London Times* in November 1970, when he described how the ASEAN states had crafted a "crisscrossing network" that collectively reinforced them all. He pointed to Malaysia's joint operations with Thailand, which continued to hunt the tattered bands of MCP fighters along the Malay-Thai border. He mentioned, too, the "security/military arrangements" that Malaysia and Indonesia had established for protecting the Sarawak-Kalimantan border in Borneo. Ghazali even boasted about the FPDA, though he could not have known how far *Bersatu Padu* had adversely affected Russian ambitions in the region, or how intensely the Chinese leadership felt their strategic shortcomings in comparison with the United States.[109]

Zhou Enlai certainly discerned that the domino theory had been running "in reverse." He recognized how all the crisscrossing economic and security networks had advanced the U.S. empire deep into Asia. In early 1969, U.S. intelligence officers established that Zhou had openly conceded that ASEAN and U.S. allies in the wider region had installed a virtual cordon sanitaire around China and Vietnam.[110] When Zhou was more at ease with Kissinger some years following the success of Sino-U.S. rapprochement, he would admit to the U.S. official that the many pro-U.S. alliances of various stripes that laced the Southeast Asian region had effectively contained Chinese influence.[111] China's foreign policy challenges did not end there. The U.S. State Department had of late determined that Mao's "universal face of militancy and belligerence toward most of the world" left China "more isolated than at any previous point in the regime's history," while his fanatical Cultural Revolution had subjected the Chinese political establishment to a crippling "internal turmoil."[112] To top these off, the Sino-Soviet conflict had in March 1969 exploded into armed clashes along the Chinese border.[113]

Thus, Nixon had reason to be confident when he spoke to U.S. news reporters in Guam in July 1969. The arc of containment had restricted Chinese power to the Indochinese states. In the wider region, the former dominoes had become sturdy stanchions of U.S. empire. Unfortunately, Nixon's remarks in Guam were imprecise, confusing and alarming his Asian allies. Between navigating reporters' follow-up questions and vainly thinking of ways to articulate his foreign policy vision, he ranged through equivocations: the United States would retreat from Vietnam and eschew policies that produced such interventions, but U.S. policy was still to militarily defend Asian allies with whom it had formal treaties. Nontreaty allies of the United States must take responsibility for defending themselves militarily; nevertheless, the United States "rule[d] out withdrawal" from the Pacific and would play the role that its Asian allies "desire[d] us to play." Buried within these ambiguities, Nixon did state that China had recently become less "effective in exporting revolution."[114] Overall, he failed to clarify emphatically that he believed Beijing was now desperate to remedy its being hived off from world affairs, that the time appeared ripe for what he had earlier described in *Foreign Affairs* as "containment without isolation." The bulk of Nixon's rambling address and responses to the press proved too distracting. As he visited allied and client states in Asia on his return journey to the United States, Nixon had to expend time and energy reassuring worried leaders that the United States would uphold its security guarantees to its friends in the region.[115]

What Nixon could not explain extemporaneously in Guam, he and Kissinger did better with in dealings with Zhou and Mao over the course of 1971 and 1972. After all, U.S. officials approached the Chinese leaders with the benefit of de facto U.S. hegemony in Southeast Asia. Historian Arne Westad has pointed out that Nixon's visit to China was a "true godsend" for Mao. Politically weakened by his foreign and domestic policy miscalculations, the aging and ailing Chinese leader longed to show upstart colleagues that Nixon had "recognized China's centrality" and sought his political wisdom.[116] For Zhou, who conducted the finer negotiations with Kissinger and Nixon over the terms of rapprochement, the need to acquire U.S. recognition of China was similarly intense. Chen Jian has shown that Beijing was preoccupied with "recognition as a central part of the world revolution"; its "constant aim" was to be perceived as an "equal" to Moscow and the United States.[117] Put another way, keeping up appearances was all important for Chinese leaders faced with their nation's very real encirclement in Southeast Asia and beyond.

To Zhou's credit, he tried to take the initiative in the rapprochement talks with the U.S. officials. Transcripts of the historic Nixon–Zhou meetings in February 1972 reveal that Zhou convinced Nixon that rapprochement between their nations required the United States and China to act, and recognize each other, as equal guarantors of Southeast Asian "peace and neutrality." Nixon agreed to "accept the idea [Zhou] referred to as a neutralized area" so long as China upheld the "deal" in concert with the United States. In addition, Zhou persuaded Nixon that the "neutrality" of Southeast Asia was coterminous with the fundamental principles of the landmark Shanghai Communiqué, which kicked off the process of gradually normalizing Sino-U.S. relations. He conflated his formulation of Southeast Asia's "neutrality" (upheld by the United States and China) with the communiqué's signature declaration that "neither [the United States nor China] should seek hegemony in the Asia Pacific region"; that both must oppose "efforts by any other country [meaning the USSR] to establish such hegemony."[118]

Zhou would later intimate to Kissinger that his formulation of Southeast Asian "neutralization" drew from a preexisting ASEAN proposal named ZOPFAN (Zone of Peace, Freedom and Neutrality), which had called on the superpowers to keep Southeast Asia "free from any form or manner of interference by outside Powers."[119] Malaysian prime minister Tun Abdul Razak, who had succeeded the Tunku in late 1970, had been integral to crafting the ZOPFAN concept. And Malaysian diplomats in particular had stumped tirelessly for ZOPFAN's principles throughout 1971 at multiple international forums like the UN General Assembly, various gatherings of the nonaligned nations, and more. The ASEAN leaders, having signed the ZOPFAN Declaration in November 1971, went on to preempt Nixon's visit to China by proposing to Beijing that Southeast Asia "embark on a road of neutrality."[120] Zhou had been so taken with how ZOPFAN implied that the United States and China were equal superpowers, he reworked its salient principles into the Shanghai Communiqué to at least have it on paper that the United States recognized China as an equal.[121] There is no exaggerating how greatly Beijing yearned for even this measly concession from Washington.

For Nixon, agreeing with Zhou's "neutralization" proposal would not shake the United States' hegemony in Southeast Asia given the entrenched U.S. political, military, and economic ties with the ASEAN countries. When the U.S. and Chinese governments publicized the Shanghai Communiqué on February 28, 1972, Nixon enthusiastically told U.S. journalists that his visit to China was a "journey of peace," explaining that this was why he and the Chinese had agreed to "oppose [the] domination of the Pacific by any one power."[122] If indeed there was peace in the wider region, or the scaling down of Sino-U.S. competition, it was because China had grudgingly resigned itself to U.S. dominance of the Pacific.

At any rate, Zhou and Nixon got mostly what they wanted from rapprochement. China secured some degree of U.S. recognition as a major power at little cost to Nixon. The burgeoning Sino-U.S. amity helped thaw their rivalry in Southeast Asia and opened the path to collusion against the Soviet Union. Additionally, Beijing's willingness to reduce aid to its Vietnamese allies promised Washington a slightly stronger position in peace talks with Hanoi.

Leveraging the fruits of Sino-U.S. rapprochement, the Nixon administration hoped to extricate all remaining U.S. forces from Vietnam. The route to that end was circuitous, however. Nixon and Kissinger's triangular diplomacy, by pursuing détente with Chinese leaders, sandwiched the USSR between NATO and China. This state of affairs, in turn, forced Brezhnev's hand to also pursue détente with the United States, since reconciling with Mao was an unpalatable course.[123] Indeed, U.S. officials had in August 1969 ascertained that the Kremlin detested, even feared, Mao's challenge to Soviet primacy in the communist world, which saw the Russians seeking "neutral allies" against China and signaling their "desire to improve the atmosphere of [Soviet] relations with the West."[124] Nixon's diplomatic maneuvers whittled down Beijing's as well as Moscow's reasons for supporting Hanoi's war against the United States. Eventually, despite the tenacity of North Vietnam's negotiators and military campaign, the Nixon administration got its settlement in the Paris Peace Accords of January 1973. The accords did cede some 40 percent of South Vietnam to the communists, which may have seemed no great victory for the United States. Yet, most importantly for Nixon's purposes, the United States could finally exit the war—let the Vietnamese on either side of the seventeenth parallel, those fleeing, fighting, and dying, be damned; let these dominoes fall, for those upholding the arc of containment stood strong, would endure.

Cool War

On March 29, 1973, the last cohort of U.S. troops left Vietnam. That day, several hundred South Vietnamese civilians looted the U.S. departure camp in Saigon while South Vietnamese soldiers stood by or pocketed the belongings of the departing U.S. troops for themselves. One U.S. officer later complained to reporters: "They took anything that wasn't tied down." A few dozen G.I.s waiting for their planes on the tarmac had to reenter the camp to drive the mob out.[125] Why they bothered was unclear, since none were staying behind.

ASEAN leaders did not wait long to remind U.S. officials that in manifold ways, the United States could neither leave Southeast Asia nor retreat from the Pacific. In an April 1973 speech to U.S. businessmen, Singapore's foreign minister Sinnathamby Rajaratnam warned against allowing their nation to shrink into "little America—not interested in the world . . . shut[ting] her doors [to] become a hermit nation." He exhorted them to struggle again for influence in Southeast Asia, but this time through "economic competition." This enterprise, he said, matched the "mood of the people" throughout the region. According to Rajaratnam, Southeast Asians' experience of postcolonial "poverty, uncertainty and turmoil" made them eager for the "good things of life." He assured his listeners that, via gifts of "technology, expertise, finance, organization and managerial skills," the United States would easily win the "cool war" for Southeast Asia.[126]

Old things were being made new. Rajaratnam's speech was a variation on the domino diplomacy that ASEAN statesmen had deployed repeatedly in dealings with U.S. leaders. It combined calculated taunts, wheedling, and encouragement and was directed squarely at U.S. decision makers within and outside Washington. Knowing his words would reach the ears of U.S. elites, Rajaratnam had once posed a version of this question to the International Press Institute: "Even if the Americans decide to leave Asia alone, would Asia leave the Americans alone?" The United States could not "really opt out of Asia," he argued, for this meant the United States would "opt out of the Pacific" and thereby "opt out of world history."[127]

As his regional counterparts had done incessantly before and during the Vietnam War, Rajaratnam kept inviting the United States deeper into Southeast Asia. In September 1973, while speaking to the Asia Society in New York, he again asked the United States to conduct a "second intervention" in the region. He flattered and cajoled, requesting the "skills and resources in which the Americans are unbeatable." He called for the "massive export and deployment of modern technological skills, financial resources, industrial expertise, commercial and organizational know-how [that] the Americans possess[ed] in abundance."[128]

Cold War or cool war, the United States had pursued versions of this imperial project in Southeast Asia since colonizing the Philippines by force. Following the humiliating U.S. military defeat in Vietnam, Rajaratnam's speeches were an exercise in pretending that a benign U.S. empire of trade and business with Southeast Asia could exist separate from, and unsullied by, the United States' war machine (and its bloody legacy). The invitation Rajaratnam extended to the United States, on behalf of Singapore and the ASEAN countries, was simply to join in this post–Vietnam War pretense.

The United States embraced the invitation. U.S.-ASEAN economic relations would continue to expand rapidly. By the mid-1970s, U.S. trade across the Pacific would exceed in volume what business the United States did with its Atlantic partners.[129]

Meanwhile, South Vietnam slid into disaster. The chaos and spectacle of Saigon's fall in April 30, 1975, coupled with U.S. officials racing to evacuate the country and bring various South Vietnamese with them, removed the most conspicuous sign of the U.S. imperial misadventure in Southeast Asia.

Much else remained in view, however, not least the tragedy of those U.S. soldiers who had gone to their graves in Vietnam, joined by their allies from South Korea, Australia, Thailand, and more, as well as the estimated two million Vietnamese who perished during the U.S. war. The fallout of U.S. intervention in Vietnam unleashed terrible bloodbaths in Laos and Cambodia.

Then again, all these horrors, trailing the tortured retreat of U.S. forces from Indochina, obscured how the United States' hegemony in Southeast Asia had outlasted its fiasco in Vietnam. The arc of containment circling the carnage had grown stronger from feeding the United States' Cold War and feeding off it. While the dominoes of Indochina fell to communism, those that made up ASEAN, the "friendly kings" long rid of their meddlesome rivals, did not.

If held to account, the "friendly kings" might intone that these deaths bought time for the arc of containment to cohere and strengthen, the better to deflect Chinese, North Vietnamese, and Soviet ambitions on Southeast Asia. They would likely insist that such blood had not been shed in vain. It was a regrettably high price, but did the ends not justify the means? Was it wrong to prosper from the war, from fixing up the U.S. military transport planes that conveyed G.I.s to the killing fields, from military procurements that supported U.S. search-and-destroy missions? In low whispers the "friendly kings" might say it was better the conflict ravaged Indochina than our homes, better that we enjoyed the political and social stability that invited investment, spurred development, and gave our children books, not bombs. In the 1980s, these authoritarians made ASEAN a zone of peace and an economic miracle. And many of them held on to power so long, too long, because the United States tolerated, supported, and feted them; loved them because they hated communism.

The arc of containment, forged in the embers of colonialism and the crucible of the Cold War, had transitioned Southeast Asia from the colonial order through Anglo-American predominance into U.S. hegemony. The arc had ensured western imperialism would evolve and endure in the region despite the calamity of World War II. The "friendly kings" of Southeast Asia would say it was all worth it.

The "Reverse Domino Effect"

On May 6, 1975, Muhammad Ghazali bin Shafie, Malaysia's minister for Home Affairs (and former minister for External Affairs), broadcast over the radio his government's response to the recent fall of Saigon. Ghazali's speech borrowed familiar themes from the playbook of ASEAN's domino diplomacy. He equivocated, both attacking and affirming the domino theory. On the one hand, he declared that "to postulate that Malaysia will succumb to Communism simply because Vietnam became Communist is to ignore the vast differences" between both countries. Unlike the "American dominoes" of Indochina, he said, Malaysia's "internal order" was not a "function of American support"— the Malaysian state could, unaided, "resist aggression from any source." Furthermore, he argued, it was "simplistic" to consider the "loss of territory by any segment of the Free World" a "gain" for the communist bloc; the global order did not turn on the Cold War's zero-sum fictions. He insisted that, in fact, the domino theory had "provided the rationale" to "build the military machine of the United States" and justify U.S. intervention in Vietnam, where "no vital American security interest was involved."[1] Scholars have for years repudiated the domino theory with similar critiques.[2]

On the other hand, Ghazali made significant concessions to the domino logic. By the time of his broadcast, communist factions had triumphed in Cambodia and Vietnam, and the Pathet Lao was making terrific advances against the pro-U.S. government in Vientiane (which would fall in August). Malaysian leaders would have recalled how, in 1954, the Viet Minh's triumph over French forces had rejuvenated the Malayan Communist Party (MCP) for a time. Furthermore, the MCP had designated 1975 "a new year of combat" in solidarity with the Indochinese communists.[3] The MCP's sporadic attacks from the Thai border, on their own, posed no existential threat to the Malaysian government. But the organization's persistence was concerning because the mostly Chinese MCP preached revolt against the conservative Malay-dominated political system. So, Ghazali acknowledged how developments in Indochina caused "nervousness" across the rest of noncommunist Southeast Asia. "Current events appear like so many portents of a dark and uncertain future," he said, and "the domino theory could well become—ironically—a self-fulfilling prophecy."[4] Perhaps Ghazali did fear that Malaysia's fate was truly intertwined with those of the "American dominoes"?

Ghazali's vacillations were deliberate. As other ASEAN statesmen had done repeatedly during the U.S. war in Vietnam, he underscored the exceptional resilience of his own government while gesturing at the region's interconnected insecurity. Which is to say that his speech was meant for not just Malaysia's citizens but also its western allies, the United States in particular. His message reprised earlier ASEAN admonitions: Washington must remain dedicated to all its Southeast Asian allies, whether strong (like Malaysia) or not (meaning: the others), else the weakest members of ASEAN would capitulate to communism and undermine the entire arc of containment. To ensure the United States paid heed, Ghazali quickly had his speech published in *Survival: Global Politics and Security*, a journal of the International Institute for Strategic Studies, a British think-tank concerned with Anglo-American foreign policy. Also, he likely pestered U.S. diplomatic staff in Kuala Lumpur to tune in to his broadcast at the scheduled time and flooded their in-trays with transcripts later. These efforts paid off. Within days, U.S. ambassador to Malaysia Francis Underhill mentioned Ghazali's "widely publicized speech on 'the domino theory'" to Secretary of State Henry Kissinger.[5] Soon after, Philip Habib, assistant secretary of state for East Asian and Pacific affairs, visited with Ghazali and Prime Minister Tun Abdul Razak to hear them out on U.S.-Southeast Asian affairs.[6]

In effect, Ghazali's speech composed a ritual invitation to his U.S. hegemon. It was an entreaty for Washington to dispatch an imperial envoy to a distant satrapy, for the "friendly king" resident there and his superpower patron to renew their commitment to each other and, by extension, to informal U.S. empire. For good measure, Ghazali's broadcast warned U.S. leaders against letting their "present strategic retreat in Indochina" become a "strategic rout worldwide."[7]

By mid-June 1975, Habib returned from visiting U.S. allies (including Ghazali) in Southeast Asia, reporting that ASEAN leaders were past the "initial

Coda

shock" of North Vietnam's victory. Now, Habib explained, they exuded "hope"—he had underlined the word for emphasis—that the United States would "be able to devote more attention to the remainder of the area." He stated that while ASEAN leaders still worried about Washington's resolve, all expressed a "uniform desire that the U.S. play a supporting—and deterrent—role in the region." In addition, he observed that ASEAN had emerged as a "mechanism for security cooperation," for each ASEAN leader had told Habib that he wanted continued U.S. collaboration with his regional organization: Lee Kuan Yew requested "selective but vital assistance"; Suharto insisted the United States play "a discreet but active role"; Thai prime minister Kukhrit Pramoj sought U.S. "security assistance"; Ferdinand Marcos affirmed the "essential" U.S.-Philippine alliance; Razak called for "quiet American support" (apparently unfamiliar with Graham Greene's novel).[8] In so doing, each man acquiesced to U.S. hegemony in Southeast Asia; each extended an invitation to empire.

Washington needed little encouragement to accept. The administration of Gerald Ford, like its predecessors, had the larger region in view. Ford's advisers were certainly alive to the new opportunities for further consolidating U.S. influence beyond Vietnam. The NSC, for one, had established that "most Asian countries are reacting to the Indochina debacle not by turning away from us . . . but by drawing closer."[9] By July 1975, Kissinger and the NSC found "virtually every Asian Embassy in Washington [was] spending more effort on the Hill" to cultivate relations with the United States against any "danger of increased Russian and Chinese activity." As one NSC staffer confided in Kissinger: "one might term it the 'reverse domino' effect."[10]

Reversals of the domino theory had been the prevailing motif of U.S. interference in Southeast Asia's fraught decolonization after 1945. Indochina's temporary embrace of communism was the exception that proved the rule of Southeast Asia's broader pro-U.S. trajectory.

For western imperialism to endure in this way, to evolve from formal colonialism to U.S. hegemony, the domino logic was key. In the early Cold War, U.S. officials as well as British and French administrators in Southeast Asia derived an embryonic domino theory from their common memories of Japan's war victories and fears of China and its diaspora, enabling them to meld their neocolonial agendas. By this, the United States opportunistically accepted the fading colonial powers' invitation to extend U.S. security and economic networks further into Asia.

To be sure, the putative author of the United States' containment policy, George F. Kennan, had objected to such deepening involvement in East and

Southeast Asia. Soon after articulating how the United States could "contain Soviet power" in a July 1947 issue of *Foreign Affairs*, he grew critical of what he considered the "militarization" of his ideas, manifest in the Truman administration's creation of the NATO alliance and determination to develop the hydrogen bomb.[11] Also, Kennan held—like many European and U.S. elites of the time—that the tropical climes of Southeast Asia could never produce sophisticated civilizations worthy of U.S. protection and commitment, that the region's indigenous nationalists were not (and might never be) capable of self-government. Southeast Asia, Kennan often expressed, must remain at the peripheries of U.S. interests, should not be part of U.S. containment strategy; it could be ceded to the communists without deleterious effect on the United States.[12] In August 1950, Kennan wrote Secretary of State Dean Acheson, insisting that the present course of U.S. policy in the Far East was "little promising" and "fraught with danger." He suggested U.S. retrenchment from Japan and Korea; advised against backing the "basically hopeless" French in Indochina; lambasted Washington's antagonism toward Beijing, writing that this position was "almost sure to run us into serious conflict with other Asian countries."[13] But Kennan's influence over U.S. policy had waned considerably by then. He was on his way out of the State Department, having been rapidly sidelined over the past year by Acheson and the rising star of Paul Nitze, the author of NSC-68.[14]

More to the point, Kennan had misjudged U.S. policy toward the Chinese communists and Southeast Asian nationalism. Indeed, conservative nationalists of Southeast Asia from the 1950s onward readily solicited U.S. support for their resistance to China, their suppression of Chinese-influenced socialist movements at home, and (in many cases) their persecution of ethnic Chinese minorities to satisfy the communalism of their nation's majorities. The domino principles, infused with anti-Chinese prejudice, allowed U.S. leaders and their Southeast Asian allies to blend their goals. True, Japan's wartime ascendancy in the region had interrupted the continuity of western imperialism. But it had been brief, not so pivotal a turn. The collapse of South Vietnam was even less consequential, producing instead another occasion for reinforcing U.S.-ASEAN relations. While Vietnam burned, the United States and ASEAN coiled the arc of containment more tightly around the South China Sea. As Ghazali had said, the domino theory "provided the rationale" for the prodigious expansion of U.S. power in Southeast Asia. Habib's trip through the region duly cycled through the established routines of collecting allies' (reissued) invitations to empire.

So, as the United States stood at the threshold of its bicentennial, Washington prepared to recommit to its imperial networks in the Asia Pacific. U.S. policymakers had already absorbed, and concurred with, their allies' many exhortations to do so. These apologetics for U.S. empire filled the "first comprehensive review" of "U.S. Policy Interests in the Asian-Pacific Area" since the fall of Saigon, a study produced by former U.S. ambassador to Thailand William R. Kintner (onetime career army officer and, later, a political scientist at the University of Pennsylvania). The NSC received Kintner's "voluminous" tome in January 1976, which included a seventy-six-page summary and a ten-page executive summary—its complete edition "occupied a third of a file drawer."[15]

Kintner's study held that the United States was permanently "intertwined" with Asia, "where the future of half the world's population, much of the world's resources, and important U.S. economic interests are at stake." According to Kintner's study, "deep U.S. involvement" in the region had "bought valuable time" for the ASEAN countries to stabilize their economies and political systems. He recommended continued U.S. assistance to ASEAN such that it matured into a "cohesive indigenous force for stability in Southeast Asia." These were familiar themes. They had circulated so long back and forth between the United States and its allies that they effectively spoke as one, their mutual goal to ensure the United States remained the hegemon of the Pacific. As such, Kintner urged that U.S. business efforts "measurably contribute to the economic development" of Asian countries (read: shoring up their pro-U.S. authoritarian leaders). He proposed that Washington keep Southeast Asia's vast resources open to U.S. allies like Japan, for the United States harbored a "significant interest" in Japan's economic success and capacity to act as a locomotive for Asian development. Importantly, he advised that the United States retain "close ties" with Indonesia, Malaysia, and Singapore "to ensure continued freedom of transit through the Straits of Malacca." It was "obvious," he remarked, that the United States and Japan had vital economic interests moving through these straits, not to mention the U.S. military's need for "free passage" to project power on both sides of the straits, into the Indian Ocean and the South China Sea. On top of these, Kintner counseled that the United States not withdraw its military power from Thailand and the Philippines, and must encourage Australia and New Zealand to maintain a security relationship with Malaysia and Singapore.[16] Three decades from the end of World War II, ASEAN and the United States, as well as U.S. allies in the Asia Pacific, had become inextricably linked in interconnected security.

Thus, the United States exited Vietnam not into decline but predominance in the wider region. By the time communist forces triumphed in Indochina, the arc of containment had for nearly a decade presided over most of Southeast Asia's resources and peoples as well as ensconced its states within the U.S. orbit. As one Singaporean diplomat would remind U.S. policymaking elites in the late 1970s, ASEAN had stayed resolutely on "the same side of the fence" as the United States, ensuring the "predicted fall of ASEAN dominoes did not materialize."[17] Rather, Soviet and Chinese influence had been mostly confined within Indochina. Per the crude calculus of a zero-sum game, the United States had won the Cold War in Southeast Asia.

Would that it was so simple. The history of what the United States and its Southeast Asian collaborators won is laced with a chronicle of loss. The anticommunist nationalists of ASEAN stifled their countrymen's political freedoms for years, citing the exigencies of the Cold War when quashing their domestic rivals with instruments of control inherited from their colonial predecessors. This process was brutal, often deadly. And the peoples living in the arc of containment, for self-preservation, for prosperity and progress, were complicit. Thereby, the ASEAN nations saw their moderate leftist movements eviscerated, and their democratic development stunted, while their rightward course fueled the bloodiest years of the United States' war in Vietnam. The present U.S. hegemony in Southeast Asia arose from these origins.

In this new century, though, China's resurgence poses a challenge to this state of affairs. Emboldened by its economic power and formidable military, Beijing has begun pushing against the limits of its sphere of influence in Southeast Asia. As U.S. leaders today mull their responses to the rise of China, the arc of containment comes back into play, and Southeast Asians return once more to the frontlines of this old rivalry between giants. The record of the Cold War shows only that the next cataclysm will bathe Southeast Asia in more blood. Surely those multitudes sacrificed to bring forth U.S. empire from the decaying colonial order would implore us to seek a different path. Their silence is deafening.

Acknowledgments

This project has incurred many debts. I would not have been able to conduct my multiarchival work without generous support from several institutions. The W. Stull Holt Dissertation Research Fellowship from the Society for Historians of American Foreign Relations (SHAFR) supported my research at the National Archives of the United Kingdom, the Durham University Library, and the Institute of Southeast Asian Studies (ISEAS)–Yusof Ishak Institute in Singapore. I was able to conduct archival research in the United States, Malaysia, and Singapore, as well as revise my book manuscript, with support from the Department of History at Northwestern University, the Rajawali Foundation, and a postdoctoral fellowship with the Nicholas D. Chabraja Center for Historical Studies. At Yale University, support from the Henry Chauncey Jr. Postdoctoral Fellowship with International Security Studies enabled me to work on revisions of my manuscript. I completed these revisions at the Nanyang Technological University, Singapore, with support from the university's Start-Up Grant No. M4081896.100.

I am much obliged for the guidance of the dedicated archivists and librarians at Durham University, the Imperial War Museum of the United Kingdom, the ISEAS–Yusof Ishak Institute, the National Archives of Singapore, the National University of Singapore, and the presidential libraries of Harry Truman, Dwight Eisenhower, John F. Kennedy, Lyndon B. Johnson, Richard Nixon, Gerald R. Ford, and Jimmy Carter.

I have been able to present my research at conferences in the United States, the United Kingdom, and Canada thanks to funding from the SHAFR

Diversity and International Fellowship, the Buffett Institute at Northwestern University, and postdoctoral fellowships from the Chabraja Center and Yale's Brady-Johnson Grand Strategy Program. Such opportunities to share my work with other scholars were invaluable. In 2013, I was fortunate enough to present my paper at the London School of Economics' Cold War Research Seminar, and the feedback from Antony Best, Luc Brunet, Tanya Harmer, Matthew Jones, and Arne Westad helped me turn that paper into a prize-winning article in the *Journal of American–East Asian Relations* (*JAER*). Portions of that 2014 article, "The Domino Logic of the Darkest Moment: The Fall of Singapore, the Atlantic Echo Chamber and 'Chinese Penetration' in U.S. Cold War Policy toward Southeast Asia," appear in this book with the permission of *JAER*'s publisher, Koninklijke Brill NV. A paper I presented at a conference of the Association of Southeast Asian Studies of the United Kingdom in 2016 developed into an article for *Diplomatic History*.

Many excellent scholars offered me indispensable advice, encouragement, and new opportunities as I prepared this book for publication: Pierre Asselin, Alice Ba, Jonathyne Briggs, the late Cheah Boon Kheng, Daniel Chua, Deborah Cohen, Nick Cullather, Craig Daigle, Ralph Emmers, Elzbieta Foeller-Pituch, John Lewis Gaddis, Laura Hein, Evelyn Hu-DeHart, Paul Kennedy, Jinah Kim, Lily Kong, William Roger Louis, Edward Miller, Nuno Monteiro, Lien-Hang Nguyen, Farish Noor, Vernie Oliveiro, Alex Owen, Kumar Ramakrishna, Johan Saravanamuttu, Pamela Sodhy, Geoffrey Stewart, Simon Toner, Tan Tai Yong, Tuong Vu, Keith Woodhouse, and Ji-Yeon Yuh. Special thanks go to my dissertation committee members, Michael Sherry, Daniel Immerwahr, and Jeffrey Winters, for their invaluable insights and critiques. Michael Allen, my mentor, was instrumental in my growth as a scholar— thanks, always. I am especially grateful to Ang Cheng Guan, David Engerman, Anne Foster, Mark Atwood Lawrence, S. R. Joey Long, Sandra Khor Manickam, Chris Miller, and Edward Miller, who read more of my evolving manuscript than anyone could have asked for and offered crucial advice. A word of thanks goes out also to my anonymous reviewers at Cornell University Press. I hope everyone will be pleasantly surprised at how the book turned out.

It was an honor to work with Mark Philip Bradley, who, as editor of the United States in the World series at Cornell University Press, gave wise counsel and recommendations as my manuscript moved toward print. The amazing people at Cornell University Press—Tonya Cook, Meagan Dermody, Karen T. Hwa, Stephanie Munson, and Bethany Wasik—helped in numerous ways to shepherd my manuscript on. Senior Editor Michael McGandy brought my prose to high polish. Mary Ribesky at Westchester Publishing Services offered indispensable editorial support. Hydar Saharudin, my graduate student, helped immensely with the work of proofreading the manuscript. My sincere thanks go to Ross Yelsey for the opportunity of including my book in the East Asian series of Columbia University's Weatherhead Institute.

I am deeply indebted to many good friends and family members who have supported me through graduate school, postdoctoral stints, and my job now in the Nanyang Technological University. Thanks go out to my colleagues and contemporaries for their scholarly advice, good cheer, friendship, and assistance: Andrew Baer, Laila Ballout, Igor Biryukov, Kyle Burke, Ian Chong, Kathleen Galo, Alex Hobson, Zachary Jacobson, Ashley Johnson, Donald Johnson, Matthew June, Charlie Keenan, Chien Wen Kung, Hayley Landman, Alexandra Lindgren-Gibson, Jack Loveridge, Michael "Marty" Martoccio, Beth Morrissey, Dani Nedal, Joe Parrot, Adam Plaiss, Nick Prime, Joy Sales, Ian Saxine, Veysel Simsek, Rachel Taylor, Elizabeth Vastaskis, and Taomo Zhou. I am especially grateful for friends who, near and far, have read my unwieldy drafts and offered feedback: Hygin Fernandez, Timothy Hia, Judith Jacob, Matthew Kahn, Eugene Lim, Jin Li Lim, Simeon Man, Gde Metera, Keith Rathbone, Shuo Yan Tan, and Evan Wilson. Thank you also to those who opened their homes to me, a traveling researcher in need of a place to sleep, home-cooked meals, and refreshing conversations (usually unrelated to history): Jin Li, Sushma Ananda and Dan Newton, Angeline Eng Radley, Hygin, Anthony and Lyn Cheong, Marten Bala, Dean and Melanie Johnson, Shuo Yan, Choon Leong and Lai King Seow, Yixian Ng, Sharanya Rao and Arvind Viswanath, Timothy Huang, and Mark and Loretta Phillips. I will always miss my circle of friends in Evanston who embraced my family and took care of us in every way: Dave and Keren Chookaszian, Ben and Stephanie Mangrich, Curtis and Stephanie Watson, Luke and Emily Anderson, Kent and Erin Wade-Lee, and Art and Shayna Counts. I am happy to have found a home in Nanyang Technological University among excellent colleagues and thank Liu Hong and Goh Geok Yian for making possible my return to Singapore.

Of course, my family shoulders the greatest burden, enduring my errands to the archives and the time consumed in the writing of this book. I am grateful for the tireless support of my parents, Foong Nghian and Evita, and my in-laws, Eric and Linda Cheng. But my greatest debt is to my wife and children. Hshia is the heart and soul of our family. Her strength, resourcefulness, and love have made this work. My children, Yong, Kai, and Rae, remind me constantly that there is a more important world beyond this book that demands my best. Thank you for making this journey with me. It is to my family that I dedicate this work.

All errors of fact and interpretation are my own.

Notes

Works frequently cited have been identified by the following abbreviations:

AJP	Alex Josey Private Papers Collection
CAB	Cabinet Office Files
CF	Country File
CO	Colonial Office
DDEL	Dwight D. Eisenhower Presidential Library
FCO	Foreign and Commonwealth Office
FOIA	Freedom of Information Act
FRUS	*Foreign Relations of the United States*
GRFL	Gerald R. Ford Presidential Library
HSTL	Harry S. Truman Presidential Library
ISEAS	Institute of Southeast Asian Studies Library, ISEAS-Yusof Ishak Institute
JFKL	John F. Kennedy Presidential Library
LBJL	Lyndon Baines Johnson Presidential Library
MDAP	Mutual Defense Assistance Program
NARA	National Archives and Records Administration
NSF	National Security File
POF	President's Office files
PREM	Prime Minister's Office Files
RG	record group
RMNL	Richard Nixon Presidential Library
SRP	Sinnathamby Rajaratnam Private Papers Collection
TARL	Tunku Abdul Rahman Library
TCL	Tan Cheng Lock Private Papers Collection
TNA	The National Archives of the United Kingdom
USDCO	U.S. Declassified Documents Online
WHO	White House Office

Introduction

1. Memorandum of Discussion at the 179th Meeting of the NSC, Friday, January 8, 1954, *Foreign Relations of the United States (FRUS)*, 1952–1954, vol. 13, pt. 1, Indochina, 1952–1954, ed. Neil H. Petersen (Washington, DC: Government Printing Office, 1982), Document 499.

2. Dwight D. Eisenhower, Inaugural Address, January 20, 1953; State of the Union Address, February 2, 1953; Address to American Society of Newspaper Editors, April 16, 1953; The President's News Conference, July 1, 1953; The President's News Conference, April 7, 1954, *The American Presidency Project*, last accessed November 20, 2017, www.presidency.ucsb.edu.

3. Kenneth T. Young Jr., "Report on Trip through Southeast Asia, Feb. 18—Mar. 21, 1955," Operations Coordinating Board 091.4 Southeast Asia file no. 3 (2) [March–August 1955], White House Office (WHO), NSC Staff Papers, 1948–61, Operations Coordinating Board Central Files Series, box 80, Dwight D. Eisenhower Presidential Library (henceforth, DDEL).

4. Staff Study by Operations Coordinating Board, "Communist Threat to American Interests in Singapore and Malaya and Possible Countermeasures," December 14, 1955, *FRUS*, 1955–1957, vol. 22, *Southeast Asia*, ed. Robert J. McMahon, Harriet D. Schwar, and Louis J. Smith (Washington, DC: Government Printing Office, 1989), Document 448.

5. NSC, U.S. Policy in Mainland Southeast Asia: Singapore, November 3, 1959, 1–2, WHO, NSC Staff Papers, 1948–61, Disaster file, box 55, Southeast Asia (2), DDEL. This document was declassified in 2014.

6. Robert J. McMahon, *The Limits of Empire: The United States and Southeast Asia since World War II* (New York: Columbia University Press, 1999), 102–3.

7. Cable from Eisenhower to His Majesty [Paramount Ruler of the Federation of Malaya], July 26, 1960, WHO, Office of the Staff Secretary, box 11, International Series, Malaya [April 1960–January 1961], DDEL.

8. CIA, "National Intelligence Estimate: Prospects for the Proposed Malaysian Federation," July 11, 1962, CIA FOIA (Freedom of Information Act) Reading Room, last accessed November 20, 2017, https://www.cia.gov/library/readingroom/docs/DOC_0000639900.pdf.

9. Memo from Hilsman to the Secretary, "Prospects for Malaysia," September 5, 1962, 7, Personal Papers of James C. Thomson, Jr. (Thomson Papers), box 22, General 1961–66, John F. Kennedy Presidential Library (henceforth, JFKL).

10. President's News Conference, February 14, 1963, *The American Presidency Project*, last accessed November 20, 2017, www.presidency.ucsb.edu.

11. Riley Sunderland, Memorandum RM-4170-ISA: Army Operations in Malaya, 1947–60; RM-4171-ISA: Organizing Counterinsurgency in Malaya, 1947–60; RM-4172-ISA": Antiguerrilla Intelligence in Malaya, 1948–60; RM-4173-ISA: Resettlement and Food Control in Malaya; RM-4174-ISA: Winning the Hearts and Minds of the People—Malaya, 1948–60 (Santa Monica, CA: RAND Corporation, September 1964).

12. The list of major studies concerned with U.S. intervention in Vietnam is long. Historian Robert McMahon's bibliographic essay from 1999 says it best: "The literature on the Vietnam War is dauntingly voluminous and tends to overwhelm virtually all other regional issues." See McMahon, *Limits of Empire*, 259–62. This literature is also more voluminous than that of noteworthy works concerned with U.S. intervention in the other states of Indochina, which include Seth Jacobs's study, *The Universe Unraveling: American Foreign Policy in Cold War Laos* (Ithaca, NY: Cornell University Press, 2012) and Kenton J. Clymer's *The United States and Cambodia, 1969–2000: A Troubled Relationship* (London: Routledge, 2004).

In contrast, works on the U.S. relationship with other Southeast Asian countries during the Cold War remain few and far between. Despite the fact that Indonesia was the fifth most populous country in the world in the 1960s and U.S. involvement there considerable, only a handful of recent historical studies exist, such as Bradley R. Simpson's *Economists with Guns: Authoritarian Development and U.S.-Indonesian Relations, 1960–8* (Stanford, CA: Stanford University Press, 2008) and John Roosa, *Pretext for Mass Murder: The September 30th Movement and Suharto's Coup d'Etat in Indonesia* (Madison: University of Wisconsin Press, 2006). Though the United States nurtured a very close relationship with the government of Thailand after World War II, the one major work of note on the subject is Daniel Fineman's *A Special Relationship: The United States and the Military Government of Thailand, 1947–58* (Honolulu: University of Hawaii Press, 1997).

Given America's intimate history with the Philippines, it is no surprise that there have been some important recent studies of the U.S.-Philippine relationship, notably Paul A. Kramer's *The Blood of Government: Race, Empire, the United States and the Philippines* (Chapel Hill: University of North Carolina Press, 2006). However, the best work on U.S.-Philippine relations in the Cold War remains Nick Cullather's *Illusions of Influence: The Political Economy of United States–Philippines Relations, 1942– 60* (Stanford, CA: Stanford University Press, 1994), which is more than two decades old. On U.S. engagement of Britain, in addition to Malaysia and Singapore, there is only Matthew Jones's *Conflict and Confrontation in Southeast Asia, 1961–1965: Britain, the United States and the Creation of Malaysia* (Cambridge: Cambridge University Press, 2002). Jones's ambitious study also delves into U.S., British, and Malaysian relations with Indonesia, though at its core it is concerned with the U.S.-British relationship. With respect to U.S.-Singapore relations, there are S. R. Joey Long's *Safe for Decolonization: The Eisenhower Administration, Britain and Singapore* (Kent, OH: Kent State University Press, 2011) and Daniel Chua's *U.S.-Singapore Relations, 1965–1975: Strategic Non-Alignment in the Cold War* (Singapore: National University of Singapore Press, 2017). Pamela Sodhy's *The U.S.-Malaysia Nexus: Themes in Superpower-Small State Relations* (Kuala Lumpur, Malaysia: Institute of Strategic and International Studies, 1991) is the major work on this topic with little of note since. With respect to U.S.-Burma relations, almost forty years passed between John Cady's *The United States and Burma* (Cambridge, MA: Harvard University Press, 1976) and Kenton J. Clymer's *A Delicate Relationship: The United States and Burma/Myanmar since 1945* (Ithaca, NY: Cornell University Press, 2015).

13. Roosa, *Pretext for Mass Murder*, 14.

14. Jacobs, *Universe Unraveling*, 1–6.

15. Clymer, *Delicate Relationship*, 2, 4. In an H-Diplo Roundtable, Clymer reiterates how "in American eyes Burma was the equal in importance, or at least near equal, of Indochina." See H-Diplo Roundtable XIX,12 on *A Delicate Relationship: The United States and Burma/Myanmar Since 1945*, last accessed November 28, 2017, http://www.tiny.cc/Roundtable-XIX-12.

16. McMahon, *Limits of Empire*, 259. The most recent and notable work on U.S. relations with Southeast Asia that adopts this "broad, regional focus" is Anne L. Foster's *Projections of Power: The United States and Europe in Colonial Southeast Asia, 1919–41* (Durham, NC: Duke University Press, 2010).

17. Mark Philip Bradley, *Imagining Vietnam and America: The Making of Postcolonial Vietnam, 1919– 1950* (Chapel Hill: University of North Carolina Press, 2000), 9.

18. Foster, *Projections of Power*.

19. Charles S. Maier, *Among Empires: American Ascendancy and Its Predecessors* (Cambridge, MA: Harvard University Press, 2006), 7, 25, 33, 35.

20. Paul Kramer, "Power and Connection: Imperial Histories of the United States in the World," *American Historical Review* 116, no. 5 (December 2011): 1348–91.

21. Geir Lundestad, "Empire by Invitation? The United States and Western Europe, 1945–1952," *Society for Historians of American Foreign Relations Newsletter* 15 (September 1984): 1–21. Maier refers to Lundestad's lecture (in the above newsletter of the Society for Historians of American Foreign Relations) in *Among Empires*, 7. See also Lundestad's later elaborations of the "empire by invitation" principle in, for example, "Empire by Invitation? The United States and Western Europe," *Journal*

of Peace Research 23, no. 3 (1986): 263–77 and "'Empire by Invitation' in the American Century," *Diplomatic History* 23, no. 2 (1999): 188–217.

22. Wen-Qing Ngoei, "The Domino Logic of the Darkest Moment: The Fall of Singapore, the Atlantic Echo Chamber and Chinese 'Penetration' in U.S. Cold War Policy toward Southeast Asia," *Journal of American–East Asian Relations* 21, no. 3 (2014): 215–45.

23. Leo Suryadinata, *China and the ASEAN States: The Ethnic Chinese Dimension* (Singapore: National University of Singapore Press, 1985), 10–11, 23. Suryadinata has written extensively along these lines concerning Malaysian and Indonesian Chinese. Also see Wang Gungwu's *The Chinese Overseas: From Earthbound China to the Quest for Autonomy* (Cambridge, MA: Harvard University Press, 2002). Wang has produced many more works on this subject. For a sampling of the literature on the Chinese diaspora in Southeast Asia, see G. William Skinner, *Chinese Society in Thailand* (Ithaca, NY: Cornell University Press, 1957); Fujio Hara, *Malayan Chinese and China: Conversion in Identity Consciousness, 1945–1957* (Singapore: National University of Singapore, 2002); and Philip A. Kuhn, *Chinese among Others: Emigration in Modern Times* (New York: Rowman & Littlefield, 2008). For useful comparisons between Indian and Chinese migration to Southeast Asia, see Sunil Amrith, *Migration and Diaspora in Modern Asia* (London: Cambridge University Press, 2012).

24. Amrith, *Migration and Diaspora*, 23, 42–43, 95–96.

25. See, in addition to Maier's *Among Empires*, Bernard Porter, *Empire and Superempire: Britain, America and the World* (New Haven, CT: Yale University Press, 2006) and Linda Colley, "Introduction: Some Difficulties of Empire—Past, Present, and Future," *Common Knowledge* 11, no. 2 (2005): 198–214. Earlier works of note include Donald Cameron Watt, *Succeeding John Bull: America in Britain's Place* (New York: Cambridge University Press, 1984); William Roger Louis, *The Special Relationship: Anglo-American Relations since 1945* (New York: Oxford University Press, 1984) and *Imperialism at Bay: The United States and the Decolonization of the British Empire, 1941–1945* (New York: Oxford University Press, 1978). For provocative discussions of how the United States may glean lessons in empire from the history of Britain's successes and failures, see Niall Ferguson, *Colossus: The Price of America's Empire* (New York: Penguin Books, 2004) and *Empire: The Rise and Demise of the British World Order and the Lessons for Global Power* (New York: Basic Books, 2002).

26. Fredrik Logevall, *Embers of War: The Fall of an Empire and the Making of America's Vietnam* (New York: Random House, 2012), xv–xvi.

27. Peter Busch, *All the Way with JFK?: Britain, the U.S. and the Vietnam War* (New York: Oxford University Press, 2003) and Jones, *Conflict and Confrontation in Southeast Asia*.

28. Detailed histories of the Malayan Emergency are understandably less concerned with the United States in Southeast Asia. Notable examples of this frequently studied subject include Anthony Short, *Communist Insurrection in Malaya, 1948–1960* (London: Muller, 1975; repr., Singapore: Cultured Lotus, 2000) and Richard Stubbs, *Hearts and Minds in Guerrilla Warfare: The Malayan Emergency, 1948–1960* (London: Oxford University Press, 1989; repr., Singapore: Times Academic Press, 2004). Stubbs discusses U.S. intervention in Korea and its bearing on Malaya in *Counter-Insurgency and the Economic Factor: The Impact of the Korean War Prices Boom on the Malayan Emergency* (Singapore: Institute of Southeast Asian Studies, 1974). Studies that compare the U.S. military campaign in Vietnam unfavorably against British-Malayan tactics are numerous, examples of which include Donald W. Hamilton, *Art of Counterinsurgency: American Military Policy and the Failure of Strategy in Southeast Asia* (London: Praeger, 1998) and John Nagl, *Learning to Eat Soup with a Knife: Counterinsurgency Lessons from Malaya and Vietnam* (Chicago: University of Chicago Press, 2005).

29. See J. R. Seeley, *The Expansion of England* (London: Macmillan, 1883). Seeley used this phrase to describe the growth of the British Empire in the nineteenth century. Bernard Porter maintains Seeley was being sarcastic. See Porter, *The Absent-Minded Imperialists: Empire, Society and Culture in Britain* (London: Oxford University Press, 2006), 18.

30. McMahon, *Limits of Empire*, 221–22. See also Michael H. Hunt and Steven I. Levine, *Arc of Empire: America's Wars in Asia from the Philippines to Vietnam* (Chapel Hill: University of North Carolina Press, 2012).

31. McMahon, *Limits of Empire*, 165, 175.

32. Odd Arne Westad, *The Global Cold War: Third World Interventions and the Making of Our Times* (New York: Cambridge University Press, 2005), 1–3.

33. Christopher E. Goscha and Christian F. Ostermann, introduction to *Connecting Histories: Decolonization and the Cold War in Southeast Asia, 1945–1962*, ed. Christopher E. Goscha and Christian Ostermann (Stanford, CA: Stanford University Press, 2009), 2, 7.

34. Pierre Asselin, *Hanoi's Road to the Vietnam War, 1954–1965* (Berkeley: University of California Press, 2013); Jessica M. Chapman, *Cauldron of Resistance: Ngo Dinh Diem, the United States and 1950s Southern Vietnam* (Ithaca: Cornell University Press, 2013); Edward G. Miller, *Misalliance: Ngo Dinh Diem, the United States and the Fate of South Vietnam* (Cambridge, MA: Harvard University Press, 2013); Lien-Hang T. Nguyen, *Hanoi's War: An International History of the War for Peace in Vietnam* (Chapel Hill: University of North Carolina Press, 2012).

35. Goscha and Ostermann, introduction, 2; Karl Hack, "Theories and Approaches to British Decolonization in Southeast Asia," in *The Transformation of Southeast Asia: International Perspectives on Decolonization*, ed. Marc Frey, Ronald Pruessen, and Tan Tai Yong (Armonk, NY: M. E. Sharpe, 2003), 121; Abu Talib Ahmad and Tan Liok Ee, introduction to *New Terrains in Southeast Asian History*, ed. Abu Talib Ahmad and Tan Liok Ee (Athens: Ohio University Press, 2003), xx. For older works that have explored the agency of Southeast Asian elites in the Philippines, Thailand, and Indonesia, see Cullather, *Illusions of Influence*; Fineman, *Special Relationship*; and Theodore Friend, *The Blue-Eyed Enemy: Japan against the West in Luzon and Java* (Princeton, NJ: Princeton University Press, 1988). More recent works on U.S.-Indonesian relations include Roosa, *Pretext for Mass Murder* and Simpson, *Economists with Guns*. Also see Long, *Safe for Decolonization*, for U.S.-Singapore relations during the Eisenhower administration; and Chua, *U.S.-Singapore Relations, 1965–1975*, for the Johnson and Nixon periods.

36. Andrew J. Rotter, *The Path to Vietnam: Origins of the American Commitment to Southeast Asia* (Ithaca, NY: Cornell University Press, 1987), 119–20; Betty Glad and Charles S. Taber, "Images, Learning, and the Decision to Use Force: The Domino Theory of the United States," in *The Psychological Dimensions of War*, ed. Betty Glad (Newbury Park, CA: Sage Publications, 1990), 58–59; Jerome Slater, "The Domino Theory and International Politics: The Case of Vietnam," *Security Studies* 3, no. 2 (1993/94): 188–89; Frank Ninkovich, *Modernity and Power: A History of the Domino Theory in the Twentieth Century* (Chicago: University of Chicago Press, 1994), 59–60, 65, 68, 192–93, 272, 276. Glad, Taber, and Slater studied the domino theory as political scientists. Ninkovich's prize-winning study, the one historical monograph on the subject, is more than two decades old.

See also Douglas J. MacDonald, "The Truman Administration and Global Responsibilities: The Birth of the Falling Domino Principle," in *Dominoes and Bandwagons: Strategic Beliefs and Great Power Competition in the Eurasian Rimland*, ed. Robert Jervis and Jack Snyder (New York: Oxford University Press, 1991), 112–44, for suggestions that U.S. policymakers remained sanguine about China's fall to the communists and preoccupied instead with Soviet advancements in Europe after World War II. For another political scientist's analysis of the manner by which analogies such as preventing "another Munich" prefigured and shaped U.S. policy toward Vietnam, see Yuen Foong Khong, *Analogies at War: Korea, Munich, Dien Bien Phu, and the Vietnam Decisions of 1965* (Princeton, NJ: Princeton University Press, 1992).

37. Ian F. W. Beckett, "Robert Thompson and the British Advisory Mission to South Vietnam, 1961–5," *Small Wars and Insurgencies* 8, no. 3 (1997): 41–63; Peter Busch, "Killing the 'Vietcong': The

British Advisory Mission and the Strategic Hamlet Program," *Journal of Strategic Studies* 25, no. 1 (2002): 135–62.

38. Robert W. Komer, *The Malayan Emergency in Retrospect: Organization of a Successful Counterinsurgency Effort* (Santa Monica, CA: RAND Corporation, 1972); Nagl, *Learning to Eat Soup with a Knife*; Advanced Research Project Agency, "Limited, Unconventional and Anti-Guerrilla Warfare Pacific Area," February 2, 1961, 11, folder "Far East: General, Doctrine and Tactics of Revolutionary Warfare, Chapters, 3/61," box 215, Kennedy Papers, National Security File (NSF)–Regional Security, JFKL.

39. See Tan Tai Yong, *Creating "Greater Malaysia": Decolonization and the Politics of Merger* (Singapore: Institute of Southeast Asian Studies, 2008) and "The 'Grand Design': British Policy, Local Politics, and the Making of Malaysia, 1955–1961," in *The Transformation of Southeast Asia: International Perspectives on Decolonization*, ed. Marc Frey, Ronald W. Pruessen, and Tan Tai Yong (Armonk, NY: M. E. Sharpe, 2003), 142–60. Also Karl Hack, *Defence and Decolonisation in Southeast Asia: Britain, Malaya and Singapore, 1941–1968* (Surrey, UK: Curzon, 2001); Matthew Jones, "Creating Malaysia: Singapore Security, the Borneo Territories and the Contours of British Policy, 1961–3," *Journal of Imperial and Commonwealth History* 28, no. 2 (2000): 85–109; and Anthony J. Stockwell, "Malaysia: The Making of a Neo-Colony?," *Journal of Imperial and Commonwealth History* 26, no. 2 (1998): 138–56.

40. Studies of the FPDA have focused mostly on its impact on Britain's Commonwealth Allies in Asia. For the FPDA in the context of British retrenchment, see Andrea Benvenuti, "The Heath Government and British Defense Policy in Southeast Asia at the End of Empire (1970–71)," *Twentieth Century British History* 20, no. 1 (2009): 53–73. For the Australian response to British retrenchment, see Andrea Benvenuti, "The British Military Withdrawal from Southeast Asia and Its Impact on Australia's Cold War Strategic Interests," *Cold War History* 5, no. 2 (2005): 189–210; "The British Are 'Taking to the Boat': Australian Attempts to Forestall Britain's Military Disengagement from Southeast Asia, 1965–1966," *Diplomacy & Statecraft* 20, no. 1 (2009): 86–106; and Andrea Benvenuti and Moreen Dee, "The Five Power Defence Arrangements and the Reappraisal of British and Australian Policy Interests in Southeast Asia, 1970–5," *Journal of Southeast Asian Studies* 41, no. 4 (2010): 101–23. For Malaysian and Singaporean views of the FPDA, see Kin Wah Chin, *The Defense of Malaysia and Singapore: The Transformation of a Security System, 1957–71* (Cambridge: Cambridge University Press, 1983) and Ang Cheng Guan, "Malaysia, Singapore, and the Road to the Five Power Defence Arrangements (FPDA), July 1970–November 1971," *War & Society* 30, no. 3 (2011): 207–25.

Daniel Chua's article "America's Role in the Five Power Defence Arrangement: Anglo-American Power Transition in Southeast Asia, 1967–1971," *International History Review* 39, no. 4 (2017): 615–37, examines how the United States offered aid and incentives to, as well as pressured, Australia and New Zealand to embrace the FPDA proposal. He rightly suggests that a broader power transition between Britain and the United States was underway in Southeast Asia but does not explore how the FPDA facilitated the transition by undermining the USSR's ambitions in the region.

Scholarly work on Soviet policy in Southeast Asia is sparse and dated, noting that the FPDA obstructed Moscow's ambitions but never delving into how this, in turn, shaped U.S. prospects in the region. See Leszek Buszynski, *Soviet Foreign Policy and Southeast Asia* (London: Croom Helm, 1986); R. A. Longmire, *Soviet Relations with South East Asia: An Historical Survey* (New York: Kegan Paul International, 1989); and Bilveer Singh, *Soviet Relations with ASEAN* (Singapore: National University of Singapore Press, 1989).

41. Eisenhower, President's News Conference, May 12, 1954; *The American Presidency Project*, last accessed April 27, 2018, www.presidency.ucsb.edu.

1. Darkest Moment

1. "Drive on Singapore," *New York Times*, December 8, 1941.

2. Frank L. Kluckhohn, "Guam Bombed; Army Ship Is Sunk," *New York Times*, December 8, 1941; "U.S. and Japs at War," *Chicago Daily Tribune*, December 8, 1941; John Burton, *Fortnight of Infamy: The Collapse of Allied Airpower West of Pearl Harbor* (Annapolis, MD: Naval Institute Press, 2006), 91, 324n4. Burton states that in 1941, Hawaiian time was thirty minutes behind its current setting. Thus, midnight on December 8, 1941, for Malaya and Singapore would have been 5:30 a.m. on December 7 in Hawaii. Pearl Harbor was attacked at 7:55 a.m., Hawaii time.

3. Brian P. Farrell, "Bitter Harvest: The Defense and Fall of Singapore," in *Between Two Oceans: A Military History of Singapore from First Settlement to Final British Withdrawal*, ed. Malcolm H. Murfett et al. (New York: Oxford University Press, 1999), 198.

4. Hanson W. Baldwin, "Japan's War Pattern," *New York Times*, December 9, 1941; "Japanese Gain Quick Successes in Far-Flung War of the Pacific," *New York Times*, December 21, 1941; "Bomb Hits Claimed," *New York Times*, December 10, 1941; James MacDonald, "Blow Staggers London," *New York Times*, December 11, 1941.

5. F. Tillman Durdin, "Tokyo Tanks Roll in Malay Jungle," *New York Times*, December 13, 1941.

6. Hanson W. Baldwin, "Three Weeks in the Pacific," *New York Times*, December 29, 1941.

7. Memo, "Report on the Fall of Singapore," April 25, 1942, 3, CAB (Cabinet Office Files) 66/24/7, The National Archives of the United Kingdom (TNA); Hanson W. Baldwin, "The Japanese in Malaya," *New York Times*, January 14, 1942; "The International Situation," *New York Times*, December 30, 1941; Christopher Bayly and Tim Harper, *Forgotten Armies: Britain's Asian Empire and the War with Japan* (Cambridge, MA: Belknap Press, 2005), 116.

8. "Drive on Singapore," *New York Times*, December 20, 1941.

9. Hanson W. Baldwin, "Defeat at Singapore," *New York Times*, February 12, 1942; Baldwin, "Japan's War Pattern"; Paul Gordon Lauren, *Power and Prejudice: The Politics and Diplomacy of Racial Discrimination* (Boulder, CO: Westview, 1988), 131–32.

10. John Dower, *War without Mercy: Race and Power in the Pacific War* (New York: Pantheon, 1986), 9, 98–99, 112–17.

11. Robert P. Post, "Premier Is Somber: Calls Singapore Military Disaster," *New York Times*, February 16, 1942; James B. Reston, "Washington Sees Dire Blow in the East," *New York Times*, February 16, 1942.

12. "Japanese Rename Singapore Shonan," *New York Times*, February 18, 1942; "Japanese Troops Go on Parade in 'Shonan' Today," *Chicago Tribune*, February 18, 1942. Historian John W. Dower translates "Shonan" as "Radiant South" in Dower, *War without Mercy*, 213. There are variants of the name that Imperial Japan gave to occupied Singapore. The one familiar to Singaporeans is *Syonan-To*, which is translated as "Light of the South Island."

13. "Japanese Pour Ashore," *New York Times,* February 16, 1942; "Singapore to Sumatra," *New York Times*, February 16, 1942; "Japanese Closing Pincers on Java," *New York Times*, February 18, 1942.

14. Larry Rue, "Shall We Save Burma or Java? British Problem: Danger to Australia and China Admitted," *Chicago Tribune*, February 18, 1942; "Battles in Pacific Believed Nearing," *New York Times*, May 2, 1942; Alexander D. Noyes, "Market Falls on Corregidor Surrender," *New York Times*, May 11, 1942.

15. See Anne L. Foster, *Projections of Power: The United States and Europe in Colonial Southeast Asia, 1919–41* (Durham, NC: Duke University Press, 2010), esp. chaps. 1 and 5 and the conclusion.

16. Dwight D. Eisenhower, "The President's News Conference, April 7, 1954," *The American Presidency Project*, last accessed November 29, 2017, http://www.presidency.ucsb.edu/ws/?pid=10202.

17. Dower, *War without Mercy*, 9, 98–99, 112–17; U.S. State Department quoted in Marilyn Lake and Henry Reynolds, *Drawing the Global Color Line: White Men's Countries and the International Challenge of Racial Equality* (Cambridge: Cambridge University Press, 2008), 341.

18. Nathaniel Peffer, "Southeastern Asia in the Escrow," *Foreign Affairs*, April 1942, 505–6. Italics in original.

19. Dower, *War without Mercy*, 7.

20. Dower, *War without Mercy*, 308–11.

21. NSC-51: U.S. Policy toward Southeast Asia, July 1, 1949, U.S. Declassified Documents Online (henceforth, USDCO) (Gale document no. CK2349354016), 1–4, 5–6; Lake and Reynolds, *Drawing the Global Color Line*, 4–6; Dower, *War without Mercy*, 7. For discussions about the drafting of NSC-51, see Paul J. Heer, *Mr. X and the Pacific: George F. Kennan and American Policy in East Asia* (Ithaca, NY: Cornell University Press, 2018), Kindle Edition, chap. 5.

22. Fredrik Logevall, *Embers of War: The Fall of an Empire and the Making of America's Vietnam* (New York: Random House, 2012), 223.

23. Telegram, Minister in Thailand (Hugh Gladney Grant) to the Secretary of State, January 4, 1941, *FRUS*, 1941, vol. 5, *The Far East, 1941*, ed. Elizabeth A. Vary (Washington, DC: Government Printing House, 1941, 1956), 1. Compiled by John G. Reid (Chief of the Far East Section), Louis E. Gates, and Ralph R. Goodwin. Elizabeth A. Vary of the Division of Publishing Services proofread and edited vol. 5 under the general direction of Chief of Division Robert L. Thompson. Document last accessed September 1, 2018, http://digicoll.library.wisc.edu/cgi-bin/FRUS/FRUS-idx ?type=turn&entity=FRUS.FRUS1941v05.p0007&id=FRUS.FRUS1941v05&isize=M.

24. Telegram, Ambassador in Japan to the Secretary of State, February 7, 1941, *FRUS*, 1941, vol. 5, 62–63.

25. Letter, British Prime Minister (Churchill) to President Roosevelt, February 16, 1941, *FRUS*, 1941, vol. 5, 79.

26. Memcon, Minister to the Netherlands Government in Exile to Department of State, August 6, 1941, *FRUS*, 1941, vol. 5, 260–62.

27. Note, British Embassy to the Department of State, November 30, 1941, *FRUS*, 1941 vol. 5, 360.

28. Letter, Lauchlin Currie to President Roosevelt, April 25, 1941, *FRUS*, 1941, vol. 4, *The Far East, 1941*, ed. Elizabeth A. Vary (Washington, DC: Government Printing House, 1956), 167–69. See note 23 above for details about the editorial team that worked on this volume and vol. 5.

29. Memo, Annex 1 to ABC-4 and JCCSs-1: Washington War Conference, American-British Strategy, December 24, 1941, 5, Combined Chiefs of Staff Conference Proceedings, 1941–5, box 1, Compiled Volume, "Arcadia," Dwight D. Eisenhower Presidential Library (henceforth, DDEL).

30. F. Tillman Durdin, "Foe Seeks to Ring Singapore; Plan to Take It Intact Seen," *New York Times*, December 28, 1941.

31. "British Fall Back in Malaya Despite Australians' Attacks," "Malaya Line Sags," *New York Times*, January 30, 1942; "Drive on Singapore," *New York Times*, December 20, 1941; "Australia Fears Jap Drive," *Chicago Daily Tribune*, February 16, 1942; "The Meaning of Disasters," *Time*, February 23, 1942, 20. The joint chiefs of the British and American military planned to "prevent further Japanese penetration of the Southwestern Pacific Theater" by "establish[ing] security of essential land, air and sea communication" including "approaches to Singapore . . . through the Dutch East Indies, to the Philippines." See Letter, Annex 1 to JCCSs-4: Proposed Draft of Instructions to the Supreme Commander, Southwestern Pacific Theater, December 24, 1941, 1–2, Combined Chiefs of Staff Conference Proceedings, 1941–5, box 1, Compiled Volume, "Arcadia," DDEL.

32. Baldwin, "Japan's War Pattern"; Baldwin, "Defeat at Singapore"; "Question over Singapore," *Los Angeles Times*, February 12, 1942.

33. "Editorial: The Battle of Singapore," *Los Angeles Times*, February 11, 1942.

34. "Singapore Falls to Japs," *Los Angeles Times*, February 16, 1942; "Question over Singapore"; "Singapore: Key to the Pacific," *New York Times*, January 4, 1942; "Britain's Fleet Secretly Built Up in Far East, Many Powerful Ships Face the Japs," *Chicago Daily Tribune*, December 8, 1941.

35. Andre De La Varre, "Singapore—Crossroads of the East (1938)," The Travel Film Archive, last accessed November 20, 2017, http://www.travelfilmarchive.com/item.php?id=10982&clip=n&num=10&startrow=0&keywords=Singapore.

36. *Alert in the East* (1941), British Movietone News, Ministry of Information, Great Britain, Colonial Film, last modified 2010, http://www.colonialfilm.org.uk/node/2467.

37. "Singapore Stormed," *New York Times*, February 15, 1942.

38. Reston, "Washington Sees Dire Blow."

39. "Sumatra, Too," *Time*, February 23, 1942.

40. "Japs Eye Indies and India," *Time*, February 23, 1942.

41. See Dower, *War without Mercy*.

42. Memo, Appreciation and Plan for the Defeat of Japan, August 18, 1943, 155–61; minutes, 1st Meeting of the President and Prime Minister with the Combined Chiefs of Staff, August 19, 1943, 402, Combined Chiefs of Staff Conference Proceedings, 1941–5, box 2, Compiled Volume, "Quadrant Conference August 1943," DDEL.

43. Summary Notes, Appendix: Appreciation and Outline Plan for the Defeat of Japan, August 18, 1943, 166, 169, Combined Chiefs of Staff Conference Proceedings, 1941–5, box 2, Compiled Volume, "Quadrant Conference August 1943," DDEL.

44. Minutes, First Plenary Meeting of Octagon Conference, September 13, 1944, 238–40, Combined Chiefs of Staff Conference Proceedings, 1941–5, box 3, Compiled Volume, "Octagon Conference September 1944," DDEL.

45. Michael S. Sherry, *In the Shadow of War: The United States since the 1930s* (New Haven, CT: Yale University Press, 1995), 32.

46. "Lessons of the Pacific," *New York Times*, February 17, 1942.

47. Paul Nitze, NSC 68: United States Objectives and Programs for National Security, April 14, 1950, last accessed November 20, 2017, https://www.mtholyoke.edu/acad/intrel/nsc-68/nsc68-1.htm.

48. Directive, Combined Chiefs of Staff to the Supreme Allied Commander (Southeast Asia), July 20, 1945, 176–78, Combined Chiefs of Staff Conference Proceedings, 1941–5, box 3, Compiled Volume, "Terminal Conference July 1945," DDEL.

49. Report, State Department—Joint Mutual Defense Assistance Program (henceforth, MDAP) Survey Mission to Southeast Asia, "Malaya," undated, 9; Report, U.S. Navy—Joint MDAP Survey Mission in Southeast Asia, "Malaya," August 17, 1950, 16, Papers of John Melby (hereafter, Melby Papers), box 12, Melby—Chronological File 1950 (August 1–15), Harry S. Truman Presidential Library (henceforth, HSTL).

50. Report, H. Merle Cochran to John F. Melby, "Indonesia: Information Desired by Survey Mission," September 22, 1950, 3, Melby Papers, box 12, "Melby—Chronological File 1950 (September 16–30), HSTL.

51. Memo, Secretary of State for Foreign Affairs to the Cabinet, November 26, 1949, CAB 129/37, 2–3, TNA.

52. CAB 129/37, 2–3.

53. "Defense Policy and Global Strategy—Report by The United Kingdom Chiefs of Staff," July 9, 1952, 13, PREM (Prime Minister's Office) 11/49, TNA. By 1949, the British government had decided that Hong Kong could not remain its choice outpost against communist China. Its proximity to the mainland and the ease with which it could be infiltrated by communist agents instead meant Malaya (for its rubber production representing Britain's largest dollar earner) and Singapore

(for its naval and air bases) were the more logical focus for Britain to preserve its imperial interests in the Far East. See Conclusions of Meeting, "China and Southeast Asia," March 8, 1949, CAB 128/15, TNA.

54. Sir William Strang, "Tour in South-East Asia and the Far East," March 17, 1949, CAB 129/33, 11.

55. NSC-51, 5–6.

56. For a study of the British role in convincing the United States to support the French, see Andrew J. Rotter, *The Path to Vietnam: Origins of the American Commitment to Southeast Asia* (Ithaca, NY: Cornell University Press, 1987). For the French role (as well as a discussion of Britain's) that few U.S. historians have studied, see Mark Atwood Lawrence, *Assuming the Burden: Europe and the American Commitment to War in Vietnam* (Berkeley: University of California Press, 2005).

57. Memo, Secretary of State for Foreign Affairs to the Cabinet, November 26, 1949, CAB 129/37, 4; telegram, Foreign Office to Washington, July 13, 1952, 1–2, PREM 11/49, TNA.

58. Among others, Jessup also visited Afghanistan, Burma, Formosa, India, Japan, and Pakistan.

59. Memcon, "Oral Report by Ambassador-at-Large Philip C. Jessup upon His Return from the East," April 3, 1950, *FRUS*, 1950, vol. 6, *East Asia and the Pacific*, ed. Neal H. Petersen, William Z. Slany, Charles S. Sampson, John P. Glennon, and David W. Mabon (Washington, DC: Government Printing Office, 1976), 68–76.

60. Memcon, Jessup, "Notes on Conference at Commissioner-General's at Bukit Serene (Johore Bahru)," February 6, 1950, *FRUS*, 1950, vol. 6, *East Asia and the Pacific*, 11–18.

61. Memcon, "Oral Report by Ambassador-at-Large Philip C. Jessup upon His Return from the East," April 3, 1950, 68–76; telegram, Ambassador in Thailand (Stanton) to the Secretary of State, February 27, 1950, *FRUS*, 1950, vol. 6, *East Asia and the Pacific*, 29–30. For the same expression "weak Thailand," see, for example, Durdin, "Tokyo Tanks Roll."

62. Oral history interview with Colonel R. Allen Griffin, conducted by James R. Fuchs, February 15, 1974, 59, Oral History Program, HSTL, last accessed November 20, 2017, http://www.trumanlibrary.org/oralhist/griffinr.htm.

63. Record, "Interdepartmental Meeting on the Far East at the Department of State," May 11, 1950, *FRUS*, 1950, vol. 6, *East Asia and the Pacific*, 87–92.

64. Memo, Rusk to Webb, Budgetary Plans for Fiscal Year 1951 for Assistance to Countries Eligible under Section 303 of the Mutual Defense Assistance Act, April 25, 1950, *FRUS*, 1950, vol. 6, *East Asia and the Pacific*, 83–84.

65. Schedule, Melby Mission in Indochina, July 17, 1950, Melby Papers, box 12, Melby Mission File, file no. 1, 1950 (May–July), HSTL.

66. Report, Melby and Erskine to Foreign Military Assistance Correlation Committee, Joint State-Defense MDAP Survey Mission to Southeast Asia, August 6, 1950, 4–5, Melby Papers, box 12, Melby Chronological File no. 1, 1950 (May–July), HSTL.

67. "Japanese Rename Singapore Shonan," *New York Times*, February 18, 1942.

68. For studies of how race featured in U.S. colonial administration of the Philippines, in particular the U.S. civilizing mission, see Foster, *Projections of Power*, esp. chaps. 2 and 3.

69. Dower, *War without Mercy*, 9, 10–11, 29, 72–73.

70. Sunil Amrith, *Migration and Diaspora in Modern Asia* (London: Cambridge University Press, 2012), 122–23. Amrith's figures are obtained from the findings of Virginia Thompson and Richard Adloff, *Minority Problems in Southeast Asia* (Stanford, CA: Stanford University Press, 1955). The figure of more than eight million is derived from calculating the combined total of the different Chinese populations in each Southeast Asian state. According to Amrith, Malaya and Singapore had about 2.95 million Chinese; Indonesia had about the same number; more than one million lived in

Thailand (though intermarriage and assimilation made this figure problematic); Indochina also had more than one million Chinese. Amrith does not mention the Chinese population of the Philippines. The U.S. State Department in 1949 estimated that there were three hundred thousand ethnic Chinese in the former American colony, which may have been on the low side. See chart, Mutual Defense Assistance Program, "South and Southeast Asia: Chart 11—Distribution of Chinese," undated, Papers of Harry S. Truman (hereafter, Truman Papers), box 40, White House Confidential File, State Department, Correspondence, 1949 [3 of 3], box 40, HSTL.

71. Amrith, *Migration and Diaspora*, 22–23. Amrith's account of all these historical processes of Chinese as well as Indian migration draws from the detailed studies of Philip Kuhn, *Chinese among Others: Emigration in Modern Times* (New York: Rowman & Littlefield, 2008); Leonard Blusse, "Batavia, 1619–1740: The Rise and Fall of a Chinese Colonial Town," *Journal of Southeast Asian Studies* 12, no. 1 (1981): 159–78; and Carl A. Trocki, *Opium and Empire: Chinese Society in Colonial Singapore, 1800–1910* (Ithaca, NY: Cornell University Press, 1990).

72. Amrith, *Migration and Diaspora*, 26–27, 38, 40–41. Here, Amrith relies on Jonathan D. Spence, *God's Chinese Son: The Taiping Heavenly Kingdom of Hong Xiquan* (New York: W. W. Norton, 1996); Adam McKeown, "Chinese Emigration in Global Context, 1850–1940," *Journal of Global History* 5, no. 1 (2010): 95–124; and Walton Look Lai, "Asian Diasporas and Tropical Migration in the Age of Empire: A Comparative Overview," *Journal of the Chinese Overseas* 5, no. 1 (2009): 28–54.

73. J. E. M. Mitchell (for Chief of the Intelligence Staff, British Pacific Fleet) to Staff Officer (Intelligence) Singapore Area, "The Post War Emigration Policy of China," August 27, 1947, 1, FCO (Foreign and Commonwealth Office) 141/16975, TNA.

74. Amrith, *Migration and Diaspora*, 47–48, 74–76. Also see Kaoru Sugihara, "Patterns of Chinese Emigration to Southeast Asia, 1869–1939," in *Japan, China and the Growth of the Asian International Economy, 1850–1949*, ed. Kaoru Sugihara, 244–274 (Oxford: Oxford University Press, 2005); and Kuhn, *Chinese among Others*.

75. See, for example, Ernest Koh, *Diaspora at War: The Chinese of Singapore between Empire and Nation, 1937–1945* (Leiden: Brill, 2013).

76. Dower, *War without Mercy*, 5; Memcon, "Oral Report by Ambassador-at-Large Philip C. Jessup upon His Return from the East," 68–76.

77. Central Intelligence Group, "Chinese Minorities in Southeast Asia," December 2, 1946, 1–2, 7, CIA FOIA, last accessed November 28, 2017, https://www.cia.gov/library/readingroom/docs/CIA-RDP78-01617A002800100004-6.pdf.

78. Chart, Mutual Defense Assistance Program, "South and Southeast Asia: Chart 11—Distribution of Chinese."

79. Lake and Reynolds, *Drawing the Global Color Line*, 9–10. See esp. chap. 1 for Chinese immigration to the United States and the interconnected construction and inspiration for white solidarity between the United States, Australia, and other white settler nations. Also see Erika Lee, *At America's Gates: Chinese Immigration during the Exclusion Era, 1882–1943* (Chapel Hill: University of North Carolina Press, 2003); and Alexander Saxton, *The Indispensable Enemy: Labor Immigration and the Anti-Chinese Movement in California* (Berkeley: University of California Press, 1971).

80. NSC-51, 1–4, 5–6.

81. CAB 129/33, 2.

82. Joint Intelligence Committee (Singapore), "The Chinese Factor in the Problem of the Security and Defense of Southeast Asia," February 20, 1947, 3, 7–9, FCO 141/16999.

83. Commissioner of Police, "The Emergency in Singapore," 1949, 5–6, FCO 141/16744.

84. "Emergency in Singapore," 1949, 5–6, FCO 141/16744.

85. Director (Special Branch, Singapore), "Emergency Legislation and the Emergency—Singapore," December 8, 1951, 2, FCO 141/14484.

86. Pan-Malayan Review of Political and Security Intelligence, December 8, 1948, 73, FCO 141/15654, TNA.

87. S. R. Joey Long, *Safe for Decolonization: The Eisenhower Administration, Britain and Singapore* (Kent, OH: Kent State University Press, 2011), 11.

88. "The Emergency in Singapore," 1949, 6, FCO 141/16744, TNA.

89. "Emergency Legislation and the Emergency—Singapore," December 8, 1951, 3–4, FCO 141/14484, TNA.

90. Governor of Singapore, "Singapore Situation Report for January 1951," March 10, 1951, 2, FCO 141/14484, TNA.

91. "Report for the Third Quarter, 1950," 1–2; "Report for the Fourth Quarter, 1950," FCO 141/14484, TNA.

92. Pan Malaya Review, April 1952, 2–3, FCO 141/15952/2, TNA.

93. Special Branch (Singapore), "Report for Second Quarter, 1950," 2, FCO 141/14484, TNA.

94. Grace Kennan, *Communism in the Chinese Middle Schools of Singapore* (Cambridge, MA: Center for International Studies at the Massachusetts Institute of Technology, February 1957), 6–7, 27, 39–41, Record Group (hereafter, RG with reference numbers) 469: Malaya Subject Files 1951–1961, box 10, Malaya—Subversive Activities, National Archives and Records Administration (NARA).

95. CIA, "Current Situation in Malaya," November 17, 1949, USDCO (Gale document no. CK2349007952).

96. Memcon, "Oral Report by Ambassador-at-Large Philip C. Jessup upon His Return from the East," 70–71.

97. Memcon, "Oral Report by Ambassador-at-Large Philip C. Jessup upon His Return from the East," 70–71.

98. Taomo Zhou, "Ambivalent Alliance: Chinese Policy toward Indonesia, 1960–1965," *China Quarterly* 221 (2015): 216–18.

99. Logevall, *Embers of War*, 223.

100. Jessup delivered his oral report to members of the State Department and other U.S. officials (including George F. Kennan) on March 23, 1950. The Griffin Mission visited Malaya and Singapore between March 16 and March 23, 1950. Griffin's itinerary included Indochina (March 6 to 16), Burma (March 23 to April 4), Thailand (April 4 to 12), and Indonesia (April 12 to 22). See Samuel P. Hayes, *The Beginning of American Aid to Southeast Asia: The Griffin Mission of 1950* (Lexington, MA: Lexington Heath Books, 1971). Hayes was Griffin's chosen deputy for the mission.

101. R. Allen Griffin, Report No. 2 of the United States Economic Survey Mission to Southeast Asia: Needs for United States Economic and Technical Aid in the Colony of Singapore and the Federation of Malaya, May 1950, iii–iv, 1–7, Melby Papers, box 9, Southeast Asia File, Miscellaneous, General—1950–1952, HSTL.

102. Griffin, Report No. 2 of the United States Economic Survey Mission to Southeast Asia, iv, 2–4.

103. Griffin, Report No. 2 of the United States Economic Survey Mission to Southeast Asia, iv, 2–4.

104. Griffin, Report No. 2 of the United States Economic Survey Mission to Southeast Asia, 1.

105. Griffin, Report No. 3 of the United States Economic Survey Mission to Southeast Asia: Needs for United States Economic and Technical Aid in Burma, May 1950, 1, 3, Melby Papers, box 9, Southeast Asia File, Miscellaneous, General—1950–1952, HSTL.

106. Griffin, Report No. 4 of the United States Economic Survey Mission to Southeast Asia: Needs for United States Economic and Technical Aid in Thailand, May 1950, ii, 3, Melby Papers, box 9, Southeast Asia File, Miscellaneous, General—1950–1952, HSTL.

107. Telegram, Stanton (U.S. Ambassador to Thailand) to Secretary of State, April 12, 1950, *FRUS*, 1950, vol. 6, *East Asia and the Pacific*, 79–81.

108. Griffin, Report No. 4 of the United States Economic Survey Mission to Southeast Asia, ii, 3.

109. Griffin, Report No. 5 of the United States Economic Survey Mission to Southeast Asia: Needs for United States Economic and Technical Aid in Indonesia, May 1950, ii, 2–3, 9, Melby Papers, box 9, Southeast Asia File, Miscellaneous, General—1950–1952, HSTL.

110. Transcript of Bukit Serene Conference, August 8, 1950, 1, 3, Melby Papers, box 9, Chronological File (1950 May–December), Melby Chronological File 1950 (August 1–15), HSTL.

111. Transcript of Bukit Serene Conference, 1, 3.

112. State Department, Report of the Joint MDAP Survey Mission to Southeast Asia— Thailand, September 30, 1950, 5, Melby Papers, box 12, Melby Chronological File 1950 (September 16–30), HSTL.

113. Transcript of Bukit Serene Conference, 1, 3.

114. Transcript of Bukit Serene Conference, 3–5.

115. "American Mission," *Malay Mail*, August 11, 1950.

116. "Appropriate Aid for Malaya to Be Recommended—Melby," *Singapore Standard*, August 10, 1950.

117. "Leader of U.S. Far East Military Aid Mission Makes Groundless Statement that Chinese Troops Threaten Indo-China. But Unable to Name Evidence to Support Statement," *Nan Chiao Jit Pao*, August 10, 1950. The colonial authorities of Singapore shut down the paper just over a month later on September 20 ("Singapore Chapter Banned," *Cairns Post* [Queensland, Australia], September 22, 1950).

118. Letter from Melby to John Davies (Policy Planning Staff, Department of State), August 31, 1950, 2, Melby Papers, box 12, Melby Chronological File 1950 (August 16–31), HSTL.

119. State Department, Report of the Joint MDAP Survey Mission to Southeast Asia—Malaya, undated, 1, 9, Melby Papers, box 12, Melby Chronological File 1950 (August 1–15), HSTL.

120. U.S. Navy, Joint MDAP Survey Mission in Southeast Asia: Malaya, August 17, 1950, 16, Melby Papers, box 12, Melby Chronological File 1950 (August 1–15), HSTL.

121. Logevall, *Embers of War*, 263; Michael James, "De Lattre of Rhine, Danube and Tonkin," *New York Times*, August 26, 1951.

122. "Vital Singapore Conference on Red Threat," *Examiner* (Tasmania), May 14, 1951; Memcon by the Assistant Secretary of State for Far Eastern Affairs (Rusk), August 29, 1951, *FRUS*, 1951, vol. 6, pt. 1, "Asia and the Pacific, 1951," ed. Paul Claussen, John P. Glennon, David W. Mabon, Neal H. Petersen, and Carl N. Raether (Washington, DC: Government Printing Office, 1977), 489.

123. CIA, "Consequences to the U.S. of Communist Domination of Mainland Southeast Asia," October 13, 1950, 1–2, CIA FOIA Reading Room, last accessed November 20, 2017, https://www.cia.gov/library/readingroom/docs/DOC_0000258837.pdf.

124. For a study of Indonesia's rise to independence in the immediate aftermath of World War II, see Robert J. McMahon, *Colonialism and the Cold War: The United States and the Struggle for Indonesian Independence, 1945–49* (Ithaca, NY: Cornell University Press, 1981). A more recent work on roughly this same period in Indonesian history is Frances Gouda and Thijs Brocades Zaalberg's *American Visions of the Netherlands East Indies/Indonesia: US Foreign Policy and Indonesian Nationalism, 1920–1949* (Amsterdam: Amsterdam University Press, 2002).

125. CIA, "The Break-Up of the Colonial Empires and Its Implications for U.S. Security," September 3, 1948, 2, 5, CIA FOIA Reading Room, last accessed November 20, 2017, https://www.cia.gov/library/readingroom/docs/DOC_0000258342.pdf.

126. NSC-51, 3, 5–6, 7, 10.

127. Eisenhower, First Inaugural Address, January 20, 1953, Bartleby, last accessed November 20, 2017, http://www.bartleby.com/124/pres54.html.

2. Patriot Games

1. NSC-51, 3, 5–6, 15. Acheson noted that Burmese communists were, for the time being, less troubling because they were "factionalized, less disciplined and far from completely Stalinized." See also Pamela Sodhy, "America's Melby Mission to Southeast Asia in 1950: The Case of Malaya," *Jebat* 18 (1990): 263–87.

2. Melby and Erskine, Joint MDAP Survey Mission to Southeast Asia, August 20, 1950, 1–4, Melby Papers, box 12, Melby—Chronological File, 1950 (August 1–15), Harry S. Truman Presidential Library (henceforth, HSTL).

3. Melby and Erskine, Joint MDAP Survey Mission to Southeast Asia, August 20, 1950, 1–4.

4. Malcolm MacDonald, Draft Response to Parliamentary Question: "The Future of the British in Malaya, 1949–50," March 13, 1949, FCO 141/14375.

5. See Cheah Boon Kheng, *Red Star over Malaya: Resistance and Conflict during and after the Japanese Occupation of Malaya, 1941–6* (Singapore: Singapore University Press, 1983, rev. ed. 2012), esp. chaps. 6, 7, and 8.

6. Melby, Joint State-Defense MDAP Survey Mission to Southeast Asia, December 6, 1950, 8, Melby Papers, box 12, Melby-Chronological File 1950 (November–December), HSTL.

7. Congressional Briefing Paper: Singapore-Malaya, March 18, 1957, RG 59, Subject Files Relating to Malaya and Singapore, 1950–8, box 22, 1957 Briefing Papers—General, January–June, NARA.

8. Paul Kramer, "Power and Connection: Imperial Histories of the United States in the World," *American Historical Review* 116 (December 2011): 1357, 1366, 1370.

9. Paul J. Heer, *Mr. X and the Pacific: George F. Kennan and American Policy in East Asia* (Ithaca, NY: Cornell University Press, 2018), Kindle Edition, chap. 5. Heer clarifies that NSC-51 was originally a paper of the State Department's policy planning staff entitled PPS (Policy Planning Staff)-51, drafted over the course of 1948 and the first half of 1949 by John Paton Davies Jr., George Kennan, the putative father of U.S. containment policy, and several others.

10. NSC-51, 2, 3–5, 13; CIA, "The Break-Up of the Colonial Empires: Its Implications for U.S. Security," September 3, 1948, 2, 5.

11. CIA, "Strategic Importance of Japan," May 24, 1948, 1, 3, USDCO (Gale document no. CK2349420615).

12. NSC-51, 4, 10, 17.

13. Heer, *Mr. X and the Pacific*, chap. 5. As Heer and other historians have pointed out, George Kennan harbored racist attitudes toward Southeast Asians and did not think the United States should be preoccupied with keeping the region from communist influence. Such condescension was rife among U.S. policymakers of the time.

Yet as my book shows, Acheson had no plans to cede Southeast Asia to the communist camp. The United States' deepening commitment to the French in Indochina and eagerness to cultivate relations with Thailand, Indonesia, and Burma all signal that Acheson's State Department did not share Kennan's fatalism. In any case, Acheson marginalized Kennan, who in turn stepped out of American policymaking circles by late 1950.

14. For U.S. policy in the Philippines, see Nick Cullather, *Illusions of Influence: The Political Economy of United States–Philippines Relations, 1942–60* (Stanford, CA: Stanford University Press, 1994).

15. Stanley Karnow, *In Our Image: America's Empire in the Philippines* (New York: Random House, 1989), esp. chap. 12.

16. Kramer, "Power and Connection," 1351, 1382.

17. For the so-called Bao Dai solution, see Mark Atwood Lawrence, *Assuming the Burden: Europe and the American Commitment to War in Vietnam* (Berkeley: University of California Press, 2005).

18. For detailed studies of the U.S. decision to support Diem, see Edward G. Miller, *Misalliance: Ngo Dinh Diem, the United States and the Fate of South Vietnam* (Cambridge, MA: Harvard University Press, 2013); Jessica M. Chapman, *Cauldron of Resistance: Ngo Dinh Diem, the United States and 1950s Southern Vietnam* (Ithaca, NY: Cornell University Press, 2013); and Seth Jacobs, *America's Miracle Man in Vietnam: Ngo Dinh Diem, Religion, Race and U.S. Intervention in Southeast Asia, 1950–7* (Durham, NC: Duke University Press, 2004).

19. For U.S. colonial policy in the Philippines and its cultivation of Filipino elites, see Paul Kramer, *The Blood of Government: Race, Empire, the United State and the Philippines* (Chapel Hill: University of North Carolina Press, 2006). For U.S. collaboration with other colonial powers in the pre-1941 period, see Anne L. Foster, *Projections of Power: The United States and Europe in Colonial Southeast Asia, 1919–41* (Durham, NC: Duke University Press, 2010).

20. See Theodore Friend, *Blue-Eyed Enemy: Japan against the West in Luzon and Java* (Princeton, NJ: Princeton University Press, 1988), esp. chaps. 3 and 4; and Kenton Clymer, *A Delicate Relationship: The United States and Burma/Myanmar since 1945* (Ithaca, NY: Cornell University Press, 2015), introduction and chap. 1.

21. Joint Intelligence Committee, Nationalist Movements in dependent territories in the Far East, July 10, 1947, 1, FCO 141/17034, TNA.

22. CIA, "Current Situation in Malaya," November 17, 1949, 1, USDCO (Gale document no. CK2349007952).

23. Paul H. Kratoska, "Dimensions of Decolonization," in *Transformation of Southeast Asia: International Perspectives on Decolonization*, ed. Marc Frey, Ronald Pruessen, and Tan Tai Yong (Armonk, NY: M. E. Sharpe, 2003), 17. Also see James P. Ongkili, "The British and Malayan Nationalism, 1946–57," *Journal of Southeast Asian Studies* 5, no. 2 (1974): 255–77.

24. Christopher Bayly and Tim Harper, *Forgotten Wars: Freedom and Revolution in Southeast Asia* (Cambridge, MA: Harvard University Press, 2007), 98–100, 130–36, 209–17. See also Cheah, *Red Star over Malaya*, chaps. 6, 7, and 8.

25. "Precis of the Basic Paper on the Malayan Communist Party," November 23, 1950, pt. 1, pt. 2, FCO 141/16835, TNA.

26. "Pan-Malayan Review," October 13, 1948, 33–34; "Pan-Malayan Review," September 1, 1948, 6, FCO 141/15654, TNA.

27. Mona Brand and Lesley Richardson, *Two Plays about Malaya* (London: Lawrence and Wishart, 1954), 142. The appendices of this book contain four authentic "Malayan guerrilla songs" translated from the Chinese that date between 1948 and 1953.

28. "Precis of the Basic Paper on the Malayan Communist Party," November 23, 1950, pt. 1, pt. 2, FCO 141/16835.

29. Sunil Amrith, *Migration and Diaspora in Modern Asia* (London: Cambridge University Press, 2012), 95, 124; Philip Kuhn, *Chinese among Others: Emigration in Modern Times* (New York: Rowman & Littlefield, 2008), 271, 287–89, 296–97; Taomo Zhou, "Ambivalent Alliance: Chinese Policy toward Indonesia, 1960–1965," *China Quarterly* (2015): 219.

30. "Appreciation of the Chinese Factor in the Defence of Southeast Asia, 1946–7," FCO 141/14359; letter, W. L. Blythe, "Malayan Communist Party," December 1950–January 1951, FCO 141/14485; "Communism in Southeast Asia, 1947–8," FCO 141/16943, TNA; CIA, "Current Situation in Malaya," 3–5. See also Fujio Hara, *Malayan Chinese and China: Conversion in Identity*

Consciousness, 1945–1957 (Singapore: National University of Singapore, 2002), for a discussion of why the MCP, at least until the height of the Emergency, did not perceive contradictions between its Malayan nationalism and statements that China remained its homeland.

31. James Wong, *From Pacific War to Merdeka: Reminiscences of Abdullah CD, Rashid Maidin, Suraini Abdullah and Abu Sam* (Kuala Lumpur, Malaysia: Strategic Information Research Division, 2005), 19; CIA, "Current Situation in Malaya," 3–5.

32. "Precis of the Basic Paper on the Malayan Communist Party," November 27, 1950, pt. 1, 2–3, pt. 2, 1–3, FCO 141/16835. Rashid Maidin, the first Malay to join the Malayan Communist Party in 1941, recounted decades later that the party leaders assigned him to organize and recruit Malays on an anticolonial and interracial platform. See Rashid Maidin, *The Memoirs of Rashid Maidin: From Armed Struggle to Peace* (Kuala Lumpur, Malaysia: Strategic Information Research Division, 2009), 13.

33. "Pan-Malayan Review," December 22, 1948, FCO 141/15654, TNA.

34. F. Brewer (Acting Secretary for Chinese Affairs), "The Chinese Problem in the Federation of Malaya," April 1955, FCO 141/7365; Report for the Foreign Office: "The Overseas Chinese in Southeast Asia," April 26, 1955, 3–8, 15–17, FCO 141/7363, TNA.

35. Sir Henry Gurney to Frank Gimson (copied to Malcolm MacDonald), April 30, 1949, 1–2, FCO 141/14548, TNA.

36. Malcolm MacDonald, "Broadcast in Singapore: The Conflict in Malaya," July 7, 1948, Malcolm MacDonald Papers GB-00330-MAC 97/1/1-5, Durham University Library.

37. See, for example, Lucian W. Pye, *Guerrilla Communism in Malaya: Its Social and Political Meaning* (Princeton, NJ: Princeton University Press, 1956) and *Lessons from the Malayan Struggle against Communism* (Cambridge, MA: MIT Center for International Studies, 1958); John A. Nagl, *Learning to Eat Soup with a Knife: Counterinsurgency Lessons from Malaya and Vietnam* (Chicago: University of Chicago Press, 2005).

38. Kumar Ramakrishna's *Emergency Propaganda: The Winning of Malayan Hearts and Minds, 1948–58* (Richmond, UK: Curzon, 2001), is likely the best work on the propaganda side of winning "hearts and minds." However, his valuable study is less interested in the rhetorical strategies of key players in the British-Malayan effort against the MCP. Presuming that the MCP and its supporters remained chiefly motivated by their economic welfare, Ramakrishna focuses on the practical rather than discursive work involved in defeating the MCP.

39. Amrith, *Migration and Diaspora*, 48. See also chap. 1 of this book.

40. S. R. Joey Long, *Safe for Decolonization: The Eisenhower Administration, Britain and Singapore* (Kent, OH: Kent State University Press, 2011), 61–65, esp. chap. 4.

41. MacDonald, "Broadcast in Singapore: The Conflict in Malaya," July 7, 1948 (MAC 97/1/2).

42. MacDonald, "Broadcast in Singapore," October 7, 1948 (MAC 97/1/63, 65).

43. MacDonald, "Broadcast Speech in Singapore," June 6, 1948 (MAC 96/8/41, 43).

44. MacDonald, "Broadcast in Singapore," October 6, 1948 (MAC 97/1/41, 43, 61–4).

45. MacDonald, "Broadcast in Singapore," October 6, 1948 (MAC 97/1/62). Italics mine.

46. Pan-Malayan Review, September 1, 1948, 3.

47. Pan Malayan Review of Political and Security Intelligence, October 27, 1948, 43, FCO 141/15654, TNA.

48. MacDonald, "Broadcast in Singapore," October 6, 1948 (MAC 97/1/ 63–4, 65, 68).

49. MacDonald, "[DRAFT] Memorandum on Relations between the Malays and Chinese in Malaya," February 8, 1949; Communities Liaison Committee Issues Communique, September 16–18, 1949 (MAC 18/2/9–10). According to the communiqué, those present at the meeting included E. E. C. Thuraisingham, Tan Cheng Lock, Lee Kong Chian, Sir Roland Bradell, Dato Onn bin

Jaafar, Mustaffa bin Osman, and Mohamed Eusuf bin Yusoff, among others. The communiqué was published in the *Singapore Free Press*. See "Charter for a Free Nation," *Singapore Free Press*, September 19, 1949.

50. Long, *Safe for Decolonization*, 61–64.

51. MacDonald, "[DRAFT] Memorandum on Relations between the Malays and Chinese in Malaya," September 16–18, 1949 (MAC 18/2/11).

52. Dato Onn bin Jaafar, "Address to General Assembly of UMNO," undated (MAC 18/2/11).

53. Letter, MacDonald to Tan, December 15, 1948 (MAC 22/4/48).

54. For Sino-Malay rivalry, see Cheah, *Red Star over Malaya*.

55. Extract from the *Singapore Standard* editorial "Knight of Malacca," January 1, 1952, folio 38 (172), Tan Cheng Lock Private Papers Collection (hereafter, TCL). Courtesy of Institute of Southeast Asian Studies (ISEAS) Library, ISEAS–Yusof Ishak Institute, Singapore.

56. Progress of Malayan Chinese League, August 11, 1948, folio 38 (96); On Revised Constitutional Proposal for Malaya, September 1947, folio 38 (Speeches 14), TCL.

57. MacDonald, "Notes on Talks with Dato' Onn," December 15, 1949 (MAC 18/1/9–10).

58. On Revised Constitutional Proposals for Malaya, September 1947, folio 38 (Speeches 14).

59. Letter, J. J. Paskin (Colonial Office) to Gurney, March 8, 1949, folder "Malayan Chinese Association," FCO 141/7395, TNA.

60. Letter, MacDonald to Gurney, March 21, 1949, folder "Malayan Chinese Association," FCO 141/7395.

61. Letter, Gurney to Colonial Office, April 4, 1949, folder "Malayan Chinese Association," FCO 141/7395.

62. "The True Malayan Spirit," August 1957, folio 38 (Printed Matters 144)/pp. 8–10, TCL. In this article, Tan said of the scrolls of Chinese lettering hanging in his house: "Unfortunately, I cannot read Chinese. . . . I have never been to China. . . . But I don't suppose I ever shall go. I am old and there is much to do in Malaya."

63. Speech at the Inaugural Meeting of the Proposed Malayan Chinese Association at Kuala Lumpur, February 27, 1949, folio 38 (21), TCL.

64. Speech at the Inaugural Meeting of the Malacca Branch of the Malayan Chinese Association at Malacca, March 11, 1949, folio 38 (22), TCL.

65. Speech at the Inaugural Meeting of the Proposal Malayan Chinese Association at Kuala Lumpur, February 27, 1949, folio 38 (21), TCL.

66. Letter, Secretary for Chinese Affairs (Federation of Malaya) to High Commissioner for Malaya, February 2, 1949, "Malayan Chinese Association," FCO 141/7935.

67. Speech at the Inaugural Meeting of the Proposal Malayan Chinese Association at Kuala Lumpur, February 27, 1949, folio 38 (21), TCL.

68. Speech at the Inaugural Meeting of the Proposal Malayan Chinese Association at Kuala Lumpur, February 27, 1949, folio 38 (21), TCL; MacDonald, "Draft: Parliamentary Question and Answer," March 13, 1949, "Future of the British in Malaya 1949–50," FCO 141/14375, TNA.

69. See Hara, *Malayan Chinese and China*, chap. 4.

70. T. N. Harper, *The End of Empire and the Making of Malaya* (London: Cambridge University Press, 1999), 260.

71. Speech at Squatter Resettlement Area, January 12, 1951, folio 38 (Speeches 34), TCL. See also Broadcast over Radio Malaya, Kuala Lumpur, January 15, 1950, folio 38 (Speeches 26); Address at Taiping and Ipoh on "The Chinese in Malaya," April 9 & 11, 1949, folio 38 (Speeches 23), TCL.

72. Speech at Squatter Resettlement Area, January 12, 1951, folio 38 (Speeches 34), TCL.

73. Harper, *End of Empire*, 260.

74. Speech at Squatter Resettlement Area, January 12, 1951, folio 38 (Speeches 34), TCL.

75. Cheah Boon Kheng, *Malaysia: The Making of a Nation* (Singapore: Institute of Southeast Asian Studies, 2002), 27–28.

76. Harper, *End of Empire*, 320.

77. Speech by Col. H. S. Lee at Chinese Assembly Hall, February 12, 1952, folio 38 (Speeches 43), TCL.

78. "Note on a Meeting between the High Commissioner and a Deputation from the MCA at King's House," June 18, 1953, 1, "Malayan Chinese Association, 1952–4," FCO 141/7478, TNA.

79. MacDonald, "Notes on Talks with Dato' Onn," December 15, 1949 (MAC 18/1/6).

80. "Notes on a Discussion concerning Consultative Liaison Committees," June 5, 1954, 1, "Malayan Chinese Association, 1952–4," FCO 141/7478.

81. Letter, Mohamed Ali bin Mohamed (Education Office, Kuala Lumpur) to Secretary for Defense (Federal Secretariat, Kuala Lumpur), August 8, 1949, "Malayan Chinese Association," FCO 141/7395, TNA.

82. Letter, Sir Henry Gurney (British High Commissioner to Malaya) to J. D. Higham (The Colonial Office), February 10, 1949, "Malayan Chinese Association," FCO 141/7395, TNA.

83. Telegram from Gurney to Colonial Office, March 1, 1949, "Malayan Chinese Association," FCO 141/7395.

84. Harper, *End of Empire*, 170–71.

85. "Grenade Wounds Tan Cheng Lock," *Straits Times*, April 11, 1949.

86. Telegram, Gurney to Colonial Office, April 18, 1949, "Malayan Chinese Association," FCO 141/7395.

87. Secretary for Chinese Affairs (Federation of Malaya), "The Public Relations Department and the Malayan Chinese Association," May 11, 1949, "Malayan Chinese Association," FCO 141/7395.

88. Letter from Chinese Secretariat Kuala Lumpur to Malayan Chinese Association, July 7, 1949, folio 38 (144), TCL.

89. Broadcast over Radio Malaya, Kuala Lumpur, January 15, 1950, folio 38 (Speeches 26), TCL.

90. Speech at the Inaugural Meeting of the Malacca Branch of the Malayan Chinese Association, March 11, 1949, folio 38 (22), 7, TCL.

91. Speech at Squatter Resettlement Area, January 12, 1951, folio 38 (Speeches 34), TCL.

92. Extract from the *Singapore Standard* editorial "Knight of Malacca," January 1, 1952, folio 38 (172), TCL.

93. Memorandum from Tan to James Griffiths (UK Secretary of State for the Colonies) and John Strachey (Secretary of State for War), May 19, 1950, 1, 8–9, Melby Papers, box 12, Melby-Chronological File, 1950 (May–July), file no. 1, HSTL.

94. Report, Melby and Erskine to FMACC (Foreign Military Assistance Correlation Committee), "Joint MDAP Survey Mission to Southeast Asia," August 20, 1950, 1–4, folder "Melby—Chronological File, 1950 (Aug 1–15)," box 12, Melby Papers, Chronological File 1950 (May–December), HSTL.

95. "American Mission," *Malay Mail*, August 11, 1950.

96. Sodhy, "America's Melby Mission," 279–80.

97. U.S. Air Force, Report of the Joint MDAP Survey Mission in Southeast Asia—Malaya, undated, 5, Melby Papers, box 12, Melby—Chronological File, 1950 (August 1–15), HSTL.

98. Letter from MacDonald to Melby, May 23, 1951, Melby Papers, box 9, Southeast Asia File, General—1950–1952, Miscellaneous File, HSTL.

99. Robert J. McMahon, *Limits of Empire: The United States and Southeast Asia since World War II* (New York: Columbia University Press, 1999), 56–57.

100. "Malaya an Example to Others," *Malay Mail*, August 15, 1950; "Indo-China Most Critical Spot in South-East Asia," *Malaya Tribune*, August 15, 1950.

101. "Specific Requests for Aid Made to U.S. Missions," *Straits Times*, August 15, 1950.

102. Melby, Joint State-Defense MDAP Survey Mission to Southeast Asia, December 6, 1950, 4, Melby Papers, box 12, Melby—Chronological File, 1950 (November–December), HSTL.

103. Melby and Erskine, Joint MDAP Survey Mission to Southeast Asia, August 20, 1950, 5.

104. Letter, Melby to MacDonald, August 29, 1950, 3, folder "Melby—Chronological File 1950 (August 16–31)," box 12, Melby Papers, Chronological File 1950 (May–December), HSTL.

105. A Note in the Handwriting of the Late Sir Henry Gurney, November 19, 1951, folio 38 (158), TCL.

106. "British Chief in Malaya Slain; Draws Red Fire, Saves Wife," *New York Times*, October 7, 1951; "British Chief in Malaya Gives Life to Save Wife," *Los Angeles Times*, October 7, 1951.

107. Cheah, *Malaysia*, 30.

108. Cheah, *Malaysia*, 26–27.

109. Tunku Abdul Rahman, "UMNO Thirty Years After"; "The Case for English and Malay," *Viewpoints* (Kuala Lumpur, Malaysia: Heinemann Books, 1978), 100, 193.

110. Harper, *End of Empire*, 266.

111. MacGillivray to Martin, "Federation of Malaya Monthly Political Report for February 1955," March 8, 1955, CO (Colonial Office) 1030/312, TNA.

112. Memorandum on the Economic Position of the Malays, February 5, 1953, folio 38 (143), 1–2, 6–7, TCL.

113. Zhou, "Ambivalent Alliance," 219.

114. Memorandum on the Economic Position of the Malays, folio 38 (143), 1–2, 6–7.

115. Memorandum on the Economic Position of the Malays, folio 38 (143), 7.

116. Far Eastern Department, "Monthly Emergency and Political Reports: Federation of Malaya and Singapore," November 15 to December 15, 1956, 1–2, CO 1030/248, TNA.

117. British Cabinet Meeting, "Malaya: Review of the Situation," April 6, 1955, 2, CAB 129/74, TNA.

118. MacGillivray to Martin, "Federation of Malaya Monthly Political Report for February 1955," March 8, 1955.

119. Pamela Sodhy, *The U.S.-Malaysian Nexus: Themes in Superpower–Small State Relations* (Kuala Lumpur, Malaysia: Institute of Strategic and International Studies, 1991), 166.

120. Joseph M. Fernando, "Sir Ivor Jennings and the Malayan Constitution," *Journal of Imperial and Commonwealth History* 34, no. 4 (2006): 577–79.

121. Fernando, "Sir Ivor Jennings," 577–80.

122. Visu Sannadurai, "The Citizenship Laws of Malaysia," in *The Constitution of Malaysia, Its Development: 1957–77*, ed. Mohamed Suffian, H. P. Lee, and F. A. Trindade (Oxford: Oxford University Press, 1978), 76–80.

123. Tunku Abdul Rahman, "Speech Given to the National Press Club, Washington D.C., October 27, 1960," 1–2, RG 59: Office of Secretary, Office of Chief of Protocol, Files of Visits by Heads of Government, 1928–76, box 77, Malaya: Visit of P.M. Tunku Abdul Rahman, MISC, October–November 1960, NARA.

124. "The Visit of His Excellency, the Prime Minister of the Federation of Malaya," 6, 8, folder "Malaya: Visit of P.M. Tunku Abdul Rahman, NEW YORK CITY, Oct–Nov 1960," box 77, RG 59, Office of Secretary, Office of the Chief of Protocol, Files of Visits by Heads of Government, Dignitaries and Delegations, 1928–76, NARA.

125. Dorothy McCardle, "Malayan Official Arrives: Tunku is a U.S. Prestige Booster," *Washington Post, Time Herald*, October 26, 1960.

126. James W. Gould, *The United States and Malaysia* (Cambridge, MA: Harvard Belknap Press, 1969).

127. Tunku Abdul Rahman, "UMNO Thirty Years After"; "The Case for English and Malay"; "Seventy-Five and Still Going Strong," *Viewpoints*, 43, 93, 100.

128. Monthly Report for Federation of Malaya (July), High Commissioner (Malaya) to Secretary of State for the Colonies, August 11, 1955, 1, FCO 141/7306, TNA.

129. Memorandum, Fisher Howe to Frederick Dearborn, "Governor Herter's Far East Trip," October 23, 1957, 2, folder "Far East," box 2, WHO, Office of the Special Assistant for National Security Affairs, Records, Operations Coordinating Board Series, Subject Subseries; Memo, Herter to President, "Official Visit of the Prime Minister of Malaya, October 25–November 5, 1960," October 22, 1960, 4–5, folder "Malaya [April 1960–January 1961]," 2, box 11, WHO, Office of the Staff Secretary, International Series, Dwight D. Eisenhower Presidential Library.

130. British Cabinet Meeting, "Malaya: Review of the Situation," April 6, 1955, 1–2, CAB 129/74.

131. Cheah, *Malaysia*, 30–32.

132. Monthly Report for Federation of Malaya (October), High Commissioner (Malaya) to Secretary of State for the Colonies, November 8, 1955, 2, FCO 141/7306.

133. Rashid, *Memoirs of Rashid Maidin*, 68.

134. Question and Answer regarding Federation of Malaya, Awberry to Hopkinson, March 23, 1955, "Incentives to Facilitate Voluntary Surrender of Communist Terrorists," FCO 141/7308, TNA.

135. Telegram, Officer Administering the Government (Federation of Malaya) to Secretary of State for the Colonies, January 7, 1955, FCO 141/7308.

136. Telegram, Officer Administering the Government (Malaya) to Secretary of State, January 19, 1955, 2, FCO 141/7308.

137. Monthly Report for Federation of Malaya (July), High Commissioner (Malaya) to Secretary of State for the Colonies, August 11, 1955, 1, FCO 141/7306.

138. Harper, *End of Empire*, 346–47.

139. Telegram, Officer Administering the Government (Malaya) to Secretary of State, January 19, 1955, 2, FCO 141/7308.

140. "Draft Report by the Chief Minister of the Federation of Malaya on the Baling Talks," May 1, 1956, CO1030/29, TNA.

141. Monthly Report for Federation of Malaya (November), High Commissioner (Malaya) to Secretary of State for the Colonies, December 8, 1955, 1–3, FCO 141/7306.

142. Chin Peng (as told to Ian Ward and Norma Miraflor), *My Side of History* (Singapore: Media Masters, 2003), 371, 375–77.

143. Rashid, *Memoirs of Rashid Maidin*, 70–71.

144. Chin, *My Side of History*, 371, 375–77.

145. Chin, *My Side of History*, 370–71, 375–77, 381.

146. Rashid, *Memoirs of Rashid Maidin*, 72.

147. "Dialogues Session VIII: The Baling Talks of 1955," in *Dialogues with Chin Peng: New Light on the Malayan Communist Party*, ed. C. C. Chin and Karl Hack (Singapore: Singapore University Press, 2004), 180.

148. Harper, *End of Empire*, 347.

149. Chin, *My Side of History*, 377.

150. "Draft Report by the Chief Minister on the Baling Talks," May 1956, 4–5, 8–9, CO 1030/29.

151. "Draft Report by the Chief Minister on the Baling Talks," 13–14.

152. "Malaya: Crucial Area in Southeast Asia," undated (likely mid-1956), 23, RG 59: Subject Files Relating to Malaya and Singapore, 1950–8, 1957 Briefing Papers—General, January–June, NARA.

153. "Draft Report by the Chief Minister on the Baling Talks," 13–14.

154. "Draft Report by the Chief Minister on the Baling Talks," 6, 10; Chin, *My Side of History*, 379–81.

155. Rashid, *Memoirs of Rashid Maidin*, 74–75.

156. Draft Report by the Chief Minister on the Baling Talks," 12–13; "Appendix A—"Declaration of Amnesty."

157. "Draft Report by the Chief Minister on the Baling Talks," 12–13; "Appendix A—"Declaration of Amnesty"; Cheah, *Malaysia*, 32.

158. Sodhy, *U.S.-Malaysian Nexus*, 166.

159. "Malaya: Crucial Area in Southeast Asia," 23.

160. "First Reactions to the Outcome of the London Talks," undated (likely January–February 1956), 1, folder "Miscellaneous Political Reports," FCO 141/7459, TNA.

161. Congressional Briefing Paper: Singapore-Malaya, March 18, 1957, RG 59: Subject Files Relating to Malaya and Singapore, 1950–8, box 22, 1957 Briefing Papers—General, January–June.

162. "Short-Range Problems and Prospects: Malaya and Singapore," March 22, 1957, RG 59: Subject Files Relating to Malaya and Singapore, 1950–8, box 22, 1957 Briefing Papers—General, January–June.

163. "Fanfare of Trumpets and Roll of Drums," *Straits Times*, August 30, 1957.

164. "Eyes of the World Will Be on Kuala Lumpur," *Straits Times*, August 30, 1957.

165. "Malaya Celebrates Independence," *BBC News*, August 31, 1957, last accessed November 28, 2017, http://news.bbc.co.uk/onthisday/hi/dates/stories/august/31/newsid_3534000/3534340.stm.

166. "Malaya Greets Merdeka," *Straits Times*, September 1, 1957.

167. Cheah, *Malaysia*, 109.

168. "Malaya Celebrates Independence," *BBC News*, August 31, 1957.

169. Tunku Abdul Rahman, "Prime Minister's Broadcast to America," August 31, 1957, Prime Minister's Speech File, Tunku Abdul Rahman Memorial Library (henceforth, TARL).

170. Sodhy, *U.S.-Malaysia Nexus*, 166–68.

171. Tunku Abdul Rahman, "Prime Minister's Broadcast to America," August 31, 1957.

172. "Malaya Celebrates Independence," *BBC News*, August 31, 1957.

3. Manifest Fantasies

1. Memo, Christian Herter to President Eisenhower, July 25, 1960, folder "Malaya [April 1960–January 1961]," box 11, White House Office (WHO), Office of the Staff Secretary, International Series, Dwight D. Eisenhower Presidential Library (henceforth, DDEL).

2. Cable, Eisenhower to His Majesty [Paramount Ruler of the Federation of Malaya], July 26, 1960, folder "Malaya [April 1960–January 1961], box 11, WHO, Office of the Staff Secretary, International Series, DDEL.

3. Dwight D. Eisenhower, "Toasts of the President and the Prime Minister of Malaya," October 26, 1960, *The American Presidency Project*, last accessed November 21, 2017, http://www.presidency.ucsb.edu/ws/index.php?pid=11994&st=Malaya&st1=.

4. Memcon, "Call on the President by the Prime Minister of the Federation of Malaya," October 26, 1960, 1, 3; memo, Herter to President, "Official Visit of the Prime Minister of Malaya, October 25–November 5, 1960," October 22, 1960, 4–5, folder "Malaya [April 1960–January 1961]," box 11, WHO, Office of the Staff Secretary, International Series, DDEL.

5. Department of the United States Army, *Counter Insurgency Operations: A Handbook for the Sup-pression of Communist Guerrilla/Terrorist Operations*, December 1960, 2, 6, folder "Justice: Counterinsurgency (U.S. Army Report) 05/61," box 80, President's Office Files (henceforth POF): Departments and Agencies, Papers of President Kennedy, John F. Kennedy Presidential Library (henceforth, JFKL).

6. Andrew J. Birtle, *U.S. Army Counterinsurgency and Contingency Operations Doctrine 1942–1976* (Fort McNair, DC: U.S. Army Center of Military History, 2006), 8; Aaron B. O'Connell, *Underdogs: The Making of the Modern Marine Corps* (Cambridge, MA: Harvard University Press, 2012), 13, 117.

7. O'Connell, *Underdogs*, 13, 117.

8. Birtle, *U.S. Army Counterinsurgency*, 8–11.

9. Alfred W. McCoy, *Policing America's Empire: The United States, the Philippines, and the Rise of the Surveillance State* (Madison: University of Wisconsin–Madison Press, 2009). Also see Paul Kramer, "The Water Cure: Debating Torture and Counterinsurgency—A Century Ago," *New Yorker*, February 25, 2008, and H. W. Brands, *Bound to Empire: The United States and the Philippines* (New York: Oxford University Press, 1992).

10. Birtle, *U.S. Army Counterinsurgency*, 22–26, 229.

11. Department of Defense, "Guerrilla Warfare and Related Matters—Status Report," February 19, 1961, 6, folder "Department of Defense, Subjects, Special Warfare, 2/61–5/61," box 279, Kennedy Papers, NSF—Departments and Agencies, JFKL; Charles Maechling Jr., "Camelot, Robert Kennedy, and Counter-Insurgency—a Memoir," *Virginia Quarterly Review* 93, no. 4 (1999), last accessed June 29, 2014, http://www.vqronline.org/essay/camelot-robert-kennedy-and-counter-insurgency-memoir.

12. Paul Kramer, "Power and Connection: Imperial Histories of the United States in the World," *American Historical Review* 116 (December 2011): 1369. Kramer's discussion of imperial formations is most useful in describing the nature of "limited liability" in the rise of the U.S. empire in the postcolonial era, for it "profited from both the presence and the disintegration of the older, European colonial worlds . . . [and so] cast [itself] as liberatory, anti-imperial polities that preserved and encouraged their subjects' nationalities," in this case, client governments of the United States. Most importantly, as Kramer points out, "empires organized in this way employed the fiction of discrete and autonomous nations to insulate themselves from the claims and movements of the majority of their subjects: residents and citizens of other peoples' countries."

13. Memorandum, Acheson to James S. Lay (Executive Secretary, NSC), October 26, 1950; NSC, "Collaboration with Friendly Governments on Exchange of Information Concerning Operations against Guerrillas," May 8, 1951, 1–4, folder "Basic National Security Policy (Miscellaneous Papers) (1)," box 6, WHO, NSC Staff, Papers 1948–61, Disaster File, DDEL.

14. U.S. Consulate-General (Singapore), "Assessment of the Situation in Malaya in the First Half of 1954: The Emergency," February 8, 1954, 1–2, folder "Malaya Reports," box 6, RG 469: Malaya Subject Files, 1951–61, NARA.

15. Birtle, *U.S. Army Counterinsurgency*, 162.

16. Riley Sunderland, memorandum RM-4170-ISA: Army Operations in Malaya, 1947–60, 7.

17. NSC 5405: United States Objectives and Courses of Action with Respect to Southeast Asia, January 16, 1954, *FRUS*, 1952–1954, vol. 12, pt. 1, "East Asia and the Pacific," ed. David W. Mabon (Washington, DC: Government Printing Office, 1984), 366–67, 370, 376.

18. Dwight D. Eisenhower, The President's News Conference, April 7, 1954, *The American Presidency Project*, last accessed November 29, 2017, http://www.presidency.ucsb.edu/ws/?pid=10202.

19. Operations Coordinating Board Secretariat Staff, Memorandum for the Record of Briefing by Mr. Malcolm MacDonald, October 14, 1954, folder "Operations Coordinating Board 091.4 Southeast Asia (File#2) (3) [August–December 1954]," box 79, WHO, NSC Staff Papers, 1948–61, Operations Coordinating Board Central File Series, DDEL; Richard Stubbs, *Hearts and Minds*

in Guerrilla Warfare, 1948–1960 (London: Oxford University Press, 1989); Karl Hack, "Everyone Lived in Fear: Malaya and the British Way of Counterinsurgency," *Small Wars & Insurgencies* 23, nos. 4–5 (2012): 671–99.

20. Office of Research and Analysis (United States Information Agency), "The Communist Threat to Malaya," September 25, 1959, 4, folder "50-11-59," box 14, RG 306: United States Information Agency, Special Reports (S), 1953–97, NARA.

21. Karl Hack, "Detention, Deportation and Resettlement: British Counterinsurgency and Malaya's Rural Chinese, 1948–1960," *Journal of Imperial and Commonwealth History* 43, no. 4 (2015): 611–40. Hack examines key techniques used to control rural Chinese during the Emergency and Britain's highly repressive measures.

22. "Smiling Tiger," *Time*, December 15, 1952, 26–32; Edward G. Miller, *Misalliance: Ngo Dinh Diem, the United States and the Fate of South Vietnam* (Cambridge, MA: Harvard University Press, 2013).

23. "Malaya: The Undeclared War," 1998, British Broadcasting Corporation (YouTube), last accessed January 25, 2018, https://www.youtube.com/watch?v=pBRMRf0JVJc; Moritz Feightinger, Stephan Malinowski, and Chase Richards, "Transformative Invasions: Western Post-9/11 Counterinsurgency and the Lessons of Colonialism," *Humanity: An International Journal of Human Rights, Humanitarianism and Development* 3, no. 1 (2012): 40–41.

24. Feightinger, Malinowski, and Richards, "Transformative Invasions," 40–41.

25. David French, *The British Way in Counter-Insurgency, 1945–67* (Oxford: Oxford University Press, 2011), 116–17, 173, 251. For an in-depth study of similar British brutality in Kenya, see Caroline Elkins, *Imperial Reckoning: The Untold Story of Britain's Gulag in Kenya* (New York: Henry Holt, 2005). For an analysis of Britain's violent late colonial polices in comparison to that of France, see Martin Thomas, *Fight or Flight: Britain, France and Their Roads from Empire* (Oxford: Oxford University Press, 2014).

26. Feightinger, Malinowski, and Richards, "Transformative Invasions," 40–41.

27. French, *British Way in Counter-Insurgency*, 116–17, 173, 251.

28. Hack, "Detention, Deportation and Resettlement," 625.

29. "Smiling Tiger."

30. Letter, Eisenhower to Templer, undated (likely October 1953), folder "Nixon, Richard M. (5)," box 28, Dwight D. Eisenhower, Papers as President, 1953–61, Ann Whitman File, Administration Series; Letter, Gerald Templer to Eisenhower, October 31, 1953, folder "Malaya (3)," box 38, Dwight D. Eisenhower, Papers as President, 1953–61, Ann Whitman File, International Series, DDEL.

31. "Malaya: The Undeclared War," 1998, British Broadcasting Corporation.

32. McCoy, *Policing America's Empire*, 374–79. See also Daniel Fineman, "Phibun, the Cold War and Thailand's Foreign Policy Revolution of 1950" in *Connecting Histories: Decolonization and the Cold War in Southeast Asia, 1945–1962*, ed. Christopher Goscha and Christian Ostermann, 275–300 (Stanford, CA: Stanford University Press, 2009); and Fineman, *A Special Relationship: The United States and the Military Government of Thailand, 1947–58* (Honolulu: University of Hawaii Press, 1997), chaps. 1 to 3.

33. Director of Operations (Malaya), *Review of Emergency Situation in Malaya at the End of 1955*, 2, folder "Review of the Emergency Situation," FCO 141/ 7340, TNA.

34. Chin Peng, *Alias Chin Peng: My Side of History* (Singapore: Media Masters, 2003), 302–9. See also Mark Curtis, *Web of Deceit: Britain's Real Role in the World* (London: Vintage, 2003), 338–43.

35. Sunil Amrith, *Migration and Diaspora in Modern Asia* (London: Cambridge University Press, 2012), 95, 124; Philip Kuhn, *Chinese among Others: Emigration in Modern Times* (New York: Rowman & Littlefield, 2008), 271, 287–89, 296–97; Taomo Zhou, "Ambivalent Alliance: Chinese Policy toward Indonesia, 1960–1965," *China Quarterly* (2015): 216–19.

36. "Review of Emergency Situation in Malaya at the End of 1955," 2, folder "Review of the Emergency Situation," FCO 141/ 7340.

37. "Report on Subversive Activities in Malaya—December 1956," folder "Monthly Subversives Report (December 1956–July 1957)," FCO 141/7259, TNA.

38. Telegram, Colonial Office to Officer Administering the Government (Federation of Malaya), July 30, 1955, FCO 141/7306, TNA.

39. "Smiling Tiger."

40. "Malaya: Crucial Area in Southeast Asia," undated (likely between January and June 1957), 35, folder "1957 Briefing Papers—General January–June," box 22, RG 59: General Records of the Department of State: Miscellaneous Lot Files, Subject Files Relating to Malaya and Singapore 1950–8, NARA.

41. Ian Cobain, Owen Bowcott and Richard Norton-Taylor, "Britain Destroyed Records of Colonial Crimes," *Guardian*, April 17, 2012.

42. "Batang Kali Massacre Ruling Clears Way for UK Supreme Court Appeal," *Guardian*, March 19, 2014, last accessed July 10, 2014, http://www.theguardian.com/world/2014/mar/19/batang-kali-massacre-judges-reject-inquiry-malaysia; "UK to Compensate Kenya's Mau Mau Torture Victims," *Guardian*, June 6, 2013, last accessed July 10, 2014, http://www.theguardian.com/world/2013/jun/06/uk-compensate-kenya-mau-mau-torture.

43. Paul Kramer, *The Blood of Government: Race, Empire, the United States and the Philippines* (Chapel Hill: University of North Carolina Press, 2006); John W. Dower, *War without Mercy: Race and Power in the Pacific War* (New York: Pantheon, 1986), 11.

44. "Malaya: Crucial Area in Southeast Asia."

45. Memorandum, Frank Wisner (Deputy Director for Plans of the CIA) to Rockefeller (President's Special Assistant), June 1, 1955, *FRUS, 1955–1957*, vol. 22, *Southeast Asia*, ed. Robert J. McMahon, Harriet D. Schwar and Louis J. Smith (Washington, DC: Government Printing Office, 1989), 735–36.

46. Letter, Lucian W. Pye to General Sir Gerald Templer (United Kingdom Director of Operations, Malaya), March 17, 1953; Letter, Pye to John Adam Watson (British Embassy, Washington, DC), January 20, 1953, folder "Relations with the U.S.A.," FCO 141/7498, TNA.

47. Letter, W. J. Rayner (Regional Information Officer, Office of UK Commissioner-General for Southeast Asia) to J. H. A. Watson, November 14, 1955; letter, F. Brewer (Chief Secretary's Office, Kuala Lumpur) to Pye, February 10, 1956, folder "(1) The Appeal of Communism in Asia, (2) The Case of the Chinese in Malaya by Dr. Lucian Pye," FCO 141/7309, TNA.

48. Lucian W. Pye, *Lessons from the Malayan Struggle against Communism* (Cambridge, MA: MIT Press, 1957), 1, 60.

49. Pye, *Lessons from the Malayan Struggle*, 40, 42, 50, 52, 57; Chin Peng, *Alias Chin Peng*, 268–72.

50. "Smiling Tiger."

51. "Smiling Tiger."

52. Department of the United States Army, *Counter Insurgency Operations*, 2, 6.

53. Birtle, *U.S. Army Counterinsurgency*, 166–68.

54. Department of the United States Army, *Counter Insurgency Operations: A Handbook for the Suppression of Communist Guerrilla/ Terrorist Operations*, 4–5, 15, 37–39, 47–49.

55. Birtle, *U.S. Army Counterinsurgency*, 62–66, 118.

56. National Security Action Memorandum (NSAM) 119, Subject: Civic Action, December 18, 1961, *John F. Kennedy Presidential Library and Museum Website*, last accessed October 30, 2012, http://www.JFKLlibrary.org/Asset-Viewer/pyvGIsw6gEqxdYR8dLGJgQ.aspx.

57. Department of the Army, "Concept of Employment of U.S. Army Forces in Paramilitary Operations," January 2, 1962, 6, folder "Department of Defense, Subjects, Special Warfare, 2/61–5/61," box 279, Kennedy Papers, NSF—Departments and Agencies, JFKL.

58. Wallace M. Greene Jr., memorandum for the Naval Aide to the President, February 13, 1961; *Guerrilla and Anti-Guerrilla Operations*, September 12, 1960, 1, folder "Counter-Insurgency," box 98, Kennedy Papers, POF, Subjects, JFKL.

59. Letter, Robert F. Kennedy to the president, May 22, 1961, folder "Justice: Counterinsurgency (U.S. Army Report) 05/61," box 80, POF: Departments and Agencies, Papers of President Kennedy.

60. For Kennedy's deliberate focus on Africa, see Philip E. Muehlenbeck, *Betting on the Africans: John F. Kennedy's Courting of African Nationalist Leaders* (New York: Oxford University Press, 2012). Robert B. Rakove, *Kennedy, Johnson, and the Non-aligned World* (New York: Cambridge University Press, 2012) examines Kennedy's efforts to engage the nonaligned movement, and the United States' retreat from his nuanced approach to world affairs under President Lyndon B. Johnson.

61. Elizabeth N. Saunders, *Leaders at War: How Presidents Shape Military Interventions* (Ithaca, NY: Cornell University Press, 2011), 93. See esp. chap. 4 for Saunders's detailed study of Kennedy's prepresidential views of Third World nationalism and how these birthed his later emphasis on reforming newly independent countries' internal conditions.

62. John F. Kennedy, Remarks of Senator Kennedy in the United States Senate, National Defense, February 29, 1960, John F. Kennedy Speeches, JFKL Presidential Library Online, last accessed August 8, 2014, http://www.JFKLlibrary.org/Research/Research-Aids/JFKL-Speeches/United-States-Senate-National-Defense_19600229.aspx.

63. Maechling, "Camelot"; Roger Hilsman, *To Move a Nation: The Politics of Foreign Policy in the Administration of John F. Kennedy* (Garden City, NY: Doubleday, 1967), 413, qtd. in John A. Nagl, *Learning to Eat Soup with a Knife: Counterinsurgency Lessons from Malaya and Vietnam* (Chicago: University of Chicago Press, 2005), 124, 145n41.

64. Hannah Gurman, introduction to *Hearts and Minds: A People's History of Counterinsurgency*, ed. Hannah Gurman (New York: New Press, 2013), 2, 10.

65. Maechling, "Camelot."

66. Maechling, "Camelot."

67. Robert W. Komer, "The Deterrence of Guerrilla Warfare," undated (likely March 1961), folder "Counterinsurgency: Special Group, 2/61–4/62 and Undated), box 414, Robert W. Komer Papers, JFKL.

68. Maechling, "Camelot."

69. Komer, "Deterrence of Guerrilla Warfare"; William J. Jorden, "South Vietnam: Communist Tactics of Subversion and Covert Aggression in Action," November 15, 1961, folder "Vietnam, Subjects, Jorden Report, November 15, 1961," box 202, NSF—Counterinsurgency, Kennedy Papers, JFKL.

70. Coordination Group (Office of Chief of Staff), "An Approach to the Creation of the Capability to Conduct Unconventional Warfare," April 13, 1961, 9, box 326, folder "Staff Memoranda, Walt W. Rostow, Guerrilla and Unconventional Warfare, 4/12/61–5/31/61," Kennedy Papers, NSF—Meetings and Memoranda, JFKL.

71. Policy Planning Council (Department of State), "Counter-Guerrilla Operations," June 13, 1961, 2, box 326, folder "Staff Memoranda, Walt W. Rostow, Guerrilla and Unconventional Warfare, 6/1/61–6/13/61," Kennedy Papers, NSF—Meetings and Memoranda, JFKL.

72. Birtle, *U.S. Army Counterinsurgency*, 226–28.

73. Memorandum for Walt Rostow, March 28, 1961; Policy Planning Council (U.S. Department of State), "Counter-Guerrilla Operations," March 20, 1961, 2, folder "Staff Memoranda, Walt W. Rostow, Guerrilla and Unconventional Warfare, 3/20/61–3/29/61," box 325, Kennedy Papers, NSF—Meetings and Memoranda, JFKL.

74. MAAG-Vietnam, *Tactics and Techniques of Counter-Insurgent Operations*, undated (likely 1961), i, folder "Subjects, MAAG, Counterinsurgency, Part 1," box 204, Kennedy Papers, NSF—Countries—Vietnam, JFKL.

75. Nagl, *Learning to Eat Soup*, 97–98.

76. Birtle, *U.S. Army Counterinsurgency*, 162, 314.

77. Memorandum, McGhee to McGeorge Bundy, November 21, 1961, folder "Department of Defense, Subject, Special Warfare, 2/61–5/61," box 279, Kennedy Papers, NSF—Departments and Agencies, JFKL.

78. National Security Action Memorandum (NSAM) 104 "Southeast Asia," October 13, 1961, box 332, Kennedy Papers, NSF—Meetings and Memoranda, JFKL.

79. Memorandum, McGhee to McGeorge Bundy, November 21, 1961.

80. George McGhee and Edward Lansdale, "Decisive Factors of the Counter-Guerrilla Campaigns in Greece, Malaya and the Philippines," November 1961, 3–5, folder, "Department of Defense, Subject, Special Warfare, 2/61–5/61," box 279, Kennedy Papers, NSF—Departments and Agencies, JFKL.

81. Bureau of Intelligence and Research (Department of State), *Internal Warfare and the Security of Underdeveloped States*, November 20, 1961, box 5, folder "Counterinsurgency Fred Greene Study (PRS-1) 11/20/61," Roger Hilsman Papers, JFKL.

82. Roger Hilsman, A Strategic Concept for South Vietnam, February 2, 1962, *FRUS*, 1962–1963, vol. 2, *Vietnam, 1962*, ed. John P. Glennon, David M. Baehler, Charles S. Sampson (Washington, DC: Government Printing Office, 1990), Document 42.

83. Report, Special Warfare Center (U.S. Army) to Chief of Staff (U.S. Army), May 2, 1962, 22, folder "Department of Defense, Subjects, Special Warfare, 2/61–5/61," box 279, Kennedy Papers, NSF—Departments and Agencies, JFKL.

84. C. C. Too, "Appendix 2: Impromptu Speech by C.C. Too" (reproduced in full) in Lim Cheng Leng, *The Story of a Psy-Warrior: Tan Sri Dr. C.C. Too* (Batu Caves, Selangor: Lim Cheng Leng, 2002), 217–31.

85. Maechling, "Camelot."

86. Stephen T. Hosmer, "Foreword to the New Edition," in *Counterinsurgency: A Symposium, April 16–20, 1962* (Santa Monica, CA: RAND Corporation, 1962), iii–v.

87. Mai Elliott, *RAND in Southeast Asia: A History of the Vietnam War Era* (Santa Monica, CA: RAND Corporation, 2010), 22.

88. Sunderland, Memorandum RM-4170-ISA: Army Operations in Malaya, 1947–60; RM-4171-ISA: Organizing Counterinsurgency in Malaya, 1947–60; RM-4172-ISA: Antiguerrilla Intelligence in Malaya, 1948–60; RM-4173-ISA: Resettlement and Food Control in Malaya; RM-4174-ISA: Winning the Hearts and Minds of the People—Malaya, 1948–60.

89. William J. Lederer, "The Guerrilla War the Reds Lost," *Reader's Digest*, May 1962. This article was condensed from Lederer's contribution, with the same title, to *The New Leader*, April 16, 1962.

90. Lederer, "Guerrilla War the Reds Lost."

91. Maechling, "Camelot."

92. Special Group (Counter-Insurgency), "U.S. Overseas Internal Defense Policy," July–August 1962, 2, folder "Special Group (CI) 7/62–11/63," box 319, Kennedy Papers, NSF-Meetings and Memoranda, JFKL.

93. See also Birtle, *U.S. Army Counterinsurgency*, 238–39.

94. Saunders, *Leaders at War*, 99.

95. Joint Chiefs of Staff, *Development Status of Military Counterinsurgency Programs, including Counterguerrilla Forces*, "Section VIII: Part I—Partial Bibliography on Counterinsurgency and Related

Matters Emphasizing Military and Political Considerations," August 1, 1963, 2–3, 5, 8, 13–16, 18, 20–21, 23–24, 30–31, 33, 36–38, 40–41, folder "Department of Defense (B): Status of Military Counterinsurgency Programs, Part VIII," box 280, Kennedy Papers, NSF—Departments and Agencies, JFKL.

96. Department of the Army, "U.S. Army Role in Guerrilla and Anti-Guerrilla Operations," undated (likely late January 1961), 1, 3–4, folder "Department of Defense, Subjects, Special Warfare, 2/61–5/61," box 279, Kennedy Papers, NSF—Departments and Agencies, JFKL.

97. Memorandum, Elvis J. Stahr Jr. (Secretary of the Army) to President Kennedy, February 5, 1962; memorandum, Lemnitzer (Chairman, Joint Chiefs of Staff) to McNamara (Secretary of Defense), "Development of Counterguerrilla Forces," March 3, 1961, 2, folder "Department of Defense, Subjects, Special Warfare, 2/61–5/61," box 279, Kennedy Papers, NSF—Departments and Agencies, JFKL.

98. Appendix, Lemnitzer to McNamara, March 3, 1961, 2, folder "Department of Defense, Subjects, Special Warfare, 2/61–5/61," box 279, Kennedy Papers, NSF—Departments and Agencies, JFKL.

99. Letter and Report, Special Warfare Center (U.S. Army) to Chief of Staff (U.S. Army), May 2, 1962, 3–4, 21–22, folder "Department of Defense, Subjects, Special Warfare, 2/61–5/61," box 279, Kennedy Papers, NSF—Departments and Agencies, JFKL.

100. "Malaya, Singapore and British Borneo," October 29, 1962, 13, folder "Southeast Asia, 1961–1966, Malaysia," box 22, Thomson Papers, JFKL.

101. Department of Defense, "Guerrilla Warfare and Related Matters—Status Report," February 19, 1961, 6, folder "Department of Defense, Subjects, Special Warfare, 2/61–5/61," box 279, Kennedy Papers, NSF—Departments and Agencies, JFKL.

102. Ian F. W. Beckett, "Robert Thompson and the British Advisory Mission to South Vietnam, 1961–5," *Small Wars and Insurgencies* 8, no. 3 (1997): 41, 44.

103. Danny Wong, *Vietnam-Malaysia: Relations during the Cold War, 1945–1990* (Kuala Lumpur, Malaysia: University of Malaya Press, 1995), 47; briefing memorandum, Rusk to JFKL, March 3, 1961, folder "Malaya/ Malaysia, 1961–3," box 121, President's Office files—Countries, JFKL.

104. Beckett, "Robert Thompson," 41, 44.

105. Beckett, "Robert Thompson," 44; memorandum of a conversation, Quai d'Orsay, Paris, August 7, 1961, *FRUS, 1961–1963*, vol. 1, *Vietnam, 1961*, eds. Ronald D. Landa and Charles S. Sampson (Washington, DC: Government Printing Office, 1988), Document 115.

106. Despatch, H. A. F. Hohler (British Embassy in Saigon) to London, January 30, 1963, folder "BRIAM Strategic Hamlet Program 1963," FO (Foreign Office) 371/ 17100, TNA.

107. Peter Busch, "Killing the 'Vietcong,': The British Advisory Mission and the Strategic Hamlet Program," *Journal of Strategic Studies* 25, no. 1 (2002): 136.

108. Miller, *Misalliance*, 231–33.

109. Busch, "Killing the 'Vietcong,'" 136.

110. From Baldwin (U.S. Embassy, Kuala Lumpur) to Secretary of State, November 8, 1961, folder "Malaya, 11/61–11/62," box 140, Kennedy Papers, NSF-Countries, JFKL.

111. Beckett, "Robert Thompson," 51; Busch, "Killing the 'Vietcong,'" 148.

112. Memorandum from Counselor and Public Affairs Office of the Embassy in Vietnam (Mecklin) to the Public Affairs Adviser in the Bureau of Far Eastern Affairs (Manelli), March 15, 1963, *FRUS, 1961–1963*, vol. 3, *Vietnam, January–August 1963*, ed. Edward C. Keefer and Louis J. Smith (Washington, DC: Government Printing Office, 1991), Document 60.

113. Memorandum for the Record by the Director of the Bureau of Intelligence and Research (Hilsman), January 2, 1963, *FRUS, 1961–1963*, vol. 3, *Vietnam, January–August 1963*, Document 2.

114. Memorandum of a Conversation (White House, Washington), April 4, 1963, *FRUS*, 1961–1963, vol. 3, *Vietnam, January–August 1963*, Document 77.

115. Minutes by E. H. Peck (Foreign Office), April 16, 1963, folder "BRIAM 1963," FO 371/17100, TNA.

116. Letter, Thompson to Edward Peck (Foreign Office), January 14, 1964, folder "BRIAM 1964," FO 371/175482, TNA.

117. Letter, Thompson (BRIAM, Saigon) to Edward Peck (Foreign Office, London), January 14, 1964; David Ormsby-Gore (Ambassador to the U.S.) to Harold Caccia (Foreign Office, London), January 24, 1964, folder "BRIAM 1964," FO 371/175482.

118. Letter, Etherington-Smith (British Embassy, Saigon) to Edward Peck (London), January 14, 1964, folder "BRIAM 1964," FO 371/175482.

119. Richard M. Nixon, "Needed in Vietnam: The Will to Win," *Reader's Digest*, August 1964, 42–43.

120. *The 7th Dawn*, dir. Lewis Gilbert, DVD (1964, Beverly Hills, CA: United Artists; MGM, 2011).

121. Michael Keon, *The Durian Tree* (New York: Simon & Schuster, 1960).

122. Sunderland, Army Operations in Malaya, 1947–60, iv.

123. For example, the secret *Briggs Report* from 1951, *Review of Emergency in Malaya from June 1948 to August 1957*, and the *Basic Paper on the MCP* from 1950, cited in Sunderland, Army Operations in Malaya, 1947–60, 14n9, 20n17, 64n76.

124. Sunderland, Army Operations in Malaya, 1947–60; 170.

125. Sunderland, Memorandum RM-4170-ISA: Army Operations in Malaya, 1947–60; RM-4171-ISA: Organizing Counterinsurgency in Malaya, 1947–60; RM-4172-ISA: Antiguerrilla Intelligence in Malaya, 1948–60; RM-4173-ISA: Resettlement and Food Control in Malaya; RM-4174-ISA: Winning the Hearts and Minds of the People—Malaya, 1948–60.

126. Sunderland, Army Operations in Malaya, 1947–60, v.

127. BRIAM, "Notes for British Advisers in Vietnam," December 30, 1964, folder "BRIAM 1965 (DV 1017/5)," FO 371/180520, TNA.

128. Personal Letter, Secretary of State to Thompson, April 13, 1965, folder "BRIAM 1965 (DV 1017/17)," FO 371/180520.

129. Note, Sir Harold Caccia, undated (likely late March 1965), folder "BRIAM 1965 (DV 1017/17)," FO 371/180520.

130. *Counterinsurgency Case History: Malaya 1948–1960* (Fort Leavenworth, KS: U.S. Army Command and General Staff College, 1965).

131. Robert G. K. Thompson, *Defeating Communist Insurgency: Experiences from Malaya and Vietnam* (London: Chatto and Windus, 1966).

132. John T. McAlister Jr., review of *Defeating Communist Insurgency: Experiences from Malaya and Vietnam*, by Robert G. K. Thompson, *American Political Science Review* 61, no. 3 (September 1967): 773–75.

133. Robert G. K. Thompson, *No Exit from Vietnam* (New York: D. McKay, 1969); David Fitzgerald, "Sir Robert Thompson, Strategic Patience and Nixon's War in Vietnam," *Journal of Strategic Studies* 37, nos. 6–7 (2014): 999–1003, 1009, 1011, 1023–24.

134. Robert W. Komer, *The Malayan Emergency in Retrospect: Organization of a Successful Counterinsurgency Effort* (Santa Monica, CA: RAND Corporation, 1972), iii–iv.

135. Gian P. Gentile, "A Strategy of Tactics: Population-Centric COIN and the Army," *Parameters: Journal of the U.S. Army War College* 41, no. 4 (2011–2012): 1–12.

4. The Best Hope

1. John F. Kennedy, President's News Conference, February 14, 1963, *The American Presidency Project*, last accessed June 24, 2014, http://www.presidency.ucsb.edu/ws/index.php?pid=9562&st =Malaysia&st1=.

2. Memo, Hilsman to the Secretary, "Prospects for Malaysia," September 5, 1962, 7, folder "General 1961–6," box 22, Personal Papers of James C. Thomson, Jr. (henceforth, Thomson Papers), John F. Kennedy Presidential Library (henceforth, JFKL).

3. Director of Central Intelligence, "National Intelligence Estimate (NIE) 54/59-62: Prospects for the Proposed Malaysian Federation," July 11, 1962, 3, CIA FOIA Reading Room, last accessed November 21, 2017, https://www.cia.gov/library/readingroom/docs/DOC_0000639900.pdf.

4. Memo, Hilsman to the Secretary, "Prospects for Malaysia," September 5, 1962.

5. Seth King, "Malaysian Union: A Potential Giant," *New York Times*, April 5, 1963.

6. Danny Wong, *Vietnam-Malaysia: Relations during the Cold War, 1945–1990* (Kuala Lumpur, Malaysia: University of Malaya Press, 1995), 48.

7. Tunku Abdul Rahman, "Prime Minister's Speech in Honor of His Excellency the President of Vietnam," February 16, 1960, Prime Minister's Speech File, The Tunku Abdul Rahman Library (henceforth, TARL).

8. Briefing memorandum, Rusk to President Kennedy, March 3, 1961, folder "Malaya/Malaysia, 1961–3," box 121, POF—Countries, JFKL.

9. Seth Jacobs, *America's Miracle Man in Vietnam: Ngo Dinh Diem, Religion, Race and U.S. Intervention in Southeast Asia, 1950–7* (Durham, NC: Duke University Press, 2004).

10. Johan Saravanamuttu, *Malaysia's Foreign Policy, the First Fifty Years: Alignment, Neutralism, Islamism* (Singapore: Institute of Southeast Asian Studies, 2010), 52.

11. Malayan Legislative Council Debates, October 2 and 3, 1957, quoted in Saravanamuttu, *Malaysia's Foreign Policy*, 51.

12. Saravanamuttu, *Malaysia's Foreign Policy*, 49–51; Draft Progress Report on U.S. Policy in Mainland Southeast Asia (NSC 5612/1), February 7, 1957, 3, folder 2, "Operations Coordinating Board 091.4 Southeast Asia (File #6)" [February–May 1957], box 81, WHO, NSC Staff Papers, Operations Coordinating Board Central Files, Dwight D. Eisenhower Presidential Library (henceforth, DDEL); Karl Hack, *Defense and Decolonization in Southeast Asia: Britain, Malaya and Singapore, 1941–1968* (Surrey, UK: Curzon, 2001), 228.

13. Peter Boyce, ed., *Malaysia and Singapore in International Diplomacy: Documents and Commentaries* (Sydney: Sydney University Press, 1968), 37–38.

14. Saravanamuttu, *Malaysia's Foreign Policy*, 50–51; "Malaya Celebrates Independence," BBC News, August 31, 1957, last accessed January 13, 2013, http://news.bbc.co.uk/onthisday/hi/dates /stories/august/31/newsid_3534000/3534340.stm.

15. "Malaya's Non-Membership of SEATO: Statement by Prime Minister," December 11, 1958, Malaya Legislative Council, *Legislative Council Debates*, 4th Session, December 1958, col. 6029, in Boyce, *Malaysia and Singapore in International Diplomacy*, 42.

16. For the best account of British-U.S.-Malayan-Singaporean support for rebellions against Sukarno in 1958, using British bases in Singapore, see Audrey R. Kahin and George McT Kahin, *Subversion as Foreign Policy: The Secret Eisenhower and Dulles Debacle in Indonesia* (New York: W. W. Norton, 1995).

17. S. R. Joey Long, *Safe for Decolonization: The Eisenhower Administration, Britain and Singapore* (Kent, OH: Kent State University Press, 2011), 155.

18. Joseph Chinyong Liow, "Tunku Abdul Rahman and Malaya's Relations with Indonesia, 1957–60," *Journal of Southeast Asian Studies* 36, no. 1 (2005): 96–98.

19. Liow, "Tunku Abdul Rahman," 96–98.

20. Liow, "Tunku Abdul Rahman," 98.

21. Bradley R. Simpson, *Economists with Guns: Authoritarian Development and U.S.-Indonesian Relations, 1960–8* (Stanford, CA: Stanford University Press, 2008), 34, 114.

22. Long, *Safe for Decolonization*, 157.

23. Liow, "Tunku Abdul Rahman," 100.

24. J. D. Legge, *Sukarno: A Political Biography* (New York: Praeger, 1972), 343, 363.

25. Matthew Jones, "Maximum Disavowable Aid: Britain, the United States and the Indonesian Rebellion, 1957–58," *English Historical Review* 114, no. 459 (1999): 1213.

26. Tunku Abdul Rahman, "Speech Given to World Affairs Councils and Asia Foundation, October 31, 1960," 2, 11–12, folder "Malaya: Visit of P.M. Tunku Abdul Rahman, SAN FRANCISCO, Oct–Nov 1960," box 76, RG 59, Office of Secretary, Office of Chief of Protocol, Files of Visits of Heads of Government, Dignitaries and Delegations (compiled 1965–70), NARA.

27. Dorothy McCardle, "Malayan Official Arrives," *Washington Post–Times Herald*, October 26, 1960; "Washington Fetes Malaya's Tunku," *Christian Science Monitor*, October 26, 1960.

28. Dwight D. Eisenhower, "Toasts of the President and the Prime Minister of Malaya," October 26, 1960.

29. Dorothy McCardle, "Malayan Orator Has Ike as Fan," *Washington Post–Times Herald*, October 27, 1960.

30. Eisenhower, "Toasts of the President and the Prime Minister of Malaya," October 26, 1960; memo, State Department to the President, October 26, 1960, 1–2, folder "Malaya (1)," box 38, Dwight D. Eisenhower: Papers as President, 1953–61, Ann Whitman File, International Series, DDEL.

31. Melani McAlister, *Epic Encounters: Culture, Media, & U.S. Interests in the Middle East since 1945* (Berkeley: University of California Press, 2001), 50–53.

32. Memo, State Department to the President, October 26, 1960, 1–2, folder "Malaya (1)," box 38, Dwight D. Eisenhower: Papers as President, 1953–61, Ann Whitman File, International Series, DDEL.

33. Memcon, "Call on the President by the Prime Minister of the Federation of Malaya," October 26, 1960, 1, folder "Malaya [April 1960–January 1961]," box 11, WHO, Office of the Staff Secretary: Records, 1952–61, International Series, DDEL.

34. Eisenhower, "Toasts of the President and the Prime Minister of Malaya," October 26, 1960.

35. Memcon, "Call on the President by the Prime Minister of the Federation of Malaya," October 26, 1960, 1, 3; memo, Herter to President, "Official Visit of the Prime Minister of Malaya, October 25–November 5, 1960," October 22, 1960, 4–5, folder "Malaya [April 1960–January 1961]," box 11, WHO, Office of the Staff Secretary, International Series, DDEL.

36. Embtel, AmEmbassy Kuala Lumpur to Department of State, "Background Material for Official Discussions during Federation Prime Minister's visit to the United States," September 13, 1960, 4, folder "Malaya: Visit of P.M. Tunku Abdul Rahman, Washington, Oct–Nov 1960," box 76, RG 59, Office of Secretary, Office of the Chief of Protocol, Files of Visits by Heads of State, Dignitaries and Delegations (compiled 1965–70), NARA.

37. Saravanamuttu, *Malaysia's Foreign Policy*, 65–66.

38. CIA, "Consequences to the US of Communist Domination of Mainland Southeast Asia," October 13, 1950, 5; NSC, "U.S. Policy in Mainland Southeast Asia," July 25, 1960, 14, USDCO (Gale document no. CK2349377947); William P. Maddox, "Singapore: Problem Child," *Foreign Affairs*, April 1962, 480.

39. U.S. Policy in Mainland Southeast Asia: Singapore, November 3, 1959, 1–2. See introduction to this book. This document was declassified in 2014.

40. Robert W. Komer, "Strategic Framework for Rethinking China Policy," April 7, 1961, 5, folder "Staff Memoranda: Robert Komer, 3/30/61–3/31/61," box 321, Kennedy Papers, NSF-Meetings and Memoranda, JFKL.

41. Maddox, "Singapore," 479–83.

42. "Prospects for the Proposed Malaysian Federation," 3.

43. Tan Tai Yong, "The 'Grand Design': British Policy, Local Politics, and the Making of Malaysia, 1955–1961," in *The Transformation of Southeast Asia: International Perspectives on Decolonization*, ed. Marc Frey, Ronald Pruessen, and Tan Tai Yong (Armonk, NY: M. E. Sharpe, 2003), 143. In this instance, Tan quotes from Mohamed Noordin Sopiee, "The Advocacy of Malaysia—Before 1961," *Modern Asian Studies* 7, no. 4 (1973): 717–32.

44. See Long, *Safe for Decolonization*, esp. chap. 8, and Matthew Jones, "Up the Garden Path? Britain's Nuclear History in the Far East, 1954–62," *International History Review* 25, no. 2 (2003): 306–33.

45. "Prospects for the Proposed Malaysian Federation," July 11, 1962, 4–5; Maddox, "Singapore," 483.

46. Memorandum: "The General Malayan Situation," Baldwin to the Under Secretary, November 15, 1961, 1–2, folder "General 1961–6," box 22, Thomson Papers, JFKL.

47. Memo, Hilsman to the Secretary, "Prospects for Malaysia," September 5, 1962, 2, 5, 7.

48. Singapore's first chief minister, David Marshall, had been at Baling with the Tunku in 1955. Marshall resigned in 1956 when he failed, unlike the Tunku, to secure full independence from Britain during talks in London. Lim Yew Hock, a pro-U.S. anticommunist, succeeded Marshall and served as chief minister from 1956 to 1959. Britain's nation-building policy of phased democratization in Singapore paralleled its approach to Malaya. Chief ministers headed the semi-autonomous Legislative Council that performed many functions of formal government but did not control internal security or defense (which remained under British administrators). The Legislative Council therefore did not enjoy formal independence. As chapter 2 of this book shows, the Tunku became chief minister of the Legislative Council in 1955. He acquired the mantle of prime minister when Britain granted Malaya independence in 1957. Also see Long, *Safe for Decolonization*, 50–51, 54–55.

49. CIA, "Singapore: Current Situation," undated (likely June 1959), CIA FOIA Reading Room, last accessed November 21, 2017, https://www.cia.gov/library/readingroom/docs/DOC_0000244661.pdf.

50. U.S. policy in Mainland Southeast Asia: Singapore, November 3, 1959, 1–2.

51. T. N. Harper, "Lim Chin Siong and the 'Singapore Story,'" in *Comet in Our Sky: Lim Chin Siong in History*, ed. Tan Jing Quee and Jomo K. S. (Kuala Lumpur: INSAN, 2001), 22; Lee Kuan Yew, "How the Communists Operate," in Lee Kuan Yew, *The Battle for Merger* (Singapore: Government Printing Office, 1961), 16.

52. UK Commissioner, "Discussion with the Prime Minister on August 13, 1959," August 14, 1959, FCO 141/15345, TNA.

53. British Defense Coordination Committee (Far East) and Joint Intelligence Committee (Far East), "The Outlook in Singapore up to the End of 1960," September 11, 1959, 3, FCO 141/12256, TNA.

54. "Who's Who: Lee Kuan Yew," June 1954, 2–3, FCO 141/15306, TNA.

55. G. C. Madoc (Director of Intelligence), "The MCP's 'Political Offensive,'" March 10, 1956, 2, FCO 141/7459, TNA.

56. UK Commissioner, "Discussion with the PM on July 30, 1959," 2, FCO 141/15345, TNA.

57. Joint Intelligence Committee (Far East), "The Outlook in Singapore for the Next Twelve Months," March 17, 1961, 3–4, FCO 141/12556, TNA.

58. Harper, "Lim Chin Siong,'" 39, 54. Here, Harper quotes from a letter, Moore to Secretary of State, July 18, 1962, CO 1030/1160, TNA.

59. UK Commissioner, "Discussion with the PM on 30 Jul 1959," 2, FCO 141/15345, TNA.

60. Long, *Safe for Decolonization*, 167.

61. Report, May 14, 1959, folder "Political Trends in Singapore," FCO 141/14651, TNA.

62. UK Commissioner, "Discussion with the PM on July 3, 1959," 9; "Discussion with the PM on November 12, 1959," 1–2, FCO 141/15345, TNA.

63. Harper, "Lim Chin Siong,'" 34–35.

64. Outgoing telegram, George Ball to American Embassies (London, Kuala Lumpur) and American Consul (Singapore), October 12, 1961, folder "Malaya and Singapore, 1/61–10/61," box 140, POF, NSF-Countries, JFKL.

65. Matthew Jones, "Creating Malaysia: Singapore Security, the Borneo Territories and the Contours of British Policy, 1961–3," *Journal of Imperial and Commonwealth History* 28, no. 2 (2000): 86, 89.

66. Tan, "'Grand Design,'" 143.

67. Tunku Abdul Rahman, "Formation of Malaysia: The Trend towards Merger Cannot Be Reversed, March 2, 1975," in Tunku Abdul Rahman Putra Al-Haj, *Looking Back: Monday Musings and Memories* (Kuala Lumpur, Malaysia: Polygraphic Press Sdn Bhd, 1977), 81–82.

68. Harper, "Lim Chin Siong,'" 4–5, 25, 35.

69. Jones, "Creating Malaysia," 88.

70. Harper, "Lim Chin Siong,'" 4–5, 25, 35.

71. *The History of Singapore Part 2—The Accidental Nation*, directed by Alex Lay (2005; Singapore: Lion Television Ltd. and Discovery Networks Asia, 2006), DVD.

72. "Roving Report: Project Malaysia (1)," November 2, 1961, ITN News (YouTube.com), last accessed April 21, 2014, http://www.youtube.com/watch?v=Raze5IozOI8.

73. Tan, "'Grand Design,'" 157.

74. Incoming telegram, Bruce (London) to Secretary of State, October 21, 1961, folder "Malaya and Singapore, 1/61–10/61," box 140, POF, NSF-Countries, JFKL. See Anthony J. Stockwell, "Malaysia: The Making of a Grand Design," *Asian Affairs* 34, no. 3 (November 2003): 227–42; and Stockwell, "Britain and Brunei, 1945–63: Imperial Retreat and Royal Ascendancy," *Modern Asian Studies* 38, no. 4 (2004): 785–819.

75. Brian Farrell, "End of Empire: From Union to Withdrawal," in *Between Two Oceans*, 390; Matthew Jones, *Conflict and Confrontation in Southeast Asia, 1961–1965: Britain, the United States and the Creation of Malaysia* (Cambridge: Cambridge University Press, 2002), 269.

76. Incoming telegram, Bruce (London) to Secretary of State, October 12, 1961, folder "Malaya and Singapore, 1/61–10/61," box 140, POF, NSF-Countries, JFKL.

77. United Kingdom Commission Report for September 1961, 1, folder "Political and Intelligence Reports on Singapore," FCO 141/12681, TNA.

78. Incoming telegram, Baldwin to Secretary of State, October 20, 1961, folder "Malaya and Singapore, 1/61–10/61," box 140, POF, NSF—Countries, JFKL.

79. Incoming telegram, Baldwin to Secretary of State, September 6, 1961, folder "Malaya and Singapore, 1/61–10/61," box 140, POF, NSF—Countries, JFKL.

80. Inward telegram, Selkirk to Secretary of State for the Colonies, April 24, 1962, DO (Dominions Office) 169/96, TNA.

81. Jones, "Creating Malaysia," 87, 91.

82. Jones, "Creating Malaysia," 87, 91–92.

83. Edward Miller, "Grand Designs: Vision, Power and Nation Building in Americas Alliance with Ngo Dinh Diem, 1954–60" (Ph.D. diss., Harvard University, 2004), 208, qtd. in Jessica

Chapman, "Staging Democracy: South Vietnam's 1955 Referendum to Depose Bao Dai," *Diplomatic History* 30, no. 4 (2006): 674.

84. Jones, "Creating Malaysia," 87, 91–92.

85. Letter, Moore (British High Commissioner, Singapore) to Lord Selkirk (British Commissioner of Singapore), November 27, 1962; letter, Moore to Wallace (Colonial Office), December 5, 1962, CO 1030/1159, TNA.

86. Notes of a Meeting with Mr. Lee Kuan Yew, November 27, 1962, CO1030/1159, TNA.

87. Jones, "Creating Malaysia," 86, 89.

88. Jones, "Creating Malaysia," 99–100.

89. United Kingdom Commission Fortnightly Summary No. 22, December 22, 1962–January 3, 1963, FCO 141/12683, TNA.

90. Category "A" (Hard Core Organizers of the Communist Conspiracy), 1, 9, 12, CO 1030/1576, TNA.

91. Jones, "Creating Malaysia," 86.

92. Jones, "Creating Malaysia," 86, 103–4.

93. Incoming telegram, Donhauser (Singapore) to Rusk (Washington), February 2, 1963, folder "Malaya and Singapore, 12/62–8/63," box 140, POF, NSF—Countries, JFKL.

94. Jones, "Creating Malaysia," 106.

95. Memorandum of a conversation, April 24, 1963, *FRUS*, 1961–1963, vol. 23, *Southeast Asia*, ed. John P. Glennon, David W. Mabon, and Edward C. Keefer (Washington, DC: Government Printing Office, 1994), document 331.

96. "Mobs Protesting Malaysia Raid Embassies," *New York Times*, September 17, 1963.

97. "Malaysians Attack Embassy," *New York Times*, September 17, 1963.

98. Flora Lewis, "British Ponder Reprisals for Jakarta Actions," *Los Angeles Times*, September 19, 1963.

99. "The High Price of Temper," *The Economist*, September 21, 1963; "Anti-British Feeling Grows in Indonesia," *Los Angeles Times*, September 18, 1963.

100. Farrell, "End of Empire," 388–90, 392–93.

101. The precise date for the coinage of *nekolim* is unclear. According to historian J. D. Legge, the word was simply the "sixties version of [Sukarno's] anti-imperialism of the twenties, designed to fit a situation where direct colonial rule had been thrown off, but where imperialism in the form of economic domination or of Western spheres of influence still existed." See Legge, *Sukarno*, 343.

However, according to political scientist Frederick P. Bunnell, *nekolim* was coined in early 1964 by Lieutenant-General Yani, commander of the Indonesian army. See Frederick P. Bunnell, "Guided Democracy Foreign Policy: 1960–5 President Sukarno Moves from Nonalignment to Confrontation," *Indonesia* 2 (October 1966): 37. Bunnell's appears to be the only work that attributes *nekolim* to someone other than Sukarno.

102. Taomo Zhou, "Ambivalent Alliance: Chinese Policy toward Indonesia, 1960–1965," *China Quarterly* (2015): 215. Zhou's study of Chinese records is singularly important to the history of the Chinese-Indonesian relationship during the Cold War.

103. Robert J. McMahon, *The Limits of Empire: The United States and Southeast Asia since World War II* (New York: Columbia University Press, 1999), 122. According to historian Adrian Vickers, the Bandung Conference eventually "produced the Nonaligned Movement . . . a separate identity for those countries that did not want to be clients of either the USSR or the USA in the Cold War." After Bandung, Vickers argues, Sukarno and Indonesia's "role in world politics was elevated." See Adrian Vickers, *A History of Modern Indonesia* (New York: Cambridge University Press, 2005), 116.

104. *A Survey on the Controversial Problems of the Establishment of the Federation of Malaysia* (Washington, DC: Information Division of the Embassy of Indonesia, 1963), 2, 5.

105. Soekarno, *Sukarno: An Autobiography as Told to Cindy Adams* (Indianapolis: Bobbs-Merrill, 1965), 302–3.

106. Taomo Zhou, "China and the Thirtieth of September Movement," *Indonesia* 98 (2014): 33.

107. For scholars concerned largely with the conflict between the British Commonwealth and Indonesia, see David Easter, *Britain and the Confrontation with Indonesia, 1960–66* (London: Tauris Academic Studies, 2004) and John Subritzky, *Confronting Sukarno: British, American, Australian and New Zealand Diplomacy in the Malaysia-Indonesia confrontation, 1961–5* (New York: St. Martin's, 2000). For those concerned with the U.S. part in *Konfrontasi*, see Simpson, *Economists with Guns* and Jones, *Conflict and Confrontation*.

108. Airgram, American Embassy (Malawi) to Department of State, "Text of Message from President Soekarno to Dr. Banda Justifying Indonesia's Withdrawal from the United Nations, January 10, 1965," January 31, 1965, folder "United Nations: Withdrawal of Indonesia, 12/64–7/65," box 294, National Security File (NSF), Country File, UN, Papers of Lyndon Baines Johnson (Johnson Papers), Lyndon Baines Johnson Presidential Library (henceforth, LBJL).

109. King, "Malaysian Union."

110. Lee Kuan Yew, *The Papers of Lee Kuan Yew: Speeches, Interviews and Dialogues*, vol. 1, *1950–1962* (Singapore: Gale Asia, 2012), 364–65.

111. Letter to "Dennis" [Dennis Bloodworth], May 2, 1962, folio 53 (13), Alex Josey Private Papers Collection (henceforth, AJP). Courtesy of ISEAS Library, ISEAS–Yusof Ishak Institute, Singapore. Lee appears to have taken as largely interchangeable the terms "neutral," "nonaligned," and "Afro-Asian," and his collaboration with Josey proceeded from this assumption. In a May 1962 radio broadcast, Lee described "neutralism" as the first incarnation of the Afro-Asian nations' attempt to keep aloof from the big power rivalries of the Cold War, which had to be turned into "nonalignment" when the Afro-Asian nations found themselves dragged in various ways into the Cold War but still sought to avoid taking sides. See Ang Cheng Guan, *Lee Kuan Yew's Strategic Thought* (London: Routledge, 2012), 15.

112. Letter to Lee Kuan Yew, February 23, 1962, folio 53 (1); letter to Peter Campbell Esq., March 31, 1962, folio 53 (9)/p. 3; letter to Director of Broadcasting, Broadcasting House Singapore, April 11, 1962, folio 53 (8)/p. 2; letter to "Dennis," May 2, 1962, folio 53 (13), AJP.

113. Inward telegram, Selkirk to Secretary of State for the Colonies, April 24, 1962, DO 169/96, TNA.

114. CIA, "Singapore on the Eve of Lee Kuan Yew's Visit to the U.S.," October 6, 1967, 7, CIA FOIA Reading Room, last accessed November 21, 2017, https://www.cia.gov/library/readingroom/docs/CIA-RDP79-00927A006000070008-3.pdf.

115. Lee Hsien Loong, "Let's Pledge to Continue Building this Exceptional Nation," *Today Online*, March 30, 2015, last accessed August 18, 2018, https://www.todayonline.com/rememberinglky/mr-lee-kuan-yews-state-funeral-service-pm-lee-hsien-loong-delivers-eulogy?singlepage=true.

116. Report, Sir Michael Creswell to Lord Home, "Visit to Yugoslavia of the Prime Minister of Singapore, Mr. Lee Kuan Yew," May 4, 1962, DO 169/97, TNA.

117. "PM's Blessings for Malaysia Secured: Lee Stresses Stabilizing Factor in S.E.-Asia," *Times of India*, April 25, 1962, folio 53 (28); Three Days in Belgrade: What Really Happened? May 10, 1962, folio 53 (21), AJP.

118. Letter, Lee to P.B.C. Moore (British High Commissioner to Singapore), February 12, 1964, FCO 141/14078, TNA.

119. Questions in Burma, Rightwing Tungku and Leftwing Lee Kuan Yew, folio 53 (16), AJP.

120. Letter to "Dennis," May 2, 1962, folio 53 (13); "PM's Blessings for Malaysia Secured: Lee Stresses Stabilizing Factor in S.E.-Asia," *Times of India*, April 25, 1962, folio 53 (28), AJP.

121. Report, British High Commissioner in India to the Lord Chancellor, "India: Visit of the Prime Minister of Singapore," May 16, 1962, DO 169/96. The British Commonwealth secretary later informed London that he did not recall Nehru "respond[ing] in any particular way" when Lee "trot[ted] out [this] thesis." Even so, the *Times of India* on April 25, 1962 reported that Nehru endorsed the formation of Malaysia.

122. Zhou, "Ambivalent Alliance," 214.

123. Letter to "Dennis," May 2, 1962, folio 53 (13), AJP.

124. Lee, "Report No. 1: United Arab Republic," February 12, 1964, folder "Visit of Mr. Lee Kuan-Yew," FCO (Foreign Commonwealth Office) 141/14078, TNA.

125. Report, Creswell to Home, "Visit to Yugoslavia of the Prime Minister of Singapore, Mr. Lee Kuan Yew."

126. Three Days in Belgrade: What Really Happened? May 10, 1962, folio 53 (21), AJP.

127. *Survey on the Controversial Problems of the Establishment of the Federation of Malaysia.*

128. Note, Hall (British Deputy High Commissioner in Kuching) to James Wong (Deputy Chief Minister of Sarawak), February 22, 1964, FCO 141/14078, TNA.

129. Letter, British High Commission (Singapore) to British High Commission (Kuala Lumpur), March 11, 1964, TNA.

130. David Easter, "British and Malaysian Covert Support for Rebel Movements in Indonesia during the 'Confrontation,' 1963–66," *Intelligence and National Security* 14, no. 4 (1999): 195–208.

131. Raffi Gregorian, "CLARET Operations and Confrontation, 1964–6," *Journal of the Center for Conflict Studies* 11, no. 1 (1991): 46–72.

132. Letter, Thompson to E.H. Peck (Foreign Office, London), January 20, 1965, FO 171/180520 (DV1017/8), TNA.

133. Lee, "Report No. 8: Ivory Coast," "Report No. 16: Kenya," February 12, 1964, FCO 141/14078, TNA.

134. Letter, Lee to P.B.C. Moore (British High Commissioner to Singapore), February 12, 1964, FCO 141/14078, TNA.

135. Zhou, "China and the Thirtieth of September Movement," 31–35, 40; Zhou, "Ambivalent Alliance," 213.

136. Lee, "Report No. 17: Ethiopia," February 12, 1964, FCO 141/14078, TNA.

137. Lee, "Report No. 9: Ghana," February 12, 1964, FCO 141/14078, TNA.

138. "Annex: The Future of Malaysia" May 1962, DO 169/96, TNA.

139. Letter, British High Commission (Singapore) to British High Commission (Kuala Lumpur), March 11, 1964, FCO 141/14078, TNA.

140. Lee, "Report No. 5: Mali," February 12, 1964, FCO 141-14078, TNA.

141. Letter and report, E.D. Hone (Governor, Northern Rhodesia) to Duncan Sandys (Secretary of State for the Colonies), February 20, 1964, FCO 141/14078, TNA.

142. Daniel Chua, *U.S.-Singapore Relations, 1965–1975: Strategic Non-Alignment in the Cold War* (Singapore: National University of Singapore Press, 2017), 73–74.

143. Zhou, "Ambivalent Alliance," 215.

144. Zhou, "China and the Thirtieth of September Movement," 33–34, 50–52.

145. Airgram, American Embassy (Malawi) to Department of State, "Text of Message from President Soekarno to Dr. Banda Justifying Indonesia's Withdrawal from the United Nations, January 10, 1965," January 31, 1965.

146. Soekarno, *Sukarno*, 302–4.

147. Far East and Pacific Department, Commonwealth Relations Office, Quadripartite Talks: Repercussions on British Policy in Southeast Asia of the Separation of Singapore, August 31, 1965, CO 968/838, TNA; Alex Josey, "Why Malaysia Failed," *New Statesman*, August 13, 1965.

148. "Aide at U.N. Shaken," *New York Times*, August 10, 1965.

149. Seth King, "Rahman Cites Tensions," *New York Times*, August 10, 1965; "Record of Talk between the Rt. Hon. Denis Healey, M.P. Secretary of State for Defence, and Mr. Lee Kuan Yew, Prime Minister of Singapore, Friday 4th February 1966," PREM (Prime Minister's Office) 13/1833, TNA.

150. "The Tengku's Statement to Parliament: A Dream Shattered . . . Now a Parting of Ways," *Straits Times*, August 10, 1965.

151. *History of Singapore Part 2—The Accidental Nation*.

152. Farrell, "End of Empire," 390.

153. Jones, *Conflict and Confrontation*, 269.

154. Farrell, "End of Empire," 390. Also see Albert Lau, *A Moment of Anguish: Singapore in Malaysia and the Politics of Disengagement* (Singapore: Times Academic Press, 1998), chaps. 5 to 8.

155. Jones, *Conflict and Confrontation*, 269, 273.

156. "Indonesians Hail Malaysia Split," *New York Times*, August 10, 1965.

157. Telegram ("Comments Made by Subandrio on August 9 about Singapore's Secession"), Djakarta to Foreign Office (London), August 10, 1965, FO 371/181454, TNA.

158. Telegram ("Further Indonesian Reactions to Singapore's Secession"), Djakarta to Foreign Office (London), August 10, 1965, FO 371/181454, TNA.

159. Zhou, "Ambivalent Alliance," 215. Here Zhou quotes from Marshall Green, *Indonesia: Crisis and Transformation, 1965–1968* (Washington, DC: Compass Press, 1990), 36.

160. Ed Meagher (of the *Los Angeles Times*), "Singapore's Secession Deals Near Fatal Blows to Malaysia," *Boston Globe*, August 12, 1965, 10.

161. Andrew Kopkind, "The First Falling Domino," *New Statesman*, August 13, 1965, 208.

162. Meagher, "Singapore's Secession," *Boston Globe*.

163. Zhou, "Ambivalent Alliance," 216.

164. Zhou, "China and the Thirtieth of September Movement," 50–52.

165. John Roosa, *Pretext for Mass Murder: The September 30th Movement and Suharto's Coup D'état in Indonesia* (Madison: University of Wisconsin Press, 2006), chap. 6.

166. Roosa, *Pretext for Mass Murder*, chaps. 5 and 6.

167. Vincent Bevins, "What the United States Did in Indonesia," *Atlantic*, October 20, 2017.

168. Sunil Amrith, *Migration and Diaspora in Modern Asia* (London: Cambridge University Press, 2012), 124.

169. Telegram, US Embassy (Jakarta) to State, October 5, 1965, *FRUS, 1964–1968*, vol. 26, *Indonesia; Malaysia-Singapore; Philippines*, ed. Edward C. Keefer (Washington, DC: Government Printing Office, 2000), document 147; Bevins, "What the United States Did." Also see "Indonesia: U.S. Documents Released on 1965–1966 Massacres," *Human Rights Watch*, October 18, 2017, last accessed October 27, 2017, https://www.hrw.org/news/2017/10/18/indonesia-us-documents-released-1965-66-massacres.

170. Zhou, "Ambivalent Alliance," 209, 219–20, 224. The events surrounding Aidit's maneuver, Suharto's coup, and the Indonesian massacres of 1965 remain mystifying to present day. Zhou's recent works are probably the most insightful on the subject and should be read in combination with Roosa, *Pretext for Mass Murder*; Simpson, *Economists with Guns*, 171–206; and Benedict Anderson, "Petrus Dadi Ratu (The Killer Becomes King)," *New Left Review* 3 (2000): 5–15.

171. Zhou, "Ambivalent Alliance," 224.

172. Telegram, Djakarta to Foreign Office (London), August 10, 1965, FO 371/181454; memorandum, "Repercussions on British Policy in Southeast Asia of the Separation of Singapore from Malaysia," September 16, 1965, DO 169/439, TNA.

173. Farrell, "End of Empire," 392–93.

174. Saki Dockrill, *Britain's Retreat from East of Suez: The Choice between Europe and the World?* (London, UK: Palgrave Macmillan, 2002), 127–28.

175. Farrell, "End of Empire," 390.

176. "Working Party on Singapore: Report to Ministers—OPD (65) 123," August 31, 1965, CO 968/838.

5. The Friendly Kings

1. Saki Dockrill, *Britain's Retreat from East of Suez: The Choice between Europe and the World?* (London: Palgrave MacMillan, 2002), 203–4.

2. Telegram (Subject "UK East of Suez"), David Bruce (U.S. Ambassador to the United Kingdom) to Department of State (Washington, DC), June 12, 1967, folder "United Kingdom (1967–1968)," box 12, Papers of Lyndon Baines Johnson (henceforth, LBJ Papers), President's Confidential File—CO 301, Lyndon Baines Johnson Presidential Library (henceforth, LBJL); Andrea Benvenuti and Moreen Dee, "The Five Power Defense Arrangements and the Reappraisal of British and Australian Policy Interests in Southeast Asia, 1970–5," *Journal of Southeast Asian Studies* 41, no. 1 (2010): 101.

3. Memorandum of a conversation, Subject: "British Budget and Defense Cuts," January 11, 1968; memorandum for the President, "British Withdrawal from the Far East and Persian Gulf," undated, folder "United Kingdom Vol. 13 [2 of 3]," box 212, LBJ Papers, NSF, Country File (henceforth CF)—United Kingdom; LBJL. In these memorandums, the phrase "fait accompli" is used by both Rusk and Brown and underlined, apparently to denote italicization.

4. Dockrill, *Britain's Retreat*, 204.

5. Letter, Rostow to the President, January 11, 1968, folder "United Kingdom Vol. 13 [2 of 3]," box 212, LBJ Papers, NSF, CF—United Kingdom; LBJL.

6. Karl Hack, *Defense and Decolonization in Southeast Asia: Britain, Malaya and Singapore 1941–68* (Surrey, UK: Curzon, 2001), 1.

7. Studies of U.S.-British relations in the latter stages of the Vietnam War are concerned with Britain's withdrawal from Singapore and focus tightly on British decision making and U.S. responses while marginalizing the Singaporeans and Malaysians. See Dockrill, *Britain's Retreat*; P. L. Pham, *Ending East of Suez: The British Decision to Withdraw from Malaysia and Singapore, 1964–1968* (Oxford: Oxford University Press, 2011); and Hack, *Defense and Decolonization*.

Works concerned with how Singapore grappled with British retrenchment sideline other nations of the region, the U.S. war in Vietnam, and the Cold War. See Malcolm Murfett, John N. Miksic, Brian P. Farrell, and Chiang Ming Shun, eds., *Between Two Oceans: A Military History of Singapore from First Settlement to Final British Withdrawal* (Oxford: Oxford University Press, 1999), 379–409.

8. See Leszek Buszynski, "The Soviet Union and Southeast Asia since the Fall of Saigon," *Asian Survey* 21, no. 5 (May 1981): 536–50; Muthiah Alagappa, "Soviet Policy in Southeast Asia: Toward Constructive Engagement," *Pacific Affairs* 63, no. 3 (1990): 321–50; Michael C. Williams, "New Soviet Policy toward Southeast Asia: Reorientation and Change," *Asian Survey* 31, no. 4 (1991): 364–77; and Susanne Birgerson, "The Evolution of Soviet Foreign Policy in Southeast Asia: Implications for Russian Foreign Policy," *Asian Affairs: An American Review* 23, no. 4 (1997): 212–34.

9. Scholars of international relations (more often than historians) have produced the major studies of how Southeast Asian elites established groupings such as ASEAN for their collective security. See Amitav Acharya, *The Making of Southeast Asia: International Relations of a Region* (Ithaca, NY: Cornell University Press, 2013), chaps. 5 and 6. Works such as this emphasize Southeast Asian regionalism and self-reliance and ignore the extent to which ASEAN upheld western imperialism.

Evelyn Goh's *The Struggle for Order: Hegemony, Hierarchy and Transition in Post-Cold War East Asia* (Oxford: Oxford University Press, 2013) shows East Asian states' complicity in bolstering U.S. hegemony in the post–Cold War era. Her book overlooks how, decades earlier, Asian anticommunist nationalists had already worked to transition the colonial order into U.S. empire.

10. CIA, National Intelligence Estimate: Communist China and Asia, March 6, 1969, 5, CIA FOIA Reading Room, last accessed November 21, 2017, http://www.foia.cia.gov/sites/default /files/document_conversions/89801/DOC_0001085113.pdf.

11. Memcon, February 17, 1973, 20, folder "Memcons and Reports (Originals) [TS 1 of 2] (3 of 4)," box 98, NSC Files—Henry A. Kissinger Office Files, CF–Far East, Richard Nixon Presidential Library (henceforth, RMNL).

12. See Niall Ferguson, ed., *Shock of the Global: The 1970s in Perspective* (Cambridge, MA: Harvard University Press, 2010); Daniel J. Sargent, *A Superpower Transformed: The Remaking of American Foreign Relations in the 1970s* (Oxford: Oxford University Press, 2015); and Jeremi Suri, *Power and Protest: Global Revolution and the Rise of Détente* (Cambridge, MA: Harvard University Press, 2003), as well as other references on this point in the introduction to this book.

13. Keith L. Nelson, "Nixon, Brezhnev, and Détente," *Peace & Change* 16, no. 2 (1991): 212–14; telegram, Soviet Ambassador Dobrynin to the Soviet Foreign Ministry, July 17, 1971, in *Soviet-American Relations: The Détente Years, 1969–1972*, ed. Edward C. Keefer, David C. Geyer, and Douglas E. Selvage, (Washington, DC: U.S. Department of State, 2007), 401–4.

14. See introduction of this book for this author's approach to the character of U.S. empire drawn from the principles discussed in Charles Maier, *Among Empires: American Ascendancy and Its Predecessors* (Cambridge, MA: Harvard University Press, 2006), 33, 35; Geir Lundestad, "Empire by Invitation? The United States and Western Europe," *Journal of Peace Research* 23, no. 3 (1986): 263–77, and Paul Kramer, "Power and Connection: Imperial Histories of the United States in the World," *American Historical Review* 116 (December 2011): 1348–91.

15. Directorate of Intelligence, Intelligence Memorandum: Britain Begins Implementation of Budget Cuts, February 6, 1968, 6, folder "United Kingdom: Memos, Vol. 13 [1 of 3]," box 212, NSF-CF-United Kingdom, LBJL.

16. Map of British Forces at Bases Overseas," undated (likely February 1968), folder "United Kingdom: Memos, Vol. 13 [1 of 3]," box 212, NSF-CF-UK, LBJL.

17. Directorate of Intelligence, Intelligence Memorandum: The Economy of the United Kingdom after Devaluation, February 8, 1968, 7, 17–18, folder "United Kingdom: Memos, Vol. 13 [1 of 3]," box 212, NSF-CF-UK, LBJL.

18. Benvenuti and Dee, "Five Power Defense Arrangements," 101–2.

19. Directorate of Intelligence, Intelligence Memorandum: Britain Begins Implementation of Budget Cuts, February 6, 1968, 6.

20. Carlyle A. Thayer, "The Five Power Defense Arrangements: The Quiet Achiever," *Security Challenges* 3, no. 1 (2007): 81.

21. Damon Bristow, "The Five Power Defense Arrangements: Southeast Asia's Unknown Regional Security Organization," *Contemporary Southeast Asia* 27, no. 1 (2005): 4.

22. Matthew Jones, *Conflict and Confrontation in Southeast Asia, 1961–1965: Britain, the United States and the Creation of Malaysia* (Cambridge: Cambridge University Press, 2002), 160–61; Memorandum of a conversation, March 8, 1966, 5, 8, folder "POL. Visits, Meetings. Singapore 1966," box 1, Subject Files of the Office of Indonesia, Malaysia and Singapore Affairs, 1965–74, RG 59, NARA; Thayer, "Five Power Defense Arrangements," 81.

23. Briefing memorandum "Malaysian Roundup," July 11, 1968, 6, folder "E-1. General Policy. Plans. Programs. 1968," box 1, Subject Files of the Office of Indonesia, Malaysia and Singapore Affairs, 1965–74, RG 59, NARA.

24. Bristow, "Five Power Defense Arrangements," 4.

25. Thayer, "Five Power Defense Arrangements," 81.

26. Ralf Emmers, "The Role of the Five Power Defense Arrangements in the Southeast Asian security architecture," RSIS (Rajaratnam School of International Studies) Working Paper No. 195, Singapore: Nanyang Technological University, 2, 7.

27. U.S. position paper: U.K. Withdrawal from Malaysia/Singapore at the SEATO/Seven Nation/ANZUS Meeting (Wellington, New Zealand), March 27, 1968, 3; Memcon, "Future Australian Role in Malaysia/Singapore Security," May 27, 1968, LBJL, USDCO (Gale document no. CK2349506586); see also Daniel Chua, "America's Role in the Five Power Defense Arrangement: Anglo-American Power Transition in Southeast Asia, 1967–1971," *International History Review* 39, no. 4 (2017): 625–28.

28. Thayer, "Five Power Defense Arrangements," 81; Benvenuti and Dee, "Five Power Defense Arrangements," 102.

29. "News in Color—Army Exercise Malaya," British MovieTone (YouTube), last accessed February 23, 2018, https://www.youtube.com/watch?v=fxDCaAcsl1o.

30. Kin Wah Chin, *The Defense of Malaysia and Singapore: The Transformation of a Security System, 1957–71* (Cambridge: Cambridge University Press, 1983), 172.

31. V. Skosyrev, "Kommivoyazher s Chuzhim Tovarom," *Izvestiya*, March 15, 1968, quoted in Leszek Buszynski, *Soviet Foreign Policy and Southeast Asia* (London: Croom Helm, 1986), 50.

32. "Prospects for the Proposed Malaysian Federation," July 11, 1962, 9; "VII. East Asia, J. Malaysia and Singapore," 18.

33. Erik Alekseev, "Zapasnyew Pozitsii," *Pravda*, March 5, 1969, quoted in Buszynski, *Soviet Foreign Policy*, 50.

34. Bilveer Singh, *The Soviet Union in Singapore's Foreign Policy: An Analysis* (Kuala Lumpur, Malaysia: Institute of Strategic and Pacific Studies, 1990), 23.

35. V. Matveev, "Krizis Politiki Sily," *Izvestiya*, November 10, 1970, quoted in Buszynski, *Soviet Foreign Policy*, 50.

36. I. Shatalov, "At the Junction of Eras and Continents," *International Affairs*, April 1971, 93–94.

37. Buszynski, *Soviet Foreign Policy*, 13–14, 24, 51. See also Odd Arne Westad, *Restless Empire: China and the World since 1750* (New York: Basic Books, 2012), 346, 418–19; and Chen Jian, *Mao's China and the Cold War* (Chapel Hill: University of North Carolina Press, 2001), 63–71.

38. Director of Central Intelligence, National Intelligence Estimate: Southeast Asia after Vietnam, November 14, 1968, 3, CIA FOIA Reading Room, last accessed July 14, 2016, http://www.foia.cia.gov/sites/default/files/document_conversions/89801/DOC_0001166458.pdf.

39. Singh, *Soviet Union*, 21. Also Buszynski, *Soviet Foreign Policy*, 40–96.

40. Bradley R. Simpson, *Economists with Guns: Authoritarian Development and U.S.-Indonesian Relations, 1960–8* (Stanford, CA: Stanford University Press, 2008); and John Roosa, *Pretext for Mass Murder: The September 30th Movement and Suharto's Coup D'état in Indonesia* (Madison: University of Wisconsin Press, 2006).

41. Buszynski, *Soviet Foreign Policy*, 69–70, 72–73, 79, 82.

42. Cheng Guan Ang, *Southeast Asia and the Vietnam War* (New York: Routledge, 2010), 56–57. Other works by this author are attributed to Ang Cheng Guan. Ang is the author's family name.

43. "Fact Sheet—Malaysia," April 29, 1971, folder "Chron 1971: Background and Briefings: Kuala Lumpur," box 10, RG 59: Subject Files of the Office of Indonesia, Malaysia and Singapore Affairs, 1965–74, NARA.

44. Shatalov, "At the Junction," 90, 92, 94.

45. Memorandum, Laird to Nixon, undated (likely January 1970), folder "NSSM [National Security Study Memorandum] 31," box H-141, Nixon Presidential Materials Staff, NSC Institutional ("H") Files—Study Memorandums (1969–74), National Security Study Memorandums, RMNL.

46. V. Kobysh, "Skolachivayut Voennyi Blok," *Izvestiya*, April 17, 1971, quoted in Buszynski, *Soviet Foreign Policy*, 51.

47. Summary of U.S. Ambassador David Bruce's conversation with Ivan Koulikov, Second Secretary of the Soviet embassy, regarding Southeast Asian issues, November 1968, LBJL, USDCO (Gale document no. CK2349522014).

48. Bilveer Singh, *Soviet Relations with ASEAN* (Singapore: National University of Singapore Press, 1989), 40. For more on the Soviet response to the FPDA, see Wen-Qing Ngoei, "A Wide Anticommunist Arc: Britain, ASEAN and Nixon's Triangular Diplomacy," *Diplomatic History* 41, no. 5 (2017): 902–32.

49. Henry Stanhope, "Britain's Rundown of Forces in Asia Is Entering the Final Phase," *Times of London*, March 27, 1971.

50. Telegram, Dobrynin to Soviet Foreign Ministry, July 17, 1971.

51. Johan Saravanamuttu, *Malaysia's Foreign Policy, the First Fifty Years: Alignment, Neutralism, Islamism* (Singapore: Institute of Southeast Asian Studies, 2010), 102.

52. Lyndon B. Johnson, "Address on Vietnam before the National Legislative Conference, San Antonio, Texas," September 29, 1967, *The American Presidency Project*, last accessed November 21, 2017, http://www.presidency.ucsb.edu/ws/?pid=28460.

53. National Intelligence Estimate: Southeast Asia After Vietnam, November 14, 1968, 1.

54. Richard M. Nixon, "Asia after Viet Nam," *Foreign Affairs*, October 1967, 111–12, 123, italics added.

55. Ngoei, "Wide Anticommunist Arc."

56. Nixon, "Asia after Viet Nam," 111–12.

57. Jeffrey Kimball, "The Nixon Doctrine: A Saga of Misunderstanding," *Presidential Studies Quarterly* 36, no. 1 (2006): 62, 70.

58. Acharya, *Making of Southeast Asia*, 161.

59. Talking points for Mr. Bundy, December 15, 1965; Briefing memorandum (Singapore) for Mr. Bundy—Tab 3: Singapore–United States Economic Relations," February 17, 1966, folder "POL 1 General Policy. Background. Singapore 1966," box 1, Subject Files of the Office of Indonesia, Malaysia and Singapore Affairs, 1965–74, RG 59, NARA.

60. Ang, *Southeast Asia*, 28–29.

61. CIA, "Singapore on the Eve of Lee Kuan Yew's Visit to the US," October 6, 1967, 7–8; Acharya, *Making of Southeast Asia*, 161.

62. *"Xin jia po ge gong tuan lian he qing zhu wu yi lao dong jie da hui tuan an"* ("Proposal on celebration of Labor Day by the various unions and clubs of Singapore"), May 1, 1966, NA 1183, Singapore Barisan Sosialis Collection, courtesy of National Archives of Singapore.

63. *"Quan xing zuo pai gong tuan lian he qing zhu wu yi guo ji lao dong jie qun zhong da hui ling shi dong yi"* (May Day Commemoration Conference Temporary Motion), May 1, 1966, NA 1183, Singapore Barisan Collection, courtesy of National Archives of Singapore.

64. Ang, *Southeast Asia*, 28–29.

65. CIA, "Singapore on the Eve of Lee Kuan Yew's Visit," 5–7.

66. Letter, Lee Kuan Yew to President Johnson c/o Bundy, October 27, 1967, LBJL, USDCO (Gale document no. CK2349493464); Thomas R. Morgan, "The Most Happy Fella in the White House," *Time*, December 1, 1967; Nicholas Tarling, *Regionalism in Southeast Asia: To Foster the Political Will* (London: Routledge, 2006), 139.

67. Memorandum for the President, March 19, 1969, folder "Singapore, Lee Kuan Yew Information Visit, May 13, 1969," box 938, Nixon Presidential Materials Staff, NSC Files—VIP Visits, RMNL.

68. Memorandum (Kissinger to Nixon), undated (likely March 19, 1969), folder "Singapore, Lee Kuan Yew Information Visit, May 13, 1969," box 938, Nixon Presidential Materials Staff, NSC Files—VIP Visits, RMNL.

69. "Malaysia, Singapore and Brunei," January 8, 1971, folder "Chron 1971: Background and Briefings: Kuala Lumpur," box 10, RG 59: Subject Files of the Office of Indonesia, Malaysia and Singapore Affairs, 1965–74, NARA.

70. "The American Presence in Singapore: Background Paper," undated (likely December 1969–January 1970), folder "V.P. Agnew's Trip—Singapore Visit Briefing Book," box 83, NSC Files—Henry A. Kissinger Office Files, CF—Far East, RMNL (exclamation mark in original).

71. Ang, *Southeast Asia*, 49.

72. Notes of the President's Meeting with the National Security Council, August 9, 1967, folder "August 9, 1967–12:20 P.M. National Security Council," box 1, Tom Johnson's Notes of Meetings, LBJL.

73. Memorandum: Meeting of NSC (Subject: Indonesia), August 9, 1967, folder "NSC Meetings, Vol. 4 Tab 55, 8/9/67, Indonesia," box 2, LBJ Papers, NSF—NSC Meetings File, LBJL.

74. Memcon (Suharto, Nixon, and Kissinger), May 26, 1970, folder "MemCon—The President/Pres. Suharto/ Kissinger, May 26, 1970," box 1024, Nixon Presidential Materials Staff, NSC Files, Presidential/Henry A. Kissinger Memcons, RMNL.

75. Memcon (Suharto, Nixon, and Henry Kissinger), May 26, 1970.

76. Memcon (Suharto, Nixon, and Henry Kissinger), May 26, 1970.

77. Memcon (H. Alamsjah, Indonesian State Secretary and Kissinger), May 27, 1970, folder "MemCon—Alamsjah/ Kissinger/ Holdridge, May 27, 1970," box 1024, Nixon Presidential Materials Staff, NSC Files, Presidential/ Henry A. Kissinger Memcons; "Background—Military Assistance to Indonesia," May 18, 1970, folder "Indonesia: President Suharto State Visit, May 26–June 1, 1970 [1 of 2]," box 919, Nixon Presidential Materials Staff, NSC Files, VIP Visits, RMNL.

78. Memcon (H. Alamsjah, Indonesian State Secretary and Kissinger), May 27, 1970.

79. Ang, *Southeast Asia*, 86–87, 80–81.

80. Memorandum (Haig to Kissinger), July 7, 1970, folder "MemCon-Sumitro/Kissinger (L.A.), July 2, 1970, box 1024, Nixon Presidential Materials Staff, NSC Files, Presidential/ Henry A. Kissinger Memcons, RMNL.

81. National Intelligence Estimate: Southeast Asia after Vietnam, November 14, 1968, 9.

82. Acharya, *Making of Southeast Asia*, 160.

83. Stanley Karnow, *In Our Image: America's Empire in the Philippines* (New York: Random House, 1989), 376–77.

84. Walden Bello, "Edging toward the Quagmire: The United States and the Philippine Crisis," *World Policy Journal* 3 (1985/6): 29–58. See also H.W. Brands, *Bound to Empire: The United States and the Philippines* (New York: Oxford University Press, 1992).

85. Kenton Clymer, *A Delicate Relationship: The United States and Burma/Myanmar since 1945* (Ithaca, NY: Cornell University Press, 2015), 215–16.

86. "VII. East Asia, A. Overview: Asian Trends and U.S. Policy," undated (likely December 1968/ January 1969), folder "Chapter 7 (East Asia): Sections A-D," box 3, LBJ Papers, Administrative History, Department of State, vol. 1, chaps. 7–9, LBJL.

87. "VII. East Asia, A. Overview: Asian Trends and U.S. Policy."

88. Fredrik Logevall, *Choosing War: The Lost Chance for Peace and the Escalation of War in Vietnam* (Berkeley: University of California Press, 1999).

89. Memo, Hilsman to the Secretary, "Prospects for Malaysia," September 5, 1962.

90. Ang, *Southeast Asia*, 50; Lyndon Baines Johnson, Remarks to the Foreign Policy Conference for Business Executives, December 4, 1967, The American Presidency Project, last accessed February 14, 2017, http://www.presidency.ucsb.edu/ws/index.php?pid=28582&st=domino&st1=.

91. Walt W. Rostow, "Commencement Address at Middlebury College: Regional and World Order," June 12, 1967, 4, folder "CO 266: Singapore," box 11, LBJ Papers, Confidential File—CO 206; Notes of the President's Meeting with the National Security Council, November 8, 1967, box 1, Tom Johnson's Notes of Meetings, LBJL.

92. Lien-Hang T. Nguyen, *Hanoi's War: An International History of the War for Peace in Vietnam* (Chapel Hill: University of North Carolina Press, 2012).

93. Fredrik Logevall, "There Ain't No Daylight: Lyndon Johnson and the Politics of Escalation," in *Making Sense of the Vietnam Wars: Local, National, and Transnational Perspectives*, ed. Mark Philip Bradley and Marilyn B. Young (Oxford: Oxford University Press, 2008), 95–96. Here, Logevall refers to Robert M. Blackburn, *Mercenaries and Lyndon Johnson's "More Flags": The Hiring of Korean, Filipino, and Thai Soldiers in the Vietnam War* (Jefferson, NC: McFarland, 1994); "VII. East Asia, J. Malaysia and Singapore," 17, folder "Chapter 7 (East Asia): Sections G-J, box 3, LBJ Papers, Administrative history, Department of State, vol. 1, chaps. 7–9, LBJL.

94. Ang, *Southeast Asia*, 31–32.

95. "Fact Sheet—Malaysia," April 29, 1971, folder "Chron 1971: Background and Briefings: Kuala Lumpur," box 10, RG 59, Subject Files of the Office of Indonesia, Malaysia and Singapore Affairs, 1965–74, NARA.

96. Tunku Abdul Rahman, "Malaysia: Key Area in Southeast Asia," *Foreign Affairs*, July 1965, last accessed November 21, 2017, https://www.foreignaffairs.com/articles/asia/1965-07-01/malaysia-key-area-southeast-asia.

97. "Malaysia's Diplomatic Support for South Vietnam/ American Effort in Vietnam," undated (likely late 1967), LBJL, USDCO (Gale document no. CK2349065959).

98. Ang Cheng Guan, "Singapore and the Vietnam War," *Journal of Southeast Asian Studies* 40, no. 2 (2009): 360–61.

99. Memorandum, John P. Roche to the President, June 29, 1967, LBJL, USDCO (Gale document no. CK2349077214).

100. "NBC Meet The Press: Interview with Lee Kuan Yew (October 22, 1967)," *PublicResourceOrg* (YouTube), last accessed November 21, 2007, https://www.youtube.com/watch?v=VexrmTacOAA.

101. Memorandum for Mr. Rostow (Subject: Southeast Asia Developments), November 3, 1966, 3, folder "Ropa Memos," box 7, LBJ Papers, NSF—Name File, LBJL.

102. Notes of the President's Meeting with the National Security Council, November 8, 1967, box 1, Tom Johnson's Notes of Meetings, LBJL.

103. Johnson, Remarks to the Foreign Policy Conference for Business Executives, December 4, 1967.

104. MemCon (Sumitro and Kissinger), July 1, 1970, folder "MemCon-Sumitro/Kissinger (L.A.), July 2, 1970, box 1024, Nixon Presidential Materials Staff, NSC Files, Presidential/ Henry A. Kissinger Memcons, RMNL.

105. Richard M. Nixon, "A Conversation with the President about Foreign Policy," July 1, 1970, The American Presidency Project, last accessed November 20, 2017, http://www.presidency.ucsb.edu/ws/index.php?pid=2567&st=domino&st1.

106. Letter, Johnson to Lee, December 25, 1967, folder "Singapore: Presidential Correspondence," box 50, LBJ Papers, NSF—Special Head of State Correspondence, LBJL.

107. Memorandum (Kissinger to Nixon), undated (likely March 19, 1969).

108. Pamela Sodhy, *The U.S.-Malaysian Nexus: Themes in Superpower-Small State Relations* (Kuala Lumpur, Malaysia: Institute of Strategic and International Studies, 1991), 327; William R. Kintner, "U.S. Policy Interests in the Asian-Pacific Area: Summary Report," 3, folder "Ambassador Kintner's Study of U.S. Policy Interest in the Asian-Pacific Area," box 1, National Security Adviser, Presidential Country Files for East Asia and the Pacific, Gerald R. Ford Presidential Library.

109. Muhammad Ghazali bin Shafie, "Malaysia in South East Asia," in Muhammad Ghazali bin Shafie, *Malaysia, International Relations: Selected Speeches* (Kuala Lumpur, Malaysia: Creative Enterprise, 1982), 160–63.

110. National Intelligence Estimate: Communist China and Asia, March 6, 1969, 5.

111. Memcon, February 17, 1973, 20, folder "Memcons and Reports (Originals) [TS 1 of 2] (3 of 4)," box 98, NSC Files—Henry A. Kissinger Office Files, CF-Far East, RMNL.

112. "VII. East Asia, C. Communist China," undated (likely December 1968/ January 1969), 3, folder "Chapter 7 (East Asia): Sections A-D, box 3, LBJ Papers, Administrative History, Department of State, vol. 1, chaps. 7–9, LBJL. See Westad, *Restless Empire*, 334, 350–53.

113. CIA, National Intelligence Estimate: The USSR and China, August 21, 1969, 1, last accessed April 28, 2017, https://www.cia.gov/library/readingroom/docs/DOC_0000261304.pdf.

114. Richard Nixon, "Informal Remarks in Guam with Newsmen, July 25, 1969," *The American Presidency Project*, last accessed April 22, 2017, http://www.presidency.ucsb.edu/ws/?pid=2140.

115. Kimball, "Nixon Doctrine," 62, 68–99.

116. Westad, *Restless Empire*, 366–69; Chen, *Mao's China*, chap. 9.

117. Chen, *Mao's China*, 63.

118. Record of Discussion: President/ Chou En-Lai—February 22 and 24, 1972, folder "February 1972 Briefing Book [TS] (1 of 4)," box 98, NSC Files, Henry A. Kissinger Office Files, CF–Far East, RMNL.

119. Record of Discussion: Henry Kissinger/ Zhou Enlai—June 21, 1972, folder "February 1973 Briefing Book [TS] (1 of 4)," box 98, NSC Files—Henry A. Kissinger Office Files, CF–Far East, RMNL; 1971 Zone of Peace, Freedom and Neutrality (ZOPFAN) Declaration, *Center of International Law*, last accessed February 25, 2015, http://www.icnl.org/research/library/files/Transnational /zone.pdf.

120. Record of Discussion: Henry Kissinger/ Zhou Enlai—June 21, 1972, folder "February 1973 Briefing Book [TS] (1 of 4)," box 98, NSC Files—Henry A. Kissinger Office Files, CF-Far East, RMNL.

121. Ngoei, "Wide Anticommunist Arc," 928–31.

122. Richard Nixon, "Remarks at Andrews Air Force Base on Returning from the People's Republic of China, February 28, 1972," *The American Presidency Project*, last accessed November 20, 2015, http://www.presidency.ucsb.edu/ws/index.php?pid=3756&st=nixon&st1=china.

123. Chen, *Mao's China*, chaps. 8 and 9.

124. CIA, National Intelligence Estimate: The USSR and China, 2.

125. "S. Viet Civilians Loot GIs' Departure Camp," *Los Angeles Times*, March 30, 1973.

126. Southeast Asia and the Great Powers, April 26, 1973, folio 15 (5), Sinnathamby Rajaratnam Private Papers Collection (henceforth, SRP). Courtesy of ISEAS Library, ISEAS–Yusof Ishak Institute, Singapore. Rajaratnam's speech was delivered to the American Business Committee at a reception in the Shangri-La Hotel, Singapore.

127. America: In or Out of Asia? May 18, 1970, folio 12 (13), SRP.

128. South-East Asia after Vietnam, September 27, 1973, folio 15 (16), SRP.

129. Sodhy, *U.S.-Malaysian Nexus*, 327; Kintner, "U.S. Policy Interests," 3.

Coda

1. Muhammad Ghazali bin Shafie, "Broadcast by Malaysia's Minister of Home Affairs," *Survival: Global Politics and Strategy*, 17, no. 4 (July 1975): 187–88. Ghazali's speech was broadcast on Malaysian radio stations two months before its publication in *Survival*.

2. Fredrik Logevall, *Embers of War: The Fall of an Empire and the Making of America's Vietnam* (New York: Random House, 2012), 223. We first encountered this view of the domino logic from Logevall in chapter 1 of this book. Also see Robert J. McMahon, *The Limits of Empire: The United States and Southeast Asia since World War II* (New York: Columbia University Press, 1999), x–xi, 221.

3. CIA, "National Intelligence Estimate: The Outlook for Malaysia," April 1, 1976, *FRUS*, 1969–76, vol. E-12, *U.S. Department of State: Office of the Historian*, last accessed March 9, 2017, http://history.state.gov/historicaldocuments/frus1969-76ve12/d302; telegram, AmEmbassy (Kuala Lumpur) to SecState (Washington, DC), June 1975, folder "Malaysia—State Department Telegrams: To SECSTATE—EXDIS," box 12, National Security Adviser, Presidential Country Files for East Asia and the Pacific, Country File, Gerald R. Ford Presidential Library (henceforth, GRFL).

4. Ghazali, "Broadcast," 186.

5. Telegram, AmEmbassy (Kuala Lumpur) to SecState (Washington, DC), May 1975, folder "Malaysia—State Department Telegrams: To SECSTATE—EXDIS," box 12, National Security Adviser, Presidential Country Files for East Asia and the Pacific, Country File, GRFL.

6. Telegram, AmEmbassy (Kuala Lumpur) to SecState (Washington, DC), June 1975.

7. Ghazali, "Broadcast," 188.

8. Philip C. Habib, "Trip Report," June 13, 1975, folder "Southeast Asia (3)," box 1, National Security Adviser, Presidential Country Files for East Asia and the Pacific, 1974–7, GRFL.

9. Memorandum, W.R. Smyser (NSC) to Brent Scowcroft (National Security Adviser), June 4, 1975, folder "Southeast Asia (3)," box 1, National Security Adviser, Presidential Country Files for East Asia and the Pacific, 1974–7, GRFL.

10. Memorandum, Smyser to Kissinger, July 15, 1975, folder "Southeast Asia (3)," box 1, National Security Adviser, Presidential Country Files for East Asia and the Pacific, 1974–7, GRFL.

11. George F. Kennan, "The Long Telegram," February 22, 1946, *National Security Archive*, last accessed December 21, 2017, https://nsarchive2.gwu.edu//coldwar/documents/episode-1/kennan.html; "The Sources of Soviet Conduct," *Foreign Affairs*, July 1947; Francis P. Sempa, "George Kennan's Other Long Telegram—About the Far East," *The Diplomat*, December 5, 2017, last accessed December 21, 2017, https://thediplomat.com/2017/12/george-kennans-other-long-telegram-about-the-far-east/.

12. Paul J. Heer, *Mr. X and the Pacific: George F. Kennan and American Policy in East Asia* (Ithaca, NY: Cornell University Press, 2018), Kindle Edition, chap. 5.

13. Memorandum, Kennan to Acheson, August 23, 1950, Acheson Papers, Secretary of State file, August 1950, Harry S. Truman Presidential Library, last accessed December 21, 2017, https://www.trumanlibrary.org/whistlestop/study_collections/koreanwar/documents/index.php?documentdate=1950-08-23&documentid=ki-14-7&pagenumber=1.

14. See Walter L. Hixson, *George F. Kennan: Cold War Iconoclast* (New York: Columbia University Press, 1989), chap. 4.

15. Memorandum, Barnes to Scowcroft, January 15, 1976, folder "Ambassador Kintner's Study of U.S. Policy Interest in the Asian-Pacific Area," box 1, National Security Adviser, Presidential Country Files for East Asia and the Pacific, GRFL.

16. William R. Kintner, "U.S. Policy Interests in the Asian-Pacific Area: Executive Summary," October 31, 1975, 3, 5; "U.S. Policy Interests in the Asian-Pacific Area: Summary Report," 19, 35,

50–51, 64–65, folder "Ambassador Kintner's Study of U.S. Policy Interest in the Asian-Pacific Area," box 1, National Security Adviser, Presidential Country Files for East Asia and the Pacific, GRFL.

17. Speech at the National Press Club Luncheon at the Woodrow Wilson Center, Washington, DC, August 3, 1978, folio 20 (9), Sinnathamby Rajaratnam Private Papers Collection. Courtesy of ISEAS Library, ISEAS–Yusof Ishak Institute, Singapore.

Bibliography

Archival Sources

United Kingdom

Imperial War Museum (London)
Malcolm MacDonald Personal Papers, Durham University
The National Archives of the United Kingdom
　　Records of the Foreign Office, Foreign and Commonwealth Office, Ministry of
　　　　Defense, Prime Minister's Office, Colonial Office, Dominions Office

United States

The American Presidency Project (University of California–Santa Barbara)
Dwight D. Eisenhower Presidential Library
Foreign Relations of the United States Collections
Gerald R. Ford Presidential Library
Harry S. Truman Presidential Library
John F. Kennedy Presidential Library
Lyndon Baines Johnson Presidential Library
National Archives and Records Administration, Archives II at College Park
　　Record Groups 59, 84, 469, and 472
RAND Corporation
Richard Nixon Presidential Library
U.S. Declassified Documents Online (formerly Declassified Documents Retrieval
　　System)

Singapore and Malaysia

Arkib Negara Malaysia (Malaysian National Archives)
East Asian Collection and Singapore-Malaysia Collections, National University of
    Singapore Library
ISEAS (Institute of Southeast Asian Studies) Library, ISEAS–Yusof Ishak Institute
    Alex A. Josey Private Papers
    Sinnathamby Rajaratnam Private Papers
    Tan Cheng Lock Private Papers
National Archives of Singapore
Tunku Abdul Rahman Memorial Library

Published Sources

Abdul Rahman, Tunku. *Looking Back: Monday Musings and Memories*. Kuala Lumpur,
    Malaysia: Polygraphic Press Sdn Bhd, 1977.
——. *Viewpoints*. Kuala Lumpur, Malaysia: Heinemann Books, 1978.
Abu Talib Ahmad and Tan Liok Ee. Introduction to *New Terrains in Southeast Asian His-
    tory*, edited by Abu Talib Ahmad and Tan Liok Ee, ix–xxv. Athens: Ohio University
    Press, 2003.
Acharya, Amitav. *Constructing a Security Community in Southeast Asia: ASEAN and the Prob-
    lem of Regional Order*. London: Routledge, 2001.
——. *The Making of Southeast Asia: International Relations of a Region*. Ithaca, NY: Cornell
    University Press, 2013.
——. *Quest for Identity: International Relations of Southeast Asia*. New York: Oxford Uni-
    versity Press, 2000.
Alagappa, Muthiah. "Soviet Policy in Southeast Asia: Toward Constructive Engagement."
    Pacific Affairs 63, no. 3 (1990): 321–50.
Amrith, Sunil. *Migration and Diaspora in Modern Asia*. London: Cambridge University
    Press, 2012.
Anderson, Benedict. "Petrus Dadi Ratu (The Killer Becomes King)." *New Left Review* 3
    (2000): 5–15.
Ang, Cheng Guan. *Lee Kuan Yew's Strategic Thought*. London: Routledge, 2012.
——. "Malaysia, Singapore, and the Road to the Five Power Defense Arrangements
    (FPDA), July 1970–November 1971." *War & Society* 30, no. 3 (2011): 207–25.
——. "Singapore and the Vietnam War." *Journal of Southeast Asian Studies* 40, no. 2 (2009):
    353–84.
——. *Southeast Asia and the Vietnam War*. New York: Routledge, 2010.
Asselin, Pierre. *Hanoi's Road to the Vietnam War, 1954–1965*. Berkeley: University of Cali-
    fornia Press, 2013.
Bayly, Christopher, and Tim Harper. *Forgotten Armies: Britain's Asian Empire and the War
    with Japan*. Cambridge, MA: Harvard Belknap Press, 2005.

———. *Forgotten Wars: Freedom and Revolution in Southeast Asia*. Cambridge, MA: Harvard University Press, 2007.

Beckett, Ian F. W. "Robert Thompson and the British Advisory Mission to South Vietnam, 1961–5." *Small Wars and Insurgencies* 8, no. 3 (1997): 41–63.

Bello, Walden. "Edging toward the Quagmire: The United States and the Philippine Crisis." *World Policy Journal* 3 (1985–86): 29–58.

Benvenuti, Andrea. "The British Are 'Taking to the Boat': Australian Attempts to Forestall Britain's Military Disengagement from Southeast Asia, 1965–1966." *Diplomacy & Statecraft* 20, no. 1 (2009): 86–106.

———. "The British Military Withdrawal from Southeast Asia and Its Impact on Australia's Cold War Strategic Interests." *Cold War History* 5, no. 2 (2005): 189–210.

———. "The Heath Government and British Defense Policy in Southeast Asia at the End of Empire (1970–71)." *Twentieth Century British History* 20, no. 1 (2009): 53–73.

Benvenuti, Andrea, and Moreen Dee. "The Five Power Defense Arrangements and the Reappraisal of British and Australian Policy Interests in Southeast Asia, 1970–5." *Journal of Southeast Asian Studies* 41, no. 4 (2010): 101–23.

Birgerson, Susanne. "The Evolution of Soviet Foreign Policy in Southeast Asia: Implications for Russian Foreign Policy." *Asian Affairs: An American Review* 23, no. 4 (1997): 212–34.

Birtle, Andrew J. *U.S. Army Counterinsurgency and Contingency Operations Doctrine 1942–1976*. Fort McNair, DC: U.S. Army Center of Military History, 2006.

Blackburn, Robert M. *Mercenaries and Lyndon Johnson's "More Flags": The Hiring of Korean, Filipino, and Thai Soldiers in the Vietnam War*. Jefferson, NC: McFarland, 1994.

Blusse, Leonard. "Batavia, 1619–1740: The Rise and Fall of a Chinese Colonial Town." *Journal of Southeast Asian Studies* 12, no. 1 (1981): 159–78.

Boyce, Peter, ed. *Malaysia and Singapore in International Diplomacy: Documents and Commentaries*. Sydney: Sydney University Press, 1968.

Bradley, Mark P. *Imagining Vietnam and America: The Making of Postcolonial Vietnam, 1919–1950*. Chapel Hill: University of North Carolina Press, 2000.

Brand, Mona, and Lesley Richardson. *Two Plays about Malaya*. London: Lawrence and Wishart, 1954.

Brands, H. W. *Bound to Empire: The United States and the Philippines*. New York: Oxford University Press, 1992.

Bresnan, John. *From Dominoes to Dynamos: The Transformation of Southeast Asia*. New York: Council on Foreign Relations, 1994.

Bristow, Damon. "The Five Power Defense Arrangements: Southeast Asia's Unknown Regional Security Organization." *Contemporary Southeast Asia* 27, no. 1 (2005): 1–20.

Bunnell, Frederick P. "Guided Democracy Foreign Policy: 1960–5 President Sukarno Moves from Nonalignment to Confrontation." *Indonesia* 2 (1966): 37–76.

Burton, John. *Fortnight of Infamy: The Collapse of Allied Airpower West of Pearl Harbor*. Annapolis, MD: Naval Institute Press, 2006.

Busch, Peter. *All the Way with JFK? Britain, the US and the Vietnam War*. New York: Oxford University Press, 2003.

———. "Killing the 'Vietcong': The British Advisory Mission and the Strategic Hamlet Program." *Journal of Strategic Studies* 25, no. 1 (2002): 135–62.

Buszynski, Leszek. *Soviet Foreign Policy and Southeast Asia*. London: Croom Helm, 1986.

———. "The Soviet Union and Southeast Asia since the Fall of Saigon." *Asian Survey* 21, no. 5 (1981): 536–50.

Cady, John. *The United States and Burma*. Cambridge, MA: Harvard University Press, 1976.

Capozzola, Christopher. "'It Makes You Want to Believe in the Country': Celebrating the Bicentennial in an Age of Limits." In *America in the Seventies*, edited by Beth Bailey and David Farber, 29–49. Lawrence: University Press of Kansas, 2004.

Chapman, Jessica M. *Cauldron of Resistance: Ngo Dinh Diem, the United States and 1950s Southern Vietnam*. Ithaca, NY: Cornell University Press, 2013.

———. "Staging Democracy: South Vietnam's 1955 Referendum to Depose Bao Dai." *Diplomatic History* 30, no. 4 (2006): 671–703.

Cheah Boon Kheng. *Malaysia: The Making of a Nation*. Singapore: Institute of Southeast Asian Studies, 2002.

———. *Red Star over Malaya: Resistance and Conflict during and after the Japanese Occupation of Malaya, 1941–6*. Rev. ed. Singapore: Singapore University Press, 2012.

Chen Jian. *Mao's China and the Cold War*. Chapel Hill: University of North Carolina Press, 2001.

Chin, C. C., and Karl Hack, eds. *Dialogues with Chin Peng: New Light on the Malayan Communist Party*. Singapore: Singapore University Press, 2004.

Chin, Kin Wah. *The Defense of Malaysia and Singapore: The Transformation of a Security System, 1957–71*. Cambridge: Cambridge University Press, 1983.

Chin Peng. *Alias Chin Peng: My Side of History*. Singapore: Media Masters, 2003.

Chua, Daniel. "America's Role in the Five Power Defense Arrangement: Anglo-American Power Transition in Southeast Asia, 1967–1971." *International History Review* 39, no. 4 (2017): 615–37.

———. *U.S.-Singapore Relations, 1965–1975: Strategic Non-Alignment in the Cold War*. Singapore: National University of Singapore Press, 2017.

Clymer, Kenton. *A Delicate Relationship: The United States and Burma/Myanmar since 1945*. Ithaca, NY: Cornell University Press, 2015.

———. *The United States and Cambodia, 1870–1969: From Curiosity to Confrontation*. London: Routledge, 2004.

———. *The United States and Cambodia, 1969–2000: A Troubled Relationship*. London: Routledge, 2004.

Colley, Linda. "Introduction: Some Difficulties of Empire—Past, Present, and Future." *Common Knowledge* 11, no. 2 (2005): 198–214.

Comber, Leon. *Malaysia's Secret Police, 1945–60: The Role of the Special Branch in the Malayan Emergency*. Singapore: Institute of Southeast Asian Studies, 2008.

Counterinsurgency Case History: Malaya 1948–1960. Fort Leavenworth, KS: U.S. Army Command and General Staff College, 1965.

Cullather, Nick. *Illusions of Influence: The Political Economy of United States–Philippines Relations, 1942–60*. Stanford, CA: Stanford University Press, 1994.

Curtis, Mark. *Web of Deceit: Britain's Real Role in the World*. London: Vintage, 2003.

Darby, Philip. *British Defense Policy East of Suez: 1948–68.* Oxford: Oxford University Press, 1973.

Darwin, John. *Britain and Decolonisation: The Retreat from Empire in the Post-War World (Making of 20th Century).* London: Macmillan, 1988.

Dean, Robert D. *Imperial Brotherhood: Gender and the Making of Cold War Foreign Policy.* Amherst: University of Massachusetts Press, 2001.

Deery, Philip. "Malaya 1948: Britain's Asian Cold War?" *Journal of Cold War Studies* 9, no. 1 (Winter 2007): 29–54.

Dockrill, Saki. *Britain's Retreat from East of Suez: The Choice between Europe and the World?* London: Palgrave MacMillan, 2002.

Dower, John W. *Embracing Defeat: Japan in the Wake of World War II.* New York: W. W. Norton, 1999.

———. *War without Mercy: Race and Power in the Pacific War.* New York: Pantheon, 1986.

Duara, Prasenjit. *Decolonization: Perspectives from Now and Then.* New York: Routledge, 2004.

Easter, David. *Britain and the Confrontation with Indonesia, 1960–66.* London: Tauris Academic Studies, 2004.

———. "British and Malaysian Covert Support for Rebel Movements in Indonesia during the 'Confrontation,' 1963–66." *Intelligence and National Security* 14, no. 4 (1999): 195–208.

Elkins, Caroline. *Imperial Reckoning: The Untold Story of Britain's Gulag in Kenya.* New York: Henry Holt, 2005.

Elliott, Mai. *RAND in Southeast Asia: A History of the Vietnam War Era.* Santa Monica, CA: RAND Corporation, 2010.

Emmers, Ralf. "The Role of the Five Power Defense Arrangements in the Southeast Asian Security Architecture." RSIS Working Paper, No. 195. Singapore: Nanyang Technological University, 1–22.

Farrell, Brian P. "Bitter Harvest: The Defense and Fall of Singapore." In *Between Two Oceans: A Military History of Singapore from First Settlement to Final British Withdrawal,* edited by Malcolm H. Murfett, John N. Miksic, Brian P. Farrell, and Chiang Ming Shun. 198–244. New York: Oxford University Press, 1999.

Feightinger, Moritz, Stephan Malinowski, and Chase Richards. "Transformative Invasions: Western Post-9/11 Counterinsurgency and the Lessons of Colonialism." *Humanity: An International Journal of Human Rights, Humanitarianism and Development* 3, no. 1 (2012): 35–63.

Ferguson, Niall. *Colossus: The Price of America's Empire.* New York: Penguin Books, 2004.

———. *Empire: The Rise and Demise of the British World Order and the Lessons for Global Power.* New York: Basic Books, 2002.

———, ed. *Shock of the Global: The 1970s in Perspective.* Cambridge, MA: Harvard University Press, 2010.

Fernando, Joseph M. "Sir Ivor Jennings and the Malayan Constitution." *Journal of Imperial and Commonwealth History* 34, no. 4 (December 2006): 577–97.

Fifield, Russell H. *Americans in Southeast Asia: The Roots of Commitment.* New York: Crowell, 1973.

———. *Diplomacy in Southeast Asia*. New York: Harper, 1958.

———. *Southeast Asia in American Policy*. New York: Praeger, 1963.

Fineman, Daniel. "Phibun, the Cold War and Thailand's Foreign Policy Revolution of 1950." In *Connecting Histories: Decolonization and the Cold War in Southeast Asia, 1945–1962*, edited by Christopher E. Goscha and Christian F. Ostermann, 275–300. Stanford, CA: Stanford University Press, 2009.

———. *A Special Relationship: The United States and the Military Government of Thailand, 1947–58*. Honolulu: University of Hawaii Press, 1997.

Fitzgerald, David. "Sir Robert Thompson, Strategic Patience and Nixon's War in Vietnam." *Journal of Strategic Studies* 37, nos. 6–7 (2014): 998–1026.

Foster, Anne L. *Projections of Power: The United States and Europe in Colonial Southeast Asia, 1919–41*. Durham, NC: Duke University Press, 2010.

French, David. *The British Way in Counter-Insurgency, 1945–67*. Oxford: Oxford University Press, 2011.

Frey, Marc. "The Tools of Empire: Persuasion and the U.S. Modernizing Mission to Southeast Asia." *Diplomatic History* 27, no. 4 (2003): 543–68.

Friend, Theodore. *The Blue-Eyed Enemy: Japan against the West in Luzon and Java*. Princeton, NJ: Princeton University Press, 1988.

Gentile, Gian P. "A Strategy of Tactics: Population-Centric COIN and the Army." *Parameters: Journal of the U.S. Army War College* 41, no. 4 (2011–2012): 1–12.

Keefer, Edward C., David C. Geyer, and Douglas E. Selvage, eds. *Soviet-American Relations: The Détente Years, 1969–1972*. Washington, DC: U.S. Department of State, 2007.

Gilbert, Lewis. *The 7th Dawn*. Beverly Hills, CA: United Artists, 1964; MGM, 2011.

Glad, Betty, and Charles S. Taber. "Images, Learning, and the Decision to Use Force: The Domino Theory of the United States." In *The Psychological Dimensions of War*, edited by Betty Glad, 56–82. Newbury Park, CA: Sage Publications, 1990.

Go, Julian, and Anne L. Foster, eds. *The American Colonial State in the Philippines: Global Perspectives*. Durham, NC: Duke University Press, 2003.

Goh, Evelyn. *Constructing the U.S. Rapprochement with China, 1961–74: From "Red Menace" to "Tacit Ally."* Cambridge: Cambridge University Press, 2005.

———. *The Struggle for Order: Hegemony, Hierarchy and Transition in Post–Cold War East Asia*. Oxford: Oxford University Press, 2013.

Goscha, Christopher E., and Christian F. Ostermann. Introduction to *Connecting Histories: Decolonization and the Cold War in Southeast Asia, 1945–1962*, edited by Christopher E. Goscha and Christian F. Ostermann, 1–12. Stanford, CA: Stanford University Press, 2009.

Gouda, Frances, and Thijs Brocades Zaalberg. *American Visions of the Netherlands East Indies/Indonesia: US Foreign Policy and Indonesian Nationalism, 1920–1949*. Amsterdam: Amsterdam University Press, 2002.

Gould, James W. *The United States and Malaysia*. Cambridge, MA: Harvard Belknap Press, 1969.

Green, Marshall. *Indonesia: Crisis and Transformation, 1965–1968*. Washington, DC: Compass, 1990.

Gregorian, Raffi. "CLARET Operations and Confrontation, 1964–6." *Journal of the Center for Conflict Studies* 11, no. 1 (1991): 46–72.

Gungwu, Wang. *The Chinese Overseas: From Earthbound China to the Quest for Autonomy*. Cambridge, MA: Harvard University Press, 2002.

Gurman, Hannah. Introduction to *Hearts and Minds: A People's History of Counterinsurgency*, edited by Hannah Gurman, 1–15. New York: New Press, 2013.

Hack, Karl. *Defense and Decolonization in Southeast Asia: Britain, Malaya and Singapore 1941–68*. Surrey, UK: Curzon, 2001.

——. "Detention, Deportation and Resettlement: British Counterinsurgency and Malaya's Rural Chinese, 1948–1960." *Journal of Imperial and Commonwealth History* 43, no. 4 (2015): 611–40.

——. "Everyone Lived in Fear: Malaya and the British Way of Counterinsurgency." *Small Wars & Insurgencies* 23, nos. 4–5 (2012): 671–99.

——. "Theories and Approaches to British Decolonization in Southeast Asia." In *The Transformation of Southeast Asia: International Perspectives on Decolonization*, edited by Marc Frey, Ronald Pruessen, and Tan Tai Yong, 105–26. Armonk, NY: M. E. Sharpe, 2003.

Hamilton, Donald W. *Art of Counterinsurgency: American Military Policy and the Failure of Strategy in Southeast Asia*. London: Praeger, 1998.

Hamilton-Merrit, Jane. *Tragic Mountains: The Hmong, the Americans, and the Secret Wars for Laos, 1942–1992*. Bloomington: Indiana University Press, 1993.

Hanngi, Heiner. *ASEAN and the ZOPFAN Concept*. Singapore: Institute of Southeast Asian Studies, 1991.

Hara, Fujio. *Malayan Chinese and China: Conversion in Identity Consciousness, 1945–1957*. Singapore: National University of Singapore, 2002.

Harper, T. N. *The End of Empire and the Making of Malaya*. London: Cambridge University Press, 1999.

——. "Lim Chin Siong and the 'Singapore Story.'" In *Comet in Our Sky: Lim Chin Siong in History*, edited by Tan Jing Quee and Jomo K. S., 1–56. Kuala Lumpur, Malaysia: Forum, 2001.

Hayes, Samuel P. *The Beginning of American Aid to Southeast Asia: The Griffin Mission of 1950*. Lexington, MA: Lexington Heath Books, 1971.

Heer, Paul J. *Mr. X and the Pacific: George F. Kennan and American Policy in East Asia*. Ithaca, NY: Cornell University Press, 2018. Kindle Edition.

Hilsman, Roger. *To Move a Nation: The Politics of Foreign Policy in the Administration of John F. Kennedy*. Garden City, NY: Doubleday, 1967.

Hixson, Walter L. *George F. Kennan: Cold War Iconoclast*. New York: Columbia University Press, 1989.

Hosmer, Stephen T. "Foreword to the New Edition." In *Counterinsurgency: A Symposium, April 16–20, 1962*, iii–v. Santa Monica, CA: RAND Corporation, 1962.

Hunt, Michael H. *American Ascendancy: How the United States Gained and Wielded Global Dominance*. Chapel Hill: University of North Carolina Press, 2007.

Hunt, Michael H., and Steven I. Levine. *Arc of Empire: America's Wars in Asia from the Philippines to Vietnam*. Chapel Hill: University of North Carolina Press, 2012.

Jacobs, Seth. *America's Miracle Man in Vietnam: Ngo Dinh Diem, Religion, Race and U.S. Intervention in Southeast Asia, 1950–7*. Durham, NC: Duke University Press, 2004.

——. *The Universe Unraveling: American Foreign Policy in Cold War Laos*. Ithaca, NY: Cornell University Press, 2012.

Jervis, Robert, and Jack Snyder, eds. *Dominoes and Bandwagons: Strategic Beliefs and Great Power Competition in the Eurasian Rimland*. New York: Oxford University Press, 1991.

Jones, Matthew. *Conflict and Confrontation in Southeast Asia, 1961–1965: Britain, the United States and the Creation of Malaysia*. Cambridge: Cambridge University Press, 2002.

——. "Creating Malaysia: Singapore Security, the Borneo Territories and the Contours of British Policy, 1961–3." *Journal of Imperial and Commonwealth History* 28, no. 2 (2000): 85–109.

——. "A Decision Delayed: Britain's Withdrawal from South East Asia Reconsidered, 1961–68." *English Historical Review* 117 (2002): 569–95.

——. "Maximum Disavowable Aid: Britain, the United States and the Indonesian Rebellion, 1957–78." *English Historical Review* 114, no. 459 (1999): 1179–1216.

——. "A 'Segregated Asia?' Race, the Bandung Conference and Pan-Asianist Fears in American Thought and Policy, 1954–1955." *Diplomatic History* 29, no. 5 (2005): 841–68.

——. "Up the Garden Path? Britain's Nuclear History in the Far East, 1954–62." *International History Review* 25, no. 2. (2003): 306–33.

Kahin, Audrey R., and George McT Kahin. *Subversion as Foreign Policy: The Secret Eisenhower and Dulles Debacle in Indonesia*. New York: W. W. Norton, 1995.

Kahin, George McT. *Nationalism and Revolution in Indonesia*. Ithaca, NY: Cornell University Press, 1952.

Karnow, Stanley. *In Our Image: America's Empire in the Philippines*. New York: Random House, 1989.

Keon, Michael. *The Durian Tree*. New York: Simon & Schuster, 1960.

Khong, Yuen Foong. *Analogies at War: Korea, Munich, Dien Bien Phu, and the Vietnam Decisions of 1965*. Princeton, NJ: Princeton University Press, 1992.

Kimball, Jeffrey. "The Nixon Doctrine: A Saga of Misunderstanding." *Presidential Studies Quarterly* 36, no. 1 (2006): 59–74.

Klein, Christina, *Cold War Orientalism: Asia in the Middlebrow Imagination, 1945–61*. Berkeley: University of California Press, 2003.

Koh, Ernest. *Diaspora at War: The Chinese of Singapore between Empire and Nation, 1937–1945*. Leiden: Brill, 2013.

Komer, Robert W. *The Malayan Emergency in Retrospect: Organization of a Successful Counterinsurgency Effort*. Santa Monica, CA: RAND Corporation, 1972.

Kramer, Paul. *The Blood of Government: Race, Empire, the United States and the Philippines*. Chapel Hill: University of North Carolina Press, 2006.

——. "Power and Connection: Imperial Histories of the United States in the World." *American Historical Review* 116 (December 2011): 1348–91.

——. "The Water Cure: Debating Torture and Counterinsurgency—A Century Ago." *New Yorker*, February 25, 2008.

Kratoska, Paul H. "Dimensions of Decolonization." In *Transformation of Southeast Asia: International Perspectives on Decolonization*, edited by Marc Frey, Ronald Pruessen, and Tan Tai Yong, 3–22. Armonk, NY: M. E. Sharpe, 2003.

Kuhn, Philip. *Chinese among Others: Emigration in Modern Times*. New York: Rowman & Littlefield, 2008.

Lai, Walton Look. "Asian Diasporas and Tropical Migration in the Age of Empire: A Comparative Overview." *Journal of the Chinese Overseas* 5 no. 1 (2009): 28–54.

Lake, Marilyn, and Henry Reynolds. *Drawing the Global Color Line: White Men's Countries and the International Challenge of Racial Equality*. Cambridge: Cambridge University Press, 2008.

Lau, Albert. *The Malayan Union Controversy, 1942–1948*. Singapore: Oxford University Press, 1991.

——. *A Moment of Anguish: Singapore in Malaysia and the Politics of Disengagement*. Singapore: Times Academic Press, 1998.

Lauren, Paul Gordon. *Power and Prejudice: The Politics and Diplomacy of Racial Discrimination*. Boulder, CO: Westview, 1988.

Lawrence, Mark Atwood. *Assuming the Burden: Europe and the American Commitment to War in Vietnam*. Berkeley: University of California Press, 2005.

Lay, Alex. Dir. *The History of Singapore Part 2—Accidental Nation*. 2005; Singapore: Lion Television and Discovery Networks Asia, 2006. DVD.

Lederer, William J. "The Guerrilla War the Reds Lost." *Reader's Digest*, May 1962.

Lee, Erika. *At America's Gates: Chinese Immigration during the Exclusion Era, 1882–1943*. Chapel Hill: University of North Carolina Press, 2003.

Lee Kuan Yew. *The Battle for Merger*. Singapore: Government Printing Office, 1961.

——. *The Papers of Lee Kuan Yew: Speeches, Interviews and Dialogues*, Vol. 1, *1950–1962*. Singapore: Gale Asia, 2012.

Leffler, Melvyn P. *A Preponderance of Power: National Security, the Truman Administration, and the Cold War*. Stanford, CA: Stanford University Press, 1992.

Legge, J. D. *Sukarno: A Political Biography*. New York: Praeger, 1972.

Leifer, Michael. *Singapore's Foreign Policy: Coping with Vulnerability*. London: Routledge, 2000.

Lim, Cheng Leng. *The Story of a Psy-Warrior: Tan Sri Dr. C.C. Too*. Batu Caves, Selangor: Lim Cheng Leng, 2002.

Lim, Yew Hock. *Reflections*. Kuala Lumpur, Malaysia: Pustaka Antara, 1986.

Liow, Joseph Chinyong. "Tunku Abdul Rahman and Malaya's Relations with Indonesia, 1957–60." *Journal of Southeast Asian Studies* 36, no. 1 (2005): 87–109.

Logevall, Fredrik. *Choosing War: The Lost Chance for Peace and the Escalation of War in Vietnam*. Berkeley: University of California Press, 1999.

——. *Embers of War: The Fall of an Empire and the Making of America's Vietnam*. New York: Random House, 2012.

——. "There Ain't No Daylight: Lyndon Johnson and the Politics of Escalation." In *Making Sense of the Vietnam Wars: Local, National, and Transnational Perspectives*, edited by Mark Philip Bradley and Marilyn B. Young, 90–107. Oxford: Oxford University Press, 2008.

Long, S. R. Joey. *Safe for Decolonization: The Eisenhower Administration, Britain and Singapore.* Kent, OH: Kent State University Press, 2011.

Longmire, R. A. *Soviet Relations with Southeast Asia: An Historical Survey.* New York: Kegan Paul International, 1989.

Louis, W. R. *British Strategy in the Far East, 1919–39.* Oxford: Oxford University Press, 1971.

———. *Imperialism at Bay, 1941–1945: The United States and the Decolonization of the British Empire.* New York: Oxford University Press, 1978.

Lundestad, Geir. "Empire by Invitation? The United States and Western Europe." *Journal of Peace Research* 23, no. 3 (1986): 263–77.

———. "Empire by Invitation? The United States and Western Europe, 1945–1952." *Society for Historians of American Foreign Relations Newsletter* 15 (1984): 1–21.

———. "'Empire by Invitation' in the American Century." *Diplomatic History* 23, no. 2 (1999): 188–217.

MacDonald, Douglas J. "The Truman Administration and Global Responsibilities: The Birth of the Falling Domino Principle." In *Dominoes and Bandwagons: Strategic Beliefs and Great Power Competition in the Eurasian Rimland,* edited by Robert Jervis and Jack Snyder, 112–44. New York: Oxford University Press, 1991.

Maechling, Charles, Jr. "Camelot, Robert Kennedy, and Counter-Insurgency—a Memoir." *Virginia Quarterly Review* 93, no. 4 (1999), last accessed June 29, 2014, http://www.vqronline.org/essay/camelot-robert-kennedy-and-counter-insurgency-memoir.

Maidin, Rashid. *The Memoirs of Rashid Maidin: From Armed Struggle to Peace.* Kuala Lumpur, Malaysia: Strategic Information Research Division, 2009.

Maier, Charles S. *Among Empires: American Ascendancy and Its Predecessors.* Cambridge, MA: Harvard University Press, 2006.

"Malaya: The Undeclared War." 1998, British Broadcasting Corporation (YouTube), last accessed January 25, 2018, https://www.youtube.com/watch?v=pBRMRf0JVJc.

Marr, David. *Vietnam: State, War, Revolution (1945–1946).* Berkeley: University of California Press, 2013.

McAlister, John T. Review of *Defeating Communist Insurgency: Experiences from Malaya and Vietnam,* by Robert G. K. Thompson. *American Political Science Review* 61, no. 3 (September 1967): 773–75.

McAlister, Melani. *Epic Encounters: Culture, Media, & U.S. Interests in the Middle East since 1945.* Berkeley: University of California Press, 2001.

McCoy, Alfred W. *Policing America's Empire: The United States, The Philippines and the Rise of the Surveillance State.* Madison: University of Wisconsin Press, 2009.

McKeown, Adam. "Chinese Emigration in Global Context, 1850–1940." *Journal of Global History* 5, no. 1 (2010): 95–124.

McMahon, Robert J. *Colonialism and the Cold War: The United States and the Struggle for Indonesian Independence, 1945–49.* Ithaca, NY: Cornell University Press, 1981.

———. *The Limits of Empire: The United States and Southeast Asia since World War II.* New York: Columbia University Press, 1999.

Miller, Edward G. *Misalliance: Ngo Dinh Diem, the United States and the Fate of South Vietnam*. Cambridge, MA: Harvard University Press, 2013.

Morais, J. Victor, ed. *Selected Speeches: A Golden Treasury of Asian Thought and Wisdom*. Petaling Jaya, Malaysia: Malayan Printers, 1967.

Muehlenbeck, Philip E. *Betting on the Africans: John F. Kennedy's Courting of African Nationalist Leaders*. New York: Oxford University Press, 2012.

Muhammad Ghazali bin Shafie. "Broadcast by Malaysia's Minister of Home Affairs." *Survival: Global Politics and Strategy* 17, no. 4 (1975): 186–88.

——. *Malaysia, International Relations: Selected Speeches*. Kuala Lumpur, Malaysia: Creative Enterprise, 1982.

Murfett, Malcolm H., John N. Miksic, Brian P. Farrell, and Chiang Ming Shun, eds. *Between Two Oceans: A Military History of Singapore from First Settlement to Final British Withdrawal*. London: Oxford University Press, 1999.

Nagl, John A. *Learning to Eat Soup with a Knife: Counterinsurgency Lessons from Malaya and Vietnam*. Chicago: University of Chicago Press, 2005.

Nelson, Keith L. "Nixon, Brezhnev, and Détente." *Peace & Change* 16, no. 2 (1991): 212–14.

Ngoei, Wen-Qing. "The Domino Logic of the Darkest Moment: The Fall of Singapore, the Atlantic Echo Chamber and Chinese 'Penetration' in U.S. Cold War Policy toward Southeast Asia." *Journal of American-East Asian Relations* 21, no. 3 (2014): 215–45.

——. "A Wide-Anti-Communist Arc: Britain, ASEAN and Nixon's Triangular Diplomacy." *Diplomatic History* 41, no. 5 (2017): 903–32.

Nguyen, Lien-Hang T. *Hanoi's War: An International History of the War for Peace in Vietnam*. Chapel Hill: University of North Carolina Press, 2012.

Ninkovich, Frank. *Modernity and Power: A History of the Domino Theory in the Twentieth Century*. Chicago: University of Chicago Press, 1994.

Nixon, Richard M. "Needed in Vietnam: The Will to Win." *Reader's Digest*, August 1964, 42–43.

O'Connell, Aaron B. *Underdogs: The Making of the Modern Marine Corps*. Cambridge, MA: Harvard University Press, 2012.

Ongkili, James P. "The British and Malayan Nationalism, 1946–57." *Journal of Southeast Asian Studies* 5, no. 2 (1974): 255–77.

Pham, P. L. *Ending East of Suez: The British Decision to Withdraw from Malaysia and Singapore, 1964–8*. Oxford: Oxford University Press, 2011.

Porter, Bernard. *The Absent-Minded Imperialists: Empire, Society and Culture in Britain*. London: Oxford University Press, 2006.

——. *Empire and Superempire: Britain, America and the World*. New Haven, CT: Yale University Press, 2006.

Pye, Lucian W. *Guerrilla Communism in Malaya: Its Social and Political Meaning*. Princeton, NJ: Princeton University Press, 1956.

——. *Lessons from the Malayan Struggle against Communism*. Cambridge, MA: Massachusetts Institute of Technology Press, 1957.

Rakove, Robert B. *Kennedy, Johnson, and the Non-Aligned World*. New York: Cambridge University Press, 2012.

Ramakrishna, Kumar. *Emergency Propaganda: The Winning of Malayan Hearts and Minds, 1948–58*. Richmond, UK: Curzon, 2001.

The Razak Touch. Kuala Lumpur, Malaysia: Department of Information Services, 1968.

Thomas, Martin. *Fight or Flight: Britain, France and Their Roads from Empire*. Oxford: Oxford University Press, 2014.

Reynolds, E. Bruce. *Thailand's Secret War: The Free Thai, OSS, and SOE during World War II*. Cambridge: Cambridge University Press, 2010.

Roosa, John. *Pretext for Mass Murder: The September 30th Movement and Suharto's Coup D'état in Indonesia*. Madison: University of Wisconsin Press, 2006.

Rotter, Andrew J. *The Path to Vietnam: Origins of the American Commitment to Southeast Asia*. Ithaca, NY: Cornell University Press, 1987.

———. "The Triangular Route to Vietnam: The United States, Great Britain and Southeast Asia, 1945–1950." *International History Review* 6, no. 3 (1984): 404–23.

Sannadurai, Visu. "The Citizenship Laws of Malaysia." In *The Constitution of Malaysia, Its Development: 1957–77*, edited by Mohamed Suffian, H. P. Lee, and F. A. Trindade, 68–100. Oxford: Oxford University Press, 1978.

Saravanamuttu, Johan. *Malaysia's Foreign Policy, the First Fifty Years: Alignment, Neutralism, Islamism*. Singapore: Institute of Southeast Asian Studies, 2010.

Sargent, Daniel J. *A Superpower Transformed: The Remaking of American Foreign Relations in the 1970s*. Oxford: Oxford University Press, 2015.

Saunders, Elizabeth N. *Leaders at War: How Presidents Shape Military Interventions*. Ithaca, NY: Cornell University Press, 2011.

Saxton, Alexander. *The Indispensable Enemy: Labor Immigration and the Anti-Chinese Movement in California*. Berkeley: University of California Press, 1971.

Schaller, Michael. *The Origins of the Cold War in Asia: The American Occupation of Japan*. New York: Oxford University Press, 1985.

Seeley, J. R. *The Expansion of England*. London: Macmillan, 1883.

Shatalov, I. "At the Junction of Eras and Continents." *International Affairs* 27 (April 1971).

Sherry, Michael S. *In the Shadow of War: The United States since the 1930s*. New Haven, CT: Yale University Press, 1995.

Short, Anthony. *Communist Insurrection in Malaya, 1948–1960*. London: Muller, 1975; repr. Singapore: Cultured Lotus, 2000.

Simpson, Bradley R. *Economists with Guns: Authoritarian Development and U.S.-Indonesian Relations, 1960–8*. Stanford, CA: Stanford University Press, 2008.

Singh, Bilveer. *Soviet Relations with ASEAN*. Singapore: National University of Singapore Press, 1989.

———. *The Soviet Union in Singapore's Foreign Policy: An Analysis*. Kuala Lumpur, Malaysia: Institute of Strategic and Pacific Studies, 1990.

———. *ZOPFAN and the New Security Order in the Asia-Pacific Region*. Kuala Lumpur, Malaysia: Pelanduk Publications, 1992.

Skinner, G. William. *Chinese Society in Thailand*. Ithaca, NY: Cornell University Press, 1957.

Slater, Jerome. "The Domino Theory and International Politics: The Case of Vietnam." *Security Studies* 3, no. 2 (1993/94): 186–224.

"Smiling Tiger." *Time*, December 15, 1952, 26–32.

Sodhy, Pamela. "America's Melby Mission to Southeast Asia in 1950: The Case of Malaya." *Jebat* 18 (1990): 263–87.

———. *The U.S.-Malaysian Nexus: Themes in Superpower–Small State Relations*. Kuala Lumpur, Malaysia: Institute of Strategic and International Studies, 1991.

Soekarno. *Sukarno: An Autobiography as Told to Cindy Adams*. Indianapolis: Bobbs-Merrill, 1965.

Sopiee, Mohamed Noordin. "The Advocacy of Malaysia—Before 1961." *Modern Asian Studies* 7, no. 4 (1973): 717–32.

Spector, Ronald H. *In the Ruins of Empire: The Japanese Surrender and the Battle for Postwar Asia*. New York: Random House, 2007.

Spence, Jonathan D. *God's Chinese Son: The Taiping Heavenly Kingdom of Hong Xiquan*. New York: W. W. Norton, 1996.

Stockwell, Anthony J. "Britain and Brunei, 1945–63: Imperial Retreat and Royal Ascendancy." *Modern Asian Studies* 38, no. 4 (2004): 785–819.

———. "Malaysia: The Making of a Grand Design." *Asian Affairs* 34, no. 3 (2003): 227–42.

———. "Malaysia: The Making of a Neo-Colony?" *Journal of Imperial and Commonwealth History* 26, no. 2 (1998): 138–56.

Stubbs, Richard. *Counter-Insurgency and the Economic Factor: The Impact of the Korean War Prices Boom on the Malayan Emergency*. Singapore: Institute of Southeast Asian Studies, 1974.

———. *Hearts and Minds in Guerrilla Warfare, 1948–1960*. London: Oxford University Press, 1989.

Subritzky, John. *Confronting Sukarno: British, American, Australian and New Zealand Diplomacy in the Malaysia-Indonesia Confrontation, 1961–5*. New York: St. Martin's, 2000.

Sugihara, Kaoru. "Patterns of Chinese Emigration to Southeast Asia, 1869–1939." In *Japan, China and the Growth of the Asian International Economy, 1850–1949*, edited by Kaoru Sugihara, 244–74. Oxford: Oxford University Press, 2005.

Suri, Jeremi. *Power and Protest: Global Revolution and the Rise of Détente*. Cambridge, MA: Harvard University Press, 2003.

Suryadinata, Leo. *China and the ASEAN States: The Ethnic Chinese Dimension*. Singapore: National University of Singapore Press, 1985.

Tan, Tai Yong. *Creating "Greater Malaysia": Decolonization and the Politics of Merger*. Singapore: Institute of Southeast Asian Studies, 2008.

———. "The 'Grand Design': British Policy, Local Politics, and the Making of Malaysia, 1955–1961." In *The Transformation of Southeast Asia: International Perspectives on Decolonization*, edited by Marc Frey, Ronald W. Pruessen, and Tan Tai Yong, 142–60. Armonk, NY: M. E. Sharpe, 2003.

Tarling, Nicholas. *Regionalism in Southeast Asia: To Foster the Political Will*. London: Routledge, 2006.

Thayer, Carlyle A. "The Five Power Defense Arrangements: The Quiet Achiever." *Security Challenges* 3, no. 1 (2007): 61–72.

Thompson, Robert G. K. *Defeating Communist Insurgency: Experiences from Malaya and Vietnam*. London: Chatto and Windus, 1966.

———. *No Exit from Vietnam*. New York: D. McKay, 1969.

Thompson, Virginia, and Richard Adloff. *Minority Problems in Southeast Asia*. Stanford, CA: Stanford University Press, 1955.

Trocki, Carl A. *Opium and Empire: Chinese Society in Colonial Singapore, 1800–1910*. Ithaca, NY: Cornell University Press, 1990.

Tyner, James A. *America's Strategy in Southeast Asia: From the Cold War to the Terror War*. Lanham, MD: Rowman & Littlefield, 2007.

Vickers, Adrian. *A History of Modern Indonesia*. New York: Cambridge University Press, 2005.

Watt, Donald Cameron. *Succeeding John Bull: America in Britain's Place*. New York: Cambridge University Press, 1984.

Westad, Odd Arne. *The Global Cold War: Third World Interventions and the Making of Our Times*. New York: Cambridge University Press, 2005.

———. *Restless Empire: China and the World since 1750*. New York: Basic Books, 2012.

Williams, Michael C. "New Soviet Policy toward Southeast Asia: Reorientation and Change." *Asian Survey* 31, no. 4 (1991): 364–77.

Wong, Danny. *Vietnam-Malaysia: Relations during the Cold War, 1945–1990*. Kuala Lumpur, Malaysia: University of Malaya Press, 1995.

Wong, James. *From Pacific War to Merdeka: Reminiscences of Abdullah CD, Rashid Maidin, Suraini Abdullah and Abu Sam*. Kuala Lumpur, Malaysia: Strategic Information Research Division, 2005.

Young, Marilyn B. *The Vietnam Wars, 1945–1990*. New York: HarperCollins, 1990.

Zaretsky, Natasha. *No Direction Home: The American Family and the Fear of National Decline, 1968–1980*. Chapel Hill: University of North Carolina Press, 2007.

Zhai Qiang. *China and the Vietnam Wars, 1950–75*. Chapel Hill: University of North Carolina Press, 2000.

Zhou, Taomo. "Ambivalent Alliance: Chinese Policy toward Indonesia, 1960–1965." *China Quarterly* (2015): 208–28.

———. "China and the Thirtieth of September Movement." *Indonesia* 98 (2014): 29–58.

Index

Studies of the Weatherhead East Asian Institute Columbia University

Selected Titles

(Complete list at: http://weai.columbia.edu/publications/studies-weai/)

The Invention of Madness: State, Society, and the Insane in Modern China, by Emily Baum. University of Chicago Press, 2018.

Idly Scribbling Rhymers: Poetry, Print, and Community in Nineteenth Century Japan, by Robert Tuck. Columbia University Press, 2018.

Forging the Golden Urn: The Qing Empire and the Politics of Reincarnation in Tibet, by Max Oidtmann. Columbia University Press, 2018.

The Battle for Fortune: State-Led Development, Personhood, and Power among Tibetans in China, by Charlene Makley. Cornell University Press, 2018.

Aesthetic Life: Beauty and Art in Modern Japan, by Miya Elise Mizuta Lippit. Harvard University Asia Center, 2018.

China's War on Smuggling: Law, Economic Life, and the Making of the Modern State, 1842–1965, by Philip Thai. Columbia University Press, 2018.

Where the Party Rules: The Rank and File of China's Communist State, by Daniel Koss. Cambridge University Press, 2018.

Resurrecting Nagasaki: Reconstruction and the Formation of Atomic Narratives, by Chad R. Diehl. Cornell University Press, 2018.

China's Philological Turn: Scholars, Textualism, and the Dao in the Eighteenth Century, by Ori Sela. Columbia University Press, 2018.

Making Time: Astronomical Time Measurement in Tokugawa Japan, by Yulia Frumer. University of Chicago Press, 2018.

Mobilizing without the Masses: Control and Contention in China, by Diana Fu. Cambridge University Press, 2018.

Post-Fascist Japan: Political Culture in Kamakura after the Second World War, by Laura Hein. Bloomsbury, 2018.

China's Conservative Revolution: The Quest for a New Order, 1927–1949, by Brian Tsui. Cambridge University Press, 2018.

Promiscuous Media: Film and Visual Culture in Imperial Japan, 1926–1945, by Hikari Hori. Cornell University Press, 2018.

The End of Japanese Cinema: Industrial Genres, National Times, and Media Ecologies, by Alexander Zahlten. Duke University Press, 2017.

The Chinese Typewriter: A History, by Thomas S. Mullaney. The MIT Press, 2017.

Forgotten Disease: Illnesses Transformed in Chinese Medicine, by Hilary A. Smith. Stanford University Press, 2017.

Borrowing Together: Microfinance and Cultivating Social Ties, by Becky Yang Hsu. Cambridge University Press, 2017.

Food of Sinful Demons: Meat, Vegetarianism, and the Limits of Buddhism in Tibet, by Geoffrey Barstow. Columbia University Press, 2017.

Youth for Nation: Culture and Protest in Cold War South Korea, by Charles R. Kim. University of Hawaii Press, 2017.

Socialist Cosmopolitanism: The Chinese Literary Universe, 1945–1965, by Nicolai Volland. Columbia University Press, 2017.

Yokohama and the Silk Trade: How Eastern Japan Became the Primary Economic Region of Japan, 1843–1893, by Yasuhiro Makimura. Lexington Books, 2017.

The Social Life of Inkstones: Artisans and Scholars in Early Qing China, by Dorothy Ko. University of Washington Press, 2017.

Darwin, Dharma, and the Divine: Evolutionary Theory and Religion in Modern Japan, by G. Clinton Godart. University of Hawaii Press, 2017.

Dictators and Their Secret Police: Coercive Institutions and State Violence, by Sheena Chestnut Greitens. Cambridge University Press, 2016.

The Cultural Revolution on Trial: Mao and the Gang of Four, by Alexander C. Cook. Cambridge University Press, 2016.

Inheritance of Loss: China, Japan, and the Political Economy of Redemption after Empire, by Yukiko Koga. University of Chicago Press, 2016.

Homecomings: The Belated Return of Japan's Lost Soldiers, by Yoshikuni Igarashi. Columbia University Press, 2016.

Samurai to Soldier: Remaking Military Service in Nineteenth-Century Japan, by D. Colin Jaundrill. Cornell University Press, 2016.

The Red Guard Generation and Political Activism in China, by Guobin Yang. Columbia University Press, 2016.

Accidental Activists: Victim Movements and Government Accountability in Japan and South Korea, by Celeste L. Arrington. Cornell University Press, 2016.

Ming China and Vietnam: Negotiating Borders in Early Modern Asia, by Kathlene Baldanza. Cambridge University Press, 2016.

Ethnic Conflict and Protest in Tibet and Xinjiang: Unrest in China's West, coedited by Ben Hillman and Gray Tuttle. Columbia University Press, 2016.

One Hundred Million Philosophers: Science of Thought and the Culture of Democracy in Postwar Japan, by Adam Bronson. University of Hawaii Press, 2016.

Conflict and Commerce in Maritime East Asia: The Zheng Family and the Shaping of the Modern World, c. 1620–1720, by Xing Hang. Cambridge University Press, 2016.

Chinese Law in Imperial Eyes: Sovereignty, Justice, and Transcultural Politics, by Li Chen. Columbia University Press, 2016.

Imperial Genus: The Formation and Limits of the Human in Modern Korea and Japan, by Travis Workman. University of California Press, 2015.

Yasukuni Shrine: History, Memory, and Japan's Unending Postwar, by Akiko Takenaka. University of Hawaii Press, 2015.

The Age of Irreverence: A New History of Laughter in China, by Christopher Rea. University of California Press, 2015.

The Knowledge of Nature and the Nature of Knowledge in Early Modern Japan, by Federico Marcon. University of Chicago Press, 2015.

The Fascist Effect: Japan and Italy, 1915–1952, by Reto Hofmann. Cornell University Press, 2015.

Empires of Coal: Fueling China's Entry into the Modern World Order, 1860–1920, by Shellen Xiao Wu. Stanford University Press, 2015.

Printed in the USA
CPSIA information can be obtained
at www.ICGtesting.com
LVHW091642250823
756268LV00025B/595/J

9 781501 716409